Copyr

MW01321124

www.urbizedge.com

All rights reserved. No part of this publication may be reproduced, distributed, or transmitted in any form or by any means, including photocopying, recording, or other electronic or mechanical methods, without the prior written permission of the publisher, except in the case of brief quotations embodied in critical reviews and certain other noncommercial uses permitted by copyright law.

Book written and formatted by mike@urbizedge.com

Preface

Microsoft Excel is the world's most used business intelligence tool. Its knowledge is even compulsory for an MBA degree and the business world depends greatly on it.

This book is aimed at making you very good in Microsoft Excel for business data analysis, teaching you with companion videos and practice files that can be accessed at **www.urbizedge.com/about** (bottom of the page). It's intended for Sales Managers, Financial Analysts, Business Analysts, Data Analysts, MIS Analysts, HR Executives and frequent Excel users.

It is written by Michael Olafusi a three time Microsoft Excel MVP (most valuable professional) and a full-time Microsoft Excel consultant. He is the founder of UrBizEdge, a business data analysis and Microsoft Excel consulting firm. He has trained hundreds of business professionals on Microsoft Excel and has used the experience gained from interacting with them both during such trainings and while consulting for companies to write this excellent guide for the busy professional who needs the improved work productivity Microsoft Excel provides.

This book is constantly being updated to cover the new features in new versions of Excel and if you purchase the kindle version you can always re-download the updated copy. Just check the book listing page **(http://www.amazon.com/gp/product/B01255TQ84)** for updates and re-download if a newer version has been published. All at no cost to you. It is the best way to give you value for your money without forcing you to buy different editions of the same book. If you feel any part of this book can be better improved or expanded, please send an email to **mike@urbizedge.com**

Table of Contents

Microsoft Excel: It's more powerful and easier to use than you think!

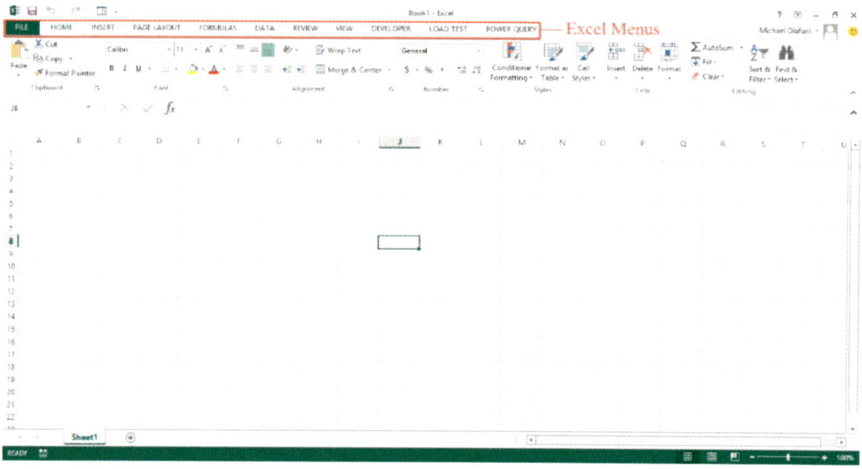

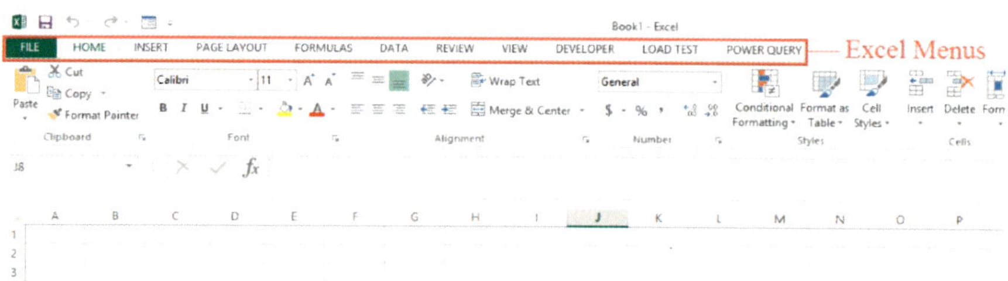

We've got Home menu, Insert menu, Page Layout menu, Formulas menu, Data menu, Review menu and View menu. Each of these menus will be discussed in practical terms.

The other menus – Developer menu, Load Test Menu and Power Query menu – are not displayed by default. I enabled them as I do a lot of programming and other advanced stuff in Excel which I need them for.

Home Menu

The home menu is Excel's most used menu. It has very straightforward sub-menus.

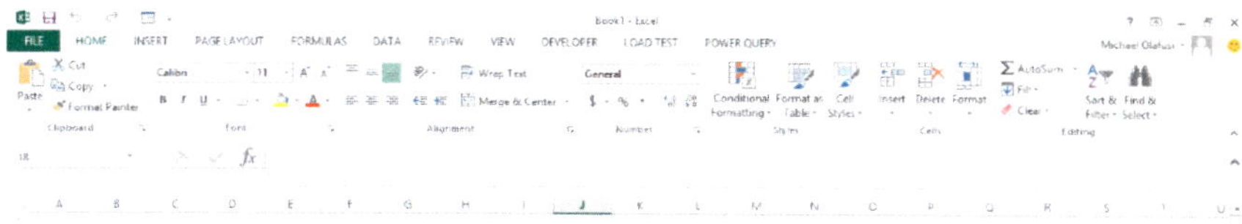

Clipboard: Allows you to copy, cut and paste in Excel
Font: Allows you to set font size, color, background color (fill) & turn on bold or italics or underline.
Alignment: Allows you to set the position of whatever you've typed (or copied) into Excel. It also allows you to set how it's written: horizontal, vertical or slanting.
Number: Allows you to set how a number is shown in Excel: regular number, currency, scientific, percentage, fraction...
Styles: Allows you to set the format of an Excel cell based on the data it holds (conditional formatting). It also allows you to convert a selection of cells to table, and to set quick formats for a cell.
Cells: Allows you to insert new cells, delete cells and change cell format.
Editing: It houses the very useful Sort and filter tools. And also Find & Select, Find & Replace. There's also AutoSum which helps you sum all numbers in a selection.

Insert Menu

The Insert menu houses some of Excel's best tools.

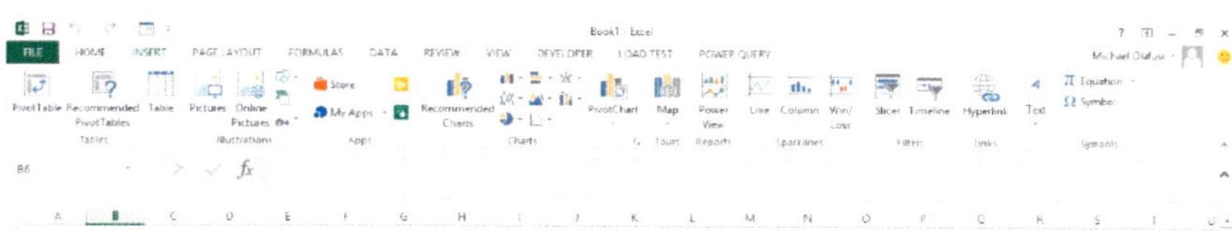

Tables: Allows you to insert PivotTable, PivotChart and Table. Inserting a table in Excel allows for quick formatting, and better formulas (via named ranges). PivotTable and PivotChart will be discussed later.
Illustrations: Allows you to insert images and shapes.
Charts: Allows you to insert charts, which will be specially discussed later.
Tours: Houses Map which takes you straight to Power Map. Power Map is part of Microsoft's new Power BI. It enables you make geo-maps and create amazing data visualization tours.

Reports: Lets you access Power View, another Power BI tool. Power View allows to create a data model, loading up many different databases and creating analysis that cuts across all the databases, allowing you to see insights that are beyond a single database.
Sparklines: Allows you to insert charts that fit into one Excel cell. They make some reports beautiful and easy to read.
Filter: Allows you to filter out field values you are not interested in.
Links: Allows you point a cell content to a website or an email address.
Text: Allows you to insert texts and objects (pretty much anything, including a PDF document)
Symbols: Allows you to type out equations and special symbols.

Page Layout Menu

The Page Layout menu does just that: setting up your Excel document's page look and for printing.

Themes: It's not often used; it sets the look of the Excel window itself.
Page Setup: It allows you to set how the page comes out when printed. Most used are the Orientation (to set as Portrait or Landscape) and Print Area (to select on the cells you want to print).
Scale to Fit: It allows you to set how much is printed per page. Most frequent use is to force Excel to print on one page, or fit all the fields (columns) on one page width.
Sheet Options: You wouldn't want to change the default. It allows you set whether Excel gridlines be printed or not, and headings too. Default is no/off (unticked).
Arrange: It lets you rearrange overlapping objects (shapes, images, textboxes…). Or align them.

Formulas Menu

The Formulas menu gives you access to Excel's built-in formulas.

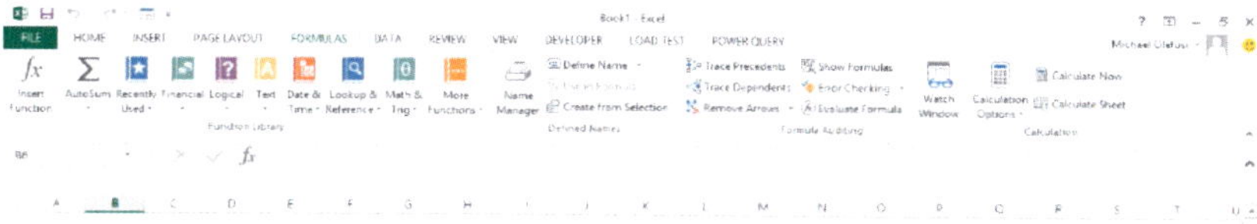

Function Library: It has the formulas grouped by category. Once you have an idea of what you want done, it helps you locate the formula to use. It's good to look through it once in a while to have an idea of the out-of-the-box analysis Excel can do.
Defined Names: Lets you name a cell or selection of cells. Can be very useful when analyzing a big database or building a model.
Formula Auditing: Allows you to check for errors in your formulas, trace formula cells and see how your final result is being calculated.
Calculation: Allows you to set when the formulas in your Excel sheet are calculated: automatic (whenever a cell value changes) or manual (at first entry and when you force them to be recalculated).

Data Menu

The Data menu allows you to work with external data and do basic data formatting.

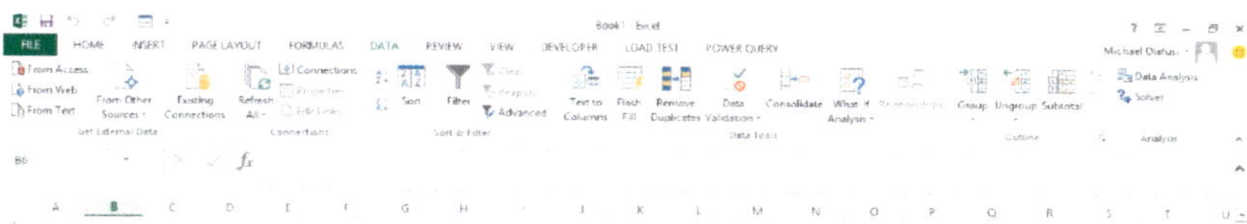

Get External Data: It allows you to import or link to an external data file (non-Excel file). You'll use it whenever you have a data in text file and need it worked on in Excel.
Connections: Allows you to make changes to the connections/links to an external data file. Or force a refresh of the connections to capture changes made in the external data file since last connection.
Sort & Filter: Allows you to sort data and do some filtering too. Filter allows you to specify values to display.
Data Tools: Allows you do very basic data analysis. Especially removing duplicate entries, and splitting one field into several (text-to-columns). Example is splitting full name into first name and last name.
Outline: Allows you to group (and hide) several rows. Useful for large data reports with few categories; helps to group categories.
Analysis: This is only visible after you enable Data Analysis add-in or Solver add-in. It allows you access a large collection of statistical analysis tools and modeling.

Review Menu

The Review menu is for spell checks, commenting and setting access restrictions.

Proofing: Allows you to carry out spell checks and word meaning checks.
Language: Allows you to translate the Excel file content from one language to another.
Comments: Allows you to include comments in an Excel sheet, view all comments at once or delete comments.
Changes: Allows you to set access restrictions and track changes to the Excel file. Also allows you to share the file.

View Menu

The View menu allows you to change the window layout of the Excel document. It doesn't change anything in the actual document, just the way it's displayed.

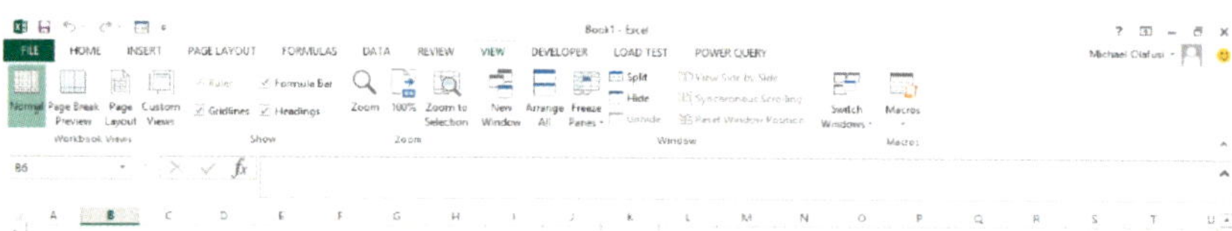

Workbook views: Allows you to set how the workbook (Excel file) is displayed.
Show: Controls what non-printing details are shown: Gridlines, Headings, Formula bar and Ruler. The one you'll be interested most in is Gridlines. If you want your Excel sheet to look more like a Word file, untick the Gridlines. That's what's done to every Excel sheet you see that has no Gridlines.
Zoom: Does what it says: sets zoom.
Window: Allows you to freeze headers so when you scroll they will never be out of view. And also allows you to split the Excel sheet display, so you can compare two different parts of the sheet.

Macros: Allows you to see the macros programmed in the Excel file (if there's any macro in it). Shows only when the developer menu is enabled.

How Excel Handles What You Type

In Excel, you type into small rectangular boxes called cells. I would be referring to everything you type or copy into Excel cells as Data.

Every cell has an address, because each cell is an intersection of a row and a column. The cell selected in the image below, is addressed as cell A1. It is the intersection of column A and row 1. A collection of millions of these cells make an Excel sheet. And an Excel file (also referred to as Excel workbook) is a collection of one or more Excel sheets.

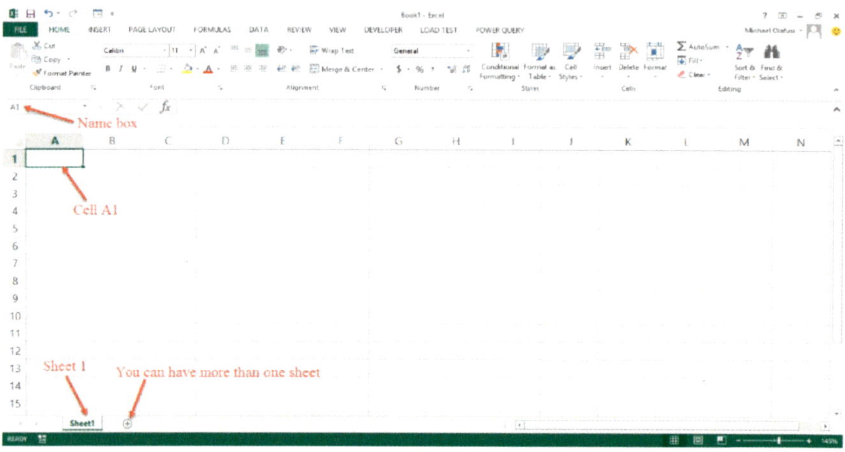

Sometimes, what you type into a cell takes more space than the cell has. Don't worry, just expand the column width by dragging the right border of the column header.

Like this:

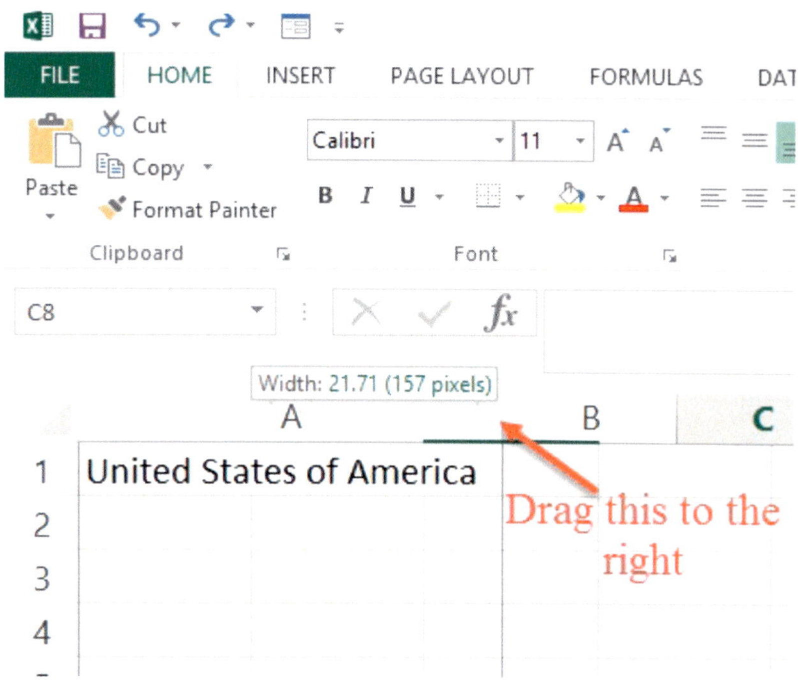

Different Data Types in Excel

Excel recognizes 4 different data types: Text, Number, Boolean & Formula. Anything you type into Excel will fall under one of these.

Text: Whenever you type alphabets, or a mix of alphabets and numbers into Excel (without proceeding with =), everything is recognized as text. By default, Excel aligns text to the left of the cell.

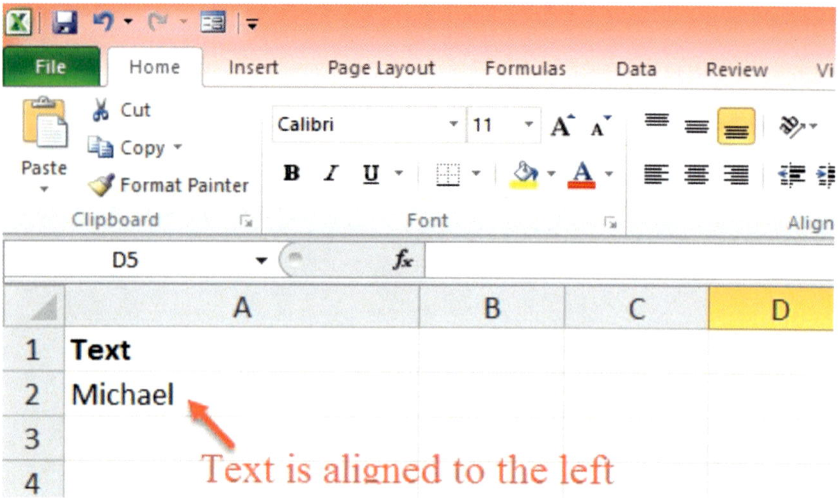

Number: If all you type into a cell are digits, they are recognized as Number by Excel. By default, Excel aligns number to the right.

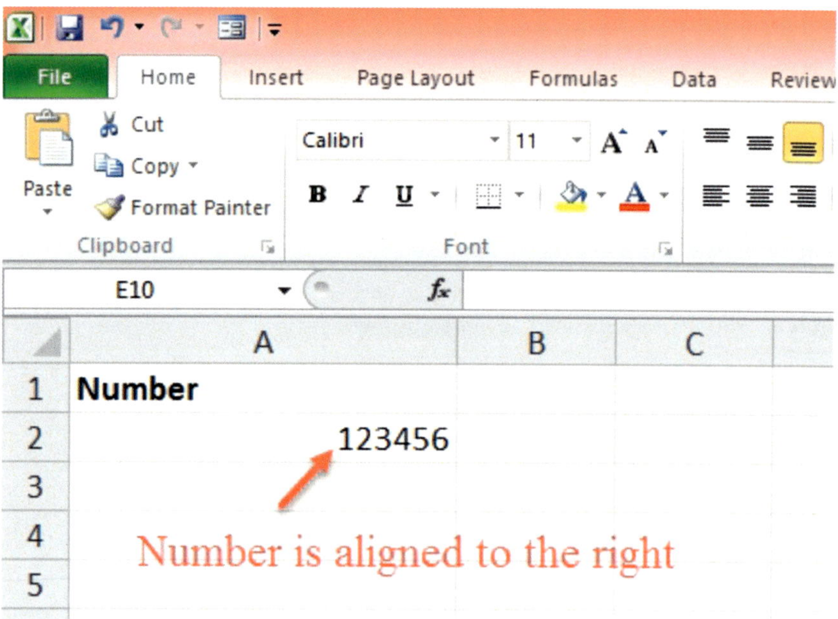

Boolean: FALSE and TRUE are Boolean entries. You'll hardly use them. They are used for setting up complex formulas. By default, whenever you type false or true in a cell, Excel will put it in upper case and align it to the center.

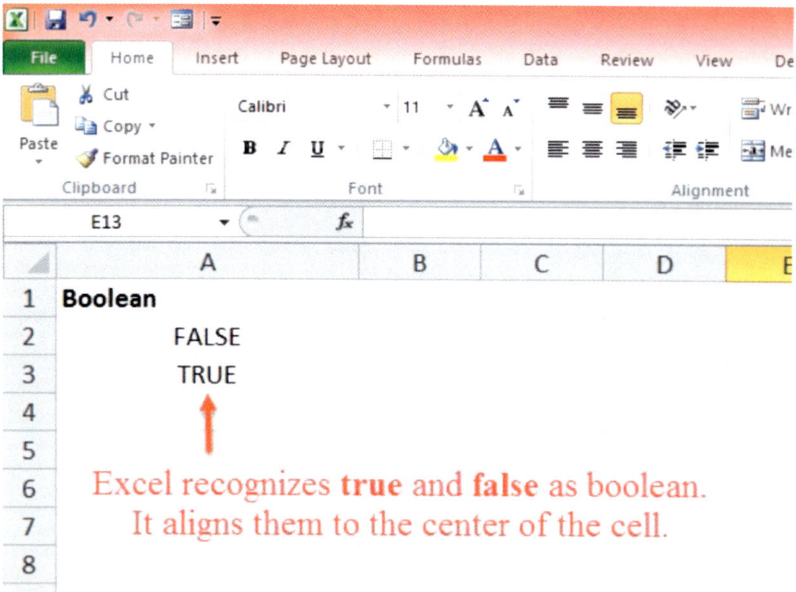

Formula: Once you begin a cell entry with =, Excel treats everything you type after as a formula.

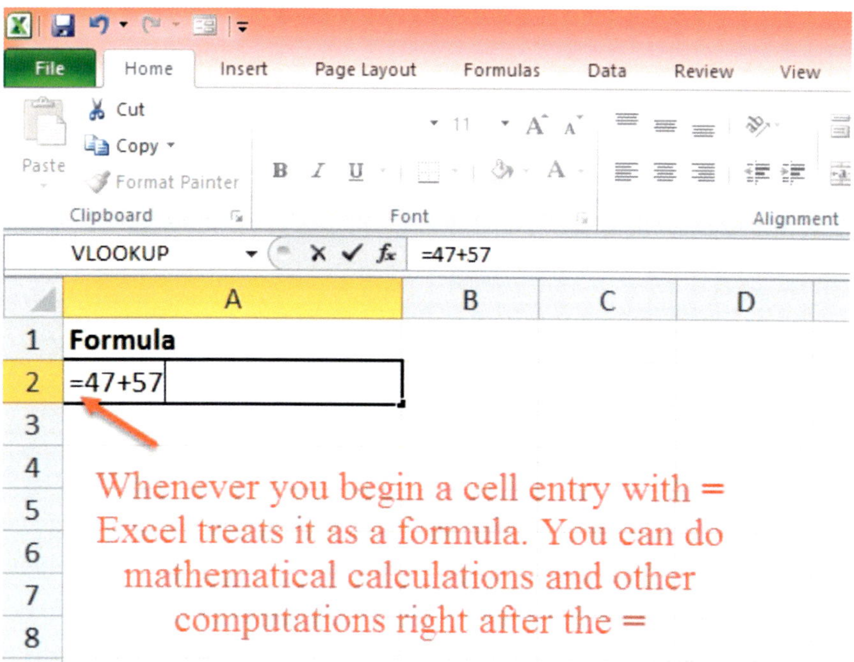

As a recap, see the image below.

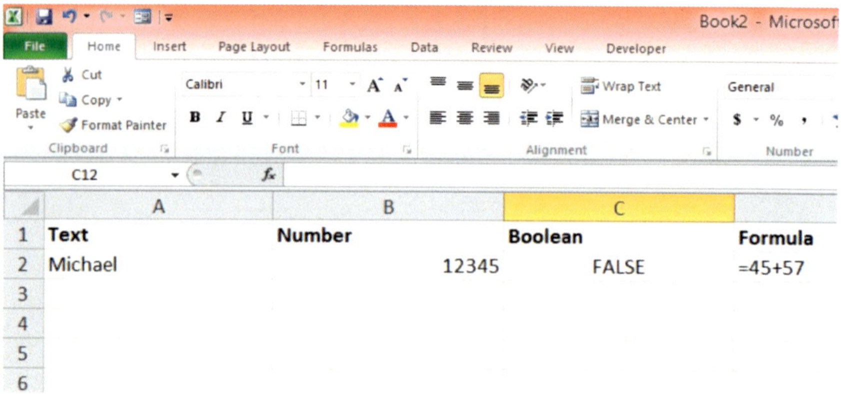

The practical importance of this is that if you receive a sales report in Excel and the numbers are aligned to left instead of right you should be concerned. There are three reasons this can happen and two of those reasons will cause some of your mathematical formulas to not work correctly. You wouldn't want to do an incorrect analysis, so it's best to check why the numbers are aligned to the left and not to the right as expected.

1. It could be that the author forced the numbers to align to the left. To find out if that's the reason, check the alignment under Home menu.

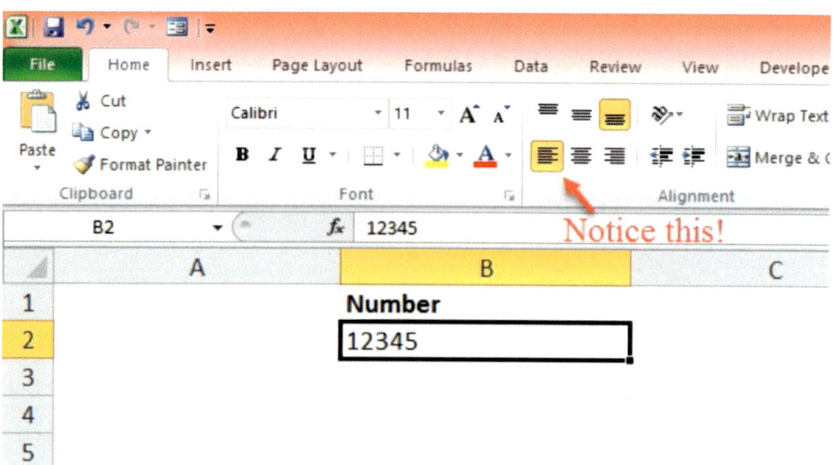

2. It could be that the author forced the number to be treated as text by setting the cell format to text

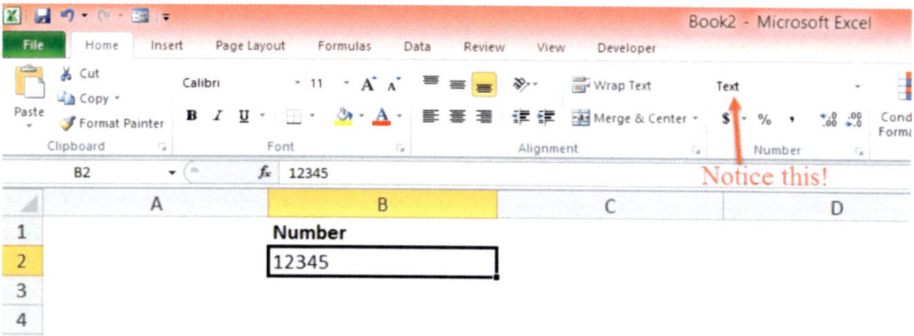

3. It could be that the author preceded the number with a single apostrophe (') before typing the number. This is a trick savvy users use to force Excel to keep the zeros at the beginning of your phone number or bank account number. Unfortunately, it forces Excel to treat the cell entry as a text and align it to the left.

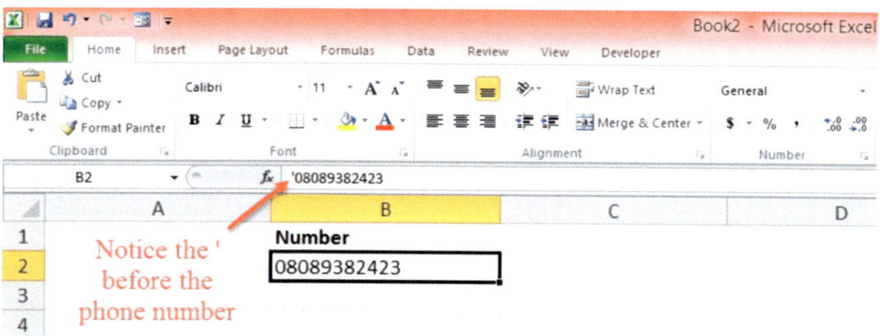

Out of these three ways of making a number show as aligned to the left, only the first one leaves the number intact. The other ways transform the number to text and will give you issues when you include them in calculations that normally would work on numbers.

Now you have an idea of how useful an understanding of the default ways Excel treat the different data types can be in your day to day use of Excel.

Data Consistency, starting with the end in view

Excel is different from every other Microsoft Office program you use. Most of the documents, reports and analysis you do with Excel will be used some day in the future for another report or analysis.

To become an expert in Excel, you have to always work with the end in mind. You have to create your Excel documents in such a way that you can easily use them for some bigger reports in the future. And there are some general rules I'll recommend you work with to achieve this.

1. Always use a compact table structure for entering you core data in Excel. This means using the minimum number of rows and minimum number of columns. Example of a compact table and non-compact table is shown below:

Monthly Revenue from Clients

Clients	Jan-14	Feb-14	Mar-14	Apr-14	May-14	Jun-14
Mobil	₦ 4,129,000	₦ 3,695,000	₦ 2,770,000	₦ 4,520,000	₦ 2,223,000	₦ 3,929,000
Nestle	₦ 1,688,000	₦ 3,300,000	₦ 4,880,000	₦ 3,730,000	₦ 2,046,000	₦ 2,326,000
NBC	₦ 3,701,000	₦ 4,361,000	₦ 4,254,000	₦ 4,550,000	₦ 4,834,000	₦ 3,116,000
Exp Nigeria	₦ 2,587,000	₦ 4,198,000	₦ 2,146,000	₦ 1,062,000	₦ 2,341,000	₦ 4,713,000
Insight Nigeria	₦ 2,408,000	₦ 4,759,000	₦ 1,300,000	₦ 4,426,000	₦ 3,521,000	₦ 3,171,000
Radisson Blu	₦ 2,485,000	₦ 2,025,000	₦ 1,603,000	₦ 3,089,000	₦ 2,841,000	₦ 3,156,000
Guinness	₦ 2,703,000	₦ 1,888,000	₦ 1,360,000	₦ 1,664,000	₦ 1,097,000	₦ 4,920,000
Chevron	₦ 3,516,000	₦ 2,988,000	₦ 4,788,000	₦ 2,425,000	₦ 4,689,000	₦ 4,080,000
Etisalat	₦ 4,475,000	₦ 3,459,000	₦ 2,701,000	₦ 2,058,000	₦ 3,562,000	₦ 3,096,000
Dangote	₦ 1,457,000	₦ 3,241,000	₦ 4,441,000	₦ 1,544,000	₦ 3,749,000	₦ 3,544,000
Dana Group	₦ 2,984,000	₦ 1,882,000	₦ 2,898,000	₦ 4,618,000	₦ 2,372,000	₦ 3,723,000
LaFarge	₦ 2,111,000	₦ 3,293,000	₦ 1,427,000	₦ 3,953,000	₦ 1,616,000	₦ 2,885,000
NB	₦ 3,396,000	₦ 4,148,000	₦ 4,569,000	₦ 3,893,000	₦ 3,871,000	₦ 3,045,000
MTN	₦ 4,410,000	₦ 2,391,000	₦ 4,180,000	₦ 3,788,000	₦ 2,669,000	₦ 4,262,000
Monacom	₦ 4,190,000	₦ 2,228,000	₦ 4,615,000	₦ 2,756,000	₦ 3,123,000	₦ 1,464,000
ARM	₦ 4,536,000	₦ 1,412,000	₦ 4,313,000	₦ 1,130,000	₦ 3,700,000	₦ 3,196,000
C & I	₦ 1,655,000	₦ 3,942,000	₦ 4,727,000	₦ 2,763,000	₦ 3,987,000	₦ 2,621,000
Total	₦ 52,431,000	₦ 53,210,000	₦ 56,972,000	₦ 51,969,000	₦ 52,241,000	₦ 57,247,000

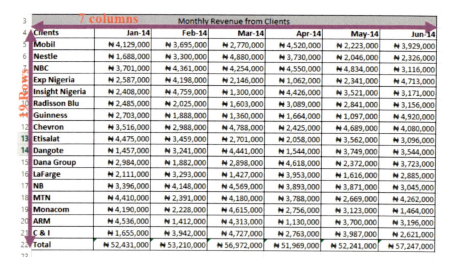

Same table but not compact, shown below.

8 Columns

21 Rows

29	Monthly Revenue from Clients						
30	**Clients**	**Jan-14**	**Feb-14**	**Mar-14**	**Apr-14**	**May-14**	**Jun-14**
31	**Mobil**	₦ 4,129,000	₦ 3,695,000	₦ 2,770,000	₦ 4,520,000	₦ 2,223,000	₦ 3,929,000
32	**Nestle**	₦ 1,688,000	₦ 3,300,000	₦ 4,880,000	₦ 3,730,000	₦ 2,046,000	₦ 2,326,000
33	**NBC**	₦ 3,701,000	₦ 4,361,000	₦ 4,254,000	₦ 4,550,000	₦ 4,834,000	₦ 3,116,000
34	**Exp Nigeria**	₦ 2,587,000	₦ 4,198,000	₦ 2,146,000	₦ 1,062,000	₦ 2,341,000	₦ 4,713,000
35	**Insight Nigeria**	₦ 2,408,000	₦ 4,759,000	₦ 1,300,000	₦ 4,426,000	₦ 3,521,000	₦ 3,171,000
36	**Radisson Blu**	₦ 2,485,000	₦ 2,025,000	₦ 1,603,000	₦ 3,089,000	₦ 2,841,000	₦ 3,156,000
37							
38							
39	**Guinness**	₦ 2,703,000	₦ 1,888,000	₦ 1,360,000	₦ 1,664,000	₦ 1,097,000	₦ 4,920,000
40	**Chevron**	₦ 3,516,000	₦ 2,988,000	₦ 4,788,000	₦ 2,425,000	₦ 4,689,000	₦ 4,080,000
41	**Etisalat**	₦ 4,475,000	₦ 3,459,000	₦ 2,701,000	₦ 2,058,000	₦ 3,562,000	₦ 3,096,000
42	**Dangote**	₦ 1,457,000	₦ 3,241,000	₦ 4,441,000	₦ 1,544,000	₦ 3,749,000	₦ 3,544,000
43	**Dana Group**	₦ 2,984,000	₦ 1,882,000	₦ 2,898,000	₦ 4,618,000	₦ 2,372,000	₦ 3,723,000
44	**LaFarge**	₦ 2,111,000	₦ 3,293,000	₦ 1,427,000	₦ 3,953,000	₦ 1,616,000	₦ 2,885,000
45	**NB**	₦ 3,396,000	₦ 4,148,000	₦ 4,569,000	₦ 3,893,000	₦ 3,871,000	₦ 3,045,000
46	**MTN**	₦ 4,410,000	₦ 2,391,000	₦ 4,180,000	₦ 3,788,000	₦ 2,669,000	₦ 4,262,000
47	**Monacom**	₦ 4,190,000	₦ 2,228,000	₦ 4,615,000	₦ 2,756,000	₦ 3,123,000	₦ 1,464,000
48	**ARM**	₦ 4,536,000	₦ 1,412,000	₦ 4,313,000	₦ 1,130,000	₦ 3,700,000	₦ 3,196,000
49	**C & I**	₦ 1,655,000	₦ 3,942,000	₦ 4,727,000	₦ 2,763,000	₦ 3,987,000	₦ 2,621,000
50	**Total**	**₦ 52,431,000**	**₦ 53,210,000**	**₦ 56,972,000**	**₦ 51,969,000**	**₦ 52,241,000**	**₦ 57,247,000**

In the non-compact table example, you can delete rows 37 and 38 without deleting any data in the table.

2. Use descriptive names for your column headers and row headers. Be as descriptive as possible in naming the fields in your table, make it easy for anyone who will view your table to understand the information it convenes.

Below is a table with field names that are descriptive enough for anyone to understand the information the table convenes.

	A	B	C	D	E	F	G
1	Monthly Revenue from Clients						
2	**Clients**	**Jan-14**	**Feb-14**	**Mar-14**	**Apr-14**	**May-14**	**Jun-14**
3	**Mobil**	₦ 4,129,000	₦ 3,695,000	₦ 2,770,000	₦ 4,520,000	₦ 2,223,000	₦ 3,929,000
4	**Nestle**	₦ 1,688,000	₦ 3,300,000	₦ 4,880,000	₦ 3,730,000	₦ 2,046,000	₦ 2,326,000
5	**NBC**	₦ 3,701,000	₦ 4,361,000	₦ 4,254,000	₦ 4,550,000	₦ 4,834,000	₦ 3,116,000
6	**Exp Nigeria**	₦ 2,587,000	₦ 4,198,000	₦ 2,146,000	₦ 1,062,000	₦ 2,341,000	₦ 4,713,000
7	**Insight Nigeria**	₦ 2,408,000	₦ 4,759,000	₦ 1,300,000	₦ 4,426,000	₦ 3,521,000	₦ 3,171,000
8	**Radisson Blu**	₦ 2,485,000	₦ 2,025,000	₦ 1,603,000	₦ 3,089,000	₦ 2,841,000	₦ 3,156,000
9	**Guinness**	₦ 2,703,000	₦ 1,888,000	₦ 1,360,000	₦ 1,664,000	₦ 1,097,000	₦ 4,920,000
10	**Chevron**	₦ 3,516,000	₦ 2,988,000	₦ 4,788,000	₦ 2,425,000	₦ 4,689,000	₦ 4,080,000
11	**Etisalat**	₦ 4,475,000	₦ 3,459,000	₦ 2,701,000	₦ 2,058,000	₦ 3,562,000	₦ 3,096,000
12	**Dangote**	₦ 1,457,000	₦ 3,241,000	₦ 4,441,000	₦ 1,544,000	₦ 3,749,000	₦ 3,544,000
13	**Dana Group**	₦ 2,984,000	₦ 1,882,000	₦ 2,898,000	₦ 4,618,000	₦ 2,372,000	₦ 3,723,000
14	**LaFarge**	₦ 2,111,000	₦ 3,293,000	₦ 1,427,000	₦ 3,953,000	₦ 1,616,000	₦ 2,885,000
15	**NB**	₦ 3,396,000	₦ 4,148,000	₦ 4,569,000	₦ 3,893,000	₦ 3,871,000	₦ 3,045,000
16	**MTN**	₦ 4,410,000	₦ 2,391,000	₦ 4,180,000	₦ 3,788,000	₦ 2,669,000	₦ 4,262,000
17	**Monacom**	₦ 4,190,000	₦ 2,228,000	₦ 4,615,000	₦ 2,756,000	₦ 3,123,000	₦ 1,464,000
18	**ARM**	₦ 4,536,000	₦ 1,412,000	₦ 4,313,000	₦ 1,130,000	₦ 3,700,000	₦ 3,196,000
19	**C & I**	₦ 1,655,000	₦ 3,942,000	₦ 4,727,000	₦ 2,763,000	₦ 3,987,000	₦ 2,621,000
20							

Below is a table that has headers that are not descriptive enough. It's hard to figure out the specific information in the table. Is it a table of revenue or expense? Are the companies clients or suppliers? What year do the months represent – January 2014 or January 2015? Whomever you send this report to will call you back for a detailed explanation of what you intended to report.

Some Data						
Companies	January	February	March	April	May	June
Mobil	₦ 4,129,000	₦ 3,695,000	₦ 2,770,000	₦ 4,520,000	₦ 2,223,000	₦ 3,929,000
Nestle	₦ 1,688,000	₦ 3,300,000	₦ 4,880,000	₦ 3,730,000	₦ 2,046,000	₦ 2,326,000
NBC	₦ 3,701,000	₦ 4,361,000	₦ 4,254,000	₦ 4,550,000	₦ 4,834,000	₦ 3,116,000
Exp Nigeria	₦ 2,587,000	₦ 4,198,000	₦ 2,146,000	₦ 1,062,000	₦ 2,341,000	₦ 4,713,000
Insight Nigeria	₦ 2,408,000	₦ 4,759,000	₦ 1,300,000	₦ 4,426,000	₦ 3,521,000	₦ 3,171,000
Radisson Blu	₦ 2,485,000	₦ 2,025,000	₦ 1,603,000	₦ 3,089,000	₦ 2,841,000	₦ 3,156,000
Guinness	₦ 2,703,000	₦ 1,888,000	₦ 1,360,000	₦ 1,664,000	₦ 1,097,000	₦ 4,920,000
Chevron	₦ 3,516,000	₦ 2,988,000	₦ 4,788,000	₦ 2,425,000	₦ 4,689,000	₦ 4,080,000
Etisalat	₦ 4,475,000	₦ 3,459,000	₦ 2,701,000	₦ 2,058,000	₦ 3,562,000	₦ 3,096,000
Dangote	₦ 1,457,000	₦ 3,241,000	₦ 4,441,000	₦ 1,544,000	₦ 3,749,000	₦ 3,544,000
Dana Group	₦ 2,984,000	₦ 1,882,000	₦ 2,898,000	₦ 4,618,000	₦ 2,372,000	₦ 3,723,000
LaFarge	₦ 2,111,000	₦ 3,293,000	₦ 1,427,000	₦ 3,953,000	₦ 1,616,000	₦ 2,885,000
NB	₦ 3,396,000	₦ 4,148,000	₦ 4,569,000	₦ 3,893,000	₦ 3,871,000	₦ 3,045,000
MTN	₦ 4,410,000	₦ 2,391,000	₦ 4,180,000	₦ 3,788,000	₦ 2,669,000	₦ 4,262,000
Monacom	₦ 4,190,000	₦ 2,228,000	₦ 4,615,000	₦ 2,756,000	₦ 3,123,000	₦ 1,464,000
ARM	₦ 4,536,000	₦ 1,412,000	₦ 4,313,000	₦ 1,130,000	₦ 3,700,000	₦ 3,196,000
C & I	₦ 1,655,000	₦ 3,942,000	₦ 4,727,000	₦ 2,763,000	₦ 3,987,000	₦ 2,621,000

3. Name your Excel sheets

Don't just go ahead with the default names – Sheet1, Sheet2, ... – rename the sheets to reflect the contents of the sheet. This makes your work better organized and future use more convenient.

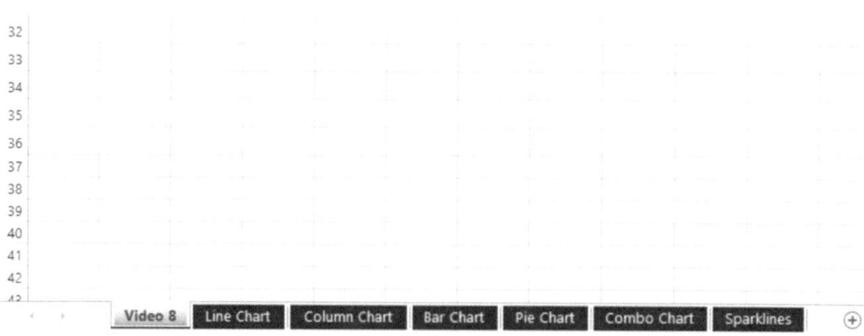

To rename a sheet, right click on the sheet name (the default names are Sheet1, Sheet2, ...) and select rename. And as you see above, you can change the color from the default too.

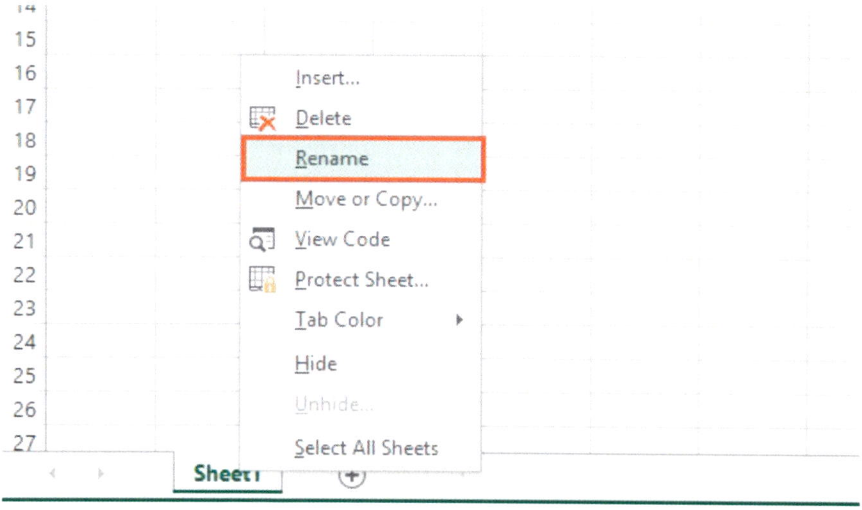

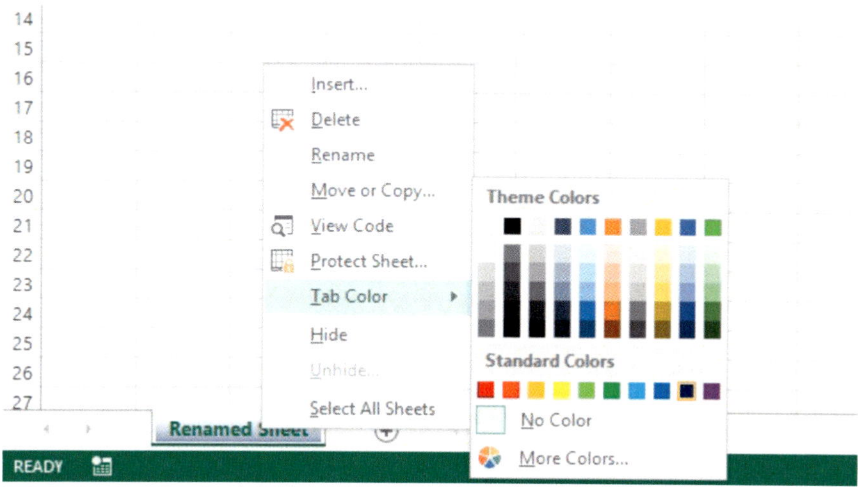

4. Also use descriptive names when renaming the Excel sheets.

12	Bayelsa	[illegible]	[illegible]	[illegible]	[illegible]
13	Rivers	₦ 4,860,256,800.00	₦ 4,459,705,200.00	₦ 2,423,028,900.00	₦ 4,148,808,
14	Anambra	₦ 1,511,863,500.00	₦ 3,015,652,900.00	₦ 2,159,322,900.00	₦ 4,060,131,
15	Enugu	₦ 2,609,372,800.00	₦ 4,581,716,900.00	₦ 1,409,979,200.00	₦ 1,990,646,
16	Benue	₦ 1,387,315,500.00	₦ 3,627,716,800.00	₦ 602,469,700.00	₦ 4,501,134,
17	Borno	₦ 1,616,065,000.00	₦ 4,166,988,100.00	₦ 2,361,614,200.00	₦ 4,908,244,
18	Gombe	₦ 2,201,453,200.00	₦ 2,523,019,700.00	₦ 620,111,300.00	₦ 1,885,641,
19	Katsina	₦ 1,293,838,700.00	₦ 2,648,689,500.00	₦ 3,589,421,500.00	₦ 638,877,
20	Kaduna	₦ 2,599,773,900.00	₦ 3,835,345,400.00	₦ 3,938,598,800.00	₦ 1,224,849,
21	Cross River	₦ 1,971,834,600.00	₦ 4,779,952,700.00	₦ 2,416,592,600.00	₦ 1,814,142,
22	Kwara	₦ 1,496,830,100.00	₦ 912,176,400.00	₦ 3,915,338,600.00	₦ 1,305,529,
23	Niger	₦ 4,592,318,900.00	₦ 1,826,747,300.00	₦ 3,002,387,100.00	₦ 3,219,870,
24	Akwa Ibom	₦ 1,691,712,500.00	₦ 2,202,014,900.00	₦ 824,782,800.00	₦ 4,927,386,
25	Plateau	₦ 2,371,220,000.00	₦ 4,894,816,200.00	₦ 4,527,323,100.00	₦ 4,471,653,
26	Taraba	₦ 785,603,400.00	₦ 3,244,525,900.00	₦ 531,248,900.00	₦ 2,475,480,
27	Zamfara	[illegible]	[illegible]	[illegible]	[illegible]

5. Avoid putting too many tables in one Excel sheet. Best to keep just related tables in the same sheet if you must put more than one table in the sheet. It makes naming the sheet easy and straightforward.

6. Use same naming conventions and table structure across all similar Excel files, especially weekly, monthly and yearly reports of the same data.

7. Don't use CAPS excessively. It makes your reports very unprofessional.

Building Datasheets that can easily scale

Occasionally, you will have to work on a table whose data grows continually. We can refer to such tables as datatables. All tables hold data and can technically be referred to as a datatable, but in this book we will refer to all tables as just tables and limit the term datatable to only tables that grow perpetually.

An example of such a table is an Employee Record table. As long as the company exists the table will keep growing and even if the company aims to not have over a 100 employees, there will always be old employees leaving and new ones taken to replace them. And they all have to be captured in the employee record table, no employee's record is deleted when he leaves, there's only a field added to capture his resignation.

There are some peculiar ways of treating a datatable.

1. Have only one datatable on a sheet. Since a datatable is a table you expect to grow over time, having only one on a sheet lets you have access to all the rows and the columns in the Excel sheet.

	A	B	C	D	E	F	
1	UrBizEdge Employees Biodata Table						
2	First Name	Last Name	Employee ID	Sex	Employment Date	Phone Number	Contact Addres
3	Michael	Olafusi	1000001	M	21-Oct-13	08089382423	21, Adigun Ala
4	John	Abiola	1000002	M	1-Apr-14	08080810251	21, Adigun Ala
5	Mary	Eze	1000003	F	1-Apr-14	08080810252	21, Adigun Ala
6	Segun	Owolabi	1000004	M	1-Apr-14	08080810253	21, Adigun Ala
7	Tolu	Owoeye	1000005	F	1-Apr-14	08080810254	21, Adigun Ala
8	Uche	Nnamdi	1000006	M	1-Apr-14	08080810255	21, Adigun Ala
9	David	Aluko	1000007	M	1-May-14	08080810256	21, Adigun Ala
10	Lekan	Bello	1000008	M	1-May-14	08080810257	21, Adigun Ala
11	Luke	Tsangi	1000009	M	1-May-14	08080810258	21, Adig

2. Start a datatable as close to cell A1 as possible. Again, this is to afford you the maximum space in the sheet for your growing table.

3. Avoid meaningless gaps in the datatable. Make it as compact as possible.

4. Arrange the fields such that the most important or basic fields come first. For example, in an Employee record table, name should come before contact address.

5. Have a field for every meaningful chunk of data. It is better to have separate fields for first name and last name than have one field hold both.

6. Avoid merging cells in a datatable. It is better to repeat cell entries than merge the cells. Merged cells aren't formula friendly.

And as a bonus, avoid hiding rows and columns in the datatable. This will save you a lot of future headaches.

Sorting

Sorting is one of the most frequent task we do in Excel. Sorting lets you re-arrange data in alphabetical order, lowest to highest, highest to lowest, and even by cell color.

We are used to having data arranged in a particular order – A to Z, January to December, 1 to 10, and so on.

Below is an example of a table that has its records haphazardly arranged. The states are not arranged alphabetically and the months are not in the natural order.

	A	B	C	D	E	F	G
1	**Internally Generated Revenue of States in Nigeria**						
2	**State**	**Feb-14**	**Jun-14**	**Jan-14**	**Mar-14**	**May-14**	**Apr-14**
3	Imo	₦ 2,521,764,800.00	₦ 2,922,241,900.00	₦ 2,591,742,600.00	₦ 2,013,994,900.00	₦ 3,014,428,300.00	₦ 4,994,515,700.00
4	Abia	₦ 821,123,500.00	₦ 4,544,916,100.00	₦ 1,297,498,300.00	₦ 1,175,454,800.00	₦ 2,265,644,000.00	₦ 967,327,400.00
5	Lagos	₦ 7,319,183,000.00	₦ 22,681,984,500.00	₦ 6,239,473,500.00	₦ 6,211,689,500.00	₦ 11,610,307,000.00	₦ 3,351,178,500.00
6	Kano	₦ 2,021,735,600.00	₦ 530,613,400.00	₦ 2,981,980,300.00	₦ 3,016,518,600.00	₦ 2,387,291,000.00	₦ 4,411,651,000.00
7	Ondo	₦ 1,690,422,800.00	₦ 4,925,747,700.00	₦ 716,222,900.00	₦ 4,362,953,800.00	₦ 4,300,936,900.00	₦ 977,876,300.00
8	Kogi	₦ 2,734,189,600.00	₦ 2,825,512,800.00	₦ 2,812,863,300.00	₦ 2,306,601,300.00	₦ 2,104,687,400.00	₦ 867,264,000.00
9	Benue	₦ 3,864,832,700.00	₦ 3,212,451,900.00	₦ 3,479,649,000.00	₦ 2,458,711,700.00	₦ 2,700,421,800.00	₦ 4,801,142,000.00
10	FCT	₦ 2,063,317,300.00	₦ 2,520,202,900.00	₦ 3,199,223,200.00	₦ 1,829,381,400.00	₦ 4,980,777,000.00	₦ 3,704,640,600.00
11	Ogun	₦ 2,586,000,100.00	₦ 3,200,451,900.00	₦ 3,434,714,900.00	₦ 3,907,557,600.00	₦ 2,265,022,600.00	₦ 1,642,410,200.00
12	Bayelsa	₦ 2,035,499,300.00	₦ 1,754,855,100.00	₦ 1,218,646,400.00	₦ 3,596,177,500.00	₦ 4,856,865,900.00	₦ 3,958,333,500.00
13	Rivers	₦ 4,860,256,800.00	₦ 4,459,705,200.00	₦ 2,423,028,900.00	₦ 4,148,808,900.00	₦ 4,882,684,300.00	₦ 859,719,700.00
14	Anambra	₦ 1,511,863,500.00	₦ 3,015,652,900.00	₦ 2,159,322,900.00	₦ 4,060,131,900.00	₦ 2,439,308,800.00	₦ 1,843,665,900.00
15	Enugu	₦ 2,609,372,800.00	₦ 4,581,716,900.00	₦ 1,409,979,200.00	₦ 1,990,646,300.00	₦ 1,893,090,400.00	₦ 3,219,650,200.00
16	Benue	₦ 1,387,315,500.00	₦ 3,627,716,800.00	₦ 602,469,700.00	₦ 4,501,134,600.00	₦ 1,687,978,600.00	₦ 2,728,902,800.00
17	Borno	₦ 1,616,065,000.00	₦ 4,166,988,100.00	₦ 2,361,614,200.00	₦ 4,908,244,600.00	₦ 581,980,000.00	₦ 4,216,846,800.00
18	Gombe	₦ 2,201,453,200.00	₦ 2,523,019,700.00	₦ 620,111,300.00	₦ 1,885,641,400.00	₦ 2,551,023,100.00	₦ 4,146,024,300.00
19	Katsina	₦ 1,293,838,700.00	₦ 2,648,689,500.00	₦ 3,589,421,500.00	₦ 638,877,300.00	₦ 1,025,989,500.00	₦ 2,969,721,400.00
20	Kaduna	₦ 2,599,773,900.00	₦ 3,835,345,400.00	₦ 3,938,598,800.00	₦ 1,224,849,400.00	₦ 450,931,500.00	₦ 1,662,248,400.00
21	Cross River	₦ 1,971,834,600.00	₦ 4,779,952,700.00	₦ 2,416,592,600.00	₦ 1,814,142,400.00	₦ 745,327,000.00	₦ 4,658,487,000.00
22	Kwara	₦ 1,496,830,100.00	₦ 912,176,400.00	₦ 3,915,338,600.00	₦ 1,305,529,900.00	₦ 2,214,504,600.00	₦ 4,919,941,300.00
23	Niger	₦ 4,592,318,900.00	₦ 1,826,747,300.00	₦ 3,002,387,100.00	₦ 3,219,870,900.00	₦ 3,979,805,300.00	₦ 1,086,334,400.00
24	Akwa Ibom	₦ 1,691,712,500.00	₦ 2,202,014,900.00	₦ 824,782,800.00	₦ 4,927,386,500.00	₦ 2,966,925,400.00	₦ 2,187,626,200.00
25	Plateau	₦ 2,371,220,000.00	₦ 4,894,816,200.00	₦ 4,527,323,100.00	₦ 4,471,653,300.00	₦ 3,593,441,000.00	₦ 932,778,800.00
26	Taraba	₦ 785,603,400.00	₦ 3,244,525,900.00	₦ 531,248,900.00	₦ 2,475,480,400.00	₦ 1,389,495,200.00	₦ 878,820,400.00
27	[illegible]	[illegible]	[illegible]	[illegible]	[illegible]	[illegible]	[illegible]

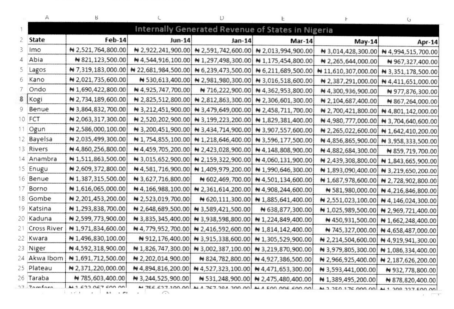

First, let's have the data sorted by State alphabetically

Below are the recommended steps to sorting a table. Select the table, go to the Home menu and click on Sort & Filter.

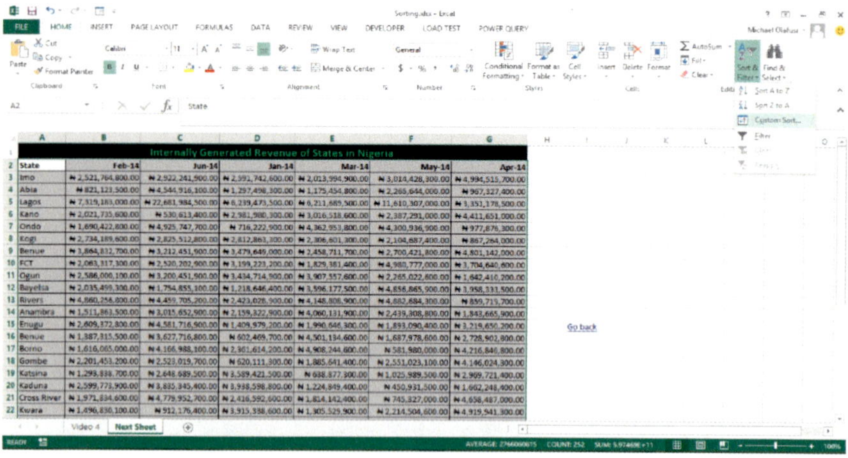

The sorting dialog box comes up.

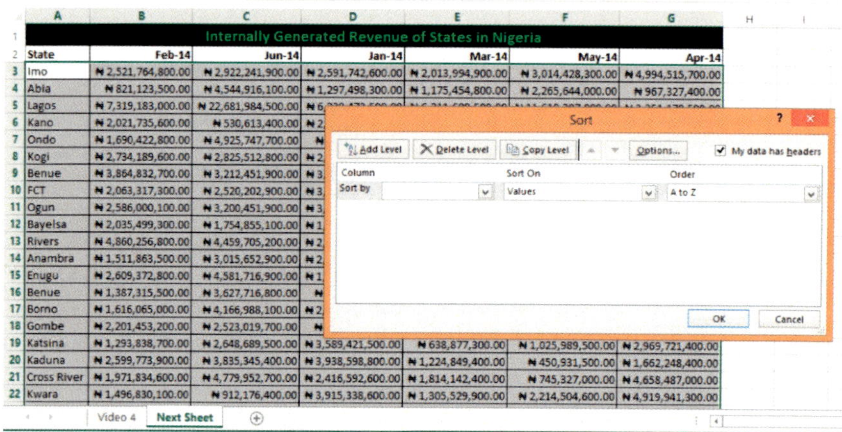

This dialog box allows you to add more than the default one level of sorting.

Select "State" in the Sort by box and A to Z in the Order box.

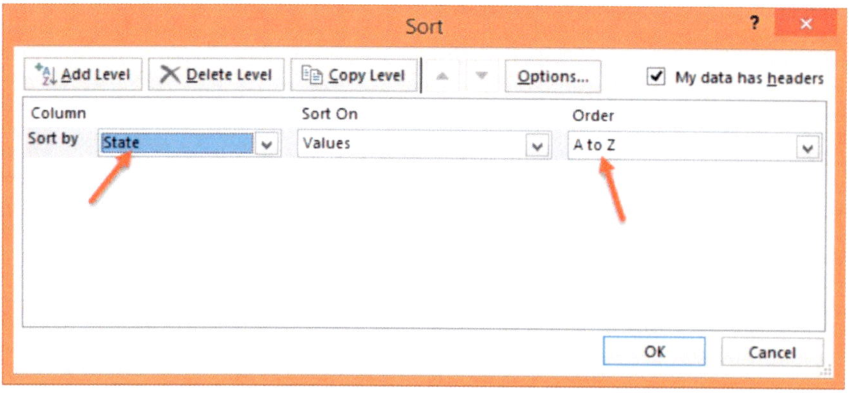

The result is shown below.

Internally Generated Revenue of States in Nigeria

State	Feb-14	Jun-14	Jan-14	Mar-14	May-14	Apr-14
Abia	₦ 821,123,500.00	₦ 4,544,916,100.00	₦ 1,297,498,300.00	₦ 1,175,454,800.00	₦ 2,265,644,000.00	₦ 967,327,400.00
Adamawa	₦ 4,317,641,300.00	₦ 1,973,059,900.00	₦ 4,022,792,500.00	₦ 1,627,470,600.00	₦ 3,493,691,500.00	₦ 1,023,694,700.00
Akwa Ibom	₦ 1,691,712,500.00	₦ 2,202,014,900.00	₦ 824,782,800.00	₦ 4,927,386,500.00	₦ 2,966,925,400.00	₦ 2,187,626,200.00
Anambra	₦ 1,511,863,500.00	₦ 3,015,652,900.00	₦ 2,159,322,900.00	₦ 4,060,131,900.00	₦ 2,439,308,800.00	₦ 1,843,665,900.00
Bauchi	₦ 3,059,451,100.00	₦ 3,000,312,200.00	₦ 764,748,600.00	₦ 2,879,985,600.00	₦ 2,609,030,900.00	₦ 3,032,115,500.00
Bayelsa	₦ 2,035,499,300.00	₦ 1,754,855,100.00	₦ 1,218,646,400.00	₦ 3,596,177,500.00	₦ 4,856,865,900.00	₦ 3,958,333,500.00
Benue	₦ 3,864,832,700.00	₦ 3,212,451,900.00	₦ 3,479,649,000.00	₦ 2,458,711,700.00	₦ 2,700,421,800.00	₦ 4,801,142,000.00
Benue	₦ 1,387,315,500.00	₦ 3,627,716,800.00	₦ 602,469,700.00	₦ 4,501,134,600.00	₦ 1,687,978,600.00	₦ 2,728,902,800.00
Borno	₦ 1,616,065,000.00	₦ 4,166,988,100.00	₦ 2,361,614,200.00	₦ 4,908,244,600.00	₦ 581,980,000.00	₦ 4,216,846,800.00
Cross River	₦ 1,971,834,600.00	₦ 4,779,952,700.00	₦ 2,416,592,600.00	₦ 1,814,142,400.00	₦ 745,327,000.00	₦ 4,658,487,000.00
Delta	₦ 2,382,209,500.00	₦ 2,363,220,900.00	₦ 4,755,914,300.00	₦ 3,361,514,600.00	₦ 4,671,269,900.00	₦ 2,060,298,000.00
Ebonyi	₦ 3,233,069,500.00	₦ 713,048,500.00	₦ 3,547,140,000.00	₦ 4,883,253,900.00	₦ 2,926,053,500.00	₦ 1,060,164,800.00
Edo	₦ 781,461,300.00	₦ 2,900,705,900.00	₦ 2,663,501,000.00	₦ 462,661,800.00	₦ 3,256,011,600.00	₦ 543,085,200.00
Ekiti	₦ 4,128,943,600.00	₦ 4,040,341,600.00	₦ 1,816,087,900.00	₦ 1,512,170,300.00	₦ 3,340,038,100.00	₦ 2,592,908,100.00
Enugu	₦ 2,609,372,800.00	₦ 4,581,716,900.00	₦ 1,409,979,200.00	₦ 1,990,646,300.00	₦ 1,893,090,400.00	₦ 3,219,650,200.00
FCT	₦ 2,063,317,300.00	₦ 2,520,202,900.00	₦ 3,199,223,200.00	₦ 1,829,381,400.00	₦ 4,980,777,000.00	₦ 3,704,640,600.00
Gombe	₦ 2,201,453,200.00	₦ 2,523,019,700.00	₦ 620,111,300.00	₦ 1,885,641,400.00	₦ 2,551,023,100.00	₦ 4,146,024,300.00
Imo	₦ 2,521,764,800.00	₦ 2,922,241,900.00	₦ 2,591,742,600.00	₦ 2,013,994,900.00	₦ 3,014,428,300.00	₦ 4,994,515,700.00
Jigawa	₦ 1,573,445,100.00	₦ 2,311,559,800.00	₦ 3,550,126,700.00	₦ 3,756,243,200.00	₦ 1,417,963,700.00	₦ 3,092,703,100.00
Kaduna	₦ 2,599,773,900.00	₦ 3,835,345,400.00	₦ 3,938,598,800.00	₦ 1,224,849,400.00	₦ 450,931,500.00	₦ 1,662,248,400.00

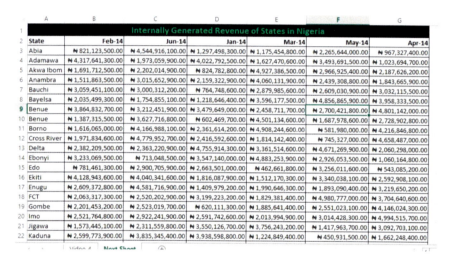

You can add an extra level of sorting in the sorting dialog box. This would be useful in sorting tables like a national population census table. You might want to sort first by state (from Abia to Zamfara) and then an extra level of sorting by Local Government Areas. So you'll have a setting similar to the one below

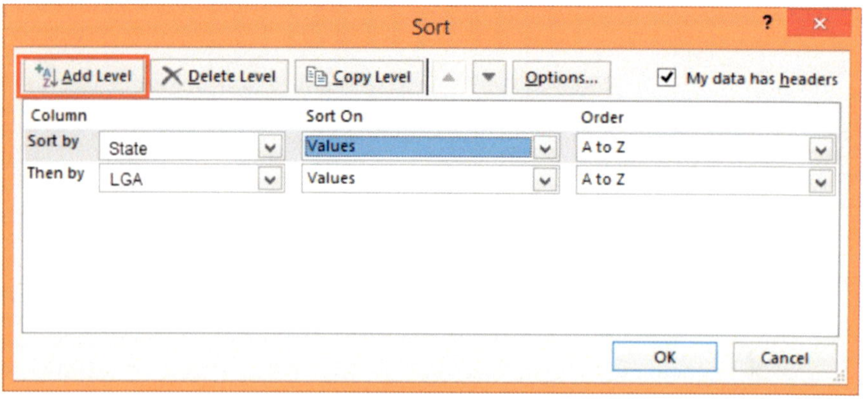

Next is to sort the months in the natural order we are used to – Jan to Dec. This will require a type of sorting called "Left to Right" as against the one we just did, called "Top to Bottom".

So to get this done, we select the table starting from the first month to the last month. We will leave the state field out because we want it to remain in the position it is.

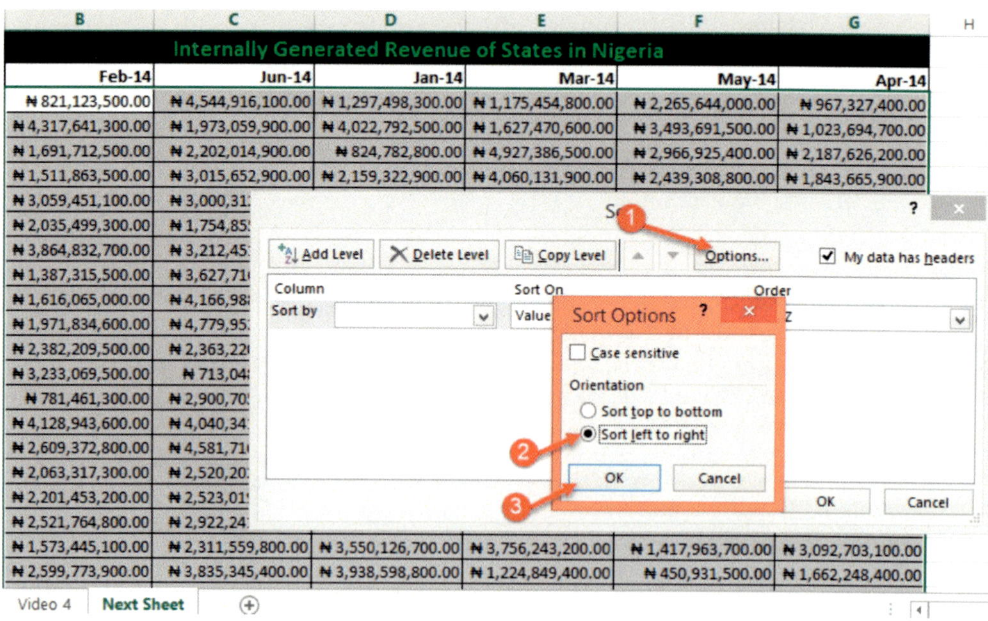

Then select the row the months are on (Row 2) and set the order to **Oldest to Newest.**

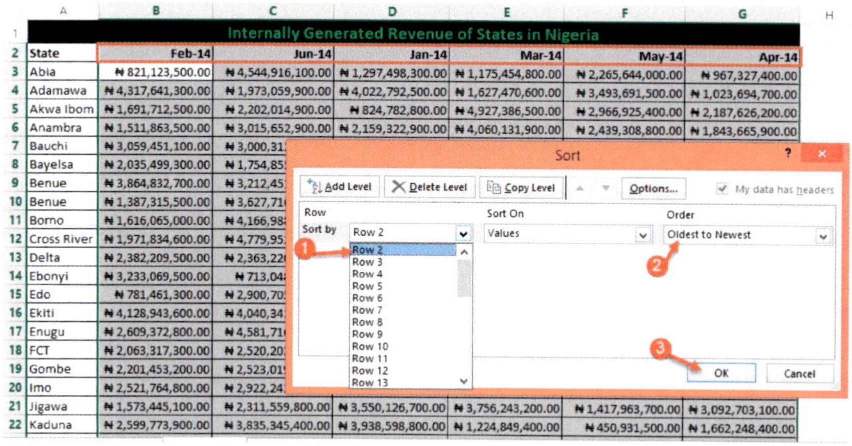

Below is the result.

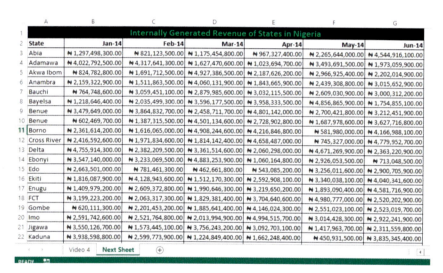

	Internally Generated Revenue of States in Nigeria					
State	Jan-14	Feb-14	Mar-14	Apr-14	May-14	Jun-14
Abia	₦ 1,297,498,300.00	₦ 821,123,500.00	₦ 1,175,454,800.00	₦ 967,327,400.00	₦ 2,265,644,000.00	₦ 4,544,916,100.00
Adamawa	₦ 4,022,792,500.00	₦ 4,317,641,300.00	₦ 1,627,470,600.00	₦ 1,023,694,700.00	₦ 3,493,691,500.00	₦ 1,973,059,900.00
Akwa Ibom	₦ 824,782,800.00	₦ 1,691,712,500.00	₦ 4,927,386,500.00	₦ 2,187,626,200.00	₦ 2,966,925,400.00	₦ 2,202,014,900.00
Anambra	₦ 2,159,322,900.00	₦ 1,511,863,500.00	₦ 4,060,131,900.00	₦ 1,843,665,900.00	₦ 2,439,308,800.00	₦ 3,015,652,900.00
Bauchi	₦ 764,748,600.00	₦ 3,059,451,100.00	₦ 2,879,985,600.00	₦ 3,032,115,500.00	₦ 2,609,030,900.00	₦ 3,000,312,200.00
Bayelsa	₦ 1,218,646,400.00	₦ 2,035,499,300.00	₦ 3,596,177,500.00	₦ 3,958,333,500.00	₦ 4,856,865,900.00	₦ 1,754,855,100.00
Benue	₦ 3,479,649,000.00	₦ 3,864,832,700.00	₦ 2,458,711,700.00	₦ 4,801,142,000.00	₦ 2,700,421,800.00	₦ 3,212,451,900.00
Benue	₦ 602,469,700.00	₦ 1,387,315,500.00	₦ 4,501,134,600.00	₦ 2,728,902,800.00	₦ 1,687,978,600.00	₦ 3,627,716,800.00
Borno	₦ 2,361,614,200.00	₦ 1,616,065,000.00	₦ 4,908,244,600.00	₦ 4,216,846,800.00	₦ 581,980,000.00	₦ 4,166,988,100.00
Cross River	₦ 2,416,592,600.00	₦ 1,971,834,600.00	₦ 1,814,142,400.00	₦ 4,658,487,000.00	₦ 745,327,000.00	₦ 4,779,952,700.00
Delta	₦ 4,755,914,300.00	₦ 2,382,209,500.00	₦ 3,361,514,600.00	₦ 2,060,298,000.00	₦ 4,671,269,900.00	₦ 2,363,220,900.00
Ebonyi	₦ 3,547,140,000.00	₦ 3,233,069,500.00	₦ 4,883,253,900.00	₦ 1,060,164,800.00	₦ 2,926,053,500.00	₦ 713,048,500.00
Edo	₦ 2,663,501,000.00	₦ 781,461,300.00	₦ 462,661,800.00	₦ 543,085,200.00	₦ 3,256,011,600.00	₦ 2,900,705,900.00
Ekiti	₦ 1,816,087,900.00	₦ 4,128,943,600.00	₦ 1,512,170,300.00	₦ 2,592,908,100.00	₦ 3,340,038,100.00	₦ 4,040,341,600.00
Enugu	₦ 1,409,979,200.00	₦ 2,609,372,800.00	₦ 1,990,646,300.00	₦ 3,219,650,200.00	₦ 1,893,090,400.00	₦ 4,581,716,900.00
FCT	₦ 3,199,223,200.00	₦ 2,063,317,300.00	₦ 1,829,381,400.00	₦ 3,704,640,600.00	₦ 4,980,777,000.00	₦ 2,520,202,900.00
Gombe	₦ 620,111,300.00	₦ 2,201,453,200.00	₦ 1,885,641,400.00	₦ 4,146,024,300.00	₦ 2,551,023,100.00	₦ 2,523,019,700.00
Imo	₦ 2,591,742,600.00	₦ 2,521,764,800.00	₦ 2,013,994,900.00	₦ 4,994,515,700.00	₦ 3,014,428,300.00	₦ 2,922,241,900.00
Jigawa	₦ 3,550,126,700.00	₦ 1,573,445,100.00	₦ 3,756,243,200.00	₦ 3,092,703,100.00	₦ 1,417,963,700.00	₦ 2,311,559,800.00
Kaduna	₦ 3,938,598,800.00	₦ 2,599,773,900.00	₦ 1,224,849,400.00	₦ 1,662,248,400.00	₦ 450,931,500.00	₦ 3,835,345,400.00

Video 4 | Next Sheet

Filtering

Filter is one of the Excel power user's most used tool. It allows you selectively choose what you want to view in a table and hide the rest.

It is very easy to access and can be accessed from three different places in Excel.

By right clicking and selecting Filter.

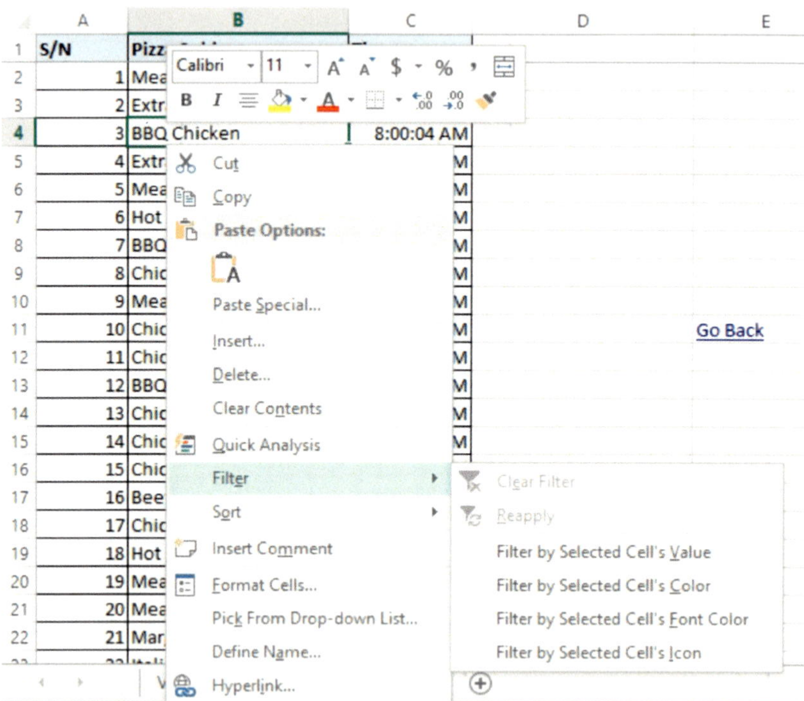

From the Home menu, clicking on Sort & Filter at the right.

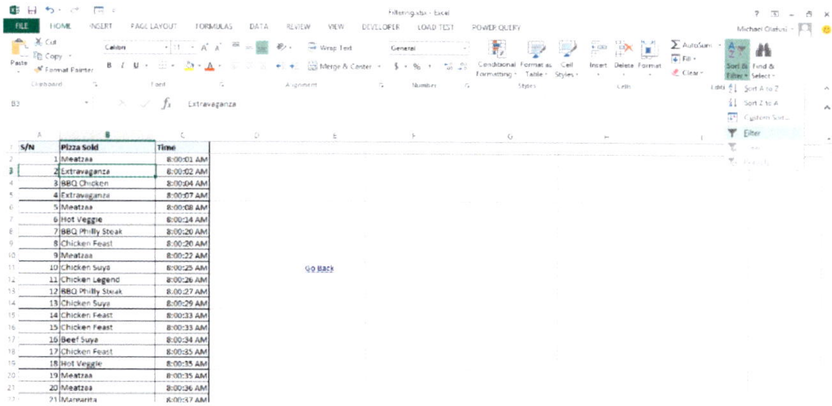

From the Data menu.

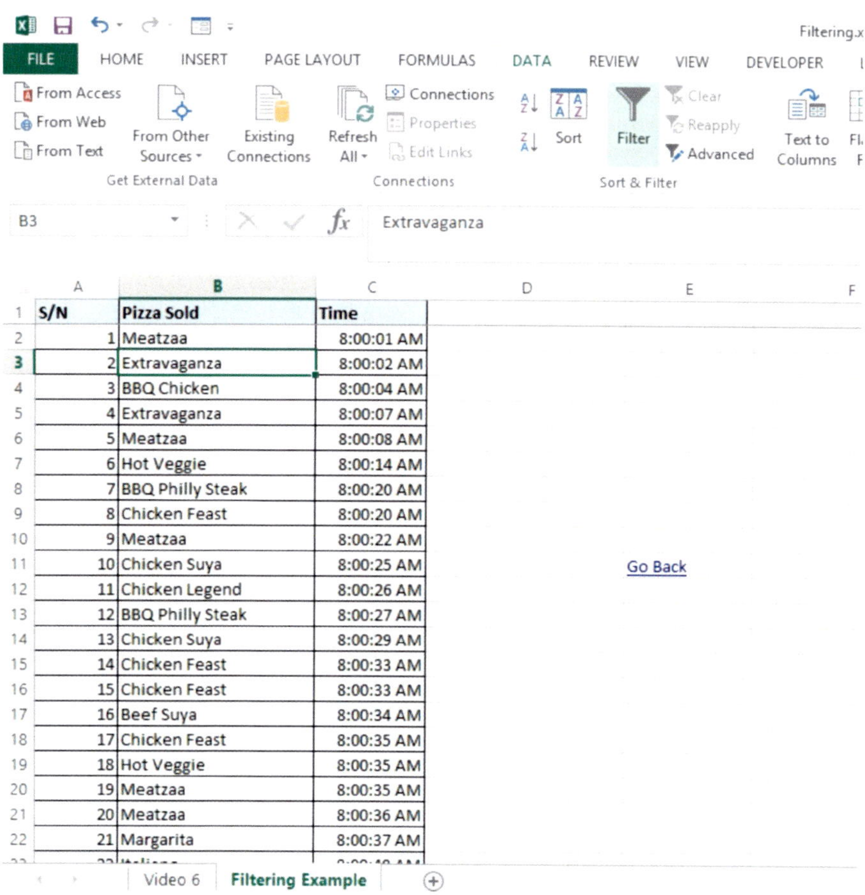

Once you've turned on the Filter tool by clicking on it, you will see a dropdown box beside the headers of the table.

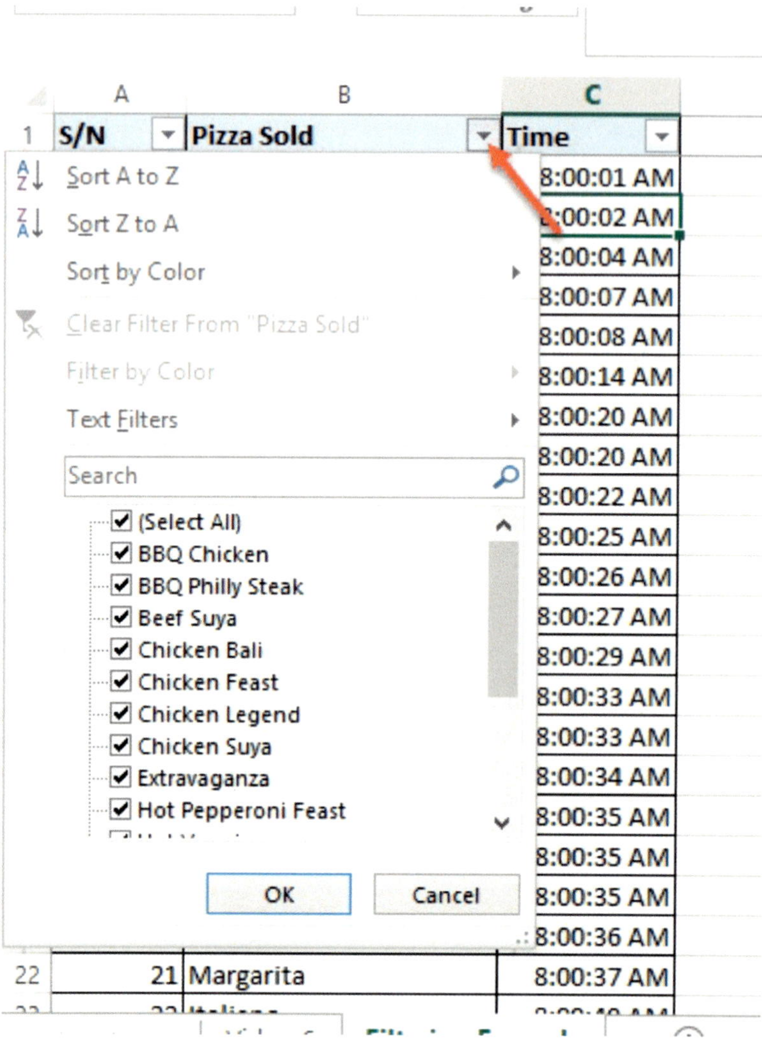

Clicking on the dropdown box shows you all the unique items in that field and you can select the ones you want to view (hiding the rest). By default, all items are selected so you will have to unselect the ones you don't want to see.

In the screenshot below, all the pizza items were unselected except the BBQ Chicken (meaning only BBQ Chicken was selected).

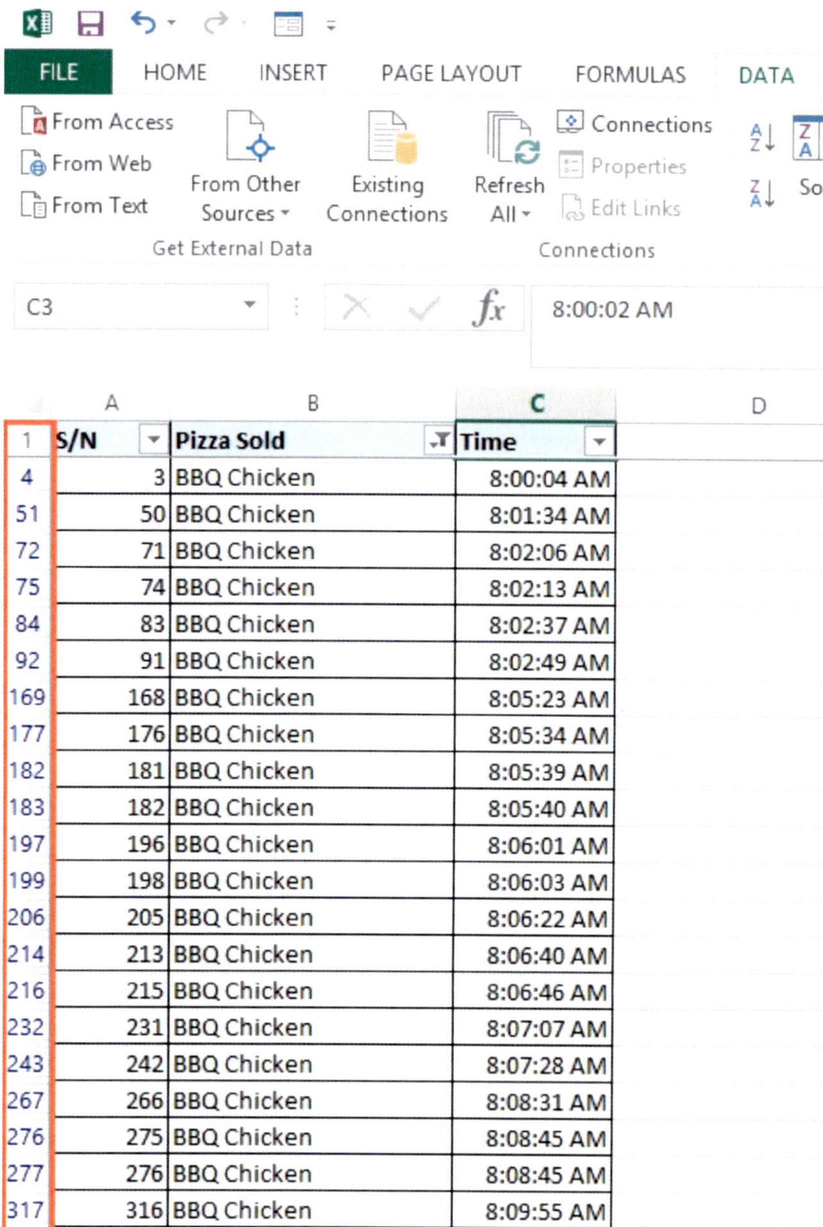

Notice the blue row numbers, it is Excel's way of visually hinting you that some rows have been hidden as they did not contain the items we want to view.

Filtering is that simple and straight forward.

Advanced Filtering

Every time you apply filter to a dataset in Excel and then copy out the filtered data, you could have saved yourself time and some mouse-strokes by using advanced filter. And despite the name, advanced filter, it is surprisingly easy to use.

As an example, I have the fictitious sales record for Dhormino's Pizza for June 5, 2016. They sell 16 Pizza types: Meatzaa, Extravaganza , BBQ Chicken, Hot Veggie, BBQ Philly Steak, Chicken Feast, Chicken Suya, Chicken Legend, Beef Suya, Margarita, Italiano, Pepperoni Suya, Veggie Supreme, Hot Pepperoni Feast, Chicken Bali and Pepperoni Feast.

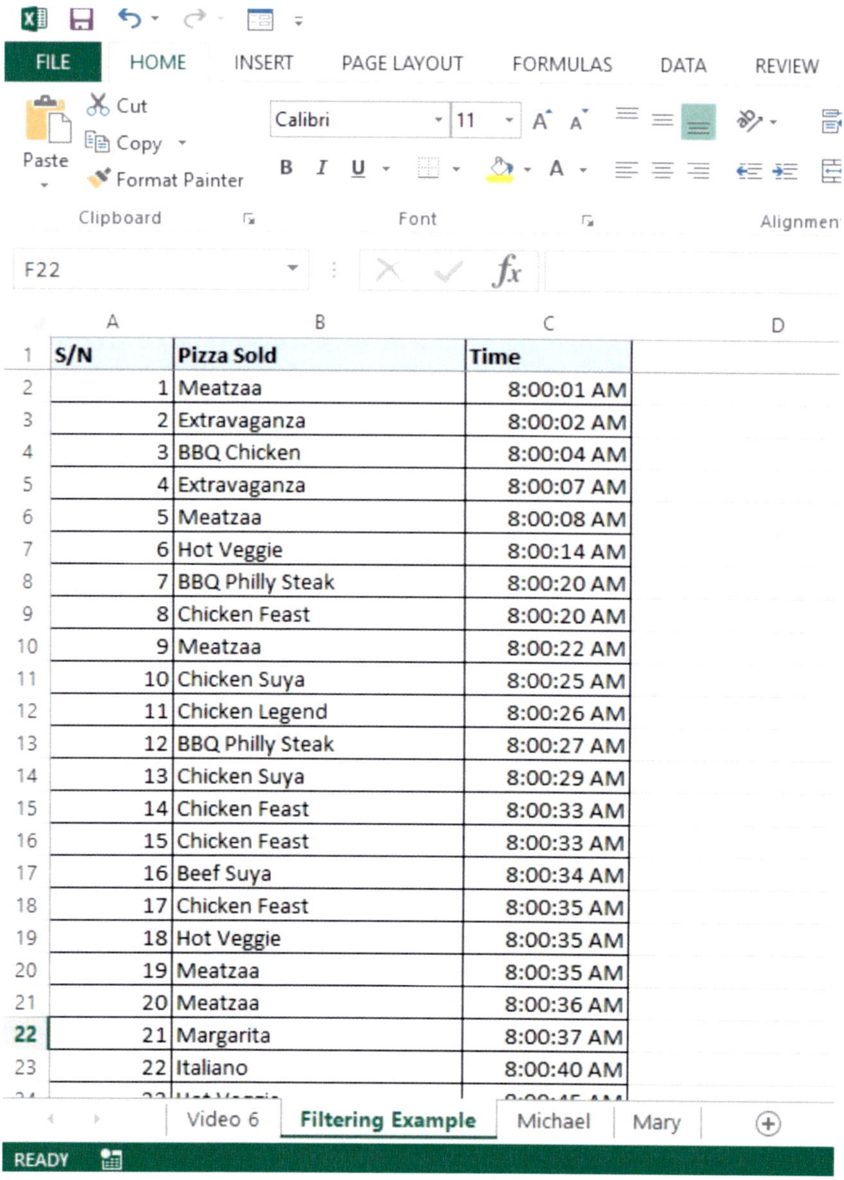

S/N	Pizza Sold	Time
1	Meatzaa	8:00:01 AM
2	Extravaganza	8:00:02 AM
3	BBQ Chicken	8:00:04 AM
4	Extravaganza	8:00:07 AM
5	Meatzaa	8:00:08 AM
6	Hot Veggie	8:00:14 AM
7	BBQ Philly Steak	8:00:20 AM
8	Chicken Feast	8:00:20 AM
9	Meatzaa	8:00:22 AM
10	Chicken Suya	8:00:25 AM
11	Chicken Legend	8:00:26 AM
12	BBQ Philly Steak	8:00:27 AM
13	Chicken Suya	8:00:29 AM
14	Chicken Feast	8:00:33 AM
15	Chicken Feast	8:00:33 AM
16	Beef Suya	8:00:34 AM
17	Chicken Feast	8:00:35 AM
18	Hot Veggie	8:00:35 AM
19	Meatzaa	8:00:35 AM
20	Meatzaa	8:00:36 AM
21	Margarita	8:00:37 AM
22	Italiano	8:00:40 AM

They got a new country manager this March, and one of his strategies is to have four brand managers owning 4 different baskets of the pizza types, like the FMCG companies do. Two of those managers are Michael and Mary. They are to ensure that the brands (pizza types) they own are performing well. They are given the latitude and resources to promote them using whatever promotional mix they want.

As the company's main business data analyst, you pull out daily sales records and extract the ones for each brand manager. With advanced filter, it will be a piece of cake. You might even hook it to a recorded macro and at a click of button all is done.

Continuing with the example, let's see how to extract for Michael and Mary.

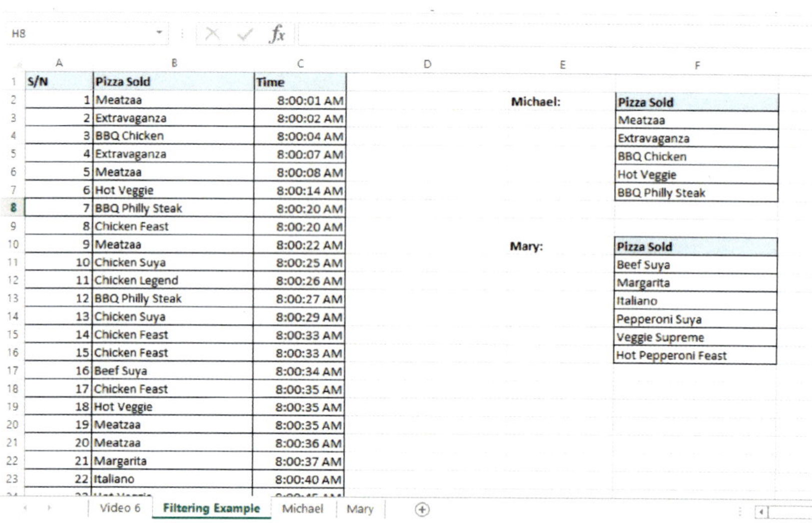

S/N	Pizza Sold	Time
1	Meatzaa	8:00:01 AM
2	Extravaganza	8:00:02 AM
3	BBQ Chicken	8:00:04 AM
4	Extravaganza	8:00:07 AM
5	Meatzaa	8:00:08 AM
6	Hot Veggie	8:00:14 AM
7	BBQ Philly Steak	8:00:20 AM
8	Chicken Feast	8:00:20 AM
9	Meatzaa	8:00:22 AM
10	Chicken Suya	8:00:25 AM
11	Chicken Legend	8:00:26 AM
12	BBQ Philly Steak	8:00:27 AM
13	Chicken Suya	8:00:29 AM
14	Chicken Feast	8:00:33 AM
15	Chicken Feast	8:00:33 AM
16	Beef Suya	8:00:34 AM
17	Chicken Feast	8:00:35 AM
18	Hot Veggie	8:00:35 AM
19	Meatzaa	8:00:35 AM
20	Meatzaa	8:00:36 AM
21	Margarita	8:00:37 AM
22	Italiano	8:00:40 AM

Michael:

Pizza Sold
Meatzaa
Extravaganza
BBQ Chicken
Hot Veggie
BBQ Philly Steak

Mary:

Pizza Sold
Beef Suya
Margarita
Italiano
Pepperoni Suya
Veggie Supreme
Hot Pepperoni Feast

Step 1 is to write out the pizza types Michael and Mary manage, separately. And to help advanced filter know where to look for those pizza names, give them a header that matches that in the sales table. See the screenshot above for what I mean.

Step 2 is to go to Michael's sheet (another Excel sheet where you want to put Michael's). Launch advanced filter from there. It is under Data menu, about the middle of the menu tools.

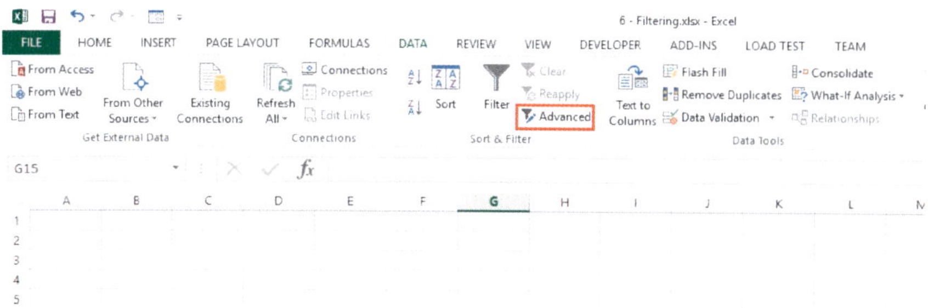

Set it to "Copy to another location"

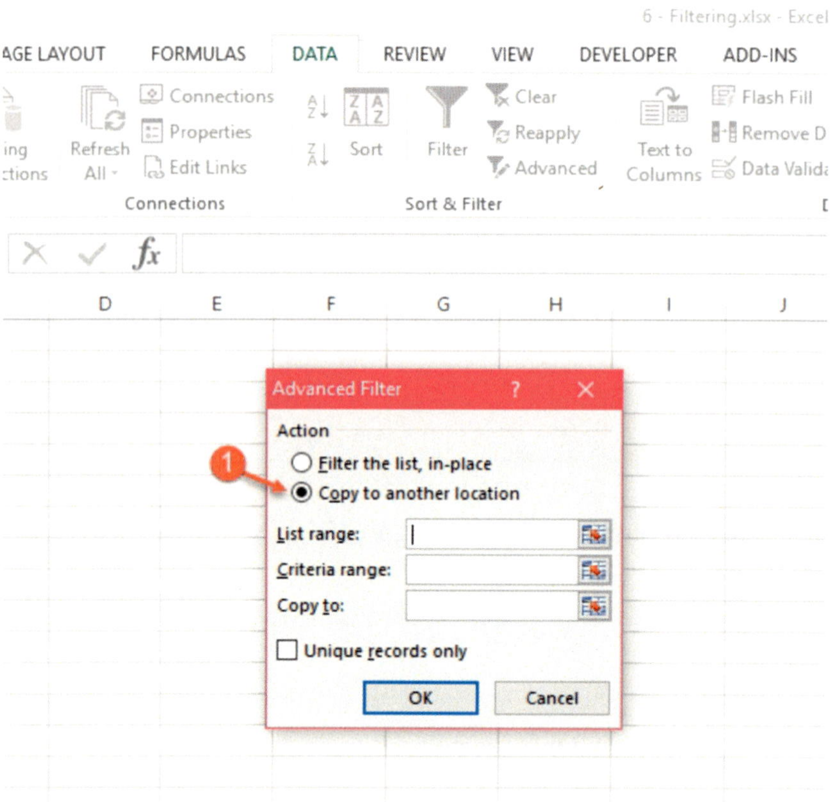

Provide the sales data range as the "list range", and Michael's pizza types with the header as the "Criteria range".

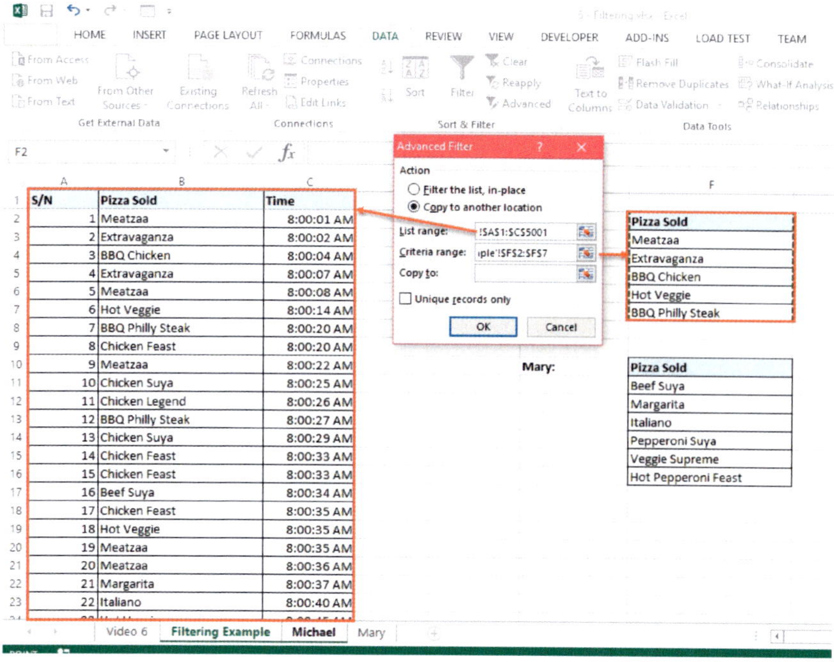

Finally, for the "Copy to", go to Michael's sheet and select where the result should be displayed. In this example, I select cell A1.

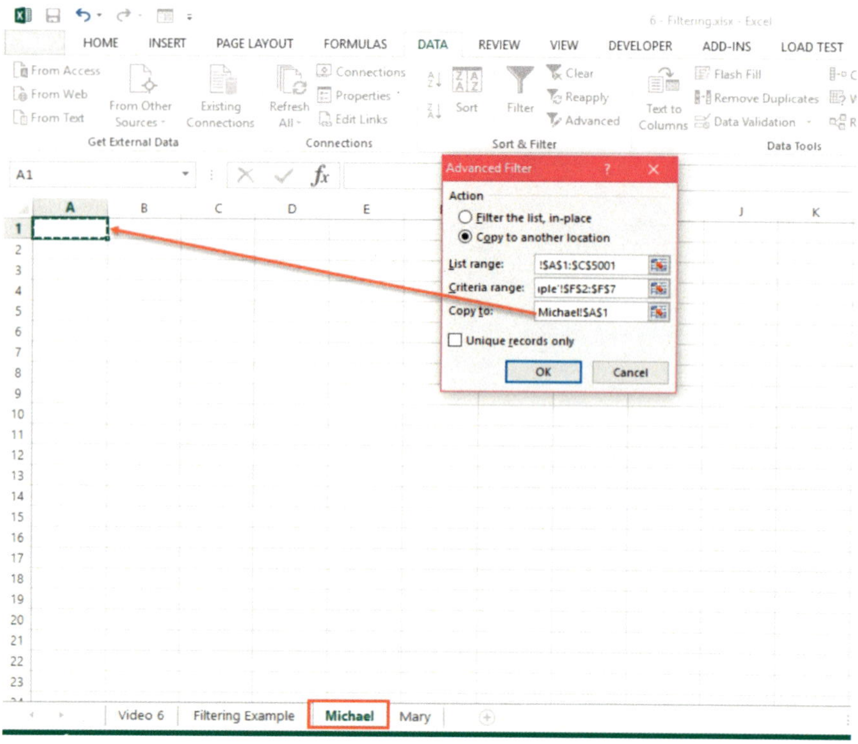

And voila! We get the results.

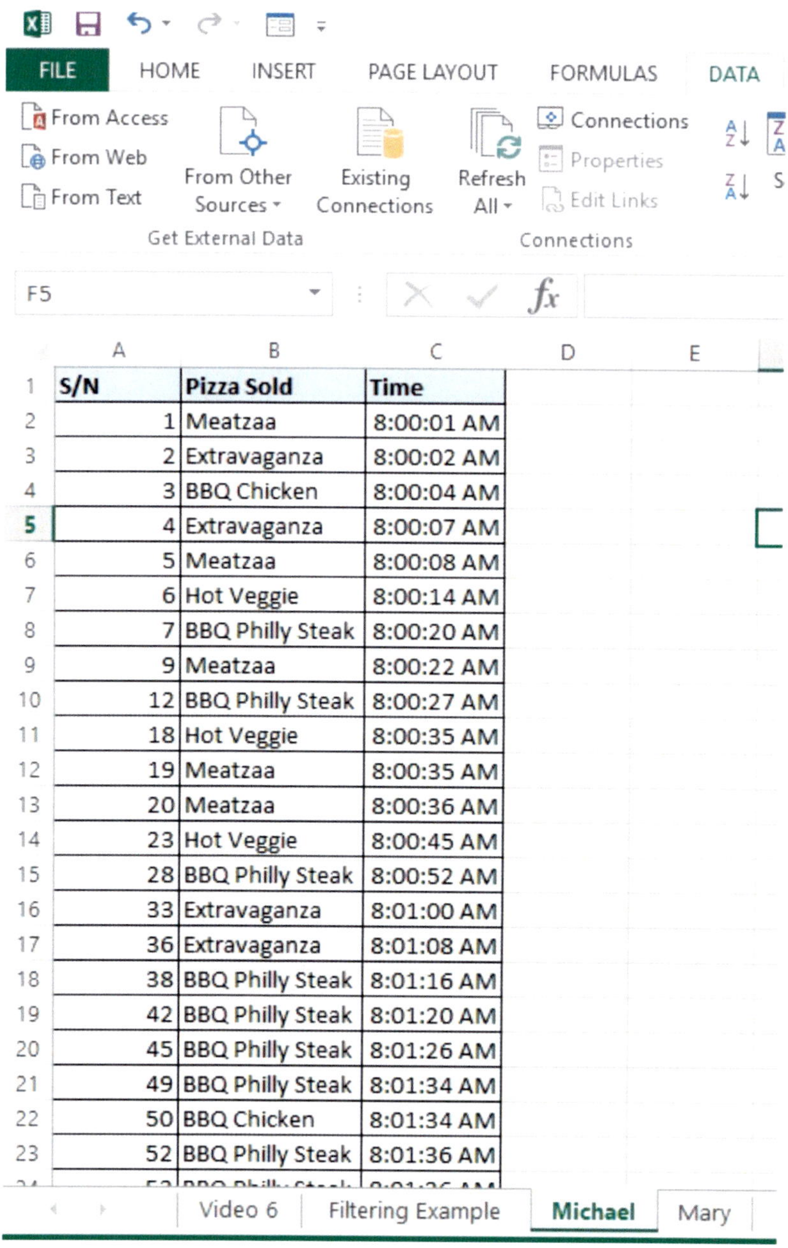

S/N	Pizza Sold	Time
1	Meatzaa	8:00:01 AM
2	Extravaganza	8:00:02 AM
3	BBQ Chicken	8:00:04 AM
4	Extravaganza	8:00:07 AM
5	Meatzaa	8:00:08 AM
6	Hot Veggie	8:00:14 AM
7	BBQ Philly Steak	8:00:20 AM
9	Meatzaa	8:00:22 AM
12	BBQ Philly Steak	8:00:27 AM
18	Hot Veggie	8:00:35 AM
19	Meatzaa	8:00:35 AM
20	Meatzaa	8:00:36 AM
23	Hot Veggie	8:00:45 AM
28	BBQ Philly Steak	8:00:52 AM
33	Extravaganza	8:01:00 AM
36	Extravaganza	8:01:08 AM
38	BBQ Philly Steak	8:01:16 AM
42	BBQ Philly Steak	8:01:20 AM
45	BBQ Philly Steak	8:01:26 AM
49	BBQ Philly Steak	8:01:34 AM
50	BBQ Chicken	8:01:34 AM
52	BBQ Philly Steak	8:01:36 AM

Very easy and cool.

And there is more to advanced filter. How about if we have a more detailed sales transaction data that captures sales value for each sales transaction, and we would like to extract sales transactions that generated more that 15,000 naira. That too is very easy with advanced filter.

Just follow me. Below is the snapshot of the detailed sales transaction data.

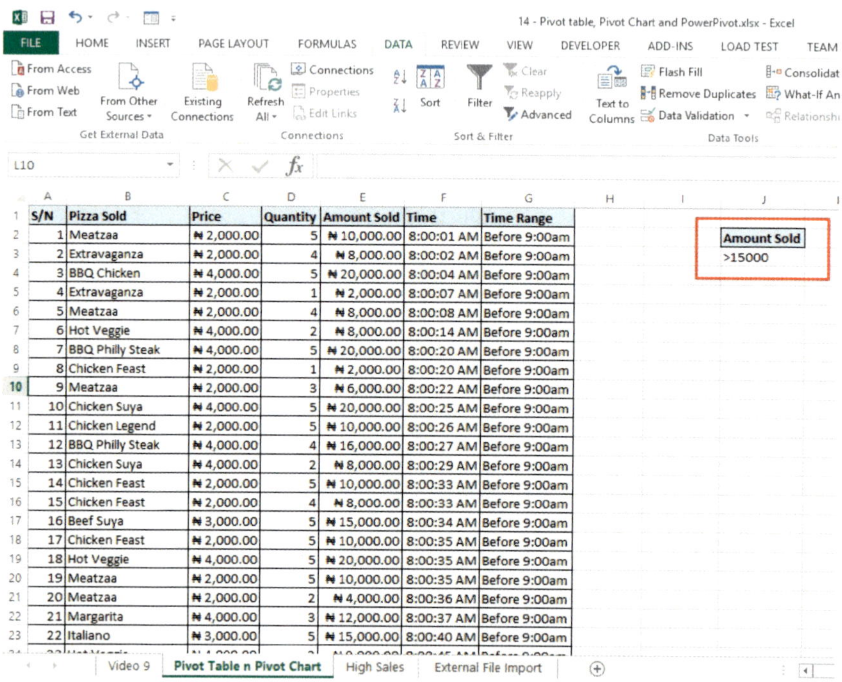

S/N	Pizza Sold	Price	Quantity	Amount Sold	Time	Time Range
1	Meatzaa	₦ 2,000.00	5	₦ 10,000.00	8:00:01 AM	Before 9:00am
2	Extravaganza	₦ 2,000.00	4	₦ 8,000.00	8:00:02 AM	Before 9:00am
3	BBQ Chicken	₦ 4,000.00	5	₦ 20,000.00	8:00:04 AM	Before 9:00am
4	Extravaganza	₦ 2,000.00	1	₦ 2,000.00	8:00:07 AM	Before 9:00am
5	Meatzaa	₦ 2,000.00	4	₦ 8,000.00	8:00:08 AM	Before 9:00am
6	Hot Veggie	₦ 4,000.00	2	₦ 8,000.00	8:00:14 AM	Before 9:00am
7	BBQ Philly Steak	₦ 4,000.00	5	₦ 20,000.00	8:00:20 AM	Before 9:00am
8	Chicken Feast	₦ 2,000.00	1	₦ 2,000.00	8:00:20 AM	Before 9:00am
9	Meatzaa	₦ 2,000.00	3	₦ 6,000.00	8:00:22 AM	Before 9:00am
10	Chicken Suya	₦ 4,000.00	5	₦ 20,000.00	8:00:25 AM	Before 9:00am
11	Chicken Legend	₦ 2,000.00	5	₦ 10,000.00	8:00:26 AM	Before 9:00am
12	BBQ Philly Steak	₦ 4,000.00	4	₦ 16,000.00	8:00:27 AM	Before 9:00am
13	Chicken Suya	₦ 4,000.00	2	₦ 8,000.00	8:00:29 AM	Before 9:00am
14	Chicken Feast	₦ 2,000.00	5	₦ 10,000.00	8:00:33 AM	Before 9:00am
15	Chicken Feast	₦ 2,000.00	4	₦ 8,000.00	8:00:33 AM	Before 9:00am
16	Beef Suya	₦ 3,000.00	5	₦ 15,000.00	8:00:34 AM	Before 9:00am
17	Chicken Feast	₦ 2,000.00	5	₦ 10,000.00	8:00:35 AM	Before 9:00am
18	Hot Veggie	₦ 4,000.00	5	₦ 20,000.00	8:00:35 AM	Before 9:00am
19	Meatzaa	₦ 2,000.00	5	₦ 10,000.00	8:00:35 AM	Before 9:00am
20	Meatzaa	₦ 2,000.00	2	₦ 4,000.00	8:00:36 AM	Before 9:00am
21	Margarita	₦ 4,000.00	3	₦ 12,000.00	8:00:37 AM	Before 9:00am
22	Italiano	₦ 3,000.00	5	₦ 15,000.00	8:00:40 AM	Before 9:00am

Amount Sold
>15000

We have specified that we want greater than 15,000 naira transactions only.

The steps are just like previous ones. Launch the advanced filter and provide both the "List range" and "Criteria range"

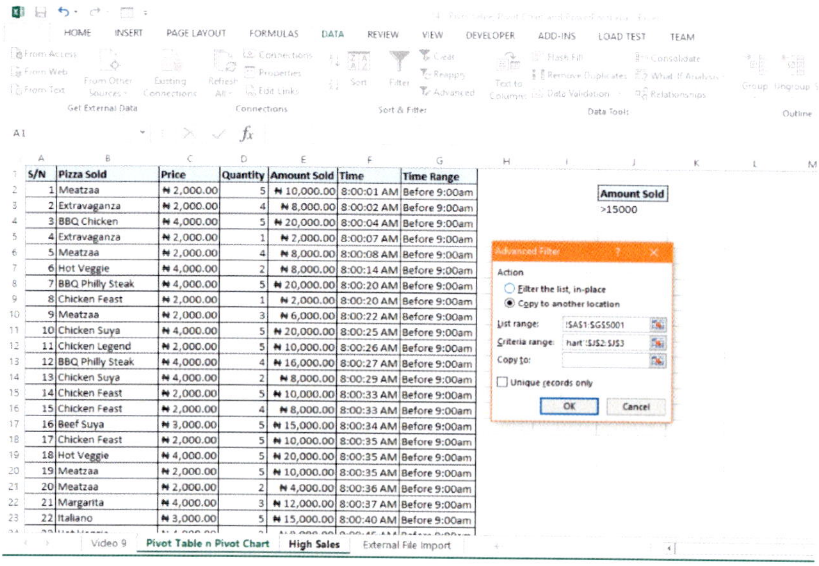

Specify where the results should be displayed.

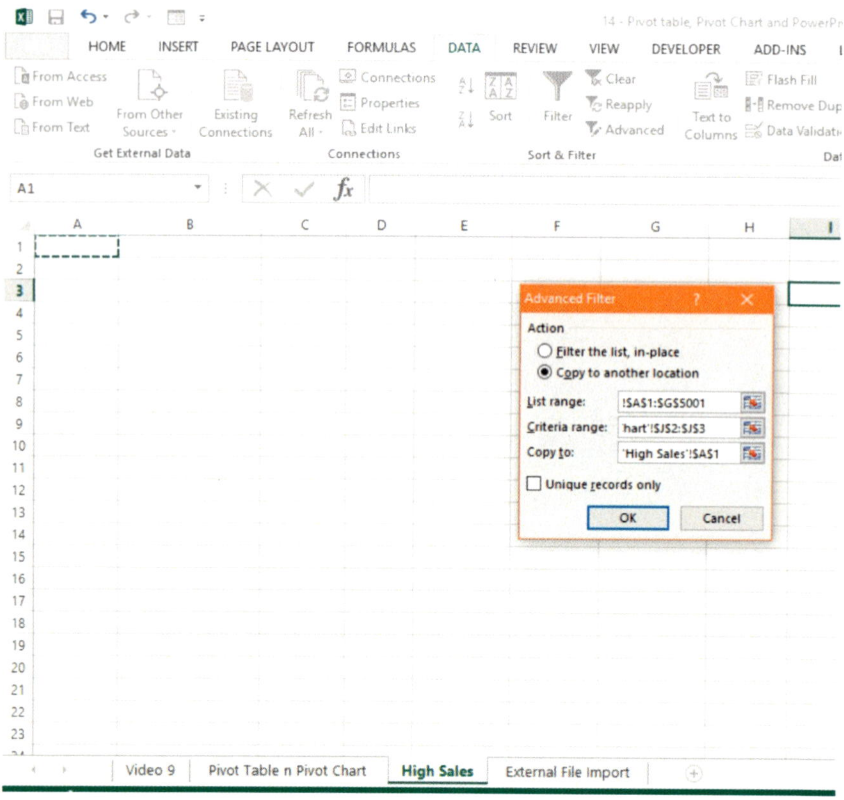

And voila, again! It's done!

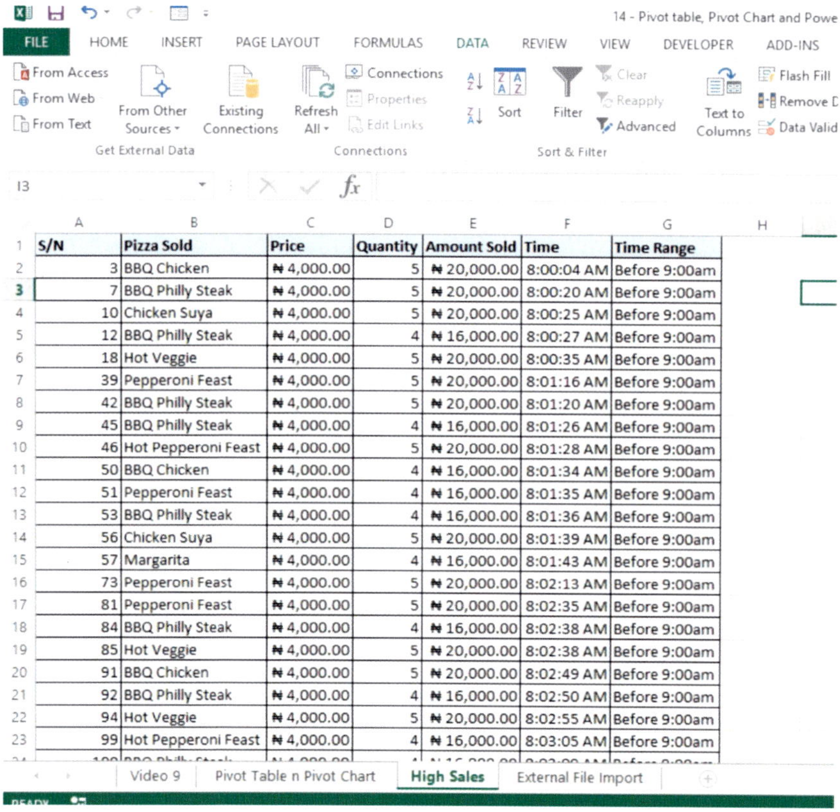

S/N	Pizza Sold	Price	Quantity	Amount Sold	Time	Time Range
3	BBQ Chicken	₦ 4,000.00	5	₦ 20,000.00	8:00:04 AM	Before 9:00am
7	BBQ Philly Steak	₦ 4,000.00	5	₦ 20,000.00	8:00:20 AM	Before 9:00am
10	Chicken Suya	₦ 4,000.00	5	₦ 20,000.00	8:00:25 AM	Before 9:00am
12	BBQ Philly Steak	₦ 4,000.00	4	₦ 16,000.00	8:00:27 AM	Before 9:00am
18	Hot Veggie	₦ 4,000.00	5	₦ 20,000.00	8:00:35 AM	Before 9:00am
39	Pepperoni Feast	₦ 4,000.00	5	₦ 20,000.00	8:01:16 AM	Before 9:00am
42	BBQ Philly Steak	₦ 4,000.00	5	₦ 20,000.00	8:01:20 AM	Before 9:00am
45	BBQ Philly Steak	₦ 4,000.00	4	₦ 16,000.00	8:01:26 AM	Before 9:00am
46	Hot Pepperoni Feast	₦ 4,000.00	5	₦ 20,000.00	8:01:28 AM	Before 9:00am
50	BBQ Chicken	₦ 4,000.00	4	₦ 16,000.00	8:01:34 AM	Before 9:00am
51	Pepperoni Feast	₦ 4,000.00	4	₦ 16,000.00	8:01:35 AM	Before 9:00am
53	BBQ Philly Steak	₦ 4,000.00	4	₦ 16,000.00	8:01:36 AM	Before 9:00am
56	Chicken Suya	₦ 4,000.00	5	₦ 20,000.00	8:01:39 AM	Before 9:00am
57	Margarita	₦ 4,000.00	4	₦ 16,000.00	8:01:43 AM	Before 9:00am
73	Pepperoni Feast	₦ 4,000.00	5	₦ 20,000.00	8:02:13 AM	Before 9:00am
81	Pepperoni Feast	₦ 4,000.00	5	₦ 20,000.00	8:02:35 AM	Before 9:00am
84	BBQ Philly Steak	₦ 4,000.00	4	₦ 16,000.00	8:02:38 AM	Before 9:00am
85	Hot Veggie	₦ 4,000.00	5	₦ 20,000.00	8:02:38 AM	Before 9:00am
91	BBQ Chicken	₦ 4,000.00	5	₦ 20,000.00	8:02:49 AM	Before 9:00am
92	BBQ Philly Steak	₦ 4,000.00	4	₦ 16,000.00	8:02:50 AM	Before 9:00am
94	Hot Veggie	₦ 4,000.00	5	₦ 20,000.00	8:02:55 AM	Before 9:00am
99	Hot Pepperoni Feast	₦ 4,000.00	4	₦ 16,000.00	8:03:05 AM	Before 9:00am

Now you should be an expert, like me, at using advanced filter.

Excel Errors

If you've used Excel consistently at work for a few months, you will be familiar with some errors Excel displays when it can't get you the answer you want. Oftentimes, we don't give some thoughts to these errors but the truth is they are not random or meaningless, they are trying to tell you something important.

Today, I will be sharing with you how to interpret those errors and uncover the gem in them. How to read the message they are trying to pass across to you.

There are eight error types in Excel:

1. #VALUE!
2. #DIV/0!
3. #N/A
4. ########
5. #NAME?
6. #REF!
7. #NUM!
8. #NULL!

#VALUE! Error

You get #VALUE! error when you do a calculation in Excel that doesn't make sense. Like Michael + 2. What is Michael + 2? Is Michael a number? What kind of answer are you expecting? Can you try it on your CASIO calculator?

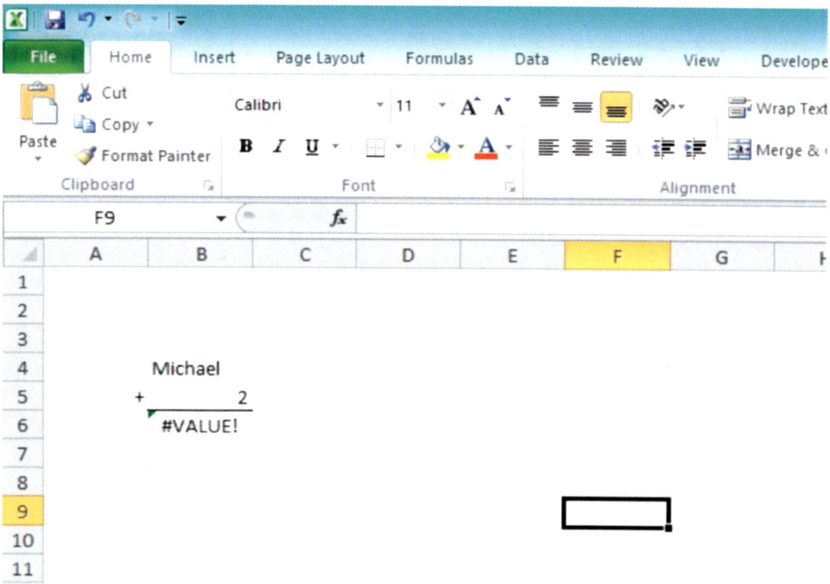

To be blunt, #VALUE! is Excel's way of saying someone is stupid. Someone has typed in a calculation that makes absolutely no sense.

#DIV/0! Error

As the name implies, division by zero, #DIV/0! is the error you get when you do any formula that divides a number by zero.

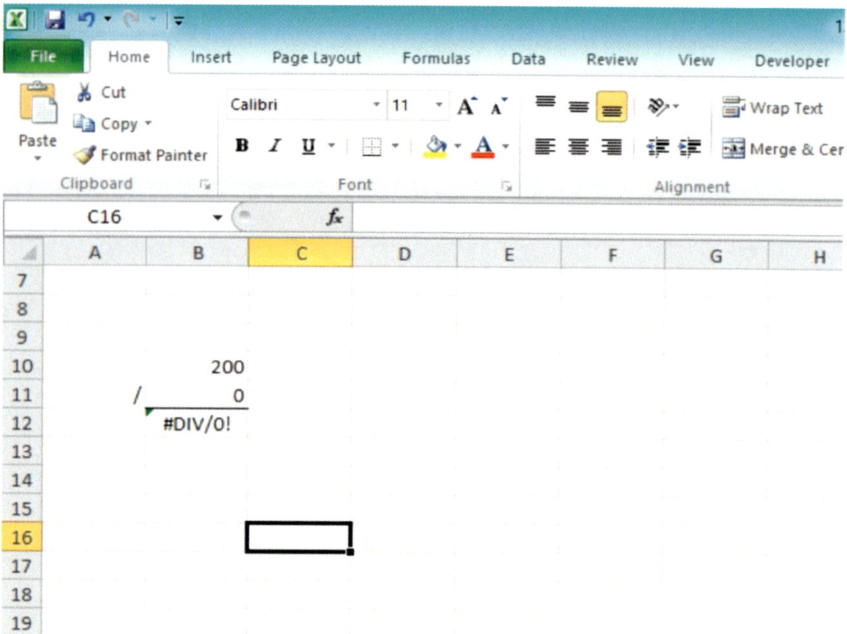

Now, I have a trick question for you: what error do you think Excel will give you when you divide Michael by zero? #VALUE! or #DIV/0!?

#N/A Error

This is the error you get when you do a lookup function (VLOOKUP, LOOKUP, MATCH etc.) and Excel can't find what you are looking for.

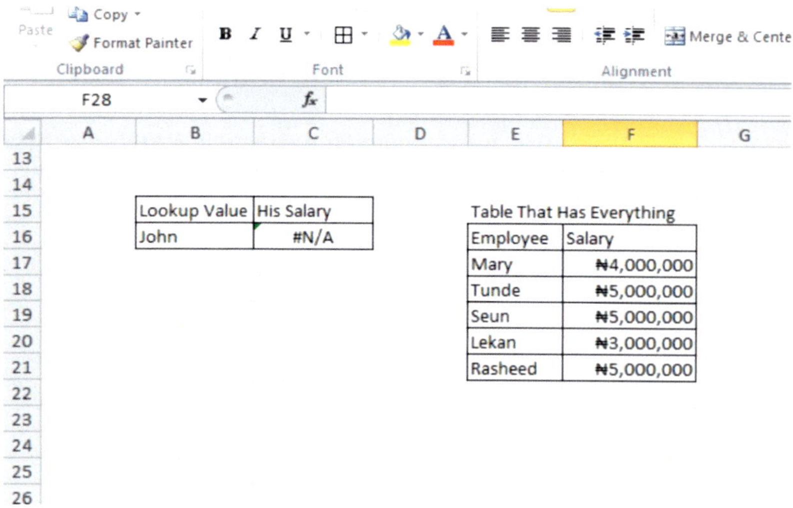

Error

You get this error for two reasons. The first and more common one is when there is not enough space in your Excel cell to display a numeric (number) value. Excel doesn't want you to take 1,000,000 as 1,000 because space was only enough to show 1,000. So it puts in ####### in the entire cell and force you to expand/widen the cell to see the entire content.

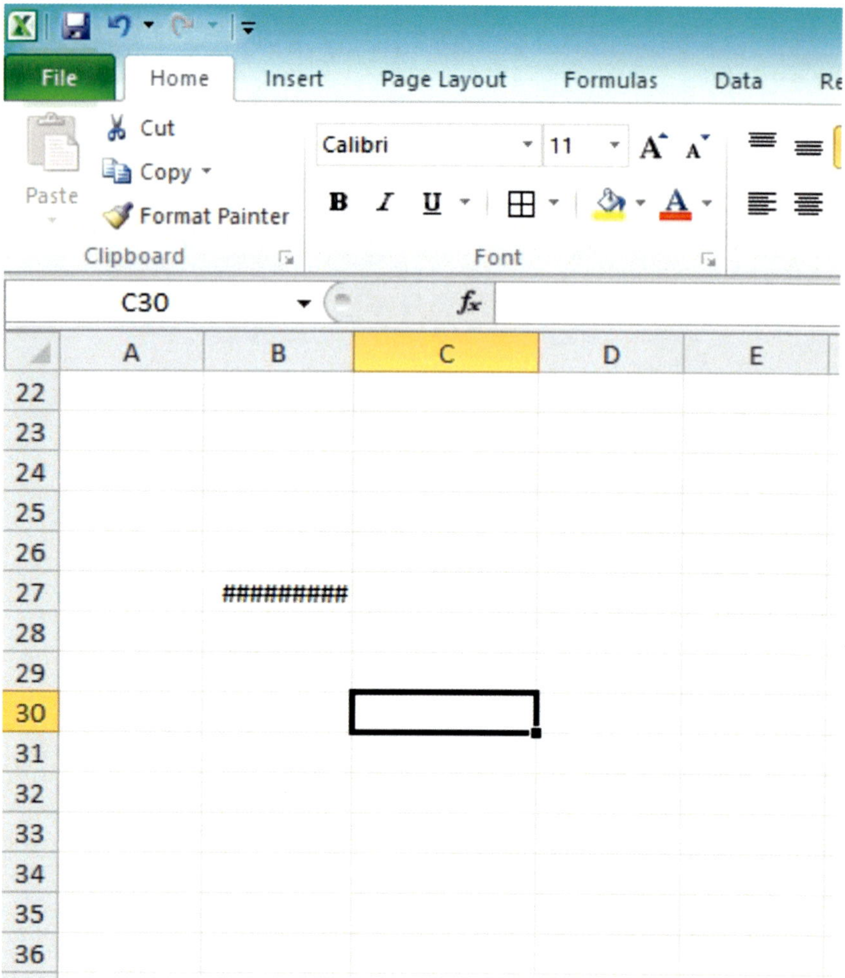
File
Home
Insert
Page Layout
Formulas
Data
Cut
Copy
Paste
Format Painter
Clipboard
Calibri
11
Font
C30
A
B
C
D
E
##########

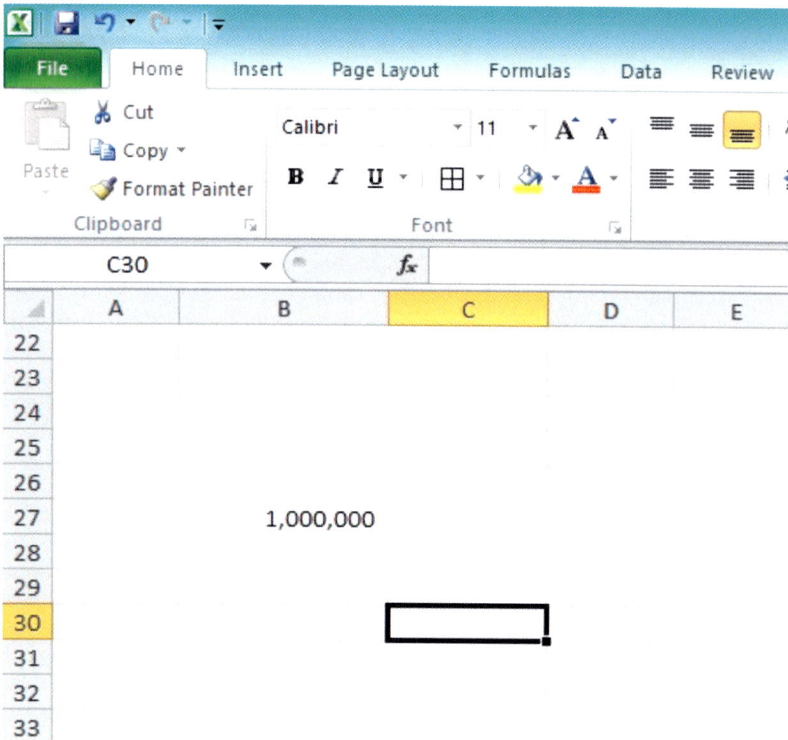

The second and less common one is when you do a calculation on date and the resulting date answer is too large or too small a value to be shown as a valid date in Excel. Here's what I mean. In Excel you can do 26-Aug-16 + 1 and you will get 27-Aug-16 (the next date).

But when you try 26-Aug-16 + 999999999 you get ######## and no amount of expanding the cell will make the error go away. You are trying to calculate a post-apocalyptic date.

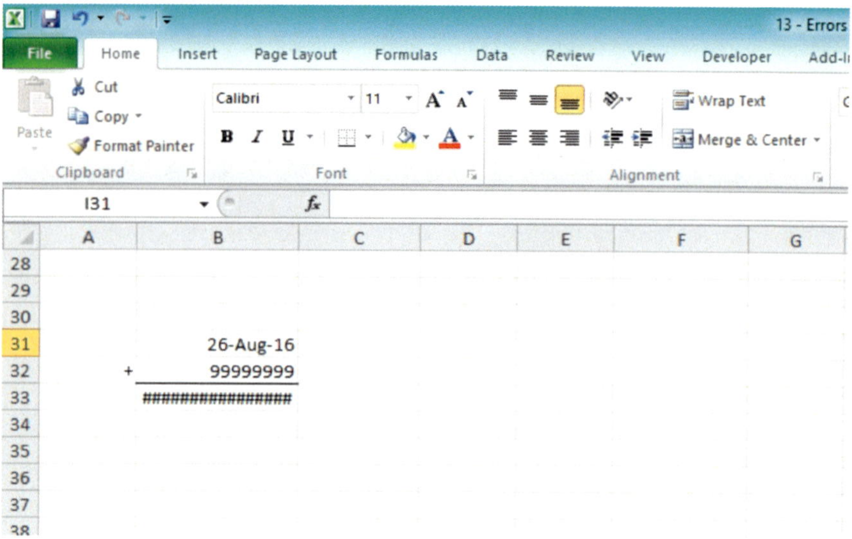

#NAME? Error

This is the error you get when you type a formula name that doesn't exist in Excel. Maybe you wanted to type SUM but mistakenly typed SUN. Well, Excel doesn't know about the solar system so t will tell you that it doesn't recognize that formula name.

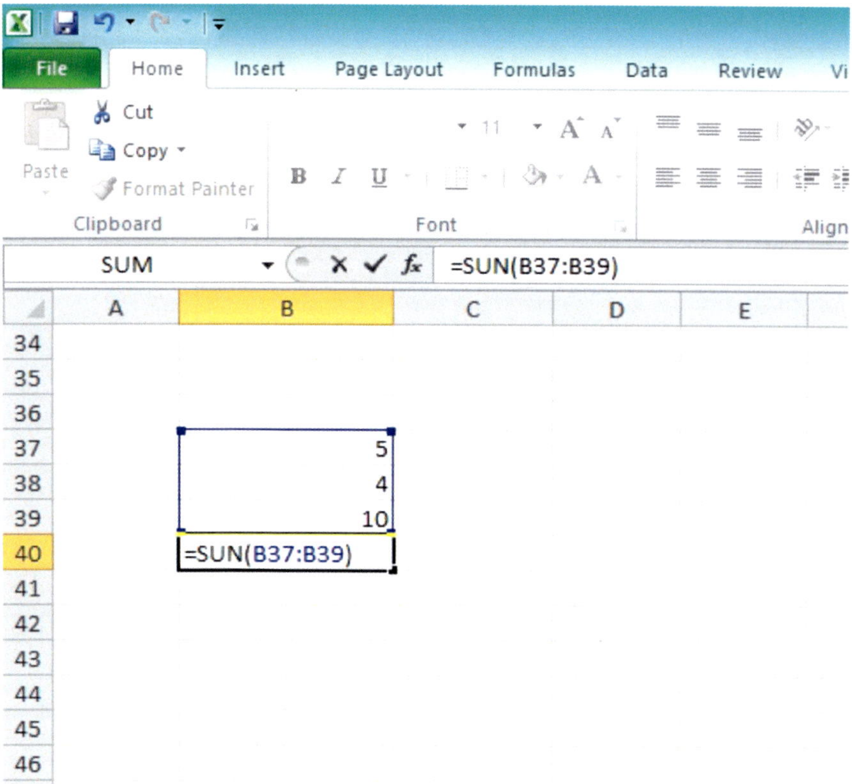
File
Home
Insert
Page Layout
Formulas
Data
Review
Cut
Copy
Paste
Format Painter
Clipboard
Font
Align
SUM
=SUN(B37:B39)
A
B
C
D
E
5
4
10
=SUN(B37:B39)

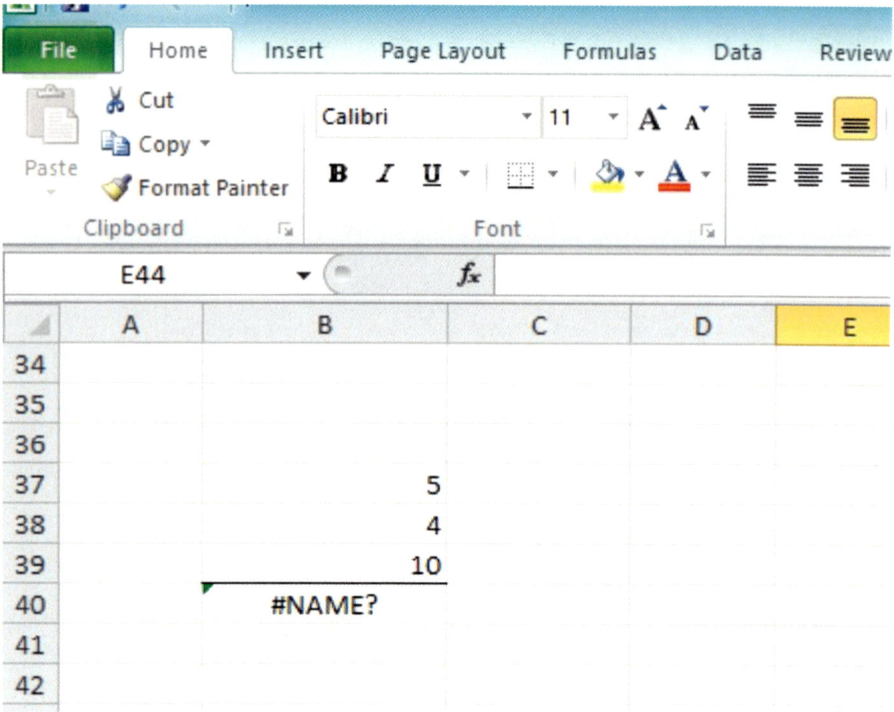

#REF! Error

This is a very popular and troublesome error. It happens when you have a formula that picks value from a different sheet or different file and somehow the file or sheet becomes inaccessible (or deleted). When Excel tries to recalculate the formula, it gives you that #REF! error because it can't access one of the reference file/sheet.

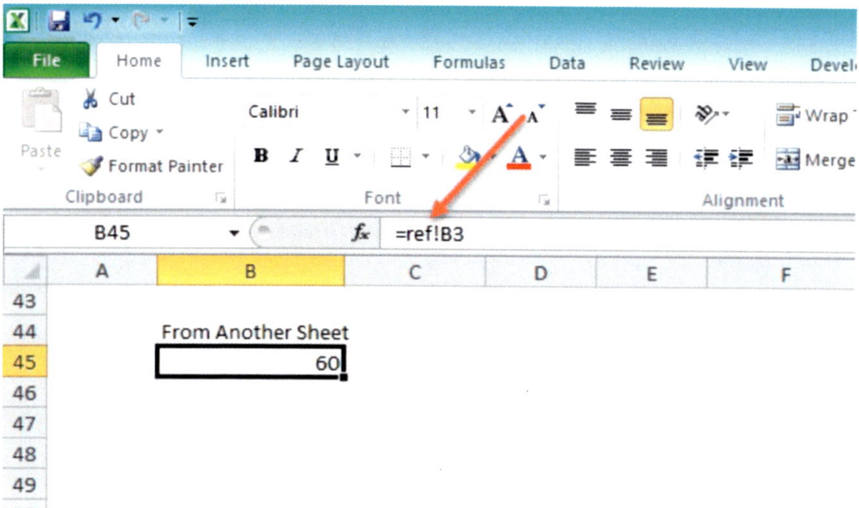
B45
=ref!B3
From Another Sheet
60

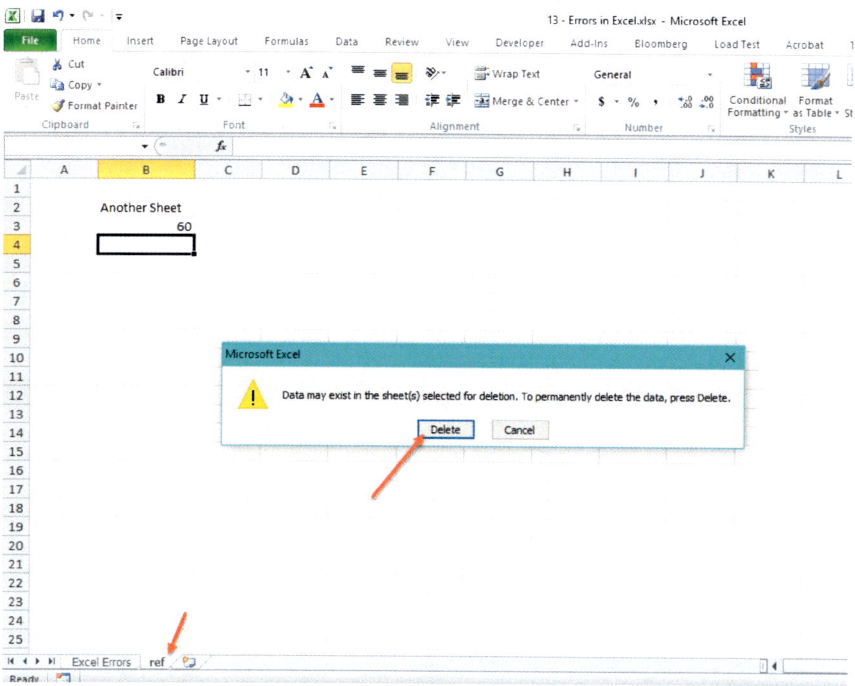
13 - Errors in Excel.xlsx - Microsoft Excel
Another Sheet
60
Microsoft Excel
Data may exist in the sheet(s) selected for deletion. To permanently delete the data, press Delete.
Delete
Cancel
Excel Errors
ref

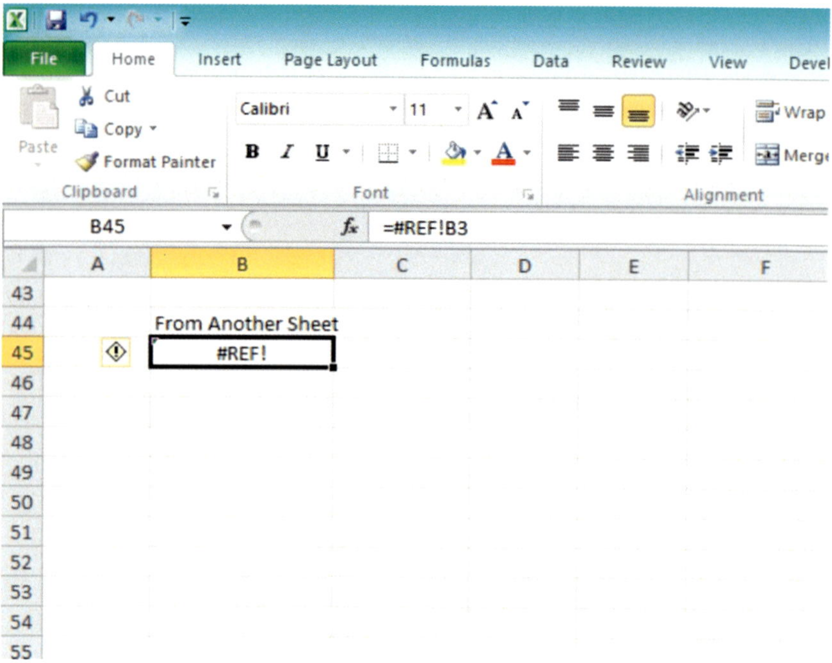

A funny case that causes it is when you drag a formula that depends on a cell above it too way up that it messes with Excel's cell reference system.

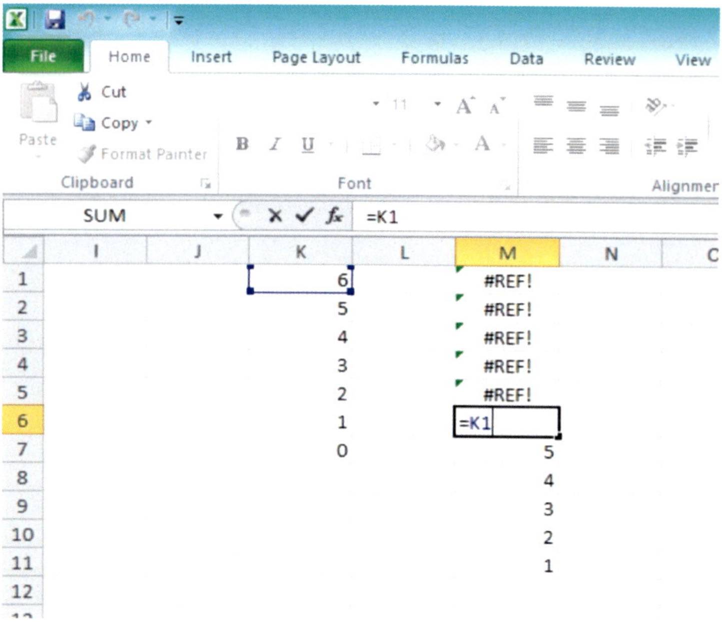

#NUM! Error

This is the error you get when you do a calculation that is too large or too small for Excel to handle. An example is 999 raised to the power of 99999

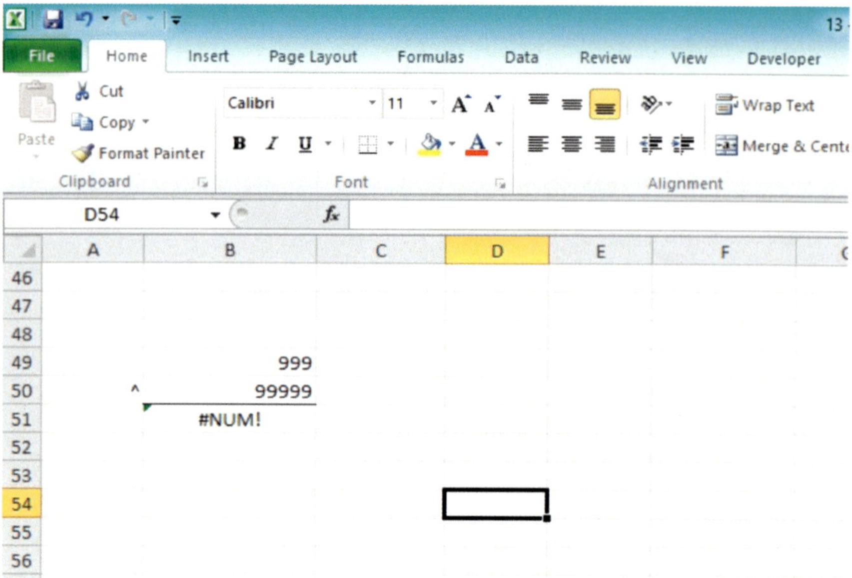

#NULL! Error

This is a very uncommon error. We are all familiar with the multiplication, addition, subtraction, division etc. operations. There is one not very commonly known -- the intersect operator. And it is simply a space. It gets you the intersect value of two different ranges.

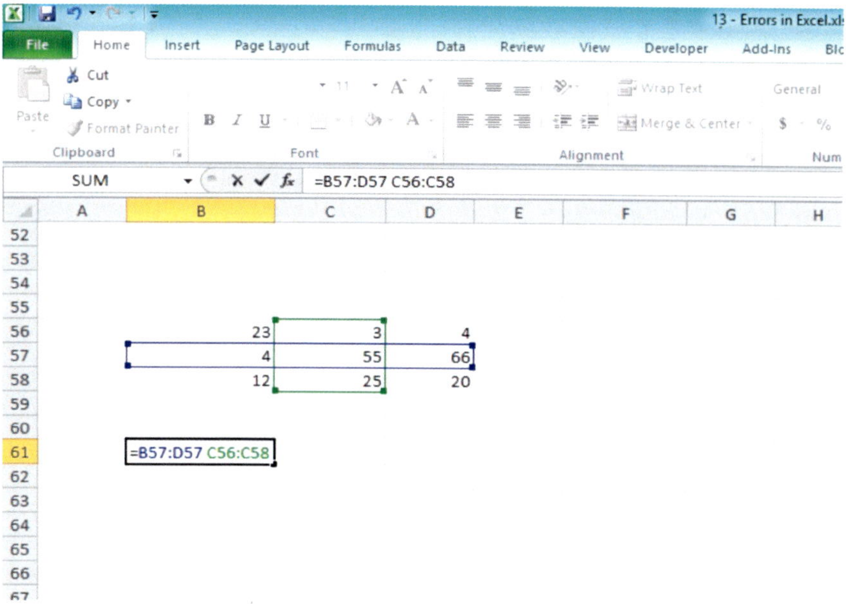

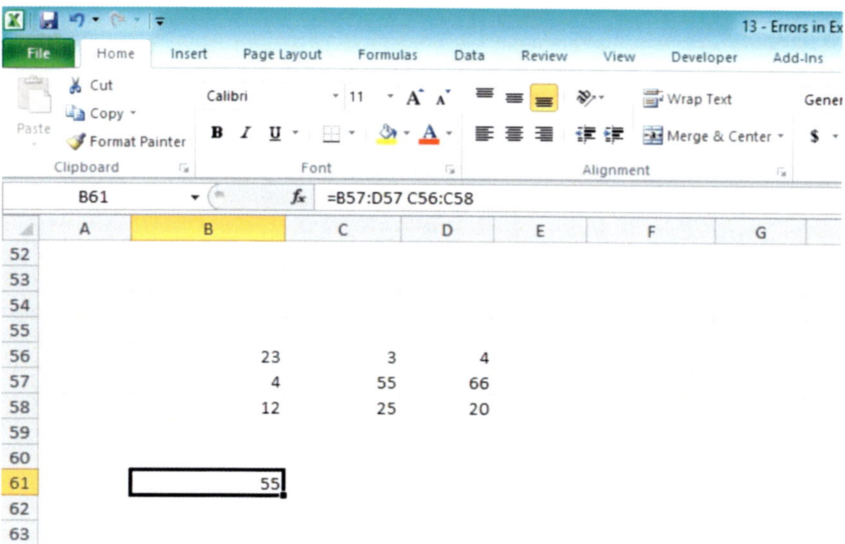

So what happens when you select ranges that do not intersect? You get #NULL! error.

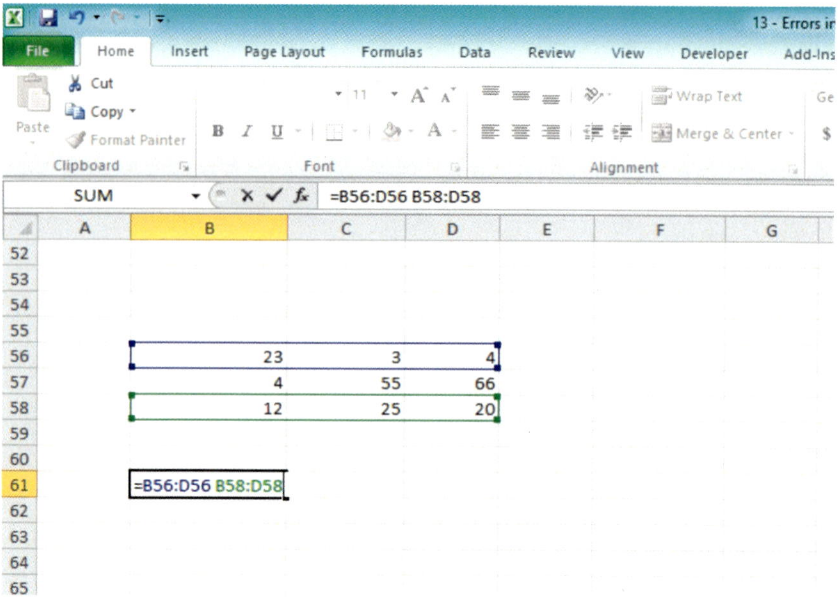
13 - Errors in
File
Home
Insert
Page Layout
Formulas
Data
Review
View
Developer
Add-Ins
Cut
Copy
Paste
Format Painter
Clipboard
Font
Wrap Text
Merge & Center
Alignment
SUM
=B56:D56 B58:D58
23
3
4
4
55
66
12
25
20
=B56:D56 B58:D58

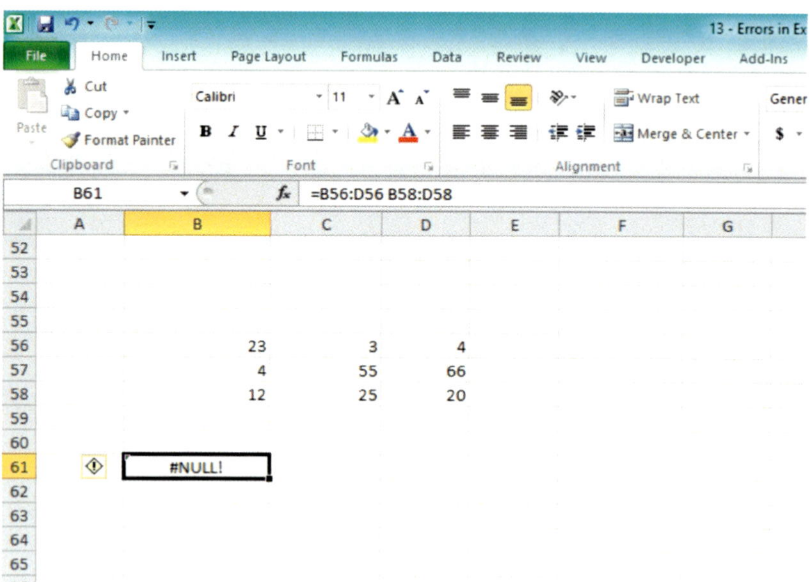
13 - Errors in Ex
File
Home
Insert
Page Layout
Formulas
Data
Review
View
Developer
Add-Ins
Cut
Copy
Paste
Format Painter
Calibri
11
Clipboard
Font
Wrap Text
Merge & Center
Alignment
Gener
B61
=B56:D56 B58:D58
23
3
4
4
55
66
12
25
20
#NULL!

And those are the errors in Excel and their interpretation. Now you know what they are telling you anytime you come across them.

Data Cleaning

A lot of times the data you are given to work on in Excel is not in a format usable for you and need some cleaning before you can go ahead with the analysis you intended doing on it. In most cases you have to manually clean the data and fix whatever issues it has one by one before progressing with the original analysis you intended to do on the data.

Fortunately, Excel has some nifty tools to help you automate some of this data cleaning process. The most common ones are,

- Removing duplicates, and
- Text to Columns

Then we'll cover a special tool that can help you do a quick categorization of your data: Subtotal. Finally we'll cover Data Validation, an ingenious tool for reducing data entry errors in your Excel files.

Removing Duplicates.

Occasionally, you will have a table and you'll want to remove duplicate entries. If it were a sales transaction table, you might want to remove the duplicate sales entries. In the example below, it is a table of items (Pizzas) and we want to remove the duplicate entries leaving only unique entries.

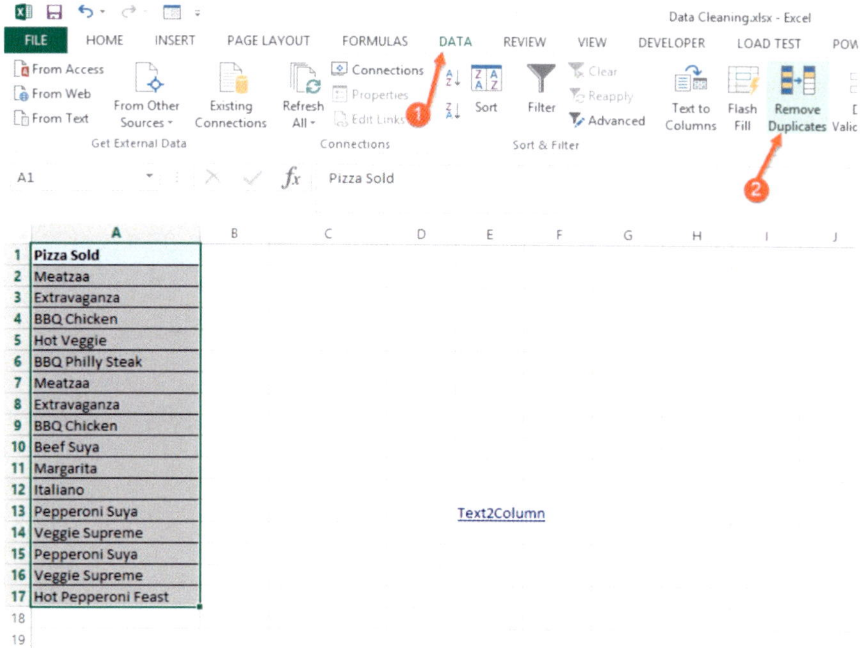

As illustrated above, you select the entire records first and then go to Data menu, click on Remove Duplicates. You will get a confirmatory dialog box. Click on OK.

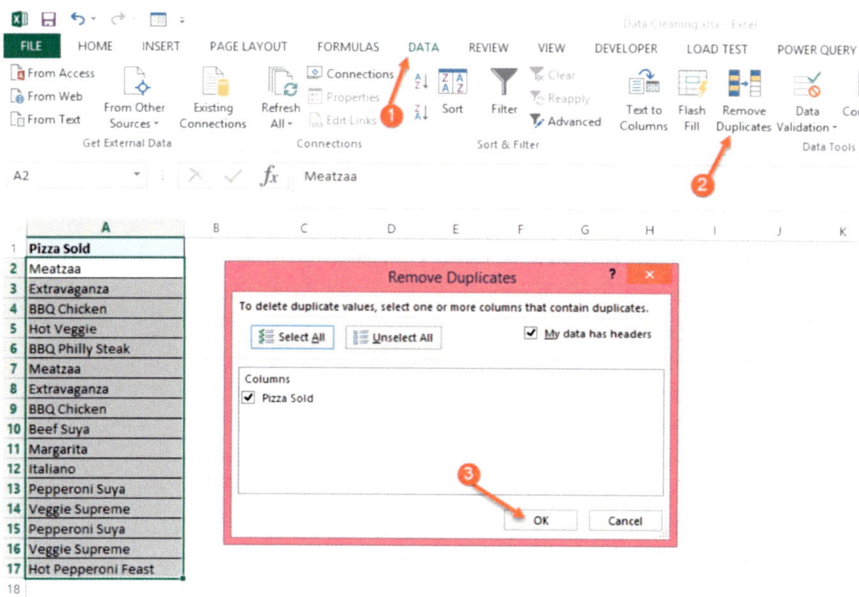

You'll see a result showing the number of duplicate values that were found and the number of unique values found. Basically, what Remove Duplicates does is it leaves one record of each item and removes all the extra record for that item that it finds.

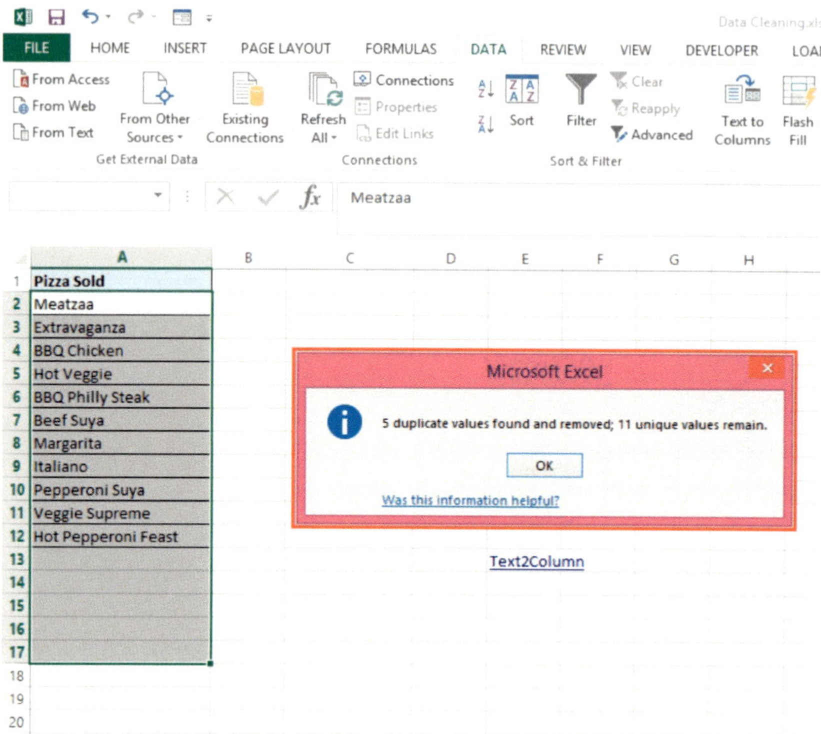

When you select a table with more than one field entry, the Remove Duplicates remove only the entries that have same value in all the fields as a previous entry except you specify which fields to exclude in the search for duplicates.

In the screenshot below, we excluded Car Sales from the fields to include in the search for duplicates. So rows that have the same entries in all the other fields will be deleted except one.

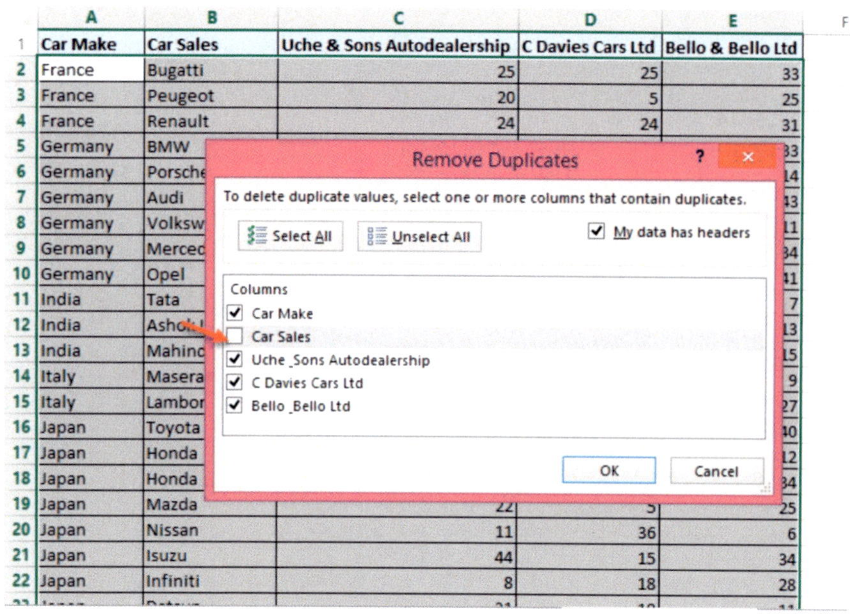

Text to Columns

There will be times you will have data you would prefer split across multiple columns squeezed into one column. This happens a lot when you copy data from an external source into Excel or you open an exported data from other business software like CRMs and ERPs.

Excel's Text to Columns tool is the magic tool for splitting such data entries into multiple columns provided there is a recognizable character separating each field or they have fixed lengths per field. Below is a simple example for splitting a full name in one column to first Name column and last Name field column.

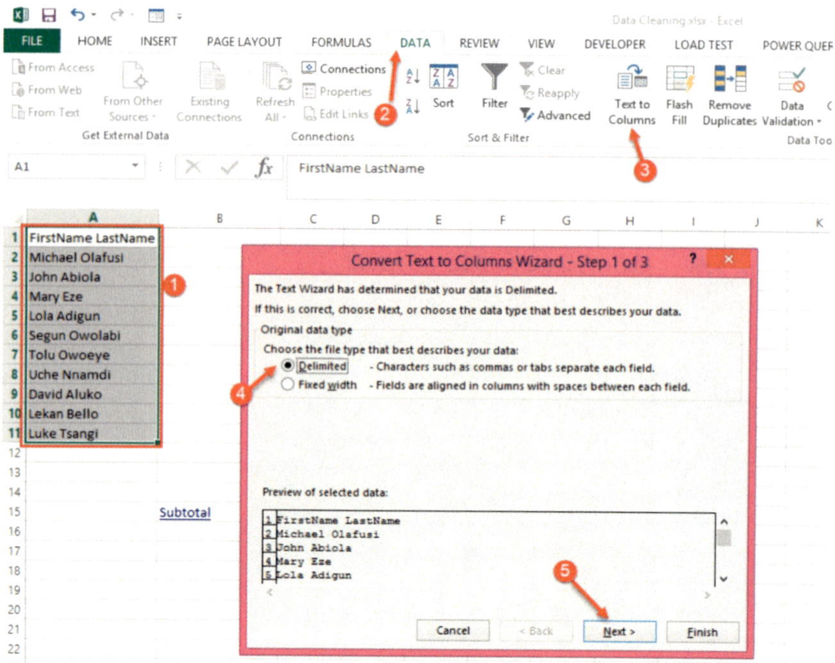

Delimited is the option to specify that there is a recognizable character separating each field. In this example, there is a space separating every first name from the last name.

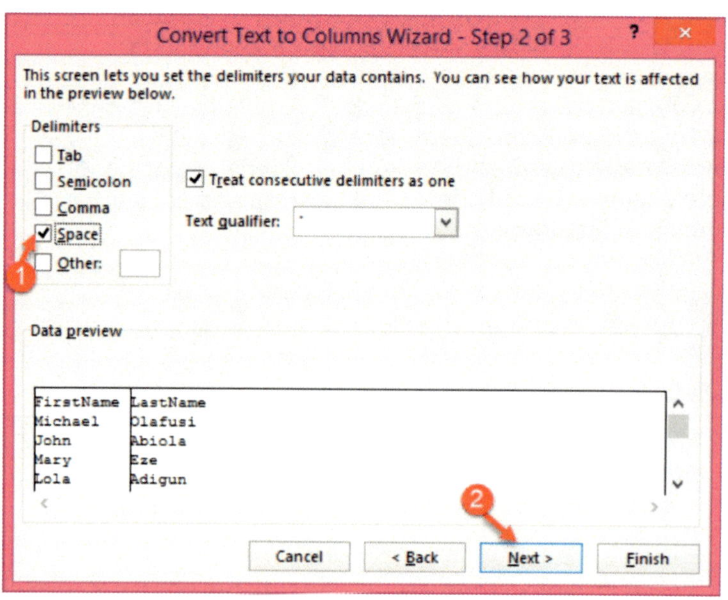

Notice how Excel shows a line between the first names and the last names once you select the appropriate delimiter (space, in this case). Click on Next and Finish.

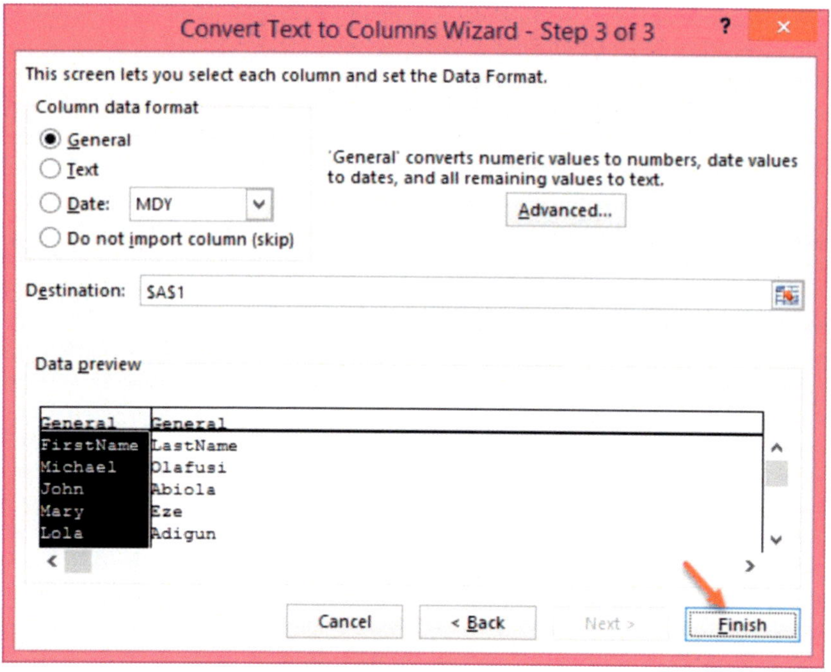

Below is the result. Just as desired.

	A	B	C
1	FirstName	LastName	
2	Michael	Olafusi	
3	John	Abiola	
4	Mary	Eze	
5	Lola	Adigun	
6	Segun	Owolabi	
7	Tolu	Owoeye	
8	Uche	Nnamdi	
9	David	Aluko	
10	Lekan	Bello	
11	Luke	Tsangi	
12			

Subtotal

Subtotal is a secret tool for doing a quick analysis of a table in Excel. It breaks the data down by categories and creates grouping that shows you different levels of details.

It is also very easy to use.

Below is an example where we'll use it.

Car Make	Car Sales	Uche & Sons Autodealership	C Davies Cars Ltd	Bello & Bello Ltd
France	Bugatti	25	25	33
France	Peugeot	20	5	25
France	Renault	24	24	31
Germany	BMW	20	6	33
Germany	Porsche	27	45	14
Germany	Audi	28	43	43
Germany	Volkswagen	16	43	11
Germany	Mercedes-Benz	23	45	34
Germany	Opel	24	16	41
India	Tata	41	29	7
India	Ashok Leyland	41	19	13
India	Mahindra	34	27	15
Italy	Maserati	13	22	9
Italy	Lamborghini	31	26	27
Japan	Toyota	30	24	40
Japan	Honda	11	42	12
Japan	Honda	36	31	34
Japan	Mazda	22	5	25
Japan	Nissan	11	36	6
Japan	Isuzu	44	15	34
Japan	Infiniti	8	18	28
Japan	Datsun	31	18	11
Japan	Subaru	24	7	20
Japan	Suzuki	13	29	43
Japan	Scion	26	18	36
South Korea	Hyundai	32	28	40

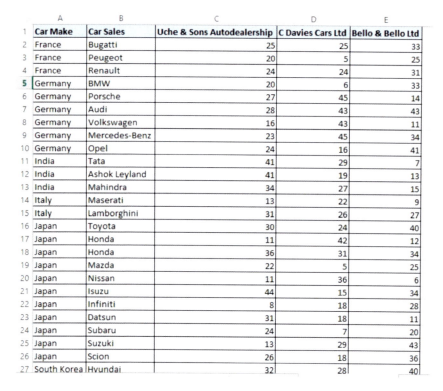

It is a market research data table showing the different car make sold in three different auto dealerships.

We can apply a subtotal to this to see some interesting analysis.

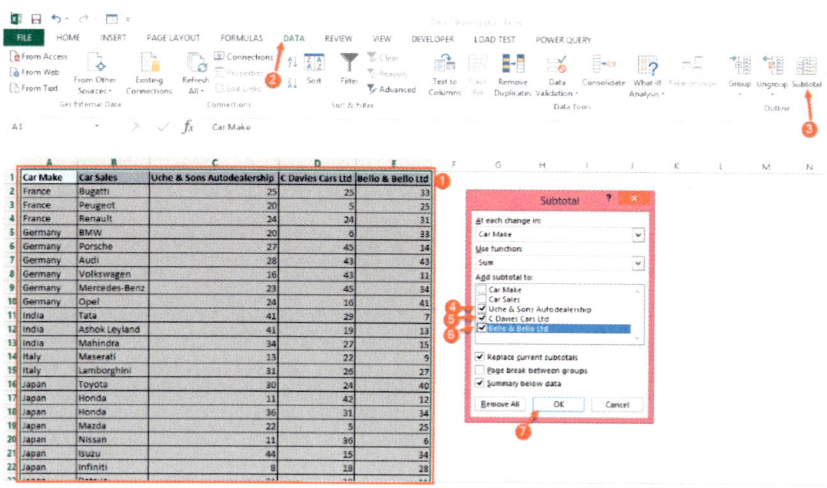

Select the table, go to Data menu and click on Subtotal. In the dialog box that comes up, in the "Add subtotal to" section tick all the fields that have numeric values (except you don't want to see a numeric analysis of them).

Once you click on OK, you get a result that looks like the following –

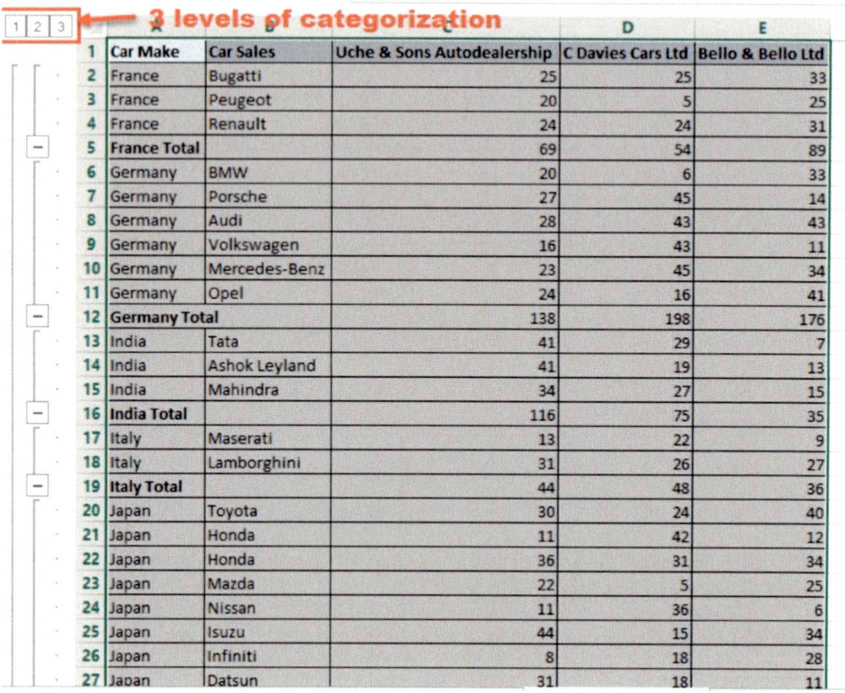

	A	B	C	D	E
1	Car Make	Car Sales	Uche & Sons Autodealership	C Davies Cars Ltd	Bello & Bello Ltd
2	France	Bugatti	25	25	33
3	France	Peugeot	20	5	25
4	France	Renault	24	24	31
5	**France Total**		69	54	89
6	Germany	BMW	20	6	33
7	Germany	Porsche	27	45	14
8	Germany	Audi	28	43	43
9	Germany	Volkswagen	16	43	11
10	Germany	Mercedes-Benz	23	45	34
11	Germany	Opel	24	16	41
12	**Germany Total**		138	198	176
13	India	Tata	41	29	7
14	India	Ashok Leyland	41	19	13
15	India	Mahindra	34	27	15
16	**India Total**		116	75	35
17	Italy	Maserati	13	22	9
18	Italy	Lamborghini	31	26	27
19	**Italy Total**		44	48	36
20	Japan	Toyota	30	24	40
21	Japan	Honda	11	42	12
22	Japan	Honda	36	31	34
23	Japan	Mazda	22	5	25
24	Japan	Nissan	11	36	6
25	Japan	Isuzu	44	15	34
26	Japan	Infiniti	8	18	28
27	Japan	Datsun	31	18	11

Level 1:

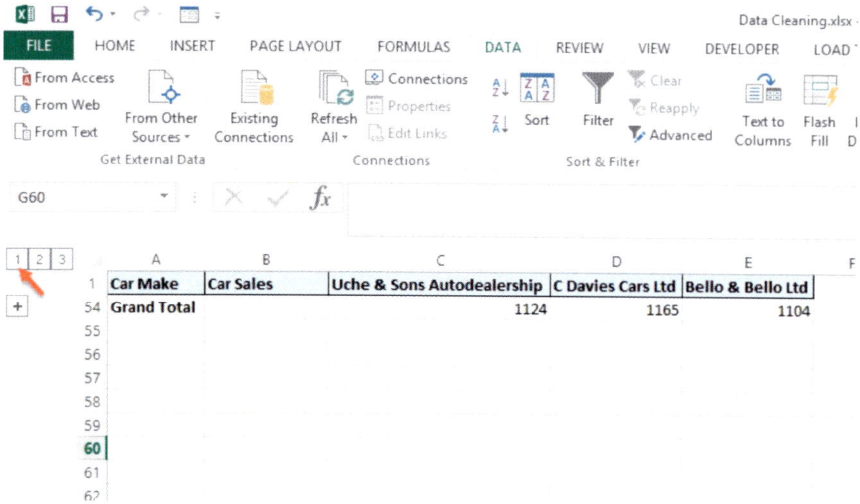

	A	B	C	D	E
1	Car Make	Car Sales	Uche & Sons Autodealership	C Davies Cars Ltd	Bello & Bello Ltd
54	Grand Total		1124	1165	1104

Level 2:

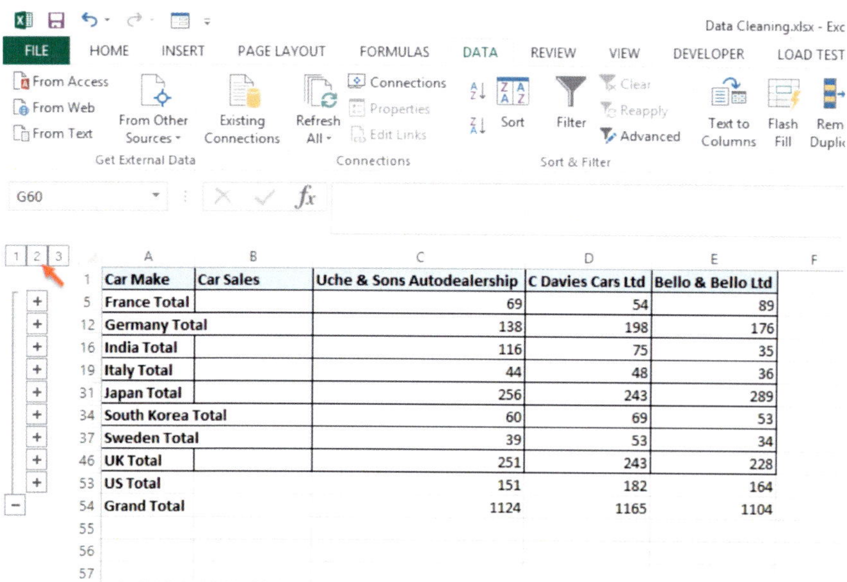

	A	B	C	D	E
1	Car Make	Car Sales	Uche & Sons Autodealership	C Davies Cars Ltd	Bello & Bello Ltd
5	France Total		69	54	89
12	Germany Total		138	198	176
16	India Total		116	75	35
19	Italy Total		44	48	36
31	Japan Total		256	243	289
34	South Korea Total		60	69	53
37	Sweden Total		39	53	34
46	UK Total		251	243	228
53	US Total		151	182	164
54	Grand Total		1124	1165	1104

Level 3:

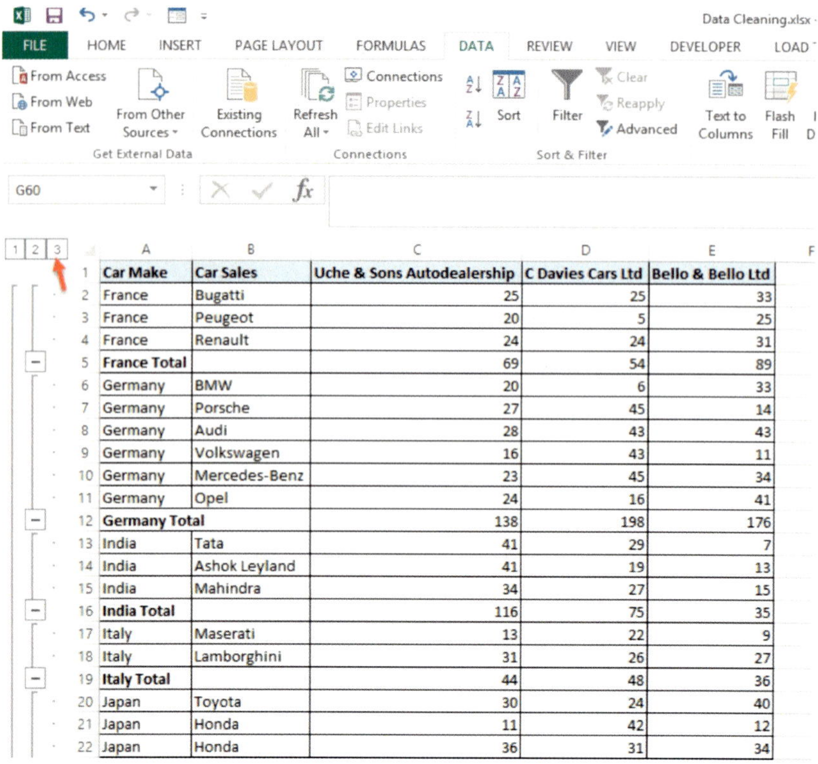

	Car Make	Car Sales	Uche & Sons Autodealership	C Davies Cars Ltd	Bello & Bello Ltd
2	France	Bugatti	25	25	33
3	France	Peugeot	20	5	25
4	France	Renault	24	24	31
5	**France Total**		69	54	89
6	Germany	BMW	20	6	33
7	Germany	Porsche	27	45	14
8	Germany	Audi	28	43	43
9	Germany	Volkswagen	16	43	11
10	Germany	Mercedes-Benz	23	45	34
11	Germany	Opel	24	16	41
12	**Germany Total**		138	198	176
13	India	Tata	41	29	7
14	India	Ashok Leyland	41	19	13
15	India	Mahindra	34	27	15
16	**India Total**		116	75	35
17	Italy	Maserati	13	22	9
18	Italy	Lamborghini	31	26	27
19	**Italy Total**		44	48	36
20	Japan	Toyota	30	24	40
21	Japan	Honda	11	42	12
22	Japan	Honda	36	31	34

And the best part is that you can remove the subtotal and have your original table data back just as it was before. To remove is as easy as clicking the Subtotal again and clicking on Remove All.

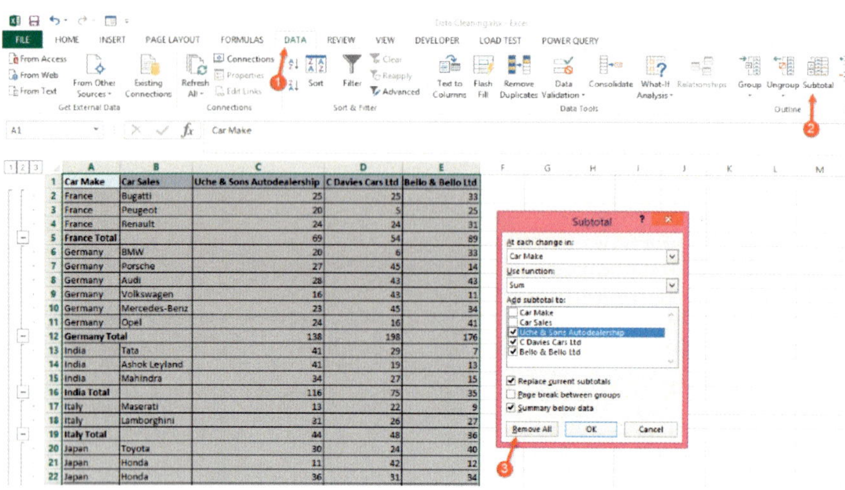

See the result below. All the level 1, 2 & 3 groupings gone.

	A	B	C	D	E
1	**Car Make**	**Car Sales**	**Uche & Sons Autodealership**	**C Davies Cars Ltd**	**Bello & Bello Ltd**
2	France	Bugatti	25	25	33
3	France	Peugeot	20	5	25
4	France	Renault	24	24	31
5	Germany	BMW	20	6	33
6	Germany	Porsche	27	45	14
7	Germany	Audi	28	43	43
8	Germany	Volkswagen	16	43	11
9	Germany	Mercedes-Benz	23	45	34
10	Germany	Opel	24	16	41
11	India	Tata	41	29	7
12	India	Ashok Leyland	41	19	13
13	India	Mahindra	34	27	15
14	Italy	Maserati	13	22	9
15	Italy	Lamborghini	31	26	27
16	Japan	Toyota	30	24	40
17	Japan	Honda	11	42	12
18	Japan	Honda	36	31	34
19	Japan	Mazda	22	5	25
20	Japan	Nissan	11	36	6
21	Japan	Isuzu	44	15	34
22	Japan	Infiniti	8	18	28
23	Japan	Datsun	31	18	11
24	Japan	Subaru	24	7	20
25	Japan	Suzuki	13	29	43
26	Japan	Scion	26	18	36
27	South Korea	Hyundai	32	28	40

Data Validation

This is another secret but powerful tool in Excel. It helps you put in place some error check mechanism and can be used by a skilled Excel user to make powerful Excel dashboards.

Let's see some of the common uses of it.

The table below is an Employee records table. In it we want to force people to enter just departments specified at the left of the table. In fact, we want them to have the easy option of seeing a pre-populated dropdown list and pick a department from the list options.

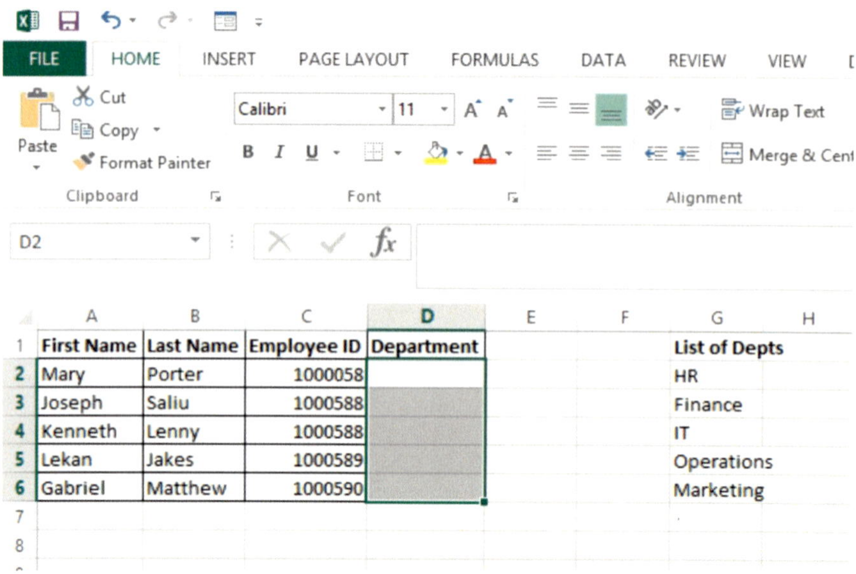

We select the cells we want to give this functionality, go to Data menu and click on Data Validation (sometimes twice).

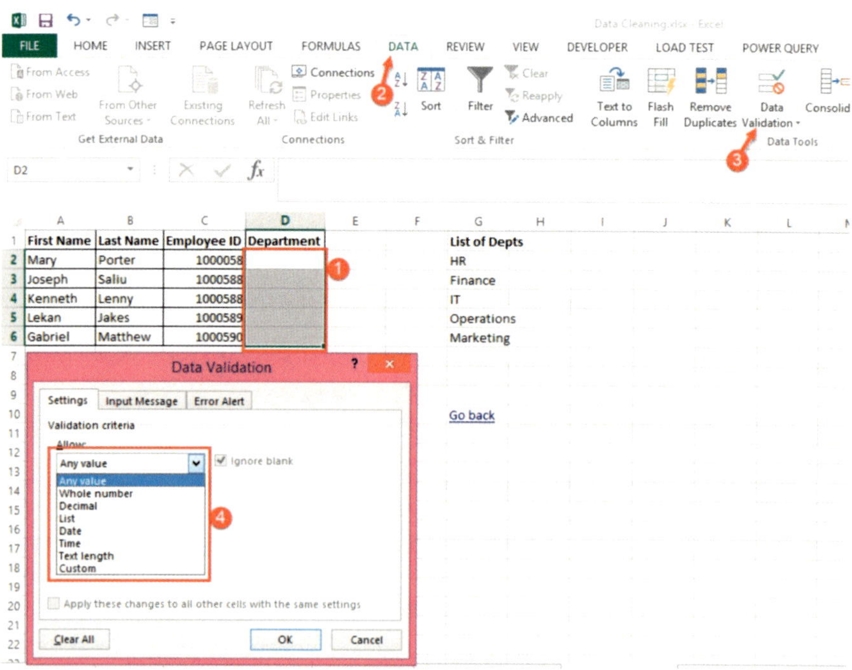

You'll see that there are many options to pick between.

1. **Any Value.** This is the default and it is same as not having any data validation. The user can enter any value into the cell.
2. **Whole Number.** This forces the user to enter only numeric values that are whole numbers. If the user enters a text or decimal entry he'll get an error. This might be applicable in an invoice sheet, for the cells that hold the order quantity if you don't sell fraction of your products.
3. **Decimal.** This forces the user to enter a whole number or decimal entry. A whole number is same as a decimal with zeros after the decimal point. This might be great in a financial model sheet, to hold values of growth assumption, exchange rates and risk premiums.
4. **List.** This is the one we are most interested in. It enables us to limit the cell entries to a list of options. We will use this in the example under review.
5. **Date.** This forces the user to enter a valid date entry.
6. **Time.** This forces the user to enter a valid time entry.
7. **Text Length.** This allows the user to enter any value as long as the character length is not more than the specified value here. It is good for fields that hold phone numbers, maybe you want to limit the entry to the +2348123456789 14 characters long entry format.
8. **Custom.** Just as the name specifies, you want to limit the cell entry to something less conventional and not covered by the other options.

In this example we are going to use the List option. So let's select it.

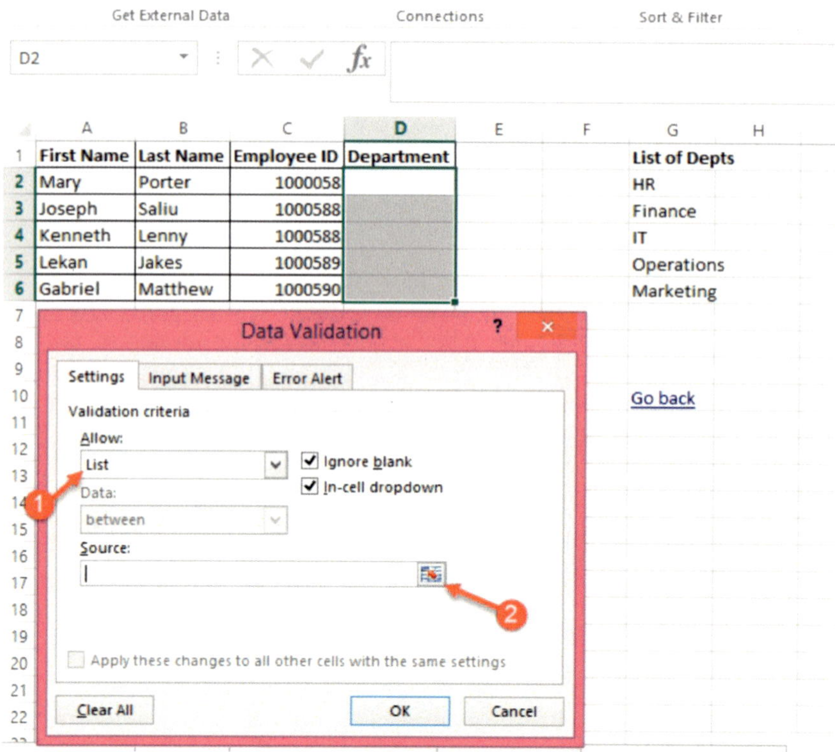

Once you click the icon on the far right corner of the Source box, select entries to limit the users to. In this case we have typed out the list options in cells G2:G6, holding the different departments.

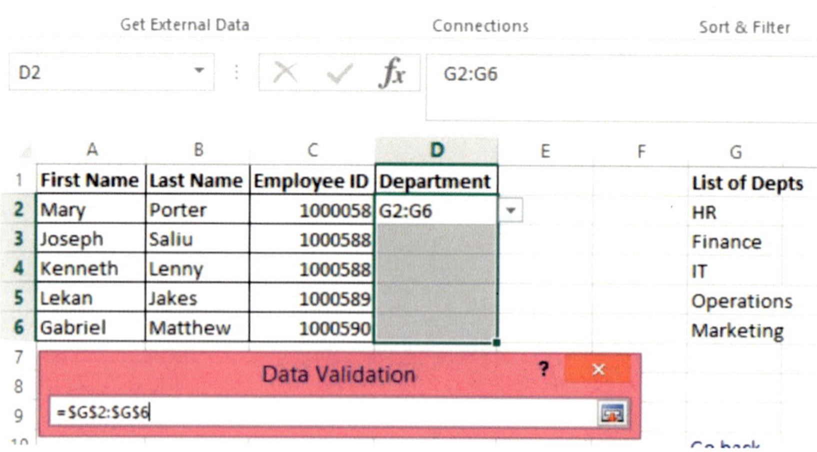

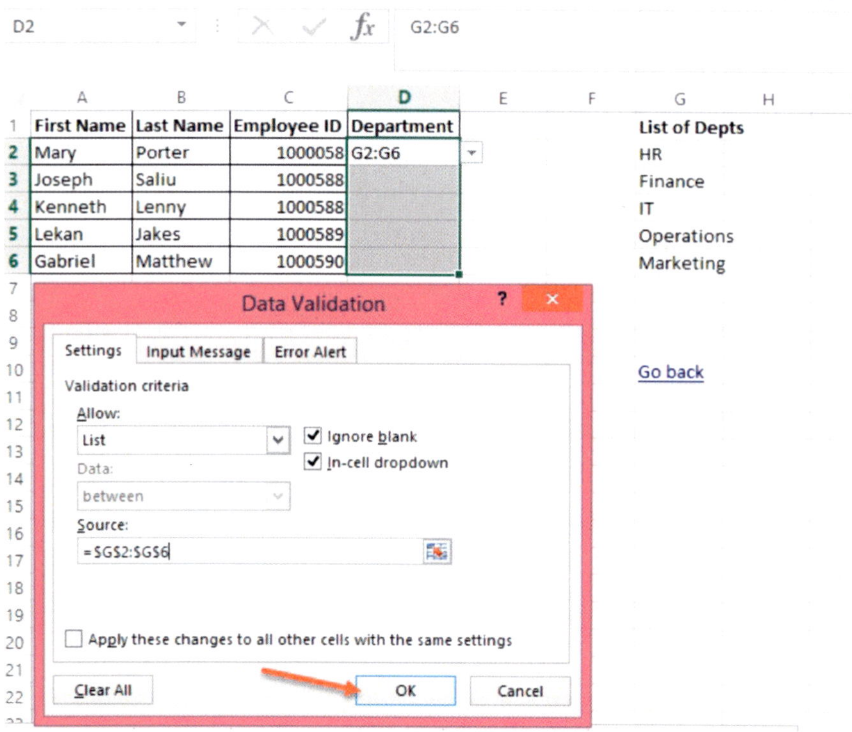

And it's done.

The user is forced to choose between the options in the list. He even sees a dropdown arrow that expands to a dropdown lists the moment he tries to fill the cell.

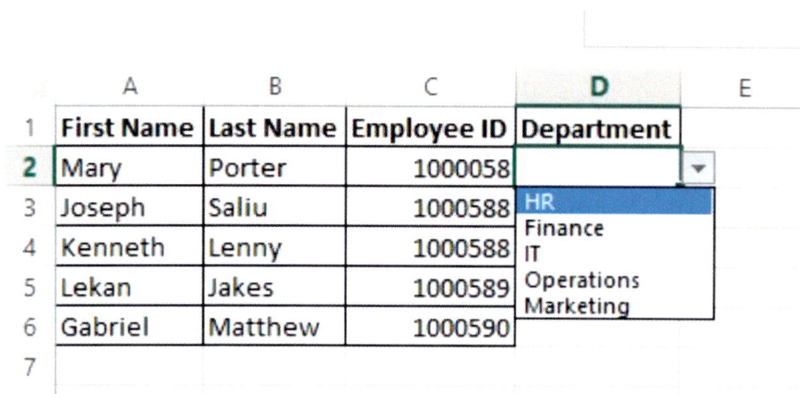

And that is how Data Validation works. When used creatively it can save you from the stress of making corrections to forms people filled and can be used in conjunction with formulas like VLOOKUP to make a dynamic report and dashboards.

Data Formatting

There are some quick tips in Excel that would turn a bland looking data into a nice looking one. One of the best tip is to apply a table formatting to the data.

An example, is taking a table like the one below and turning it in a well formatted one.

	A	B	C	D	E	F	G
1	State	Jan-14	Feb-14	Mar-14	Apr-14	May-14	Jun-14
2	Abia	₦ 1,297,498,300	₦ 821,123,500	₦ 1,175,454,800	₦ 967,327,400	₦ 2,265,644,000	₦ 4,544,916,100
3	Adamawa	₦ 4,022,792,500	₦ 4,317,641,300	₦ 1,627,470,600	₦ 1,023,694,700	₦ 3,493,691,500	₦ 1,973,059,900
4	Akwa Ibom	₦ 824,782,800	₦ 1,691,712,500	₦ 4,927,386,500	₦ 2,187,626,200	₦ 2,966,925,400	₦ 2,202,014,900
5	Anambra	₦ 2,159,322,900	₦ 1,511,863,500	₦ 4,060,131,900	₦ 1,843,665,900	₦ 2,439,308,800	₦ 3,015,652,900
6	Bauchi	₦ 764,748,600	₦ 3,059,451,100	₦ 2,879,985,600	₦ 3,032,115,500	₦ 2,609,030,900	₦ 3,000,312,200
7	Bayelsa	₦ 1,218,646,400	₦ 2,035,499,300	₦ 3,596,177,500	₦ 3,958,333,500	₦ 4,856,865,900	₦ 1,754,855,100
8	Benue	₦ 3,479,649,000	₦ 3,864,832,700	₦ 2,458,711,700	₦ 4,801,142,000	₦ 2,700,421,800	₦ 3,212,451,900
9	Benue	₦ 602,469,700	₦ 1,387,315,500	₦ 4,501,134,600	₦ 2,728,902,800	₦ 1,687,978,600	₦ 3,627,716,800
10	Borno	₦ 2,361,614,200	₦ 1,616,065,000	₦ 4,908,244,600	₦ 4,216,846,800	₦ 581,980,000	₦ 4,166,988,100
11	Cross River	₦ 2,416,592,600	₦ 1,971,834,600	₦ 1,814,142,400	₦ 4,658,487,000	₦ 745,327,000	₦ 4,779,952,700
12	Delta	₦ 4,755,914,300	₦ 2,382,209,500	₦ 3,361,514,600	₦ 2,060,298,000	₦ 4,671,269,900	₦ 2,363,220,900
13	Ebonyi	₦ 3,547,140,000	₦ 3,233,069,500	₦ 4,883,253,900	₦ 1,060,164,800	₦ 2,926,053,500	₦ 713,048,500
14	Edo	₦ 2,663,501,000	₦ 781,461,300	₦ 462,661,800	₦ 543,085,200	₦ 3,256,011,600	₦ 2,900,705,900
15	Ekiti	₦ 1,816,087,900	₦ 4,128,943,600	₦ 1,512,170,300	₦ 2,592,908,100	₦ 3,340,038,100	₦ 4,040,341,600
16	Enugu	₦ 1,409,979,200	₦ 2,609,372,800	₦ 1,990,646,300	₦ 3,219,650,200	₦ 1,893,090,400	₦ 4,581,716,900
17	FCT	₦ 3,199,223,200	₦ 2,063,317,300	₦ 1,829,381,400	₦ 3,704,640,600	₦ 4,980,777,000	₦ 2,520,202,900
18	Gombe	₦ 620,111,300	₦ 2,201,453,200	₦ 1,885,641,400	₦ 4,146,024,300	₦ 2,551,023,100	₦ 2,523,019,700
19	Imo	₦ 2,591,742,600	₦ 2,521,764,800	₦ 2,013,994,900	₦ 4,994,515,700	₦ 3,014,428,300	₦ 2,922,241,900
20	Jigawa	₦ 3,550,126,700	₦ 1,573,445,100	₦ 3,756,243,200	₦ 3,092,703,100	₦ 1,417,963,700	₦ 2,311,559,800
21	Kaduna	₦ 3,938,598,800	₦ 2,599,773,900	₦ 1,224,849,400	₦ 1,662,248,400	₦ 450,931,500	₦ 3,835,345,400
22	Kano	₦ 2,981,980,300	₦ 2,021,735,600	₦ 3,016,518,600	₦ 4,411,651,000	₦ 2,387,291,000	₦ 530,613,400

Sheet1

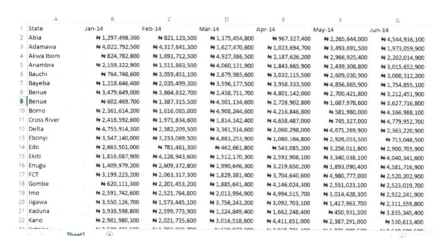

Select the data and go to Home menu, Format as Table. Choose a color theme.

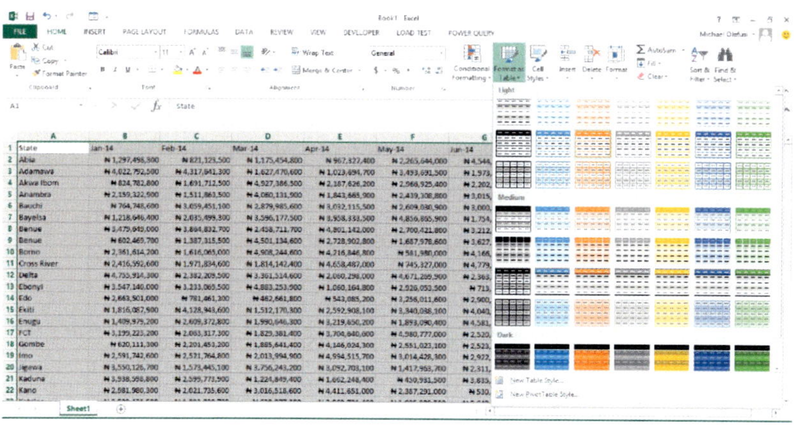

State	Jan-14	Feb-14	Mar-14	Apr-14	May-14	Jun-14
Abia	₦ 1,297,498,300	₦ 821,123,500	₦ 1,175,454,800	₦ 967,327,400	₦ 2,265,644,000	₦ 4,544,916,100
Adamawa	₦ 4,022,792,500	₦ 4,317,641,300	₦ 1,627,470,600	₦ 1,023,694,700	₦ 3,493,691,500	₦ 1,973,059,900
Akwa Ibom	₦ 824,782,800	₦ 1,691,712,500	₦ 4,927,386,500	₦ 2,187,626,200	₦ 2,966,925,400	₦ 2,202,014,900
Anambra	₦ 2,159,322,900	₦ 1,511,863,500	₦ 4,060,131,900	₦ 1,843,665,900	₦ 2,439,308,800	₦ 3,015,652,900
Bauchi	₦ 764,748,600	₦ 3,059,451,100	₦ 2,879,985,600	₦ 3,032,115,500	₦ 2,609,030,900	₦ 3,000,312,200
Bayelsa	₦ 1,218,646,400	₦ 2,035,499,300	₦ 3,596,177,500	₦ 3,958,333,500	₦ 4,856,865,900	₦ 1,754,855,100
Benue	₦ 3,479,649,000	₦ 3,864,832,700	₦ 2,458,711,700	₦ 4,801,142,000	₦ 2,700,421,800	₦ 3,212,451,900
Benue	₦ 602,469,700	₦ 1,387,315,500	₦ 4,501,134,600	₦ 2,728,902,800	₦ 1,687,978,600	₦ 3,627,716,800
Borno	₦ 2,361,614,200	₦ 1,616,065,000	₦ 4,908,244,600	₦ 4,216,846,800	₦ 581,980,000	₦ 4,166,988,100
Cross River	₦ 2,416,592,600	₦ 1,971,834,600	₦ 1,814,142,400	₦ 4,658,487,000	₦ 745,327,000	₦ 4,779,952,700
Delta	₦ 4,755,914,300	₦ 2,382,209,500	₦ 3,361,514,600	₦ 2,060,298,000	₦ 4,671,269,900	₦ 2,363,220,900
Ebonyi	₦ 3,547,140,000	₦ 3,233,069,500	₦ 4,883,253,900	₦ 1,060,164,800	₦ 2,926,053,500	₦ 713,048,500
Edo	₦ 2,663,501,000	₦ 781,461,300	₦ 462,661,800	₦ 543,085,200	₦ 3,256,011,600	₦ 2,900,705,900
Ekiti	₦ 1,816,087,900	₦ 4,128,943,600	₦ 1,512,170,300	₦ 2,592,908,100	₦ 3,340,038,100	₦ 4,040,341,600
Enugu	₦ 1,409,979,200	₦ 2,609,372,800	₦ 1,990,646,300	₦ 3,219,650,200	₦ 1,893,090,400	₦ 4,581,716,900
FCT	₦ 3,199,223,200	₦ 2,063,317,300	₦ 1,829,381,400	₦ 3,704,640,600	₦ 4,980,777,000	₦ 2,520,202,900
Gombe	₦ 620,111,300	₦ 2,201,453,200	₦ 1,885,641,400	₦ 4,146,024,300	₦ 2,551,023,100	₦ 2,523,019,700
Imo	₦ 2,591,742,600	₦ 2,521,764,800	₦ 2,013,994,900	₦ 4,994,515,700	₦ 3,014,428,300	₦ 2,922,241,900
Jigawa	₦ 3,550,126,700	₦ 1,573,445,100	₦ 3,756,243,200	₦ 3,092,703,100	₦ 1,417,963,700	₦ 2,311,559,800
Kaduna	₦ 3,938,598,800	₦ 2,599,773,900	₦ 1,224,849,400	₦ 1,662,248,400	₦ 450,931,500	₦ 3,835,345,400
Kano	₦ 2,981,980,300	₦ 2,021,735,600	₦ 3,016,518,600	₦ 4,411,651,000	₦ 2,387,291,000	₦ 530,613,400
Katsina	₦ 3,589,421,500	₦ 1,293,838,700	₦ 638,877,300	₦ 2,969,721,400	₦ 1,025,989,500	₦ 2,648,689,500
Kebbi	₦ 1,684,273,500	₦ 4,790,202,900	₦ 991,721,500	₦ 4,897,014,100	₦ 4,131,210,900	₦ 3,990,418,100
Kogi	₦ 2,812,863,300	₦ 2,734,189,600	₦ 2,306,601,300	₦ 867,264,000	₦ 2,104,687,400	₦ 2,825,512,800
Kwara	₦ 3,915,338,600	₦ 1,496,830,100	₦ 1,305,529,900	₦ 4,919,941,300	₦ 2,214,504,600	₦ 912,176,400
Lagos	₦ 6,239,473,500	₦ 7,319,183,000	₦ 6,211,689,500	₦ 3,351,178,500	₦ 11,610,307,000	₦ 22,681,984,500

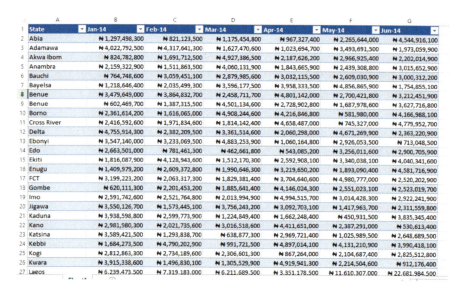

If you want to email the Excel file to a colleague, you can copy the table and paste in Outlook and you'll have the beautiful looking table in the body of the email. Your colleague will have no excuse to give regarding not seeing or acting on the data.

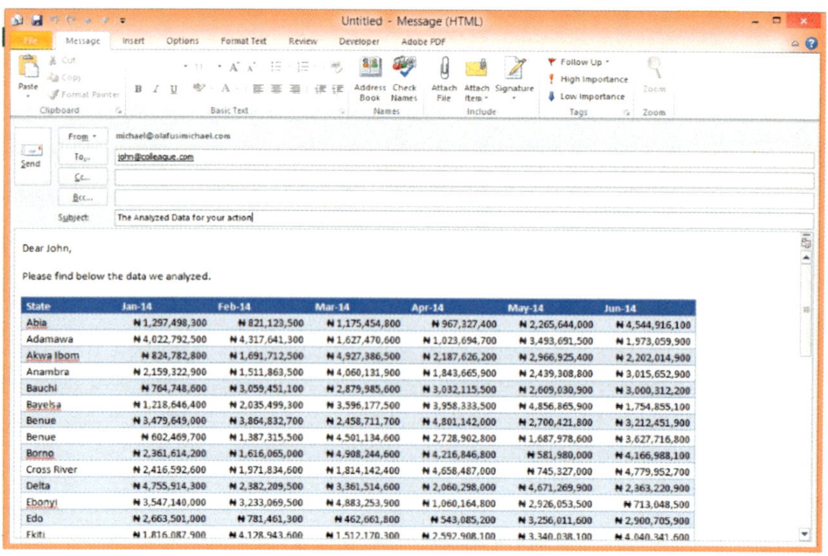

So what if you needed to print it for your boss.

Here's what you get from Print Preview.

State	Jan-14	Feb-14	Mar-14	Apr-14
Abia	₦ 1,297,498,300	₦821,123,500	₦ 1,175,434,800	₦ 967,327,400
Adamawa	₦ 4,022,792,500	₦4,317,641,300	₦ 1,627,470,600	₦ 1,023,694,700
Akwa Ibom	₦ 824,782,800	₦1,691,712,500	₦ 4,927,386,500	₦ 2,187,626,200
Anambra	₦ 2,139,322,900	₦1,511,863,500	₦ 4,060,131,900	₦ 1,843,665,900
Bauchi	₦ 764,748,600	₦3,059,451,100	₦ 2,879,985,600	₦ 3,032,115,500
Bayelsa	₦ 1,218,646,400	₦2,035,499,300	₦ 3,596,177,500	₦ 3,958,333,500
Benue	₦ 3,479,649,000	₦3,864,832,700	₦ 2,458,711,700	₦ 4,801,142,000
Benue	₦ 602,469,700	₦1,387,315,500	₦ 4,501,134,600	₦ 2,728,902,800
Borno	₦ 2,361,614,200	₦1,616,065,000	₦ 4,908,244,600	₦ 4,216,846,800
Cross River	₦ 2,416,592,600	₦1,971,834,600	₦ 1,814,142,400	₦ 4,658,487,000
Delta	₦ 4,755,914,300	₦2,382,209,500	₦ 3,361,514,600	₦ 2,060,298,000
Ebonyi	₦ 3,547,140,000	₦3,233,069,500	₦ 4,883,253,900	₦ 1,060,164,800
Edo	₦ 2,663,501,000	₦781,461,300	₦ 462,661,800	₦ 543,085,200
Ekiti	₦ 1,816,087,900	₦4,128,943,600	₦ 1,512,170,300	₦ 2,592,908,100
Enugu	₦ 1,409,979,200	₦2,609,372,800	₦ 1,990,646,300	₦ 3,219,650,200
FCT	₦ 3,199,223,200	₦2,063,317,300	₦ 1,829,381,400	₦ 3,704,640,600
Gombe	₦ 620,111,300	₦2,201,453,200	₦ 1,885,641,400	₦ 4,146,024,300
Imo	₦ 2,591,742,600	₦2,521,764,800	₦ 2,013,994,900	₦ 4,994,515,700
Jigawa	₦ 3,550,126,700	₦1,573,445,100	₦ 3,756,243,200	₦ 3,092,703,100
Kaduna	₦ 3,938,598,800	₦2,599,773,900	₦ 1,224,849,400	₦ 1,662,248,400
Kano	₦ 2,981,980,300	₦2,021,735,600	₦ 3,016,518,600	₦ 4,411,651,000
Katsina	₦ 3,589,421,500	₦1,293,838,700	₦ 638,877,300	₦ 2,969,721,400
Kebbi	₦ 1,684,273,500	₦4,790,202,900	₦ 991,721,500	₦ 4,897,014,100
Kogi	₦ 2,812,863,300	₦2,734,189,600	₦ 2,306,601,300	₦ 867,264,000
Kwara	₦ 3,915,338,600	₦1,496,830,100	₦ 1,305,529,900	₦ 4,919,941,300
Lagos	₦ 6,239,473,500	₦7,319,183,000	₦ 6,211,689,500	₦ 3,351,178,500
Nasarawa	₦ 430,732,700	₦4,852,095,900	₦ 1,411,838,200	₦ 743,233,200
Niger	₦ 3,002,387,100	₦4,592,318,900	₦ 3,219,870,900	₦ 1,086,334,400
Ogun	₦ 3,434,714,900	₦2,586,000,100	₦ 3,907,557,600	₦ 1,642,410,200
Ondo	₦ 716,222,900	₦1,690,422,800	₦ 4,362,953,800	₦ 977,876,300
Plateau	₦ 4,527,323,100	₦2,371,220,000	₦ 4,471,653,300	₦ 932,778,800
Rivers	₦ 2,423,028,900	₦4,860,256,800	₦ 4,148,808,900	₦ 839,719,700
Taraba	₦ 531,248,900	₦785,603,400	₦ 2,475,480,400	₦ 878,820,400
Yobe	₦ 2,187,894,400	₦2,500,320,500	₦ 3,497,511,100	₦ 829,030,800
Zamfara	₦ 4,767,284,200	₦1,622,967,600	₦ 4,509,006,600	₦ 1,308,237,500
Total	₦ 90,504,729,800	₦91,889,335,900	₦ 101,344,816,300	₦ 87,169,591,800

May-14	Jun-14
₦ 2,265,644,000	₦ 4,544,916,100
₦ 3,493,691,500	₦ 1,973,059,900
₦ 2,966,925,400	₦ 2,202,014,900
₦ 2,439,308,800	₦ 3,015,652,900
₦ 2,609,030,900	₦ 3,000,312,200
₦ 4,836,865,900	₦ 1,754,855,100
₦ 2,700,421,800	₦ 3,212,451,900
₦ 1,687,978,600	₦ 3,627,716,800
₦ 581,980,000	₦ 4,166,988,100
₦ 745,327,000	₦ 4,779,952,700
₦ 4,671,269,900	₦ 2,363,220,900
₦ 2,926,053,500	₦ 713,048,500
₦ 3,256,011,600	₦ 2,900,705,900
₦ 3,340,038,100	₦ 4,040,341,600
₦ 1,893,090,400	₦ 4,581,716,900
₦ 4,980,777,000	₦ 2,520,202,900
₦ 2,551,023,100	₦ 2,523,019,700
₦ 3,014,428,300	₦ 2,922,241,900
₦ 1,417,963,700	₦ 2,311,559,800
₦ 450,931,500	₦ 3,835,345,400
₦ 2,387,291,000	₦ 530,613,400
₦ 1,025,989,500	₦ 2,648,689,500
₦ 4,131,210,900	₦ 3,990,418,100
₦ 2,104,687,400	₦ 2,825,512,800
₦ 2,214,504,600	₦ 912,176,400
₦ 11,610,307,000	₦ 22,681,984,500
₦ 492,081,500	₦ 1,310,892,700
₦ 3,979,805,300	₦ 1,826,747,300
₦ 2,265,022,600	₦ 3,200,451,900
₦ 4,300,936,900	₦ 4,925,747,700
₦ 3,593,441,000	₦ 4,894,816,200
₦ 4,882,684,300	₦ 4,459,705,200
₦ 1,389,495,200	₦ 3,244,525,900
₦ 3,799,677,800	₦ 2,986,053,000
₦ 3,350,176,900	₦ 756,637,100
₦ 104,376,072,900	₦ 122,184,295,800

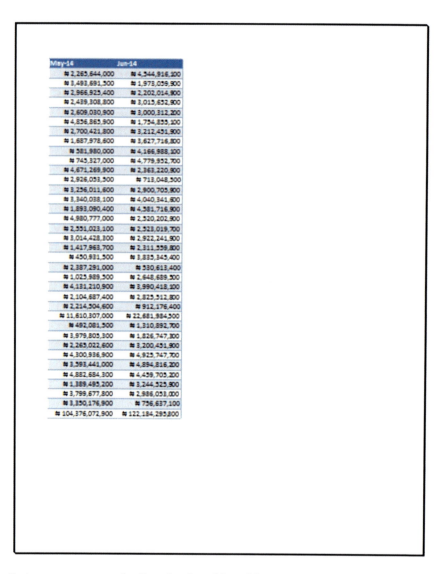

So how can you make Excel print this table on just on paper?
Very Easy.

Go to Page Layout menu, and under the Scale to Fit section, set the Width and Height to 1 page.

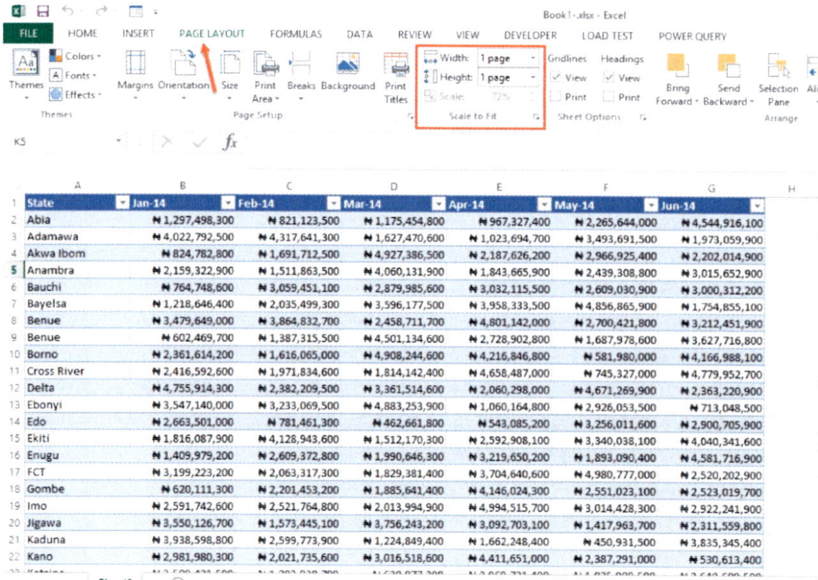

So let's see the result.

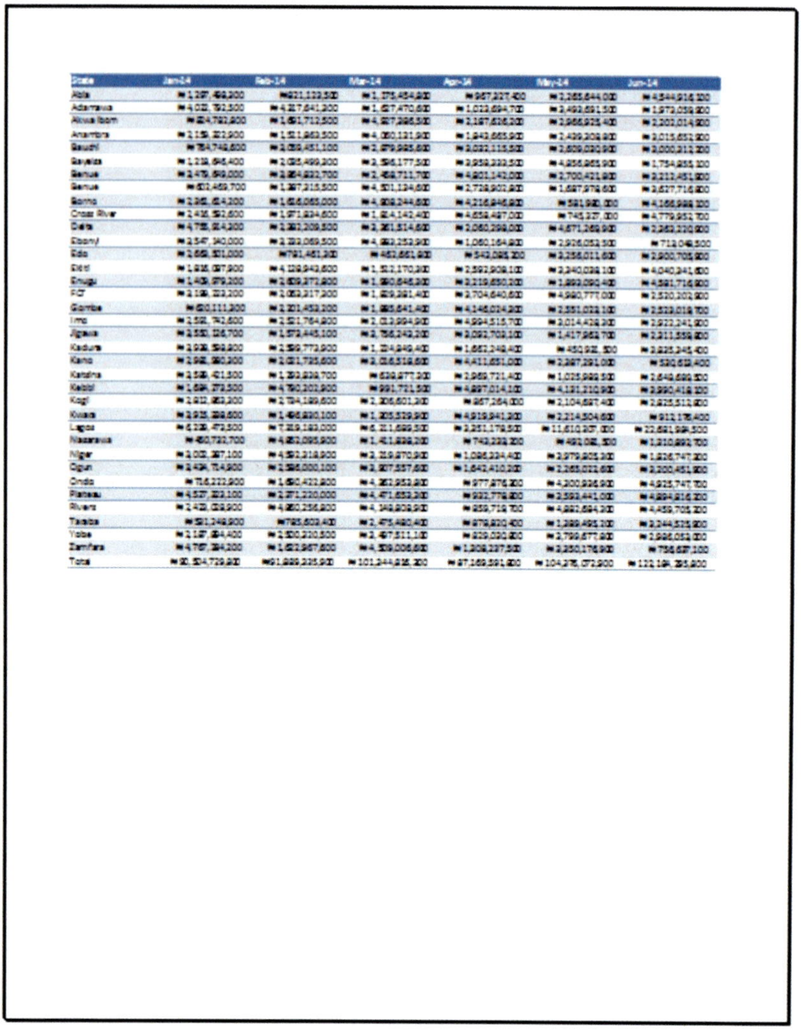

State	Jan-14	Feb-14	Mar-14	Apr-14	May-14	Jun-14
Abia	[illegible]	[illegible]	[illegible]	[illegible]	[illegible]	[illegible]
Adamawa	[illegible]	[illegible]	[illegible]	[illegible]	[illegible]	[illegible]
Akwa Ibom	[illegible]	[illegible]	[illegible]	[illegible]	[illegible]	[illegible]
Anambra	[illegible]	[illegible]	[illegible]	[illegible]	[illegible]	[illegible]
Bauchi	[illegible]	[illegible]	[illegible]	[illegible]	[illegible]	[illegible]
Bayelsa	[illegible]	[illegible]	[illegible]	[illegible]	[illegible]	[illegible]
Benue	[illegible]	[illegible]	[illegible]	[illegible]	[illegible]	[illegible]
Benue	[illegible]	[illegible]	[illegible]	[illegible]	[illegible]	[illegible]
Borno	[illegible]	[illegible]	[illegible]	[illegible]	[illegible]	[illegible]
Cross River	[illegible]	[illegible]	[illegible]	[illegible]	[illegible]	[illegible]
Delta	[illegible]	[illegible]	[illegible]	[illegible]	[illegible]	[illegible]
Ebonyi	[illegible]	[illegible]	[illegible]	[illegible]	[illegible]	[illegible]
Edo	[illegible]	[illegible]	[illegible]	[illegible]	[illegible]	[illegible]
Ekiti	[illegible]	[illegible]	[illegible]	[illegible]	[illegible]	[illegible]
Enugu	[illegible]	[illegible]	[illegible]	[illegible]	[illegible]	[illegible]
FCT	[illegible]	[illegible]	[illegible]	[illegible]	[illegible]	[illegible]
Gombe	[illegible]	[illegible]	[illegible]	[illegible]	[illegible]	[illegible]
Imo	[illegible]	[illegible]	[illegible]	[illegible]	[illegible]	[illegible]
Jigawa	[illegible]	[illegible]	[illegible]	[illegible]	[illegible]	[illegible]
Kaduna	[illegible]	[illegible]	[illegible]	[illegible]	[illegible]	[illegible]
Kano	[illegible]	[illegible]	[illegible]	[illegible]	[illegible]	[illegible]
Katsina	[illegible]	[illegible]	[illegible]	[illegible]	[illegible]	[illegible]
Kebbi	[illegible]	[illegible]	[illegible]	[illegible]	[illegible]	[illegible]
Kogi	[illegible]	[illegible]	[illegible]	[illegible]	[illegible]	[illegible]
Kwara	[illegible]	[illegible]	[illegible]	[illegible]	[illegible]	[illegible]
Lagos	[illegible]	[illegible]	[illegible]	[illegible]	[illegible]	[illegible]
Nasarawa	[illegible]	[illegible]	[illegible]	[illegible]	[illegible]	[illegible]
Niger	[illegible]	[illegible]	[illegible]	[illegible]	[illegible]	[illegible]
Ogun	[illegible]	[illegible]	[illegible]	[illegible]	[illegible]	[illegible]
Ondo	[illegible]	[illegible]	[illegible]	[illegible]	[illegible]	[illegible]
Plateau	[illegible]	[illegible]	[illegible]	[illegible]	[illegible]	[illegible]
Rivers	[illegible]	[illegible]	[illegible]	[illegible]	[illegible]	[illegible]
Taraba	[illegible]	[illegible]	[illegible]	[illegible]	[illegible]	[illegible]
Yobe	[illegible]	[illegible]	[illegible]	[illegible]	[illegible]	[illegible]
Zamfara	[illegible]	[illegible]	[illegible]	[illegible]	[illegible]	[illegible]
Total	[illegible]	[illegible]	[illegible]	[illegible]	[illegible]	[illegible]

Goal achieved! But it could have looked better if it had used more space, the space below. So we need to try out one more setting and see if it will give us a better result. We will set the Orientation to Landscape.

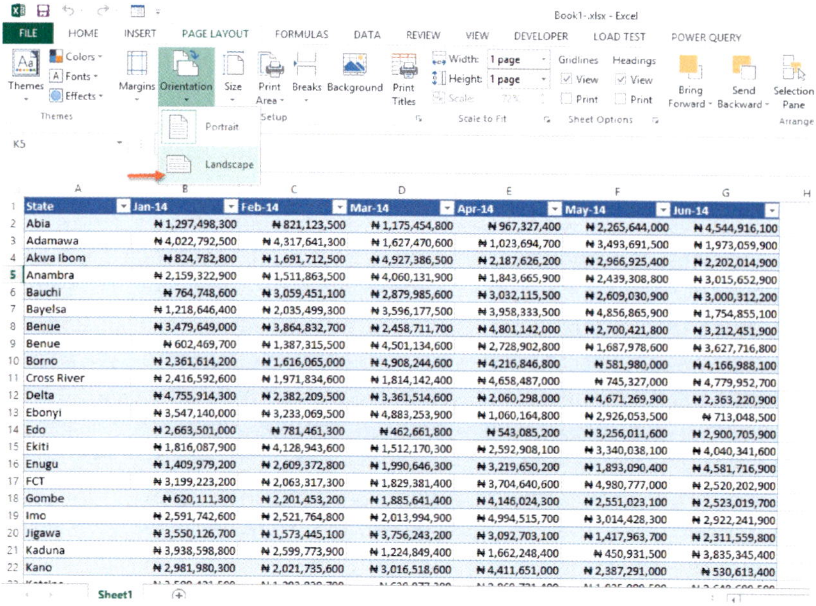

State	Jan-14	Feb-14	Mar-14	Apr-14	May-14	Jun-14
Abia	₦1,297,498,300	₦821,123,500	₦1,175,454,800	₦967,327,400	₦2,265,644,000	₦4,544,916,100
Adamawa	₦4,022,792,500	₦4,317,641,300	₦1,627,470,600	₦1,023,694,700	₦3,493,691,500	₦1,973,059,900
Akwa Ibom	₦824,782,800	₦1,691,712,500	₦4,927,386,500	₦2,187,626,200	₦2,966,925,400	₦2,202,014,900
Anambra	₦2,159,322,900	₦1,511,863,500	₦4,060,131,900	₦1,843,665,900	₦2,439,308,800	₦3,015,652,900
Bauchi	₦764,748,600	₦3,059,451,100	₦2,879,985,600	₦3,032,115,500	₦2,609,030,900	₦3,000,312,200
Bayelsa	₦1,218,646,400	₦2,035,499,300	₦3,596,177,500	₦3,958,333,500	₦4,856,865,900	₦1,754,855,100
Benue	₦3,479,649,000	₦3,864,832,700	₦2,458,711,700	₦4,801,142,000	₦2,700,421,800	₦3,212,451,900
Benue	₦602,469,700	₦1,387,315,500	₦4,501,134,600	₦2,728,902,800	₦1,687,978,600	₦3,627,716,800
Borno	₦2,361,614,200	₦1,616,065,000	₦4,908,244,600	₦4,216,846,800	₦581,980,000	₦4,166,988,100
Cross River	₦2,416,592,600	₦1,971,834,600	₦1,814,142,400	₦4,658,487,000	₦745,327,000	₦4,779,952,700
Delta	₦4,755,914,300	₦2,382,209,500	₦3,361,514,600	₦2,060,298,000	₦4,671,269,900	₦2,363,220,900
Ebonyi	₦3,547,140,000	₦3,233,069,500	₦4,883,253,900	₦1,060,164,800	₦2,926,053,500	₦713,048,500
Edo	₦2,663,501,000	₦781,461,300	₦462,661,800	₦543,085,200	₦3,256,011,600	₦2,900,705,900
Ekiti	₦1,816,087,900	₦4,128,943,600	₦1,512,170,300	₦2,592,908,100	₦3,340,038,100	₦4,040,341,600
Enugu	₦1,409,979,200	₦2,609,372,800	₦1,990,646,300	₦3,219,650,200	₦1,893,090,400	₦4,581,716,900
FCT	₦3,199,223,200	₦2,063,317,300	₦1,829,381,400	₦3,704,640,600	₦4,980,777,000	₦2,520,202,900
Gombe	₦620,111,300	₦2,201,453,200	₦1,885,641,400	₦4,146,024,300	₦2,551,023,100	₦2,523,019,700
Imo	₦2,591,742,600	₦2,521,764,800	₦2,013,994,900	₦4,994,515,700	₦3,014,428,300	₦2,922,241,900
Jigawa	₦3,550,126,700	₦1,573,445,100	₦3,756,243,200	₦3,092,703,100	₦1,417,963,700	₦2,311,559,800
Kaduna	₦3,938,598,800	₦2,599,773,900	₦1,224,849,400	₦1,662,248,400	₦450,931,500	₦3,835,345,400
Kano	₦2,981,980,300	₦2,021,735,600	₦3,016,518,600	₦4,411,651,000	₦2,387,291,000	₦530,613,400

Let's view the result.

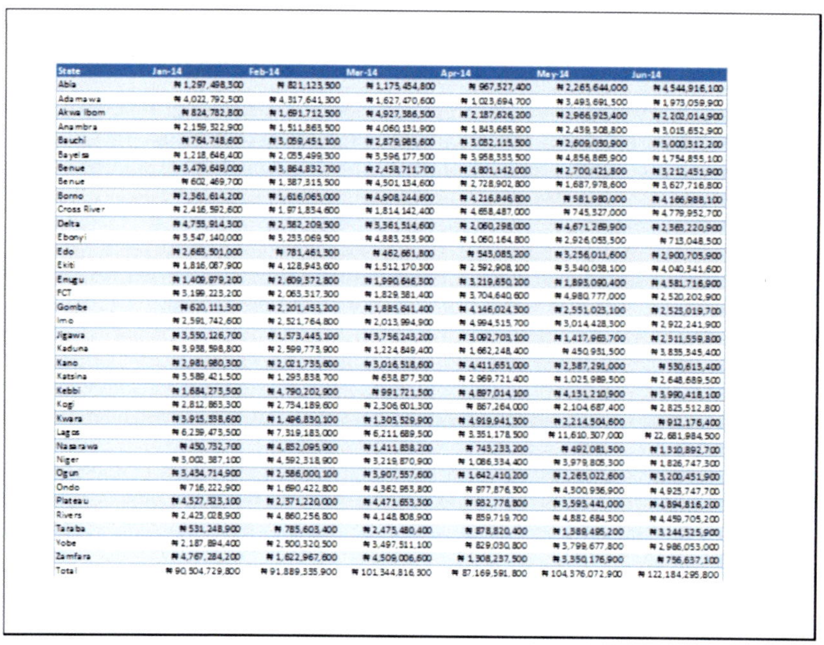

State	Jan-14	Feb-14	Mar-14	Apr-14	May-14	Jun-14
Abia	₦1,297,498,300	₦821,123,500	₦1,175,454,800	₦967,327,400	₦2,265,644,000	₦4,544,916,100
Adamawa	₦4,022,792,500	₦4,317,641,300	₦1,627,470,600	₦1,023,694,700	₦3,493,691,500	₦1,973,059,900
Akwa Ibom	₦824,782,800	₦1,691,712,500	₦4,927,386,500	₦2,187,626,200	₦2,966,925,400	₦2,202,014,900
Anambra	₦2,159,322,900	₦1,511,863,500	₦4,060,131,900	₦1,843,665,900	₦2,439,308,800	₦3,015,652,900
Bauchi	₦764,748,600	₦3,059,451,100	₦2,879,985,600	₦3,032,115,500	₦2,609,030,900	₦3,000,312,200
Bayelsa	₦1,218,646,400	₦2,035,499,300	₦3,596,177,500	₦3,958,333,500	₦4,856,865,900	₦1,754,855,100
Benue	₦3,479,649,000	₦3,864,832,700	₦2,458,711,700	₦4,801,142,000	₦2,700,421,800	₦3,212,451,900
Benue	₦602,469,700	₦1,387,315,500	₦4,501,134,600	₦2,728,902,800	₦1,687,978,600	₦3,627,716,800
Borno	₦2,361,614,200	₦1,616,065,000	₦4,908,244,600	₦4,216,846,800	₦581,980,000	₦4,166,988,100
Cross River	₦2,416,592,600	₦1,971,834,600	₦1,814,142,400	₦4,658,487,000	₦745,327,000	₦4,779,952,700
Delta	₦4,755,914,300	₦2,382,209,500	₦3,361,514,600	₦2,060,298,000	₦4,671,269,900	₦2,363,220,900
Ebonyi	₦3,547,140,000	₦3,233,069,500	₦4,883,253,900	₦1,060,164,800	₦2,926,053,500	₦713,048,500
Edo	₦2,663,501,000	₦781,461,300	₦462,661,800	₦543,085,200	₦3,256,011,600	₦2,900,705,900
Ekiti	₦1,816,087,900	₦4,128,943,600	₦1,512,170,300	₦2,592,908,100	₦3,340,038,100	₦4,040,341,600
Enugu	₦1,409,979,200	₦2,609,372,800	₦1,990,646,300	₦3,219,650,200	₦1,893,090,400	₦4,581,716,900
FCT	₦3,199,223,200	₦2,063,317,300	₦1,829,381,400	₦3,704,640,600	₦4,980,777,000	₦2,520,202,900
Gombe	₦620,111,300	₦2,201,453,200	₦1,885,641,400	₦4,146,024,300	₦2,551,023,100	₦2,523,019,700
Imo	₦2,591,742,600	₦2,521,764,800	₦2,013,994,900	₦4,994,515,700	₦3,014,428,300	₦2,922,241,900
Jigawa	₦3,550,126,700	₦1,573,445,100	₦3,756,243,200	₦3,092,703,100	₦1,417,963,700	₦2,311,559,800
Kaduna	₦3,938,598,800	₦2,599,773,900	₦1,224,849,400	₦1,662,248,400	₦450,931,500	₦3,835,345,400
Kano	₦2,981,980,300	₦2,021,735,600	₦3,016,518,600	₦4,411,651,000	₦2,387,291,000	₦530,613,400
Katsina	₦3,589,421,500	₦1,293,838,700	₦638,877,300	₦2,969,721,400	₦1,025,989,500	₦2,648,689,500
Kebbi	₦1,684,273,500	₦4,790,202,900	₦991,721,500	₦4,897,014,100	₦4,131,210,900	₦3,990,418,100
Kogi	₦2,812,863,300	₦2,734,189,600	₦2,306,601,300	₦867,264,000	₦2,104,687,400	₦2,825,512,800
Kwara	₦3,915,338,600	₦1,496,830,100	₦1,305,529,900	₦4,919,941,300	₦2,214,504,600	₦912,176,400
Lagos	₦6,239,473,500	₦7,319,183,000	₦6,211,689,500	₦3,351,178,500	₦11,610,307,000	₦22,681,984,500
Nasarawa	₦450,732,700	₦4,852,095,900	₦1,411,838,200	₦743,233,200	₦492,081,500	₦1,310,892,700
Niger	₦3,002,387,100	₦4,592,318,900	₦3,219,870,900	₦1,086,334,400	₦3,979,805,300	₦1,826,747,300
Ogun	₦3,434,714,900	₦2,586,000,100	₦3,907,557,600	₦1,642,410,200	₦2,265,022,600	₦3,200,451,900
Ondo	₦716,222,900	₦1,690,422,800	₦4,362,953,800	₦977,876,300	₦4,300,936,900	₦4,925,747,700
Plateau	₦4,527,323,100	₦2,371,220,000	₦4,471,653,300	₦932,778,800	₦3,593,441,000	₦4,894,816,200
Rivers	₦2,423,028,900	₦4,860,256,800	₦4,148,808,900	₦859,719,700	₦4,882,684,300	₦4,459,705,200
Taraba	₦531,248,900	₦785,603,400	₦2,475,480,400	₦878,820,400	₦1,389,495,200	₦3,244,525,900
Yobe	₦2,187,894,400	₦2,500,320,500	₦3,497,511,100	₦829,030,800	₦3,799,677,800	₦2,986,053,000
Zamfara	₦4,767,284,200	₦1,622,967,600	₦4,509,006,600	₦1,308,237,500	₦3,350,176,900	₦756,637,100
Total	₦90,504,729,800	₦91,889,335,900	₦101,344,816,300	₦87,169,591,800	₦104,376,072,900	₦122,184,295,800

Bravo! This is much better!

What if the boss wanted just January to May data and not the entire table?
Also very easy.

Highlight the table from the beginning up to May, leaving out June. So we are highlighting just what we want to print.

Under same Page Layout, Click on Print Area, and select Set Print Area.

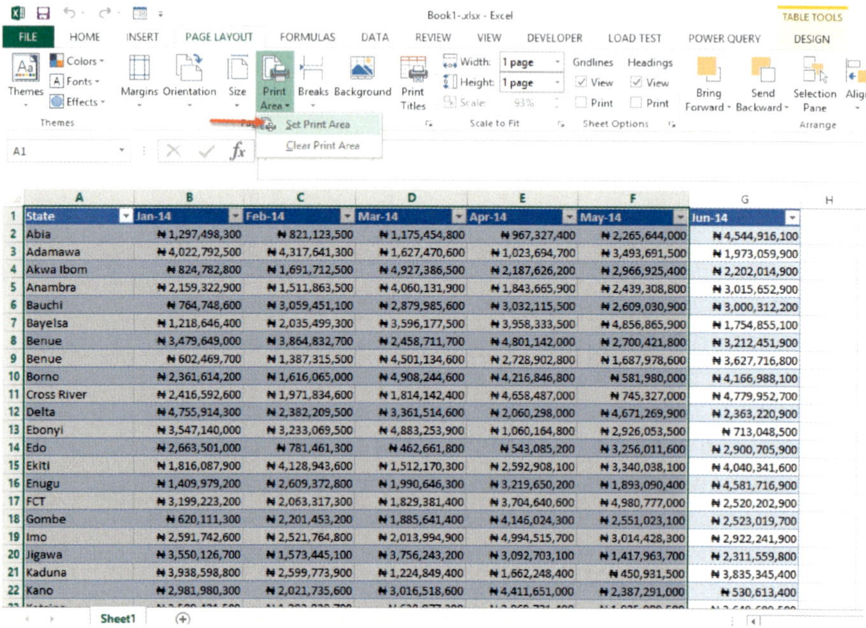

	A	B	C	D	E	F	G
1	State	Jan-14	Feb-14	Mar-14	Apr-14	May-14	Jun-14
2	Abia	₦1,297,498,300	₦821,123,500	₦1,175,454,800	₦967,327,400	₦2,265,644,000	₦4,544,916,100
3	Adamawa	₦4,022,792,500	₦4,317,641,300	₦1,627,470,600	₦1,023,694,700	₦3,493,691,500	₦1,973,059,900
4	Akwa Ibom	₦824,782,800	₦1,691,712,500	₦4,927,386,500	₦2,187,626,200	₦2,966,925,400	₦2,202,014,900
5	Anambra	₦2,159,322,900	₦1,511,863,500	₦4,060,131,900	₦1,843,665,900	₦2,439,308,800	₦3,015,652,900
6	Bauchi	₦764,748,600	₦3,059,451,100	₦2,879,985,600	₦3,032,115,500	₦2,609,030,900	₦3,000,312,200
7	Bayelsa	₦1,218,646,400	₦2,035,499,300	₦3,596,177,500	₦3,958,333,500	₦4,856,865,900	₦1,754,855,100
8	Benue	₦3,479,649,000	₦3,864,832,700	₦2,458,711,700	₦4,801,142,000	₦2,700,421,800	₦3,212,451,900
9	Benue	₦602,469,700	₦1,387,315,500	₦4,501,134,600	₦2,728,902,800	₦1,687,978,600	₦3,627,716,800
10	Borno	₦2,361,614,200	₦1,616,065,000	₦4,908,244,600	₦4,216,846,800	₦581,980,000	₦4,166,988,100
11	Cross River	₦2,416,592,600	₦1,971,834,600	₦1,814,142,400	₦4,658,487,000	₦745,327,000	₦4,779,952,700
12	Delta	₦4,755,914,300	₦2,382,209,500	₦3,361,514,600	₦2,060,298,000	₦4,671,269,900	₦2,363,220,900
13	Ebonyi	₦3,547,140,000	₦3,233,069,500	₦4,883,253,900	₦1,060,164,800	₦2,926,053,500	₦713,048,500
14	Edo	₦2,663,501,000	₦781,461,300	₦462,661,800	₦543,085,200	₦3,256,011,600	₦2,900,705,900
15	Ekiti	₦1,816,087,900	₦4,128,943,600	₦1,512,170,300	₦2,592,908,100	₦3,340,038,100	₦4,040,341,600
16	Enugu	₦1,409,979,200	₦2,609,372,800	₦1,990,646,300	₦3,219,650,200	₦1,893,090,400	₦4,581,716,900
17	FCT	₦3,199,223,200	₦2,063,317,300	₦1,829,381,400	₦3,704,640,600	₦4,980,777,000	₦2,520,202,900
18	Gombe	₦620,111,300	₦2,201,453,200	₦1,885,641,400	₦4,146,024,300	₦2,551,023,100	₦2,523,019,700
19	Imo	₦2,591,742,600	₦2,521,764,800	₦2,013,994,900	₦4,994,515,700	₦3,014,428,300	₦2,922,241,900
20	Jigawa	₦3,550,126,700	₦1,573,445,100	₦3,756,243,200	₦3,092,703,100	₦1,417,963,700	₦2,311,559,800
21	Kaduna	₦3,938,598,800	₦2,599,773,900	₦1,224,849,400	₦1,662,248,400	₦450,931,500	₦3,835,345,400
22	Kano	₦2,981,980,300	₦2,021,735,600	₦3,016,518,600	₦4,411,651,000	₦2,387,291,000	₦530,613,400

And that's it! So let's see the result.

State	Jan-14	Feb-14	Mar-14	Apr-14	May-14
Abia	₦ 1,297,498,300	₦ 821,123,500	₦ 1,175,454,800	₦ 967,327,400	₦ 2,265,644,000
Adamawa	₦ 4,022,792,500	₦ 4,317,641,300	₦ 1,627,470,600	₦ 1,023,694,700	₦ 3,493,691,500
Akwa Ibom	₦ 824,782,800	₦ 1,691,712,500	₦ 4,927,386,500	₦ 2,187,626,200	₦ 2,966,925,400
Anambra	₦ 2,159,322,900	₦ 1,511,863,500	₦ 4,060,131,900	₦ 1,843,665,900	₦ 2,439,308,800
Bauchi	₦ 764,748,600	₦ 3,059,451,100	₦ 2,879,985,600	₦ 3,052,115,500	₦ 2,609,030,900
Bayelsa	₦ 1,218,646,400	₦ 2,035,499,300	₦ 3,596,177,500	₦ 3,958,333,500	₦ 4,856,865,900
Benue	₦ 3,479,649,000	₦ 3,864,832,700	₦ 2,458,711,700	₦ 4,801,142,000	₦ 2,700,421,800
Benue	₦ 602,469,700	₦ 1,387,315,500	₦ 4,501,134,600	₦ 2,728,902,800	₦ 1,687,978,600
Borno	₦ 2,361,614,200	₦ 1,616,065,000	₦ 4,908,244,600	₦ 4,216,846,800	₦ 581,980,000
Cross River	₦ 2,416,592,600	₦ 1,971,834,600	₦ 1,814,142,400	₦ 4,658,487,000	₦ 745,327,000
Delta	₦ 4,755,914,300	₦ 2,382,209,500	₦ 3,361,514,600	₦ 2,060,298,000	₦ 4,671,269,900
Ebonyi	₦ 3,547,140,000	₦ 3,233,069,500	₦ 4,883,253,900	₦ 1,060,164,800	₦ 2,926,053,500
Edo	₦ 2,663,501,000	₦ 781,461,300	₦ 462,661,800	₦ 543,085,200	₦ 3,256,011,600
Ekiti	₦ 1,816,087,900	₦ 4,128,943,600	₦ 1,512,170,300	₦ 2,592,908,100	₦ 3,340,038,100
Enugu	₦ 1,409,979,200	₦ 2,609,372,800	₦ 1,990,646,300	₦ 3,219,650,200	₦ 1,893,090,400
FCT	₦ 3,199,223,200	₦ 2,063,317,300	₦ 1,829,381,400	₦ 3,704,640,600	₦ 4,980,777,000
Gombe	₦ 620,111,300	₦ 2,201,453,200	₦ 1,885,641,400	₦ 4,146,024,300	₦ 2,551,025,100
Imo	₦ 2,591,742,600	₦ 2,521,764,800	₦ 2,013,994,900	₦ 4,994,515,700	₦ 3,014,428,300
Jigawa	₦ 3,550,126,700	₦ 1,573,445,100	₦ 3,756,243,200	₦ 3,092,703,100	₦ 1,417,963,700
Kaduna	₦ 3,938,598,800	₦ 2,599,773,900	₦ 1,224,849,400	₦ 1,662,248,400	₦ 450,931,500
Kano	₦ 2,981,980,300	₦ 2,021,735,600	₦ 3,016,518,600	₦ 4,411,651,000	₦ 2,387,291,000
Katsina	₦ 3,589,421,500	₦ 1,293,838,700	₦ 638,877,300	₦ 2,969,721,400	₦ 1,025,989,500
Kebbi	₦ 1,684,273,500	₦ 4,790,202,900	₦ 991,721,500	₦ 4,897,014,100	₦ 4,131,210,900
Kogi	₦ 2,812,863,300	₦ 2,734,189,600	₦ 2,306,601,300	₦ 867,264,000	₦ 2,104,687,400
Kwara	₦ 3,915,338,600	₦ 1,496,830,100	₦ 1,305,529,900	₦ 4,919,941,300	₦ 2,214,504,600
Lagos	₦ 6,239,473,500	₦ 7,319,183,000	₦ 6,211,689,500	₦ 3,351,178,500	₦ 11,610,307,000
Nasarawa	₦ 450,732,700	₦ 4,852,095,900	₦ 1,411,838,200	₦ 743,233,200	₦ 492,081,500
Niger	₦ 3,002,387,100	₦ 4,592,318,900	₦ 3,219,870,900	₦ 1,086,334,400	₦ 3,979,805,300
Ogun	₦ 3,434,714,900	₦ 2,586,000,100	₦ 3,907,557,600	₦ 1,642,410,200	₦ 2,265,022,600
Ondo	₦ 716,222,900	₦ 1,690,422,800	₦ 4,362,953,800	₦ 977,876,300	₦ 4,300,936,900
Plateau	₦ 4,527,323,100	₦ 2,371,220,000	₦ 4,471,653,300	₦ 952,778,800	₦ 3,593,441,000
Rivers	₦ 2,423,028,900	₦ 4,860,256,800	₦ 4,148,808,900	₦ 859,719,700	₦ 4,882,684,300
Taraba	₦ 531,248,900	₦ 785,603,400	₦ 2,475,480,400	₦ 878,820,400	₦ 1,389,495,200
Yobe	₦ 2,187,894,400	₦ 2,500,320,500	₦ 3,497,511,100	₦ 829,030,800	₦ 3,799,677,800
Zamfara	₦ 4,767,284,200	₦ 1,622,967,600	₦ 4,509,006,600	₦ 1,308,237,500	₦ 3,350,176,900
Total	₦ 90,504,729,800	₦ 91,889,335,900	₦ 101,344,816,300	₦ 87,169,591,800	₦ 104,376,072,900

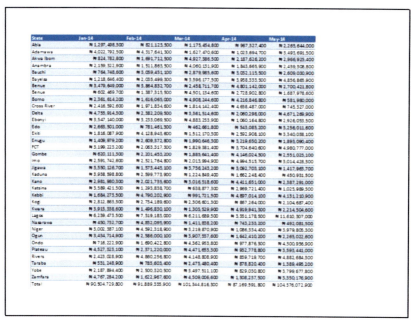

There we have it, no June data included!

One more big tip.

What if you have a big table that will print onto many pages but you want the header to repeat on the first row of every page?

Below is a sample.

S/N	Pizza Sold	Price	Quantity	Amount Sold	Time
1	Meatzaa	₦2,000.00	5	₦10,000.00	8:00:01 AM
2	Extravaganza	₦2,000.00	4	₦8,000.00	8:00:02 AM
3	BBQ Chicken	₦4,000.00	5	₦20,000.00	8:00:04 AM
4	Extravaganza	₦2,000.00	1	₦2,000.00	8:00:07 AM
5	Meatzaa	₦2,000.00	4	₦8,000.00	8:00:08 AM
6	Hot Veggie	₦4,000.00	2	₦8,000.00	8:00:14 AM
7	BBQ Philly Steak	₦4,000.00	5	₦20,000.00	8:00:20 AM
8	Chicken Feast	₦2,000.00	1	₦2,000.00	8:00:20 AM
9	Meatzaa	₦2,000.00	3	₦6,000.00	8:00:22 AM
10	Chicken Suya	₦4,000.00	5	₦20,000.00	8:00:25 AM
11	Chicken Legend	₦2,000.00	5	₦10,000.00	8:00:26 AM
12	BBQ Philly Steak	₦4,000.00	4	₦16,000.00	8:00:27 AM
13	Chicken Suya	₦4,000.00	2	₦8,000.00	8:00:29 AM
14	Chicken Feast	₦2,000.00	5	₦10,000.00	8:00:33 AM
15	Chicken Feast	₦2,000.00	4	₦8,000.00	8:00:33 AM
16	Beef Suya	₦3,000.00	5	₦15,000.00	8:00:34 AM
17	Chicken Feast	₦2,000.00	5	₦10,000.00	8:00:35 AM
18	Hot Veggie	₦4,000.00	5	₦20,000.00	8:00:35 AM
19	Meatzaa	₦2,000.00	5	₦10,000.00	8:00:35 AM
20	Meatzaa	₦2,000.00	2	₦4,000.00	8:00:36 AM
21	Margarita	₦4,000.00	3	₦12,000.00	8:00:37 AM
22	Italiano	₦3,000.00	5	₦15,000.00	8:00:40 AM
23	Hot Veggie	₦4,000.00	2	₦8,000.00	8:00:45 AM
24	Pepperoni Suya	₦3,000.00	3	₦9,000.00	8:00:45 AM
25	Veggie Supreme	₦3,000.00	5	₦15,000.00	8:00:48 AM
26	Hot Pepperoni Feast	₦4,000.00	3	₦12,000.00	8:00:49 AM
27	Chicken Legend	₦2,000.00	4	₦8,000.00	8:00:49 AM
28	BBQ Philly Steak	₦4,000.00	1	₦4,000.00	8:00:52 AM
29	Hot Pepperoni Feast	₦4,000.00	2	₦8,000.00	8:00:56 AM
30	Chicken Bali	₦2,000.00	4	₦8,000.00	8:00:56 AM
31	Chicken Feast	₦2,000.00	3	₦6,000.00	8:00:57 AM
32	Veggie Supreme	₦3,000.00	2	₦6,000.00	8:00:57 AM
33	Extravaganza	₦2,000.00	4	₦8,000.00	8:01:00 AM
34	Pepperoni Suya	₦3,000.00	4	₦12,000.00	8:01:01 AM
35	Veggie Supreme	₦3,000.00	2	₦6,000.00	8:01:02 AM
36	Extravaganza	₦2,000.00	2	₦4,000.00	8:01:08 AM
37	Italiano	₦3,000.00	2	₦6,000.00	8:01:14 AM
38	BBQ Philly Steak	₦4,000.00	2	₦8,000.00	8:01:16 AM
39	Pepperoni Feast	₦4,000.00	5	₦20,000.00	8:01:16 AM
40	Chicken Bali	₦2,000.00	4	₦8,000.00	8:01:17 AM
41	Pepperoni Suya	₦3,000.00	2	₦6,000.00	8:01:18 AM
42	BBQ Philly Steak	₦4,000.00	5	₦20,000.00	8:01:20 AM
43	Chicken Bali	₦2,000.00	3	₦6,000.00	8:01:21 AM
44	Italiano	₦3,000.00	5	₦15,000.00	8:01:22 AM
45	BBQ Philly Steak	₦4,000.00	4	₦16,000.00	8:01:26 AM
46	Hot Pepperoni Feast	₦4,000.00	5	₦20,000.00	8:01:28 AM

47	Chicken Legend	₦2,000.00	2	₦4,000.00	8:01:31 AM
48	Chicken Bali	₦2,000.00	2	₦4,000.00	8:01:32 AM
49	BBQ Philly Steak	₦4,000.00	1	₦4,000.00	8:01:34 AM
50	BBQ Chicken	₦4,000.00	4	₦16,000.00	8:01:34 AM
51	Pepperoni Feast	₦4,000.00	4	₦16,000.00	8:01:35 AM
52	BBQ Philly Steak	₦4,000.00	1	₦4,000.00	8:01:36 AM
53	BBQ Philly Steak	₦4,000.00	4	₦16,000.00	8:01:36 AM
54	Pepperoni Suya	₦3,000.00	2	₦6,000.00	8:01:37 AM
55	Veggie Supreme	₦3,000.00	5	₦15,000.00	8:01:37 AM
56	Chicken Suya	₦4,000.00	5	₦20,000.00	8:01:39 AM
57	Margarita	₦4,000.00	4	₦16,000.00	8:01:43 AM
58	Chicken Bali	₦2,000.00	5	₦10,000.00	8:01:44 AM
59	Meatzaa	₦2,000.00	5	₦10,000.00	8:01:44 AM
60	BBQ Philly Steak	₦4,000.00	3	₦12,000.00	8:01:46 AM
61	Pepperoni Suya	₦3,000.00	5	₦15,000.00	8:01:48 AM
62	Chicken Feast	₦2,000.00	5	₦10,000.00	8:01:49 AM
63	Chicken Feast	₦2,000.00	4	₦8,000.00	8:01:52 AM
64	Chicken Suya	₦4,000.00	2	₦8,000.00	8:01:54 AM
65	Chicken Legend	₦2,000.00	3	₦6,000.00	8:01:55 AM
66	Chicken Feast	₦2,000.00	4	₦8,000.00	8:01:56 AM
67	Chicken Bali	₦2,000.00	1	₦2,000.00	8:02:03 AM
68	Pepperoni Suya	₦3,000.00	1	₦3,000.00	8:02:03 AM
69	Pepperoni Feast	₦4,000.00	3	₦12,000.00	8:02:04 AM
70	Beef Suya	₦3,000.00	3	₦9,000.00	8:02:05 AM
71	BBQ Chicken	₦4,000.00	1	₦4,000.00	8:02:06 AM
72	Pepperoni Feast	₦4,000.00	3	₦12,000.00	8:02:10 AM
73	Pepperoni Feast	₦4,000.00	5	₦20,000.00	8:02:13 AM
74	BBQ Chicken	₦4,000.00	2	₦8,000.00	8:02:13 AM
75	Extravaganza	₦2,000.00	5	₦10,000.00	8:02:18 AM
76	Chicken Legend	₦2,000.00	1	₦2,000.00	8:02:18 AM
77	Pepperoni Suya	₦3,000.00	2	₦6,000.00	8:02:22 AM
78	Hot Veggie	₦4,000.00	2	₦8,000.00	8:02:22 AM
79	Extravaganza	₦2,000.00	3	₦6,000.00	8:02:30 AM
80	Chicken Suya	₦4,000.00	3	₦12,000.00	8:02:31 AM
81	Pepperoni Feast	₦4,000.00	5	₦20,000.00	8:02:35 AM
82	Pepperoni Feast	₦4,000.00	3	₦12,000.00	8:02:36 AM
83	BBQ Chicken	₦4,000.00	3	₦12,000.00	8:02:37 AM
84	BBQ Philly Steak	₦4,000.00	4	₦16,000.00	8:02:38 AM
85	Hot Veggie	₦4,000.00	5	₦20,000.00	8:02:38 AM
86	Chicken Bali	₦2,000.00	1	₦2,000.00	8:02:42 AM
87	Beef Suya	₦3,000.00	2	₦6,000.00	8:02:44 AM
88	BBQ Philly Steak	₦4,000.00	2	₦8,000.00	8:02:46 AM
89	Veggie Supreme	₦3,000.00	4	₦12,000.00	8:02:47 AM
90	Chicken Suya	₦4,000.00	1	₦4,000.00	8:02:47 AM
91	BBQ Chicken	₦4,000.00	5	₦20,000.00	8:02:49 AM
92	BBQ Philly Steak	₦4,000.00	4	₦16,000.00	8:02:50 AM
93	Meatzaa	₦2,000.00	5	₦10,000.00	8:02:50 AM

Notice that the page two has no header to help you identify what the fields are.

So here's how to fix that.

Still at Page Layout menu, click on the small icon at the bottom right corner of the Sheet Options section.

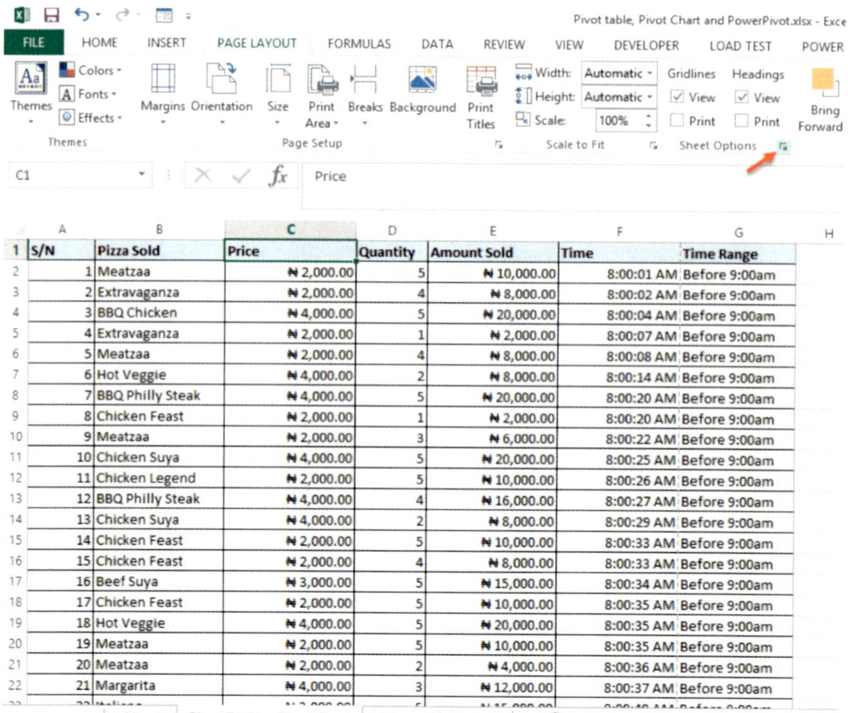

	A	B	C	D	E	F	G
1	S/N	Pizza Sold	Price	Quantity	Amount Sold	Time	Time Range
2	1	Meatzaa	₦ 2,000.00	5	₦ 10,000.00	8:00:01 AM	Before 9:00am
3	2	Extravaganza	₦ 2,000.00	4	₦ 8,000.00	8:00:02 AM	Before 9:00am
4	3	BBQ Chicken	₦ 4,000.00	5	₦ 20,000.00	8:00:04 AM	Before 9:00am
5	4	Extravaganza	₦ 2,000.00	1	₦ 2,000.00	8:00:07 AM	Before 9:00am
6	5	Meatzaa	₦ 2,000.00	4	₦ 8,000.00	8:00:08 AM	Before 9:00am
7	6	Hot Veggie	₦ 4,000.00	2	₦ 8,000.00	8:00:14 AM	Before 9:00am
8	7	BBQ Philly Steak	₦ 4,000.00	5	₦ 20,000.00	8:00:20 AM	Before 9:00am
9	8	Chicken Feast	₦ 2,000.00	1	₦ 2,000.00	8:00:20 AM	Before 9:00am
10	9	Meatzaa	₦ 2,000.00	3	₦ 6,000.00	8:00:22 AM	Before 9:00am
11	10	Chicken Suya	₦ 4,000.00	5	₦ 20,000.00	8:00:25 AM	Before 9:00am
12	11	Chicken Legend	₦ 2,000.00	5	₦ 10,000.00	8:00:26 AM	Before 9:00am
13	12	BBQ Philly Steak	₦ 4,000.00	4	₦ 16,000.00	8:00:27 AM	Before 9:00am
14	13	Chicken Suya	₦ 4,000.00	2	₦ 8,000.00	8:00:29 AM	Before 9:00am
15	14	Chicken Feast	₦ 2,000.00	5	₦ 10,000.00	8:00:33 AM	Before 9:00am
16	15	Chicken Feast	₦ 2,000.00	4	₦ 8,000.00	8:00:33 AM	Before 9:00am
17	16	Beef Suya	₦ 3,000.00	5	₦ 15,000.00	8:00:34 AM	Before 9:00am
18	17	Chicken Feast	₦ 2,000.00	5	₦ 10,000.00	8:00:35 AM	Before 9:00am
19	18	Hot Veggie	₦ 4,000.00	5	₦ 20,000.00	8:00:35 AM	Before 9:00am
20	19	Meatzaa	₦ 2,000.00	5	₦ 10,000.00	8:00:35 AM	Before 9:00am
21	20	Meatzaa	₦ 2,000.00	2	₦ 4,000.00	8:00:36 AM	Before 9:00am
22	21	Margarita	₦ 4,000.00	3	₦ 12,000.00	8:00:37 AM	Before 9:00am

In the dialog box that comes up, set the **Rows to repeat at top**

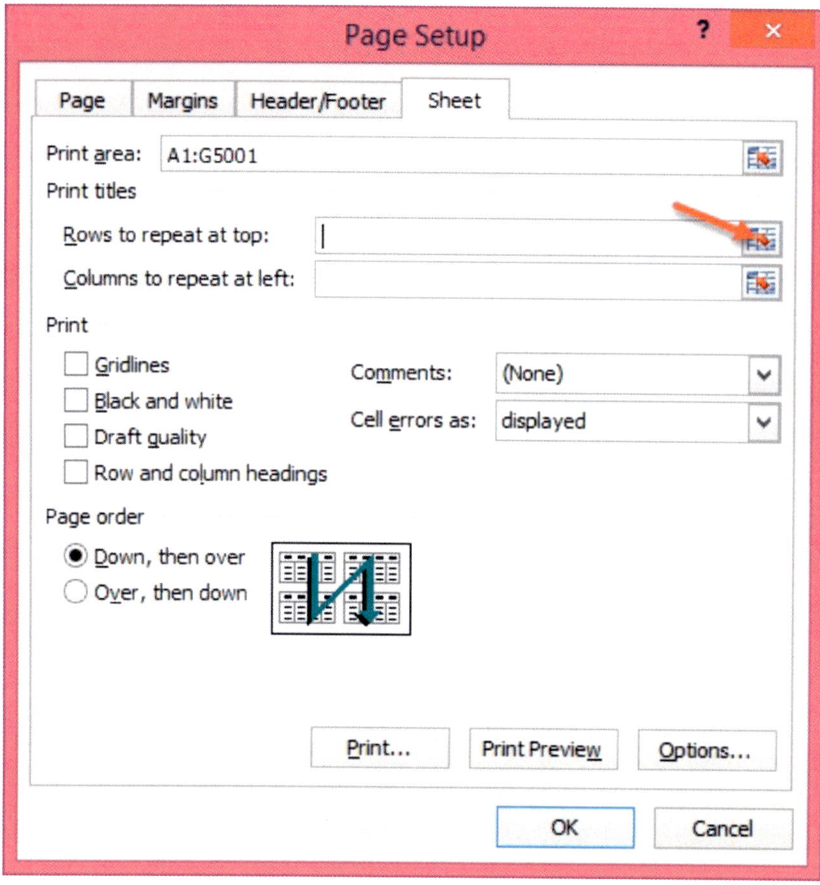

Select Row 1 that has the headers.

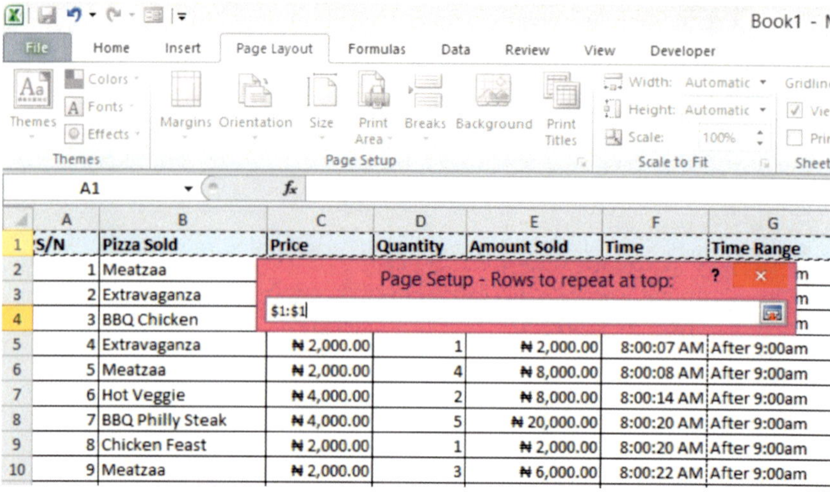
Book1 - M
File
Home
Insert
Page Layout
Formulas
Data
Review
View
Developer
Colors
Fonts
Effects
Themes
Margins
Orientation
Size
Print Area
Breaks
Background
Print Titles
Page Setup
Width: Automatic
Height: Automatic
Scale: 100%
Scale to Fit
Gridlines
View
Print
A1
S/N
Pizza Sold
Price
Quantity
Amount Sold
Time
Time Range
Page Setup - Rows to repeat at top:
$1:$1
1 Meatzaa
2 Extravaganza
3 BBQ Chicken
4 Extravaganza ₦ 2,000.00 1 ₦ 2,000.00 8:00:07 AM After 9:00am
5 Meatzaa ₦ 2,000.00 4 ₦ 8,000.00 8:00:08 AM After 9:00am
6 Hot Veggie ₦ 4,000.00 2 ₦ 8,000.00 8:00:14 AM After 9:00am
7 BBQ Philly Steak ₦ 4,000.00 5 ₦ 20,000.00 8:00:20 AM After 9:00am
8 Chicken Feast ₦ 2,000.00 1 ₦ 2,000.00 8:00:20 AM After 9:00am
9 Meatzaa ₦ 2,000.00 3 ₦ 6,000.00 8:00:22 AM After 9:00am

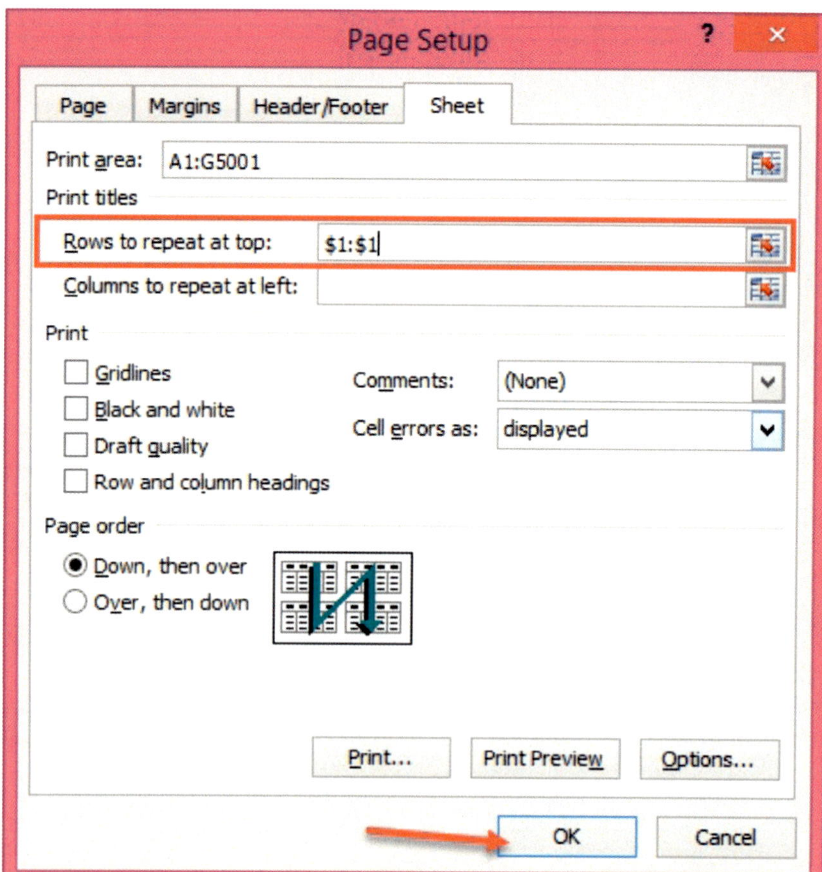
Page Setup
Page
Margins
Header/Footer
Sheet
Print area: A1:G5001
Print titles
Rows to repeat at top: $1:$1
Columns to repeat at left:
Print
Gridlines
Black and white
Draft quality
Row and column headings
Comments: (None)
Cell errors as: displayed
Page order
Down, then over
Over, then down
Print...
Print Preview
Options...
OK
Cancel

And that is all!

So let's see the result.

S/N	Pizza Sold	Price	Quantity	Amount Sold	Time
1	Meatzaa	₦ 2,000.00	5	₦ 10,000.00	8:00:01 AM
2	Extravaganza	₦ 2,000.00	4	₦ 8,000.00	8:00:02 AM
3	BBQ Chicken	₦ 4,000.00	5	₦ 20,000.00	8:00:04 AM
4	Extravaganza	₦ 2,000.00	1	₦ 2,000.00	8:00:07 AM
5	Meatzaa	₦ 2,000.00	4	₦ 8,000.00	8:00:08 AM
6	Hot Veggie	₦ 4,000.00	2	₦ 8,000.00	8:00:14 AM
7	BBQ Philly Steak	₦ 4,000.00	5	₦ 20,000.00	8:00:20 AM
8	Chicken Feast	₦ 2,000.00	1	₦ 2,000.00	8:00:20 AM
9	Meatzaa	₦ 2,000.00	3	₦ 6,000.00	8:00:22 AM
10	Chicken Suya	₦ 4,000.00	5	₦ 20,000.00	8:00:25 AM
11	Chicken Legend	₦ 2,000.00	5	₦ 10,000.00	8:00:26 AM
12	BBQ Philly Steak	₦ 4,000.00	4	₦ 16,000.00	8:00:27 AM
13	Chicken Suya	₦ 4,000.00	2	₦ 8,000.00	8:00:29 AM
14	Chicken Feast	₦ 2,000.00	5	₦ 10,000.00	8:00:33 AM
15	Chicken Feast	₦ 2,000.00	4	₦ 8,000.00	8:00:33 AM
16	Beef Suya	₦ 3,000.00	5	₦ 15,000.00	8:00:34 AM
17	Chicken Feast	₦ 2,000.00	5	₦ 10,000.00	8:00:35 AM
18	Hot Veggie	₦ 4,000.00	5	₦ 20,000.00	8:00:35 AM
19	Meatzaa	₦ 2,000.00	5	₦ 10,000.00	8:00:35 AM
20	Meatzaa	₦ 2,000.00	2	₦ 4,000.00	8:00:36 AM
21	Margarita	₦ 4,000.00	3	₦ 12,000.00	8:00:37 AM
22	Italiano	₦ 3,000.00	5	₦ 15,000.00	8:00:40 AM
23	Hot Veggie	₦ 4,000.00	2	₦ 8,000.00	8:00:45 AM
24	Pepperoni Suya	₦ 3,000.00	3	₦ 9,000.00	8:00:45 AM
25	Veggie Supreme	₦ 3,000.00	5	₦ 15,000.00	8:00:48 AM
26	Hot Pepperoni Feast	₦ 4,000.00	3	₦ 12,000.00	8:00:49 AM
27	Chicken Legend	₦ 2,000.00	4	₦ 8,000.00	8:00:49 AM
28	BBQ Philly Steak	₦ 4,000.00	1	₦ 4,000.00	8:00:52 AM
29	Hot Pepperoni Feast	₦ 4,000.00	2	₦ 8,000.00	8:00:56 AM
30	Chicken Bali	₦ 2,000.00	4	₦ 8,000.00	8:00:56 AM
31	Chicken Feast	₦ 2,000.00	3	₦ 6,000.00	8:00:57 AM
32	Veggie Supreme	₦ 3,000.00	2	₦ 6,000.00	8:00:57 AM
33	Extravaganza	₦ 2,000.00	4	₦ 8,000.00	8:01:00 AM
34	Pepperoni Suya	₦ 3,000.00	4	₦ 12,000.00	8:01:01 AM
35	Veggie Supreme	₦ 3,000.00	2	₦ 6,000.00	8:01:02 AM
36	Extravaganza	₦ 2,000.00	2	₦ 4,000.00	8:01:08 AM
37	Italiano	₦ 3,000.00	2	₦ 6,000.00	8:01:14 AM
38	BBQ Philly Steak	₦ 4,000.00	2	₦ 8,000.00	8:01:16 AM
39	Pepperoni Feast	₦ 4,000.00	5	₦ 20,000.00	8:01:16 AM
40	Chicken Bali	₦ 2,000.00	4	₦ 8,000.00	8:01:17 AM
41	Pepperoni Suya	₦ 3,000.00	2	₦ 6,000.00	8:01:18 AM
42	BBQ Philly Steak	₦ 4,000.00	5	₦ 20,000.00	8:01:20 AM
43	Chicken Bali	₦ 2,000.00	3	₦ 6,000.00	8:01:21 AM
44	Italiano	₦ 3,000.00	5	₦ 15,000.00	8:01:22 AM
45	BBQ Philly Steak	₦ 4,000.00	4	₦ 16,000.00	8:01:26 AM
46	Hot Pepperoni Feast	₦ 4,000.00	5	₦ 20,000.00	8:01:28 AM

S/N	Pizza Sold	Price	Quantity	Amount Sold	Time
47	Chicken Legend	₦ 2,000.00	2	₦ 4,000.00	8:01:31 AM
48	Chicken Bali	₦ 2,000.00	2	₦ 4,000.00	8:01:32 AM
49	BBQ Philly Steak	₦ 4,000.00	1	₦ 4,000.00	8:01:34 AM
50	BBQ Chicken	₦ 4,000.00	4	₦ 16,000.00	8:01:34 AM
51	Pepperoni Feast	₦ 4,000.00	4	₦ 16,000.00	8:01:35 AM
52	BBQ Philly Steak	₦ 4,000.00	1	₦ 4,000.00	8:01:36 AM
53	BBQ Philly Steak	₦ 4,000.00	4	₦ 16,000.00	8:01:36 AM
54	Pepperoni Suya	₦ 3,000.00	2	₦ 6,000.00	8:01:37 AM
55	Veggie Supreme	₦ 3,000.00	5	₦ 15,000.00	8:01:37 AM
56	Chicken Suya	₦ 4,000.00	5	₦ 20,000.00	8:01:39 AM
57	Margarita	₦ 4,000.00	4	₦ 16,000.00	8:01:43 AM
58	Chicken Bali	₦ 2,000.00	5	₦ 10,000.00	8:01:44 AM
59	Meatzaa	₦ 2,000.00	5	₦ 10,000.00	8:01:44 AM
60	BBQ Philly Steak	₦ 4,000.00	3	₦ 12,000.00	8:01:46 AM
61	Pepperoni Suya	₦ 3,000.00	5	₦ 15,000.00	8:01:48 AM
62	Chicken Feast	₦ 2,000.00	5	₦ 10,000.00	8:01:49 AM
63	Chicken Feast	₦ 2,000.00	4	₦ 8,000.00	8:01:52 AM
64	Chicken Suya	₦ 4,000.00	2	₦ 8,000.00	8:01:54 AM
65	Chicken Legend	₦ 2,000.00	3	₦ 6,000.00	8:01:55 AM
66	Chicken Feast	₦ 2,000.00	4	₦ 8,000.00	8:01:56 AM
67	Chicken Bali	₦ 2,000.00	1	₦ 2,000.00	8:02:03 AM
68	Pepperoni Suya	₦ 3,000.00	1	₦ 3,000.00	8:02:03 AM
69	Pepperoni Feast	₦ 4,000.00	3	₦ 12,000.00	8:02:04 AM
70	Beef Suya	₦ 3,000.00	3	₦ 9,000.00	8:02:05 AM
71	BBQ Chicken	₦ 4,000.00	1	₦ 4,000.00	8:02:06 AM
72	Pepperoni Feast	₦ 4,000.00	3	₦ 12,000.00	8:02:10 AM
73	Pepperoni Feast	₦ 4,000.00	5	₦ 20,000.00	8:02:13 AM
74	BBQ Chicken	₦ 4,000.00	2	₦ 8,000.00	8:02:13 AM
75	Extravaganza	₦ 2,000.00	5	₦ 10,000.00	8:02:18 AM
76	Chicken Legend	₦ 2,000.00	1	₦ 2,000.00	8:02:18 AM
77	Pepperoni Suya	₦ 3,000.00	2	₦ 6,000.00	8:02:22 AM
78	Hot Veggie	₦ 4,000.00	2	₦ 8,000.00	8:02:22 AM
79	Extravaganza	₦ 2,000.00	3	₦ 6,000.00	8:02:30 AM
80	Chicken Suya	₦ 4,000.00	3	₦ 12,000.00	8:02:31 AM
81	Pepperoni Feast	₦ 4,000.00	5	₦ 20,000.00	8:02:35 AM
82	Pepperoni Feast	₦ 4,000.00	3	₦ 12,000.00	8:02:36 AM
83	BBQ Chicken	₦ 4,000.00	3	₦ 12,000.00	8:02:37 AM
84	BBQ Philly Steak	₦ 4,000.00	4	₦ 16,000.00	8:02:38 AM
85	Hot Veggie	₦ 4,000.00	5	₦ 20,000.00	8:02:38 AM
86	Chicken Bali	₦ 2,000.00	1	₦ 2,000.00	8:02:42 AM
87	Beef Suya	₦ 3,000.00	2	₦ 6,000.00	8:02:44 AM
88	BBQ Philly Steak	₦ 4,000.00	2	₦ 8,000.00	8:02:46 AM
89	Veggie Supreme	₦ 3,000.00	4	₦ 12,000.00	8:02:47 AM
90	Chicken Suya	₦ 4,000.00	1	₦ 4,000.00	8:02:47 AM
91	BBQ Chicken	₦ 4,000.00	5	₦ 20,000.00	8:02:49 AM
92	BBQ Philly Steak	₦ 4,000.00	4	₦ 16,000.00	8:02:50 AM

Done.

So these are the basic ways you format your data for printing.

Custom Lists

If you are an average or above average Excel user, you will be very familiar with Excel autofill. A common example is you typing numbers 1 and 2, then dragging to have Excel do to 10 for you. Or having January and February, then dragging to have Excel do the other months of the year for you.

What if I tell you that you can create your own list. A list of states in Nigeria which you can autofill whenever you need to recreate them. Or a list of your products; you simply type the first two and drag to create the rest (autofill). It even helps you with sorting in the order you've created the list. This can be super useful for companies that use codes for aspects of their operations -- base station address code, branch code, product code and so on. Caution: The custom list has a quite limiting size limit.

So here is the example of how I created a custom list of states in Nigeria, arranged alphabetical order.

First, I have the states typed out in Excel, in the order I want it (alphabetical order).

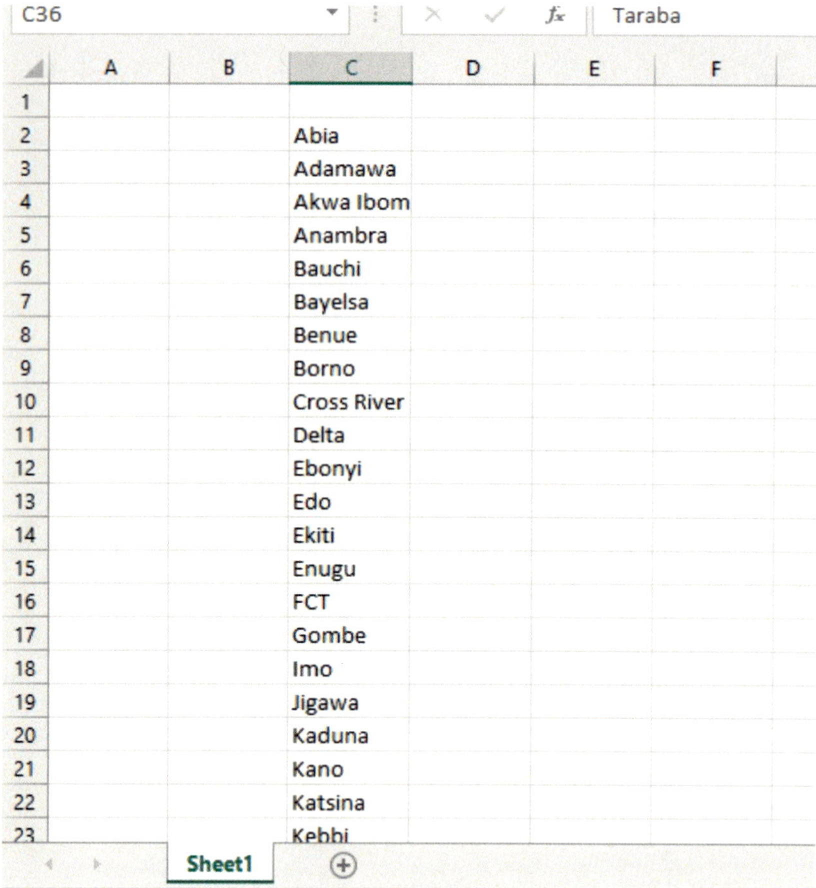

And we are half-way done to having it permanently in Excel as an autofill-able list.

Go to File, Options, Advanced, and Edit Custom Lists.

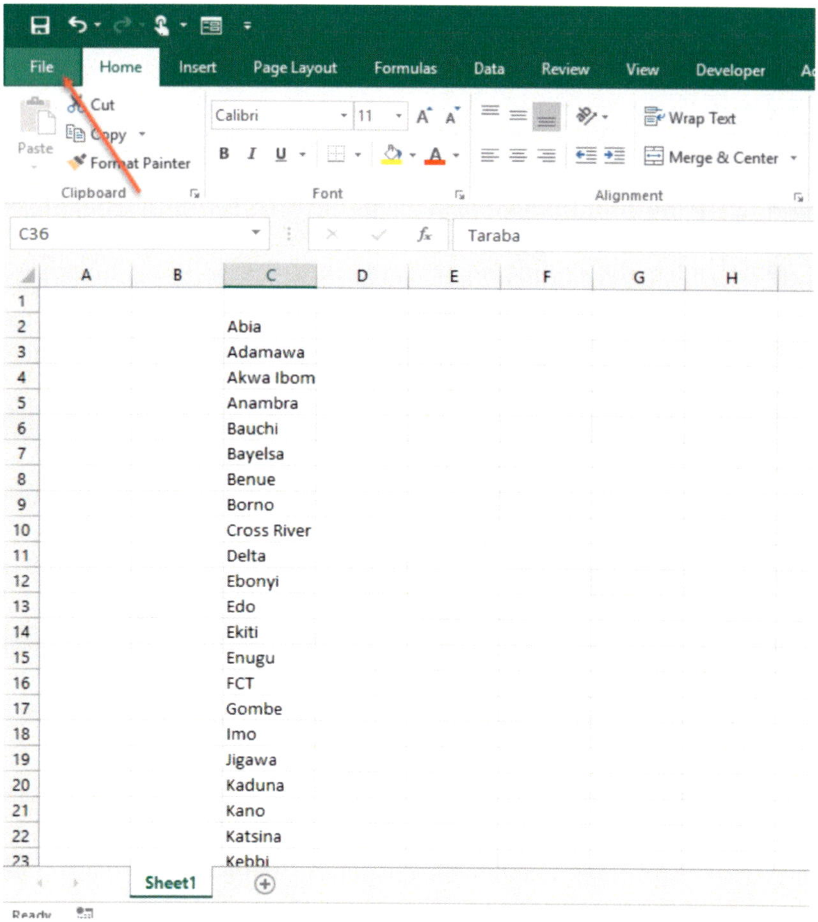
File
Home
Insert
Page Layout
Formulas
Data
Review
View
Developer
Cut
Copy
Paste
Format Painter
Clipboard
Calibri
11
Font
Wrap Text
Merge & Center
Alignment
C36
Taraba
Abia
Adamawa
Akwa Ibom
Anambra
Bauchi
Bayelsa
Benue
Borno
Cross River
Delta
Ebonyi
Edo
Ekiti
Enugu
FCT
Gombe
Imo
Jigawa
Kaduna
Kano
Katsina
Kebbi
Sheet1

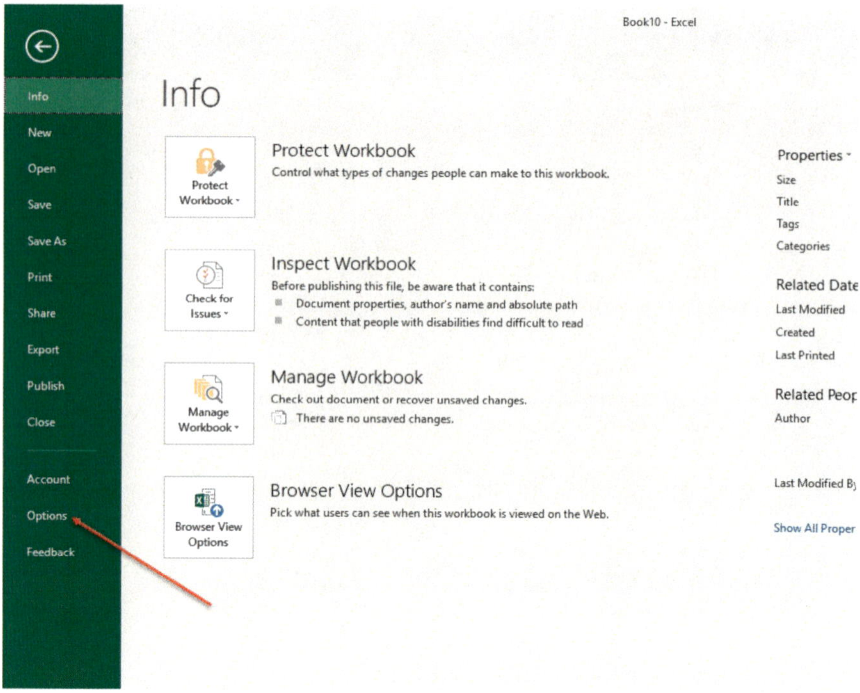
Book10 - Excel
Info
New
Open
Save
Save As
Print
Share
Export
Publish
Close
Account
Options
Feedback
Info
Protect Workbook
Protect Workbook
Control what types of changes people can make to this workbook.
Check for Issues
Inspect Workbook
Before publishing this file, be aware that it contains:
Document properties, author's name and absolute path
Content that people with disabilities find difficult to read
Manage Workbook
Manage Workbook
Check out document or recover unsaved changes.
There are no unsaved changes.
Browser View Options
Browser View Options
Pick what users can see when this workbook is viewed on the Web.
Properties
Size
Title
Tags
Categories
Related Date
Last Modified
Created
Last Printed
Related Peop
Author
Last Modified B
Show All Proper

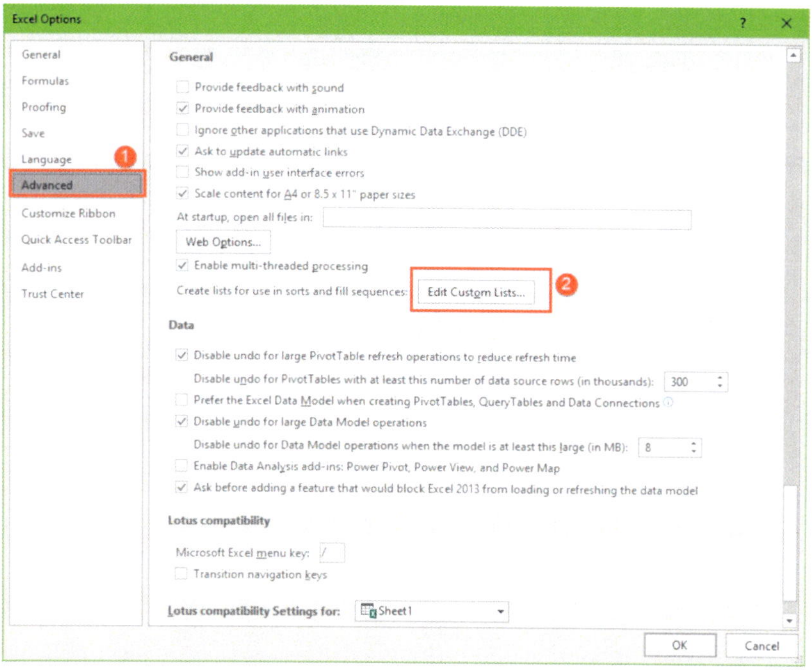

In the Custom List Dialog box that comes up, import the list of states you already have typed into Excel.

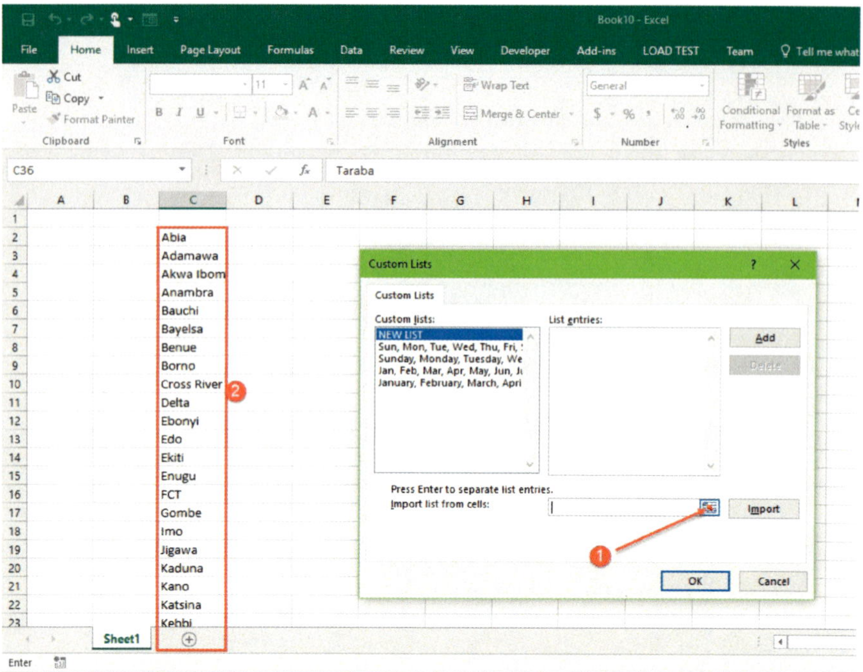
Book10 - Excel
File
Home
Insert
Page Layout
Formulas
Data
Review
View
Developer
Add-ins
LOAD TEST
Team
Tell me what
Cut
Copy
Format Painter
Paste
Clipboard
Font
Wrap Text
Merge & Center
Alignment
General
Number
Conditional Formatting
Format as Table
Styles
C36
Taraba
Abia
Adamawa
Akwa Ibom
Anambra
Bauchi
Bayelsa
Benue
Borno
Cross River
Delta
Ebonyi
Edo
Ekiti
Enugu
FCT
Gombe
Imo
Jigawa
Kaduna
Kano
Katsina
Kebbi
2
Custom Lists
Custom lists:
NEW LIST
Sun, Mon, Tue, Wed, Thu, Fri,
Sunday, Monday, Tuesday, We
Jan, Feb, Mar, Apr, May, Jun, Ju
January, February, March, Apri
List entries:
Add
Delete
Press Enter to separate list entries.
Import list from cells:
Import
1
OK
Cancel
Sheet1
Enter

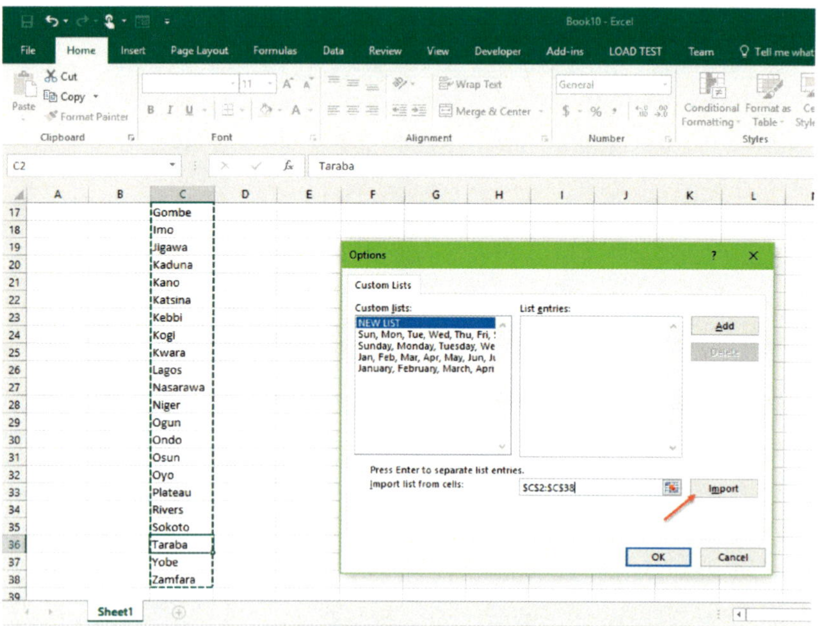
Book10 - Excel
File
Home
Insert
Page Layout
Formulas
Data
Review
View
Developer
Add-ins
LOAD TEST
Team
Tell me what
C2
Taraba
Gombe
Imo
Jigawa
Kaduna
Kano
Katsina
Kebbi
Kogi
Kwara
Lagos
Nasarawa
Niger
Ogun
Ondo
Osun
Oyo
Plateau
Rivers
Sokoto
Taraba
Yobe
Zamfara
Options
Custom Lists
Custom lists:
NEW LIST
Sun, Mon, Tue, Wed, Thu, Fri,
Sunday, Monday, Tuesday, We
Jan, Feb, Mar, Apr, May, Jun, Ju
January, February, March, Apri
List entries:
Add
Delete
Press Enter to separate list entries.
Import list from cells:
$C$2:$C$38
Import
OK
Cancel
Sheet1

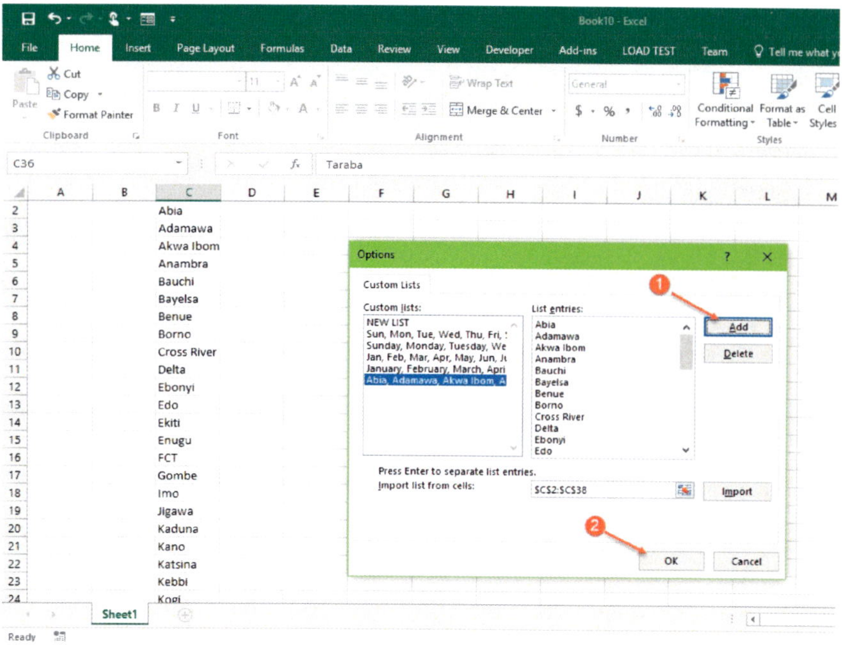

And you are done.

Now in a new Excel file or Sheet, type in the first two states, select them and drag down. Excel will start autofilling the other states.

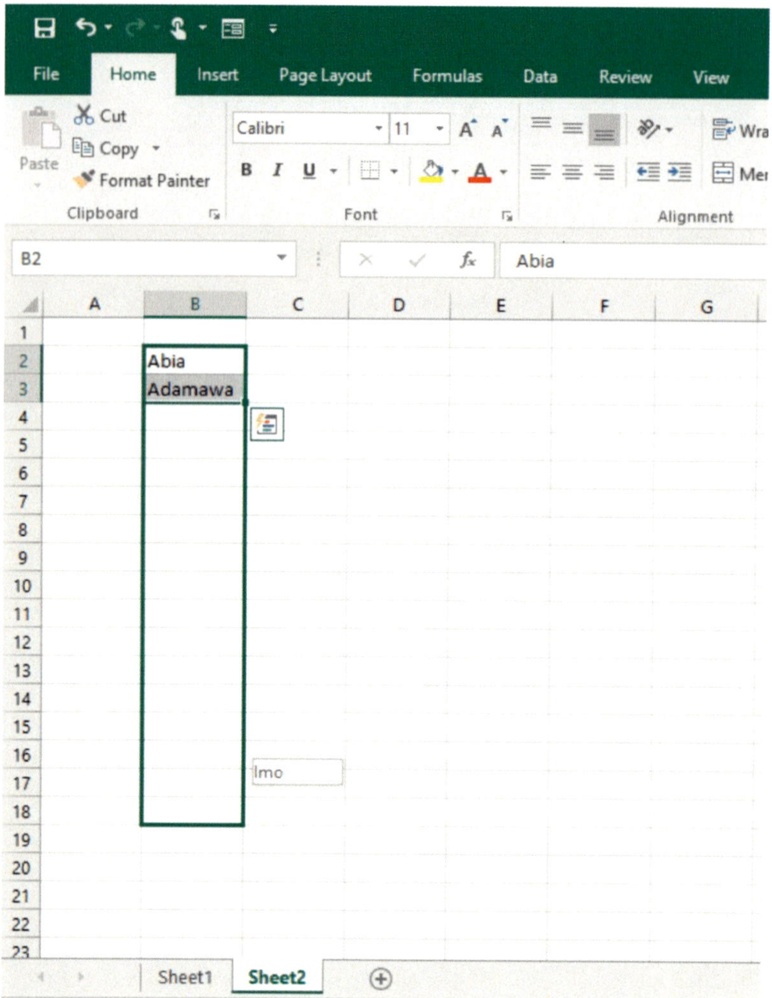
File
Home
Insert
Page Layout
Formulas
Data
Review
View
Paste
Cut
Copy
Format Painter
Clipboard
Calibri
11
Font
Alignment
B2
Abia
A
B
C
D
E
F
G
Abia
Adamawa
Imo
Sheet1
Sheet2

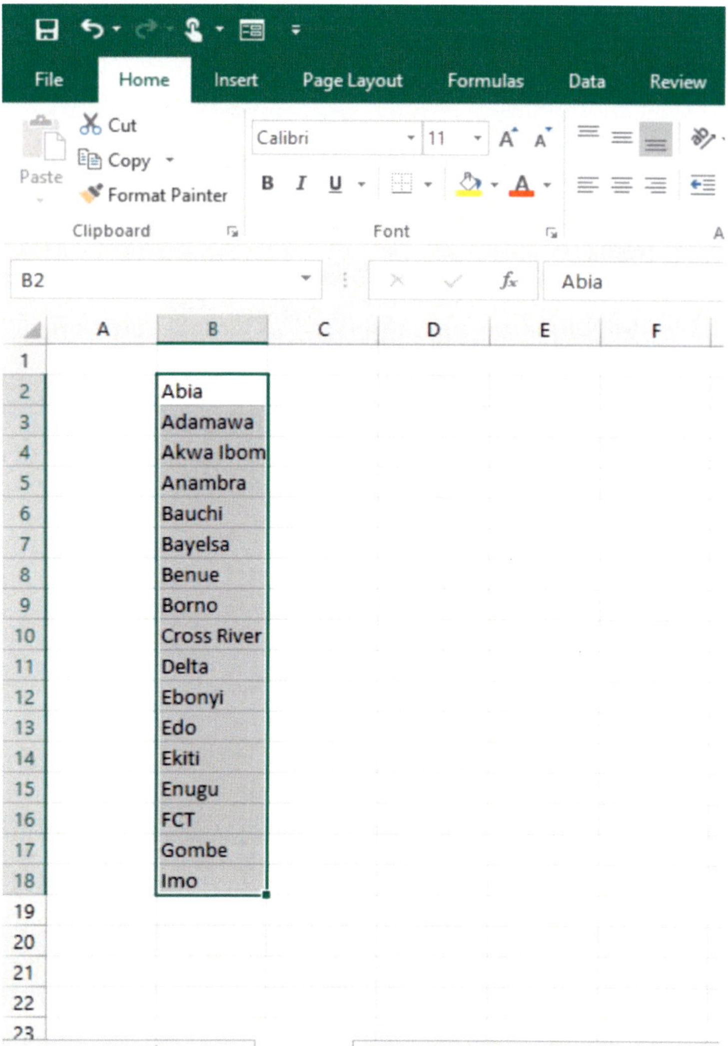

Congrats! Now you've created a custom list. No more typing out states in Nigeria, just type the first (or first two) and have Excel autofill the rest for you.

Charts

Excel 2010 has 11 main chart types.

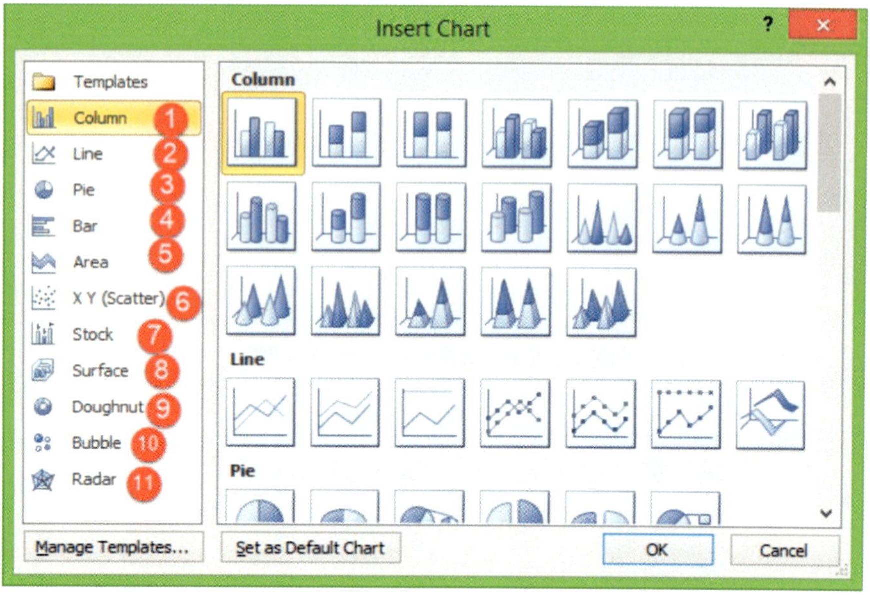

Excel 2013 and Excel 2016 have 10 main chart types. Actually, 9 If you take combo chart as a combination of two or more other chart types.

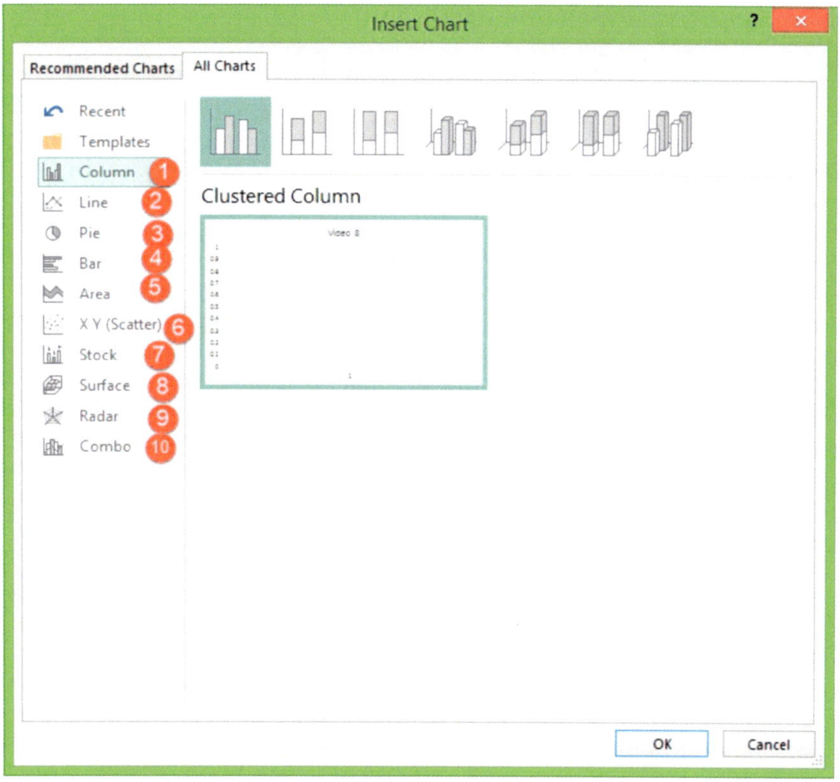

But in all you will end up using majorly,

1. Column chart
2. Line chart
3. Pie chart, and
4. Bar chart.

So let's focus on these four charts.

Column Chart and when to use it.

Column chart is used to visualize data across different categories. An example is revenue across the four different branches of a company.

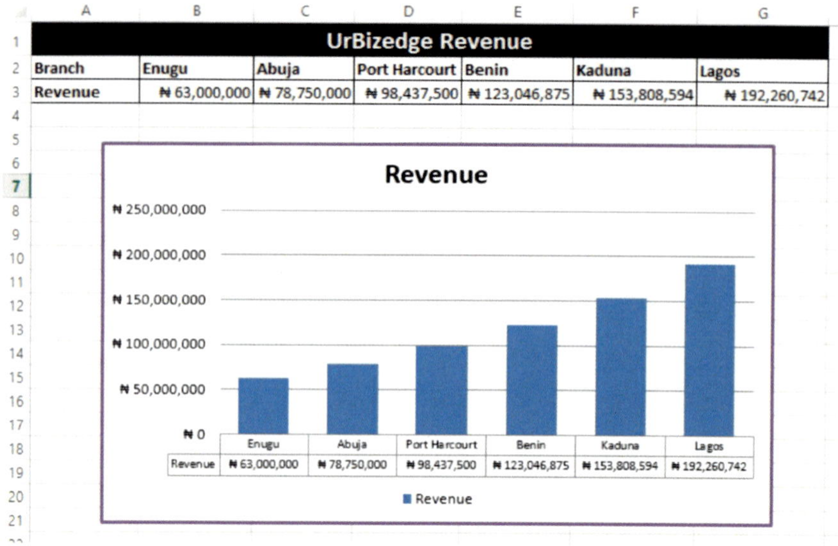

So how do you turn a boring data like this:

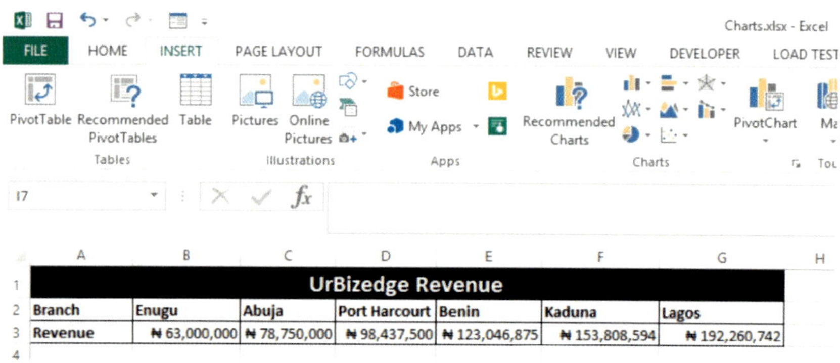

Into a beautiful insightful chart like this:

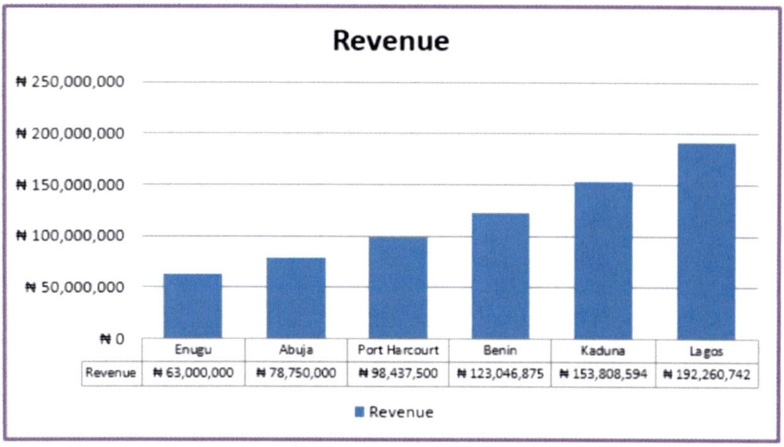

It is very easy.

Select the table data you want to make a chart of and go to the Insert menu, click on the Column chart and select the 2D Clustered Column chart (the first option).

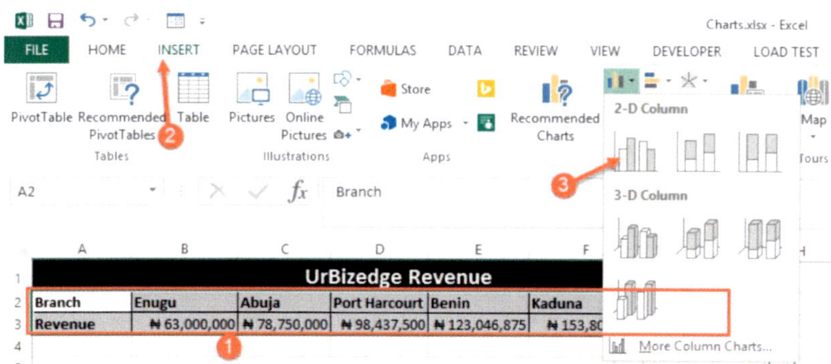

You will get a chart that looks like the one below. Not bad looking, just needs a little formatting to make great.

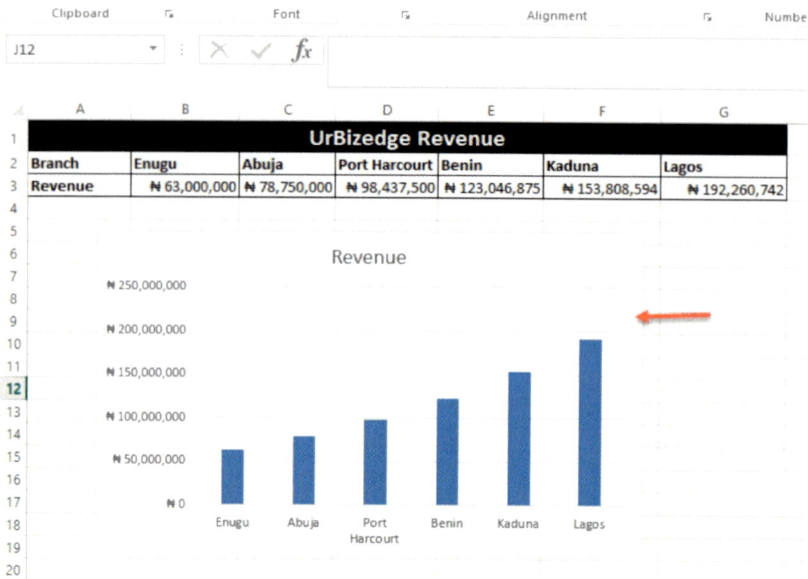

Click on the chart, and the context based menus will show up on the Excel menu bar.

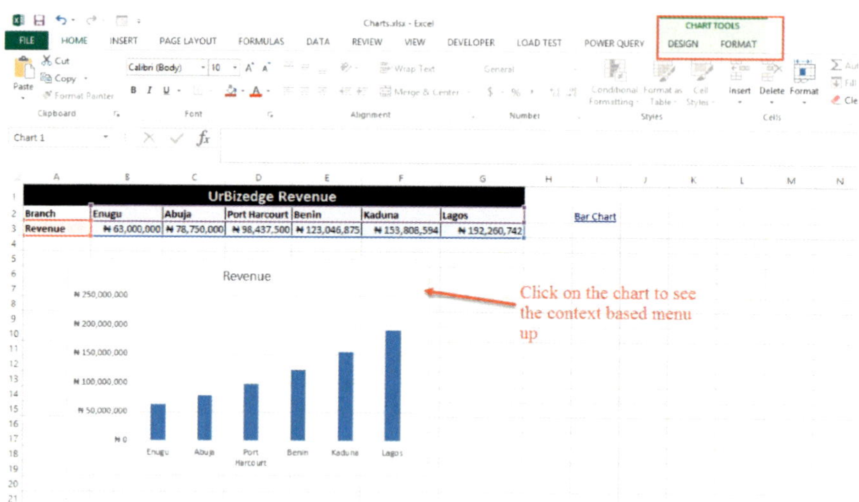

Go to the Format menu and choose a formatting you like for the entire chart. If your company's corporate color is red and purple, you might want to make charts that reflect that brand color.

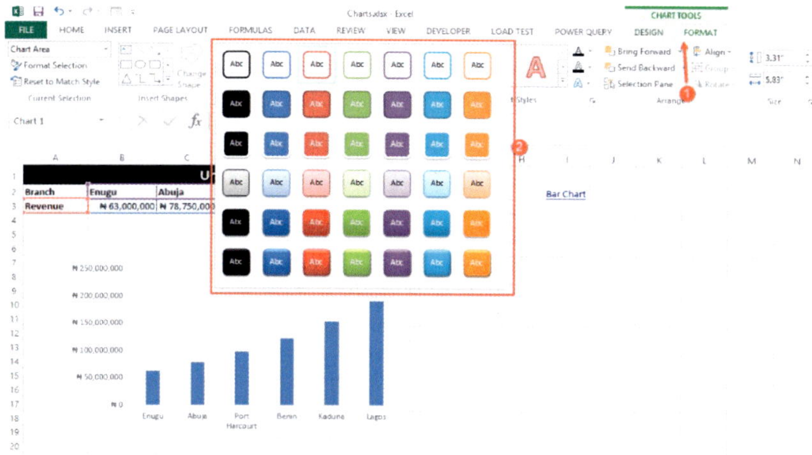

See the result red border white fill format.

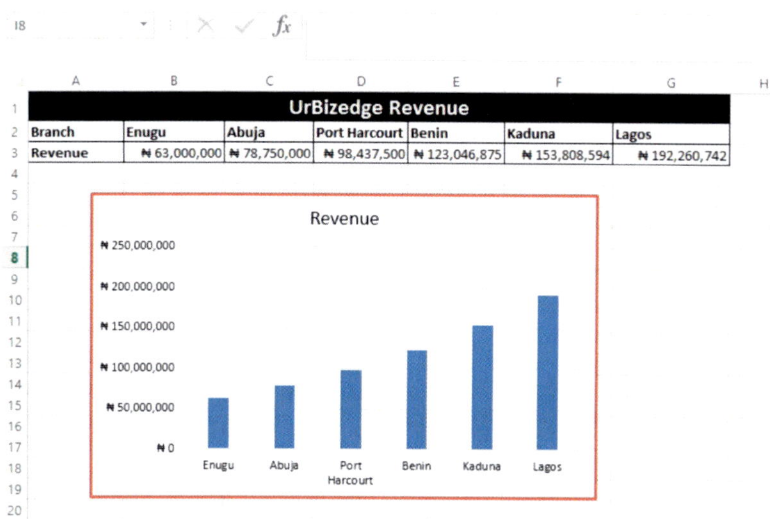

You can also change the chart background color.

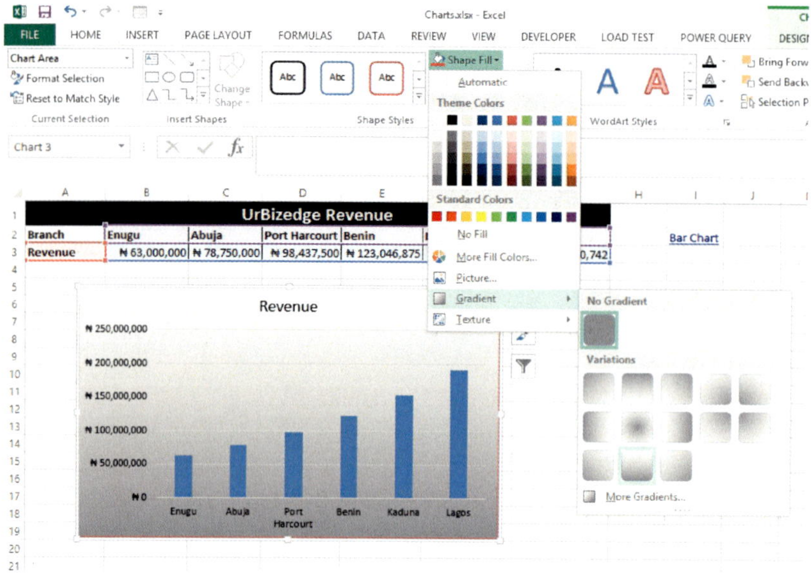

Also you can change the color of the bars by clicking on them and choosing the color you want.

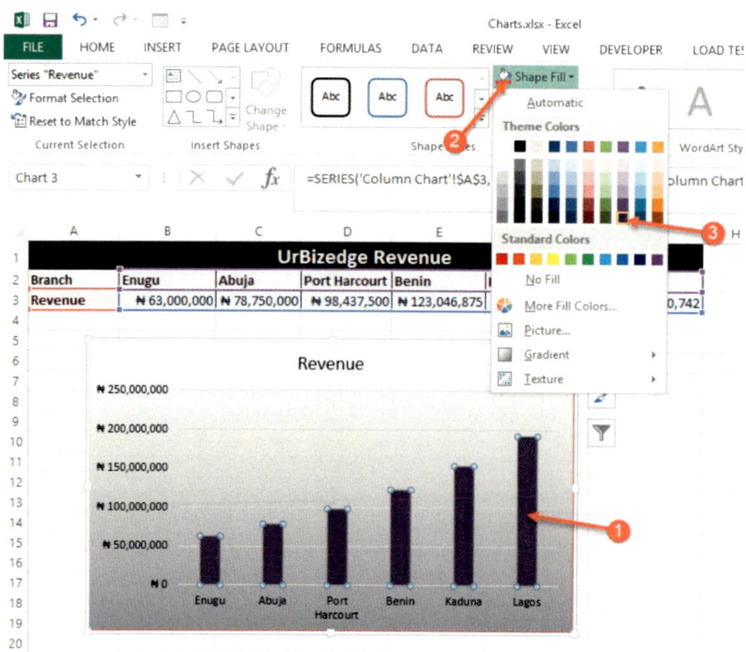

And this is the final result.

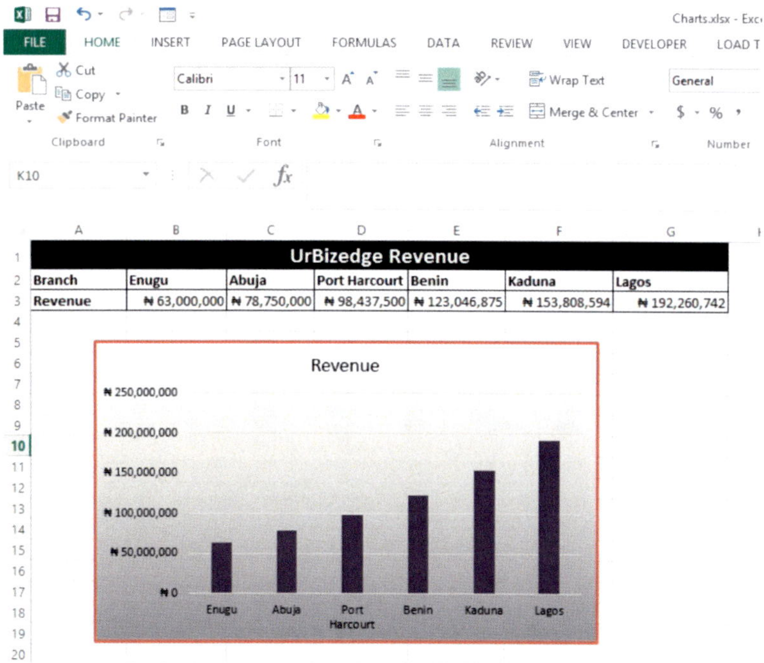

It looks better than the default and reflects your company's corporate color. Just that you might want to not use the red border. Most professionals argue that it's best to not use any border or background, just make only the important things obvious - data bar and the axis label. I suggest you do whatever looks great to you. This is not an exam and most likely what will look good to you will look good to your colleagues whom you'll share the report and charts with.

If you try out other color schemes you can end up with charts looking like the one below.

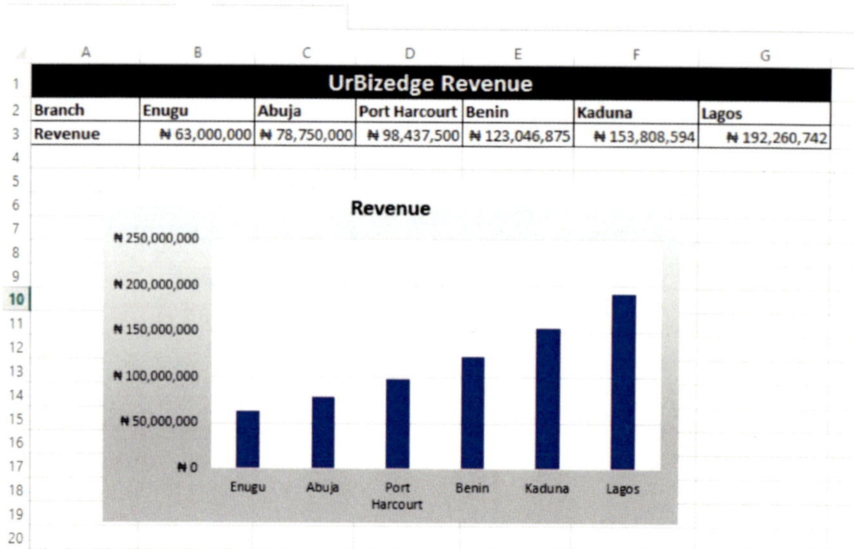

The extra step we took besides removing the red border and changing the bar color to bright blue is to change the chart area background to white.

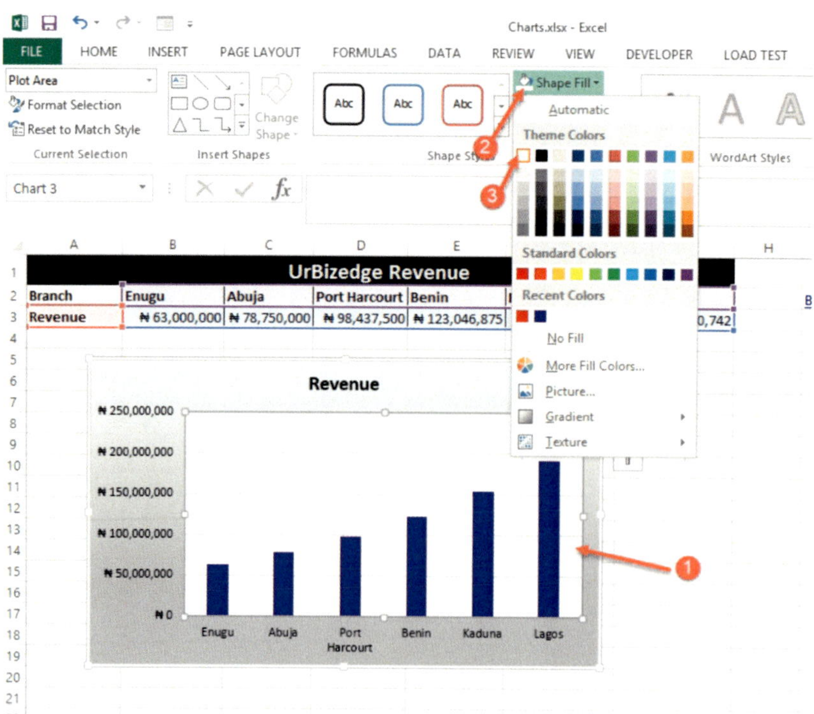

And that's basically how you insert and format a column chart. You can try inserting a 3D chart too for the same data. Follow the same steps but choose a 3D chart instead of the 2D we earlier used. And when you do the extra formatting already explained to you, you can end up with a beautiful chart like the one below.

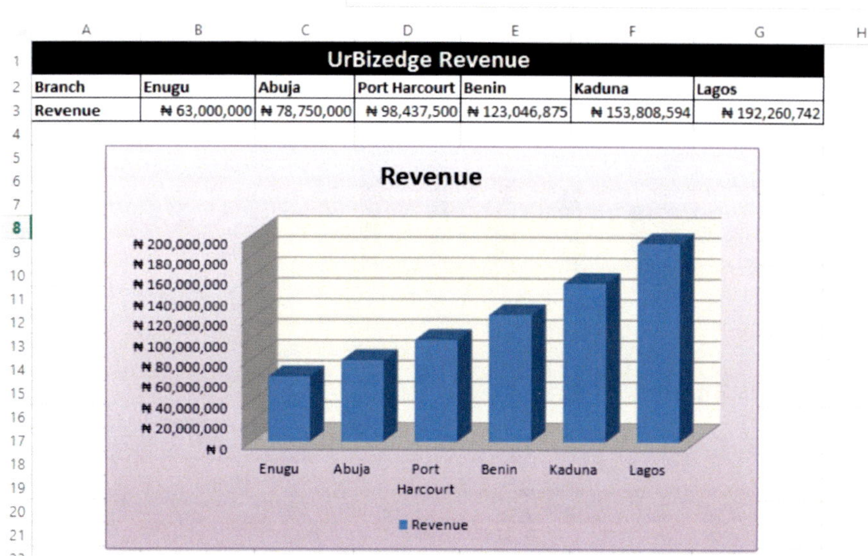

Finally, you can insert other elements on the chart like the data table, as shown below.

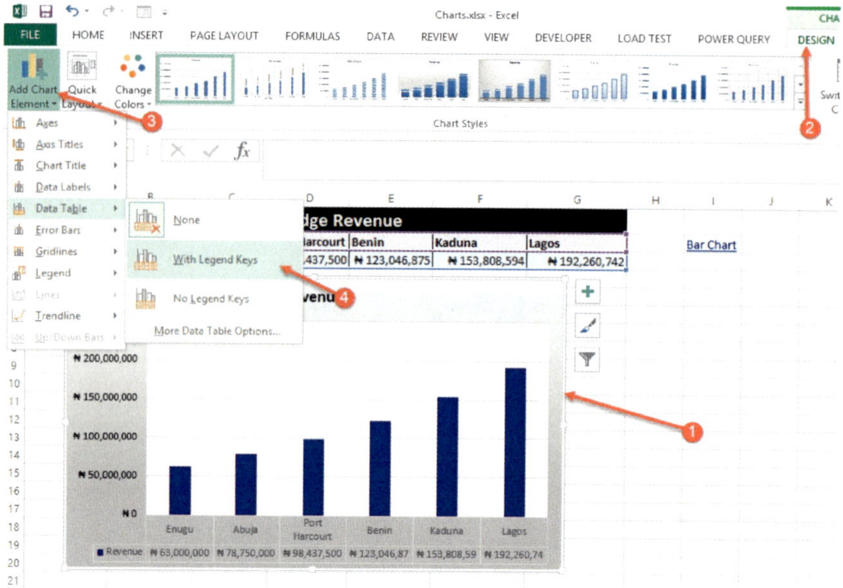

The result is shown below.

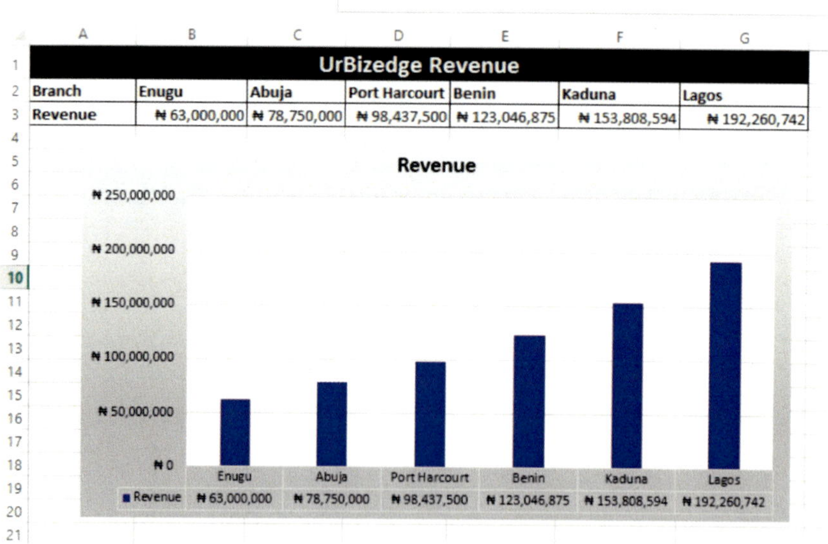

You would have noticed that there are other column chart types besides the Clustered one we selected (the first option).

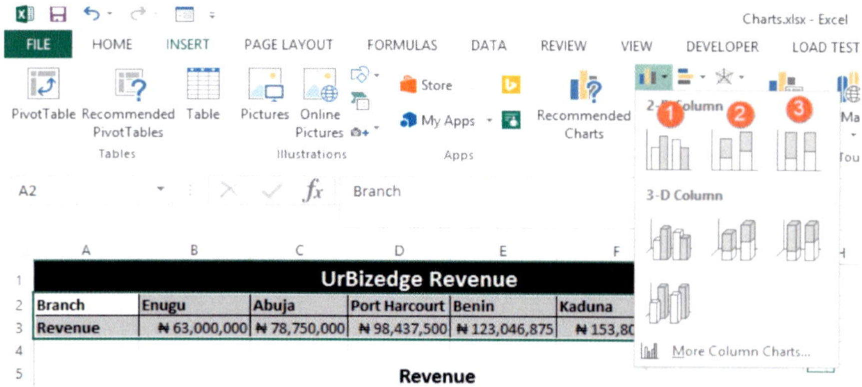

As numbered in the image above, they are

1. Clustered Column
2. Stacked Column
3. 100% Stacked Column

The clustered column is what we have used so far. It's straightforward to understand. The stacked column is useful for showing the breakdown of the data that makes up the bar. Below is an example of its use. We are going to breakdown the revenue by the products that contributed to it.

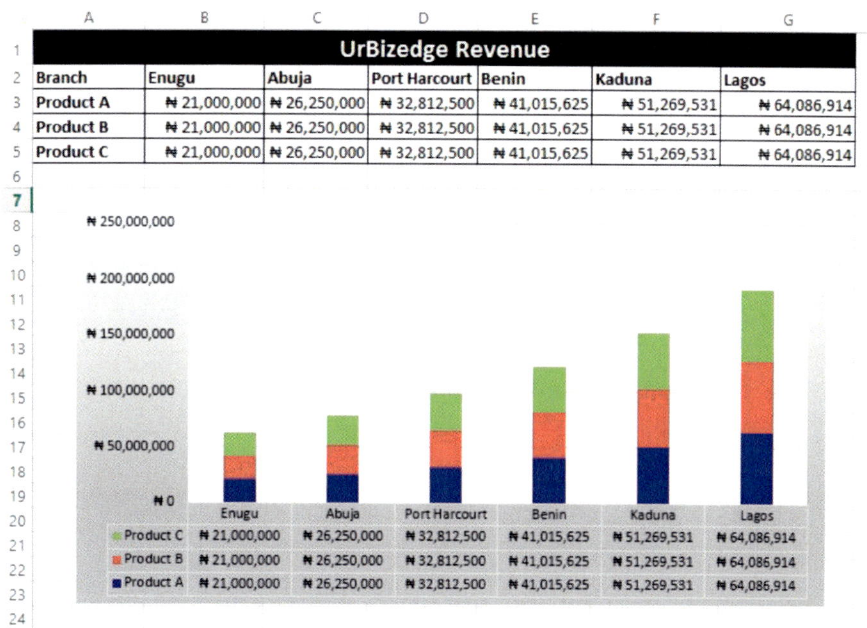

To do this stacked column chart, you simply select the entire table data, including the breakdown by products and choose the Stacked Column chart. And as you can see, it shows a breakdown of each bar by the constituting parts (products in this example)

The third one, 100% stacked column, is just slightly different. Rather than show you the breakdown by product revenue values, it shows the breakdown by the percentage contribution each product makes to the total. Below is the 100% Stacked Column output for the same data.

UrBizedge Revenue						
Branch	Enugu	Abuja	Port Harcourt	Benin	Kaduna	Lagos
Product A	₦ 21,000,000	₦ 26,250,000	₦ 32,812,500	₦ 41,015,625	₦ 51,269,531	₦ 64,086,914
Product B	₦ 21,000,000	₦ 26,250,000	₦ 32,812,500	₦ 41,015,625	₦ 51,269,531	₦ 64,086,914
Product C	₦ 21,000,000	₦ 26,250,000	₦ 32,812,500	₦ 41,015,625	₦ 51,269,531	₦ 64,086,914

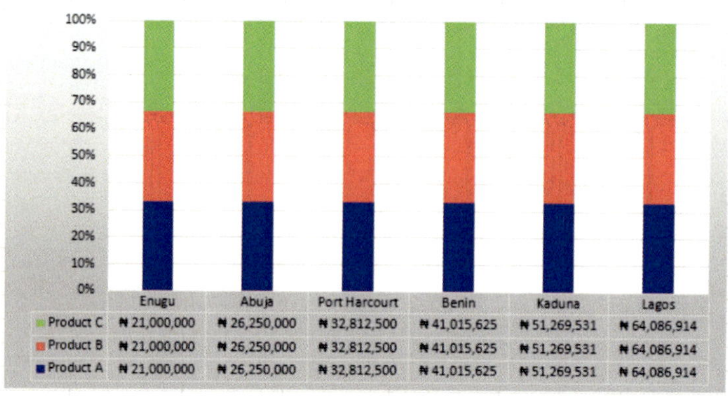

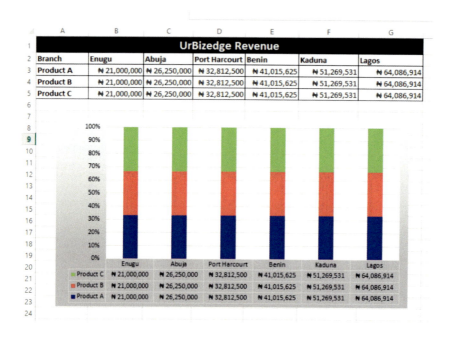

Line Chart and when to use it.

Line chart is used to show trend, usually over a time period. An example is if you want to show the trend of how the company's revenue has been growing for the last five years.

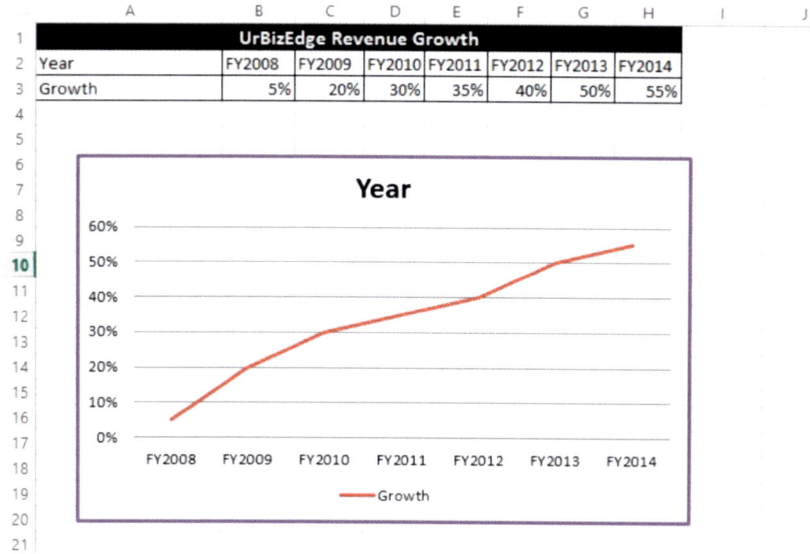

You create a line chart of a table in a similar way as we did for the column chart. You select the table's data and go to insert menu, click on the Line chart type you prefer.

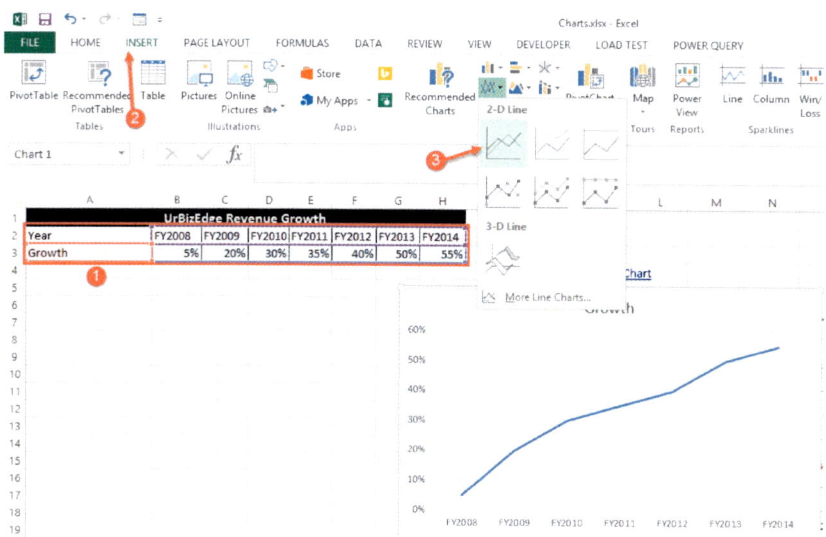

Again, Excel does a fairly good job and you can easily improve the format of the chart using the steps already explained.

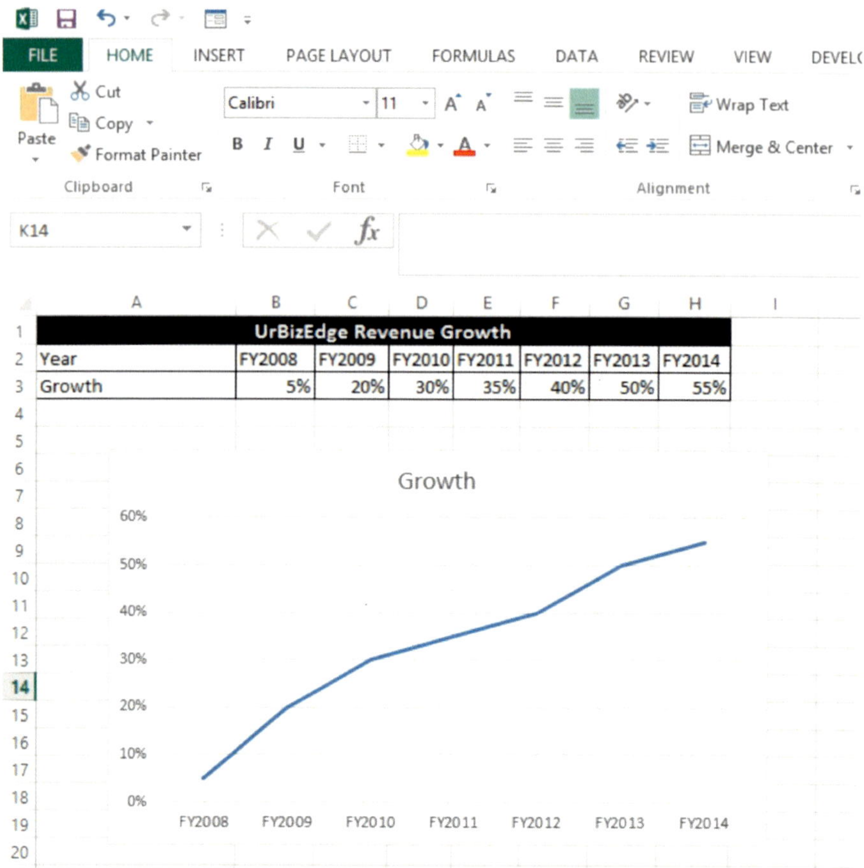

Pie Chart and when to use it.

Pie chart is used to show the contribution of each category to the pie that represents the grand total.

Below is an example showing the breakdown of Nigerian population by region. You can see how the Pie Chart makes it easy to see the contribution of each region to the total population of Nigeria.

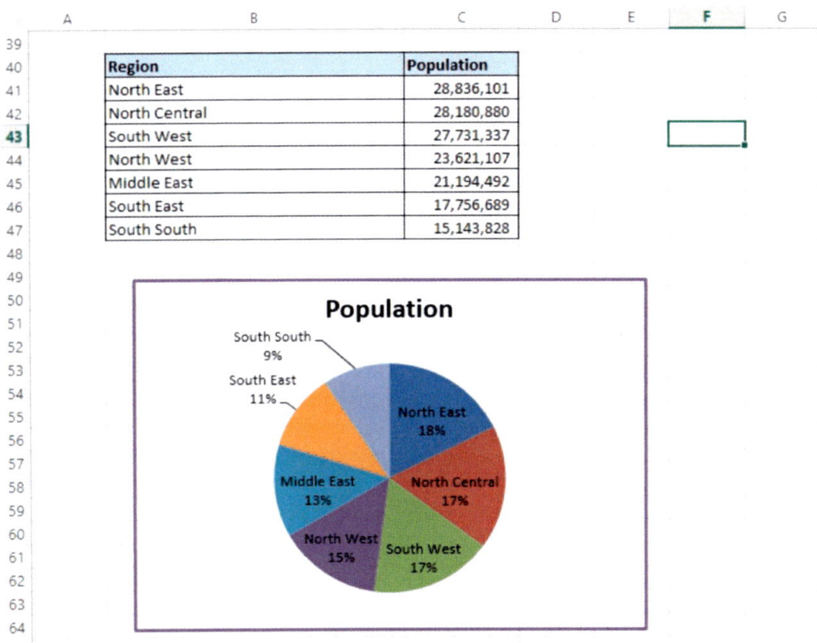

Region	Population
North East	28,836,101
North Central	28,180,880
South West	27,731,337
North West	23,621,107
Middle East	21,194,492
South East	17,756,689
South South	15,143,828

It is extremely easy to make. You, like for others, select the table's data and select Pie Chart under the Insert menu.

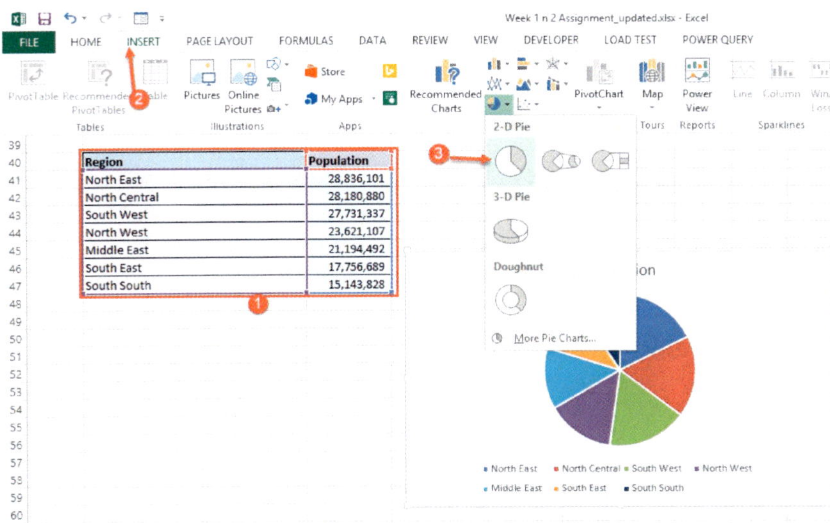

Region	Population
North East	28,836,101
North Central	28,180,880
South West	27,731,337
North West	23,621,107
Middle East	21,194,492
South East	17,756,689
South South	15,143,828

Excel does a default pie chart that you can greatly improve.

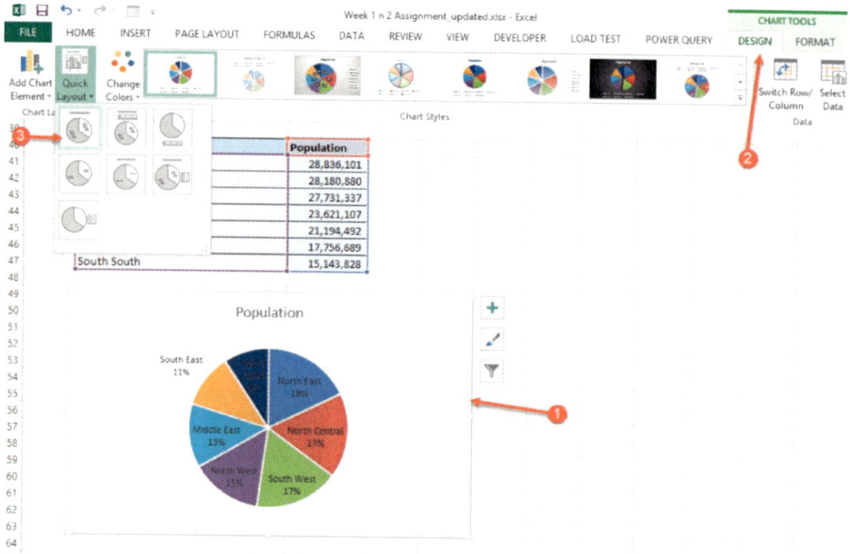

Bar Chart and when to use it.

Bar chart is technically the same as Column chart. The difference is that when you have a table with lots of entries, usually over 8, you are better off with using a bar chart rather than the column chart. Also when the entries have long label names, it's better to use bar chart even if the entries aren't many.

Below is an example.

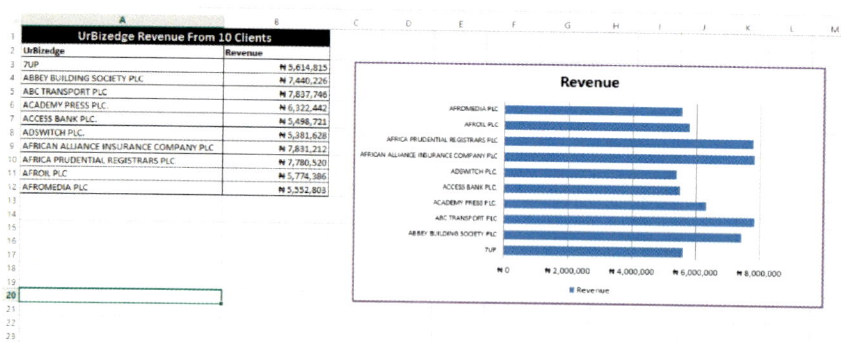

The same rules about Stacked and 100% stacked apply to bar chart and, even, line charts.

Combo Chart

Occasionally, you will have to combine two or more chart types in one visualization/graph. This is very useful if you want to show two interconnected data and their combined relevance.

An example is showing how a company's revenue has been changing in values and as a growth ratio.

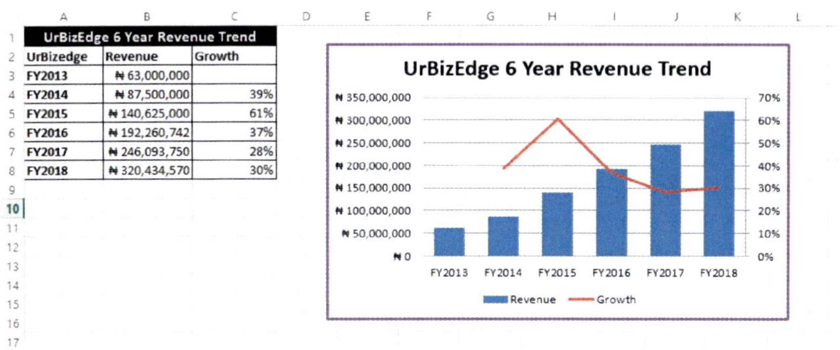

In Excel 2013 and Excel 2016, it is very easy to make.

Just select the entire table and insert a combo chart. It can be easily located under Recommended Charts.

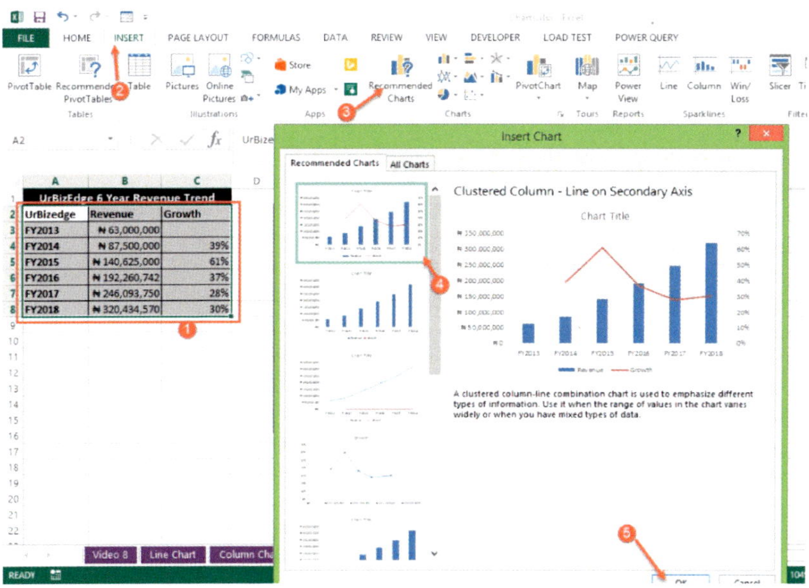

New Excel 2016 Charts

If you've felt limited by the charts in Excel or would like to do some of those amazing charts you see online, then you've got to try out the new charts in Excel 2016. And if you are in finance and always had to use a complicated way to create waterfall charts, well, those hard days are now over. Same also for our statistically inclined folks -- you can now create your histogram and Box & Whisker charts easily in Excel.

I will be showing you what those charts look like in Excel. And if you are impressed enough to want try them, all you need is Excel 2016. Better if you have the O365 subscription pack one, I think those ones get pushed new updates first.

1. Treemap.

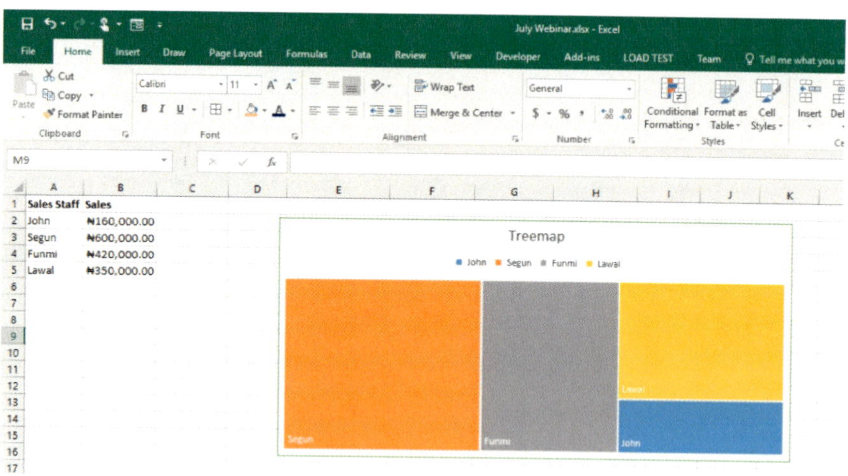

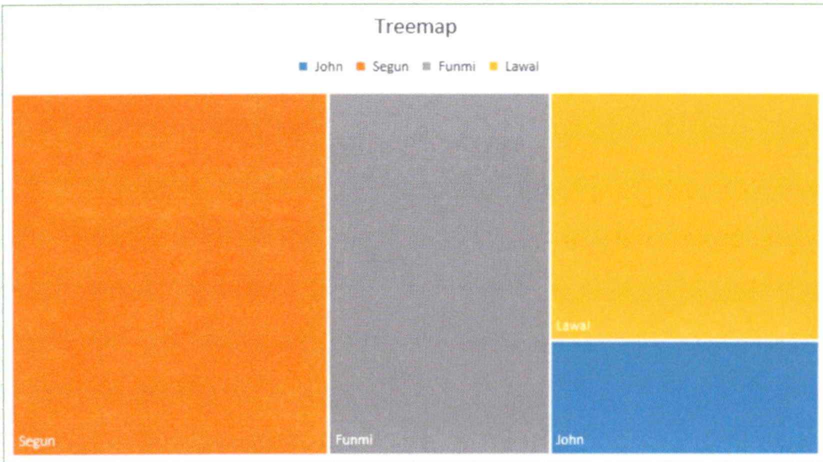

This lets you use rectangular bars of varying height and width to visualize performance or values of different entities.

2. Sunburst

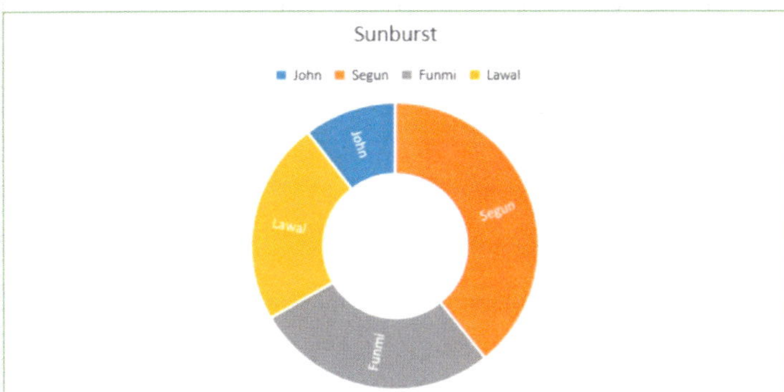

It's a lot like Pie chart and Doughnut chart, main difference is that it automatically sorts the data to be visually represented in descending order clockwise and shows multi-level (hierarchy).

3. Histogram

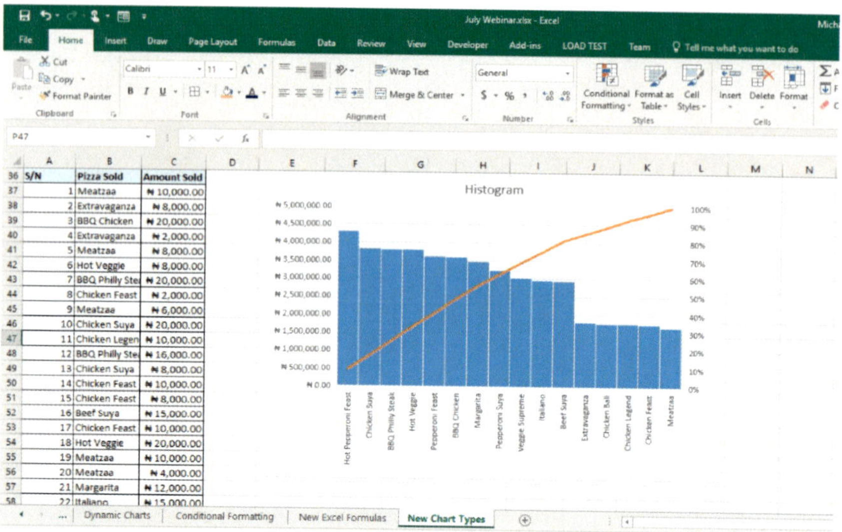

It is for showing frequency distribution. Those of us with some statistical background will be at home with it.

4. Box & Whisker

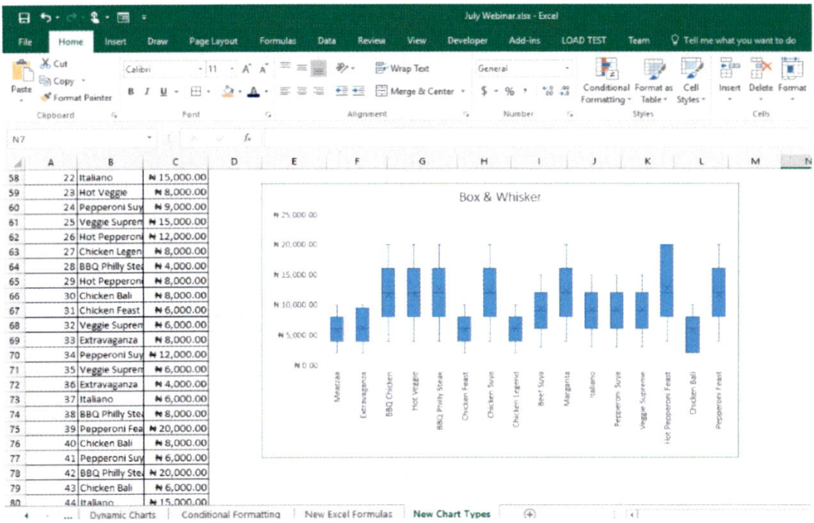

This is also a statistician's tool. It is for showing the spread of values for the different quartiles in the data.

5. Waterfall.

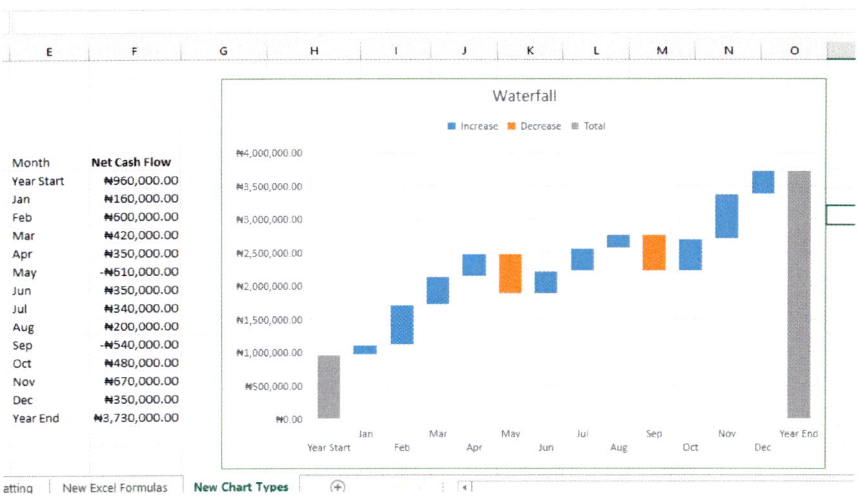

This is an accountant's staple. It shows incremental effect of connected data points.

6. Funnel

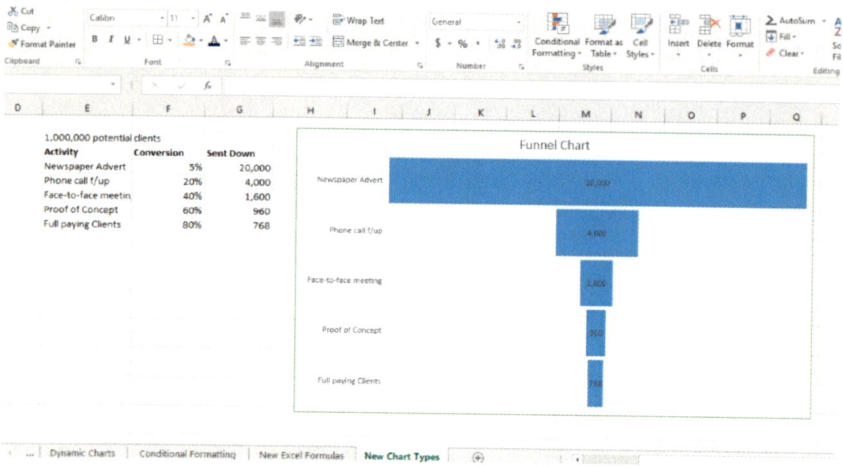

If you are into sales you will be familiar with funnels. How many leads you need to get a sale? Conversion rates? With a funnel chart you can visually depict each level of your sales activities and their conversion rates.

And those are the new chart types in Excel.

You can access them natively from the chart menu.

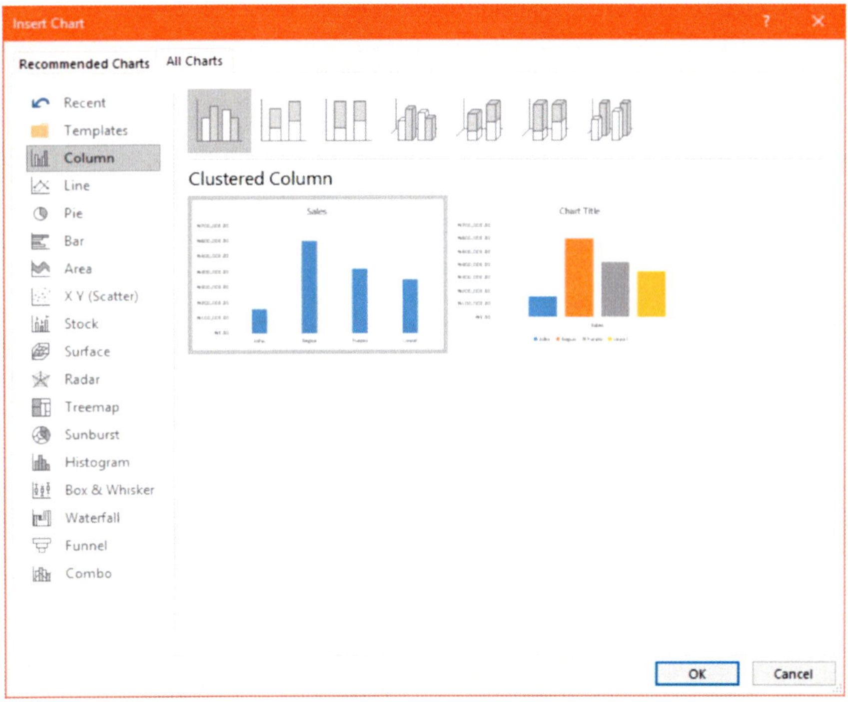
Insert Chart
Recommended Charts
All Charts
Recent
Templates
Column
Line
Pie
Bar
Area
X Y (Scatter)
Stock
Surface
Radar
Treemap
Sunburst
Histogram
Box & Whisker
Waterfall
Funnel
Combo
Clustered Column
Sales
Chart Title
OK
Cancel

PivotTable and PivotChart

PivotTable is Excel's premium tool for working with huge data table and even data stored in other database systems like Access, SQL servers and MySQL servers.

Below is an example of a large data table we will use PivotTable on to do some very relevant quick analysis. It is a table of sales for a particular Pizza Restaurant for a day and it has 5000 entries.

	A	B	C	D	E	F	G
1	S/N	Pizza Sold	Price	Quantity	Amount Sold	Time	Time Range
2	1	Meatzaa	₦ 2,000.00	5	₦ 10,000.00	8:00:01 AM	Before 9:00am
3	2	Extravaganza	₦ 2,000.00	4	₦ 8,000.00	8:00:02 AM	Before 9:00am
4	3	BBQ Chicken	₦ 4,000.00	5	₦ 20,000.00	8:00:04 AM	Before 9:00am
5	4	Extravaganza	₦ 2,000.00	1	₦ 2,000.00	8:00:07 AM	Before 9:00am
6	5	Meatzaa	₦ 2,000.00	4	₦ 8,000.00	8:00:08 AM	Before 9:00am
7	6	Hot Veggie	₦ 4,000.00	2	₦ 8,000.00	8:00:14 AM	Before 9:00am
8	7	BBQ Philly Steak	₦ 4,000.00	5	₦ 20,000.00	8:00:20 AM	Before 9:00am
9	8	Chicken Feast	₦ 2,000.00	1	₦ 2,000.00	8:00:20 AM	Before 9:00am
10	9	Meatzaa	₦ 2,000.00	3	₦ 6,000.00	8:00:22 AM	Before 9:00am
11	10	Chicken Suya	₦ 4,000.00	5	₦ 20,000.00	8:00:25 AM	Before 9:00am
12	11	Chicken Legend	₦ 2,000.00	5	₦ 10,000.00	8:00:26 AM	Before 9:00am
13	12	BBQ Philly Steak	₦ 4,000.00	4	₦ 16,000.00	8:00:27 AM	Before 9:00am
14	13	Chicken Suya	₦ 4,000.00	2	₦ 8,000.00	8:00:29 AM	Before 9:00am
15	14	Chicken Feast	₦ 2,000.00	5	₦ 10,000.00	8:00:33 AM	Before 9:00am
16	15	Chicken Feast	₦ 2,000.00	4	₦ 8,000.00	8:00:33 AM	Before 9:00am
17	16	Beef Suya	₦ 3,000.00	5	₦ 15,000.00	8:00:34 AM	Before 9:00am
18	17	Chicken Feast	₦ 2,000.00	5	₦ 10,000.00	8:00:35 AM	Before 9:00am
19	18	Hot Veggie	₦ 4,000.00	5	₦ 20,000.00	8:00:35 AM	Before 9:00am
20	19	Meatzaa	₦ 2,000.00	5	₦ 10,000.00	8:00:35 AM	Before 9:00am
21	20	Meatzaa	₦ 2,000.00	2	₦ 4,000.00	8:00:36 AM	Before 9:00am
22	21	Margarita	₦ 4,000.00	3	₦ 12,000.00	8:00:37 AM	Before 9:00am

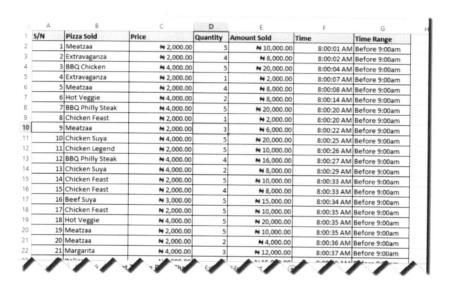

So how can we make a report that will show us the sales performance that day by the different type of Pizzas the restaurant sells. A report like the one below:

J	K	L
Pizza Type	**Sum of Quantity**	**Total Sales Amount**
BBQ Chicken	900	₦ 3,600,000.00
BBQ Philly Steak	952	₦ 3,808,000.00
Beef Suya	981	₦ 2,943,000.00
Chicken Bali	889	₦ 1,778,000.00
Chicken Feast	872	₦ 1,744,000.00
Chicken Legend	883	₦ 1,766,000.00
Chicken Suya	956	₦ 3,824,000.00
Extravaganza	907	₦ 1,814,000.00
Hot Pepperoni Feast	1,073	₦ 4,292,000.00
Hot Veggie	950	₦ 3,800,000.00
Italiano	985	₦ 2,955,000.00
Margarita	871	₦ 3,484,000.00
Meatzaa	838	₦ 1,676,000.00
Pepperoni Feast	907	₦ 3,628,000.00
Pepperoni Suya	1,077	₦ 3,231,000.00
Veggie Supreme	1,009	₦ 3,027,000.00
Grand Total	**15,050**	**₦ 47,370,000.00**

It's quite easy with Pivot Table.

You start by selecting the sales transaction table or selecting one of the cells in it. Then go to Insert menu and click on Pivot Table.

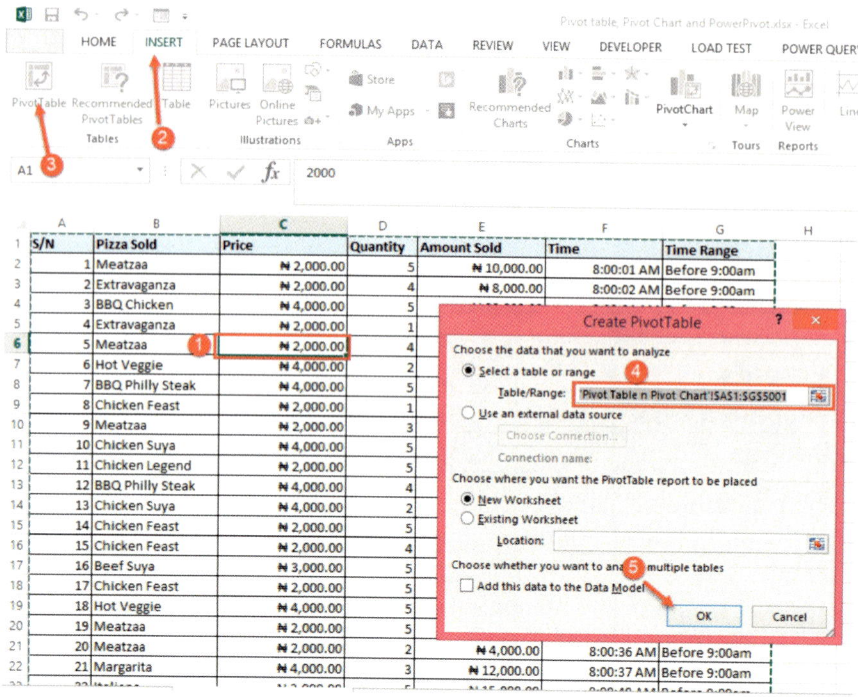

In the screenshot above, I selected one of the cells in the table, clicked on Insert menu, clicked on PivotTable, confirmed that my entire table has been selected and clicked on OK.

You will be taken to a new sheet that looks like the one below:

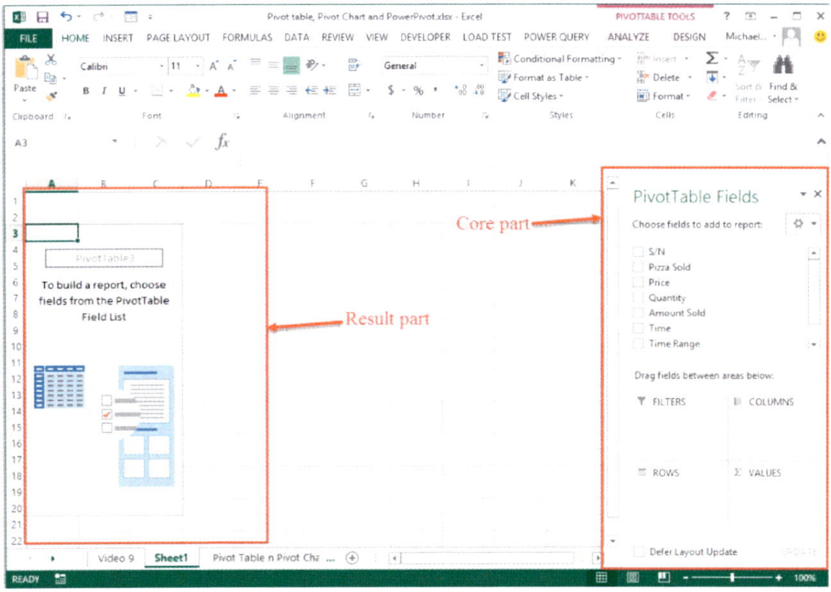

At first it looks really different, like you are no longer in Excel. But it is very easy to work with. The core part is the part on the right with the name **PivotTable Fields**. It has a list of all the fields in the original data table. The part below the field names are where you actually set up your report.

Whatever field you want to display its unique entries, one per line/row, you will drag to ROWS. Let's do that for the Pizza Sold field so we will be able to see all the pizza types the restaurant sells.

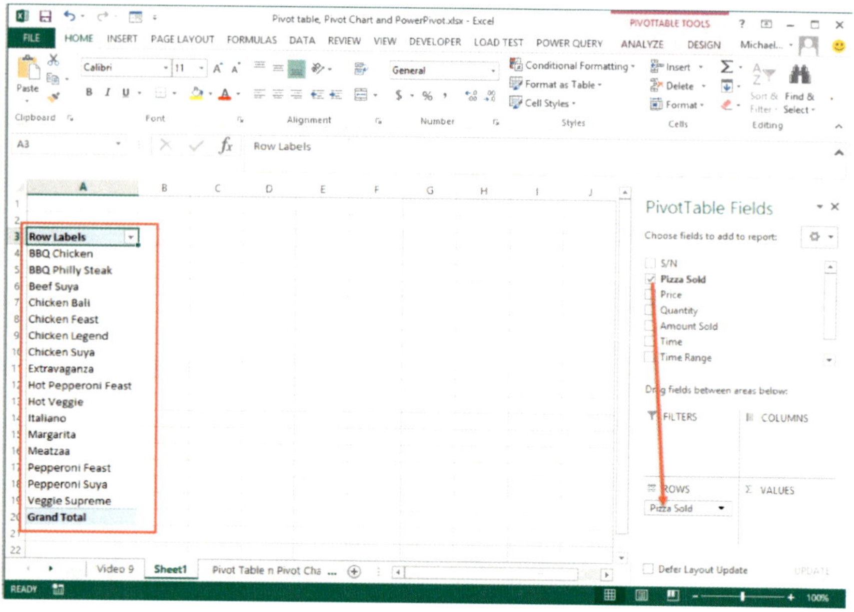

Then if it is that you want to display those unique entries one per column, drag the field to COLUMNS. Let's see what will happen if we drag that Pizza Sold field from ROWS to COLUMNS.

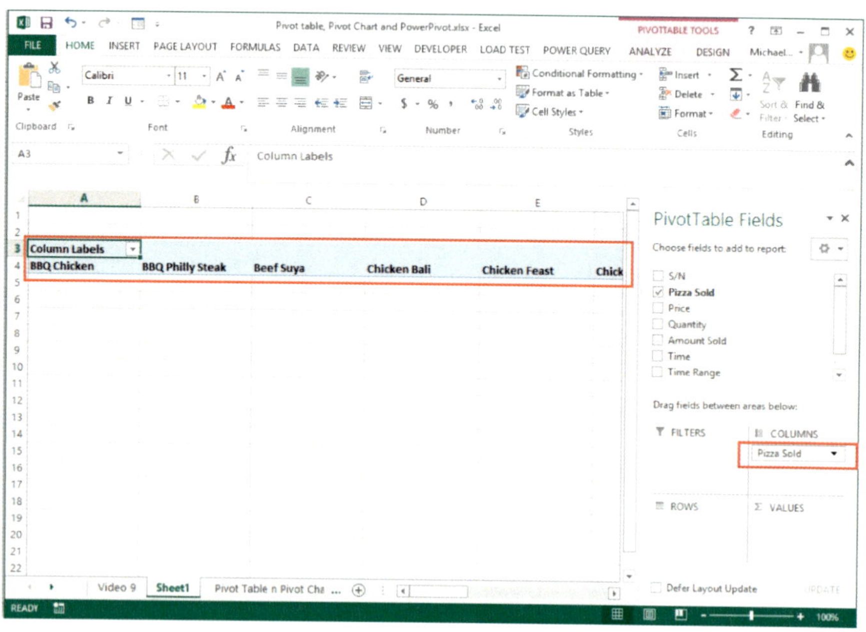

So now you understand how ROWS and COLUMNS work.

Drag Pizza Sold back to ROWS, that is where we need it for our quick analysis.

Next is VALUES. Whatever you want to do a mathematical calculation on, you drag to the VALUES part. Common calculations you will find yourself doing are counts (to see the number of time each unique entry occurred in the original table), sum (to add the values a particular field) and average (to average the values of a particular field).

In our case, let's drag Quantity and Amount Sold fields to VALUES.

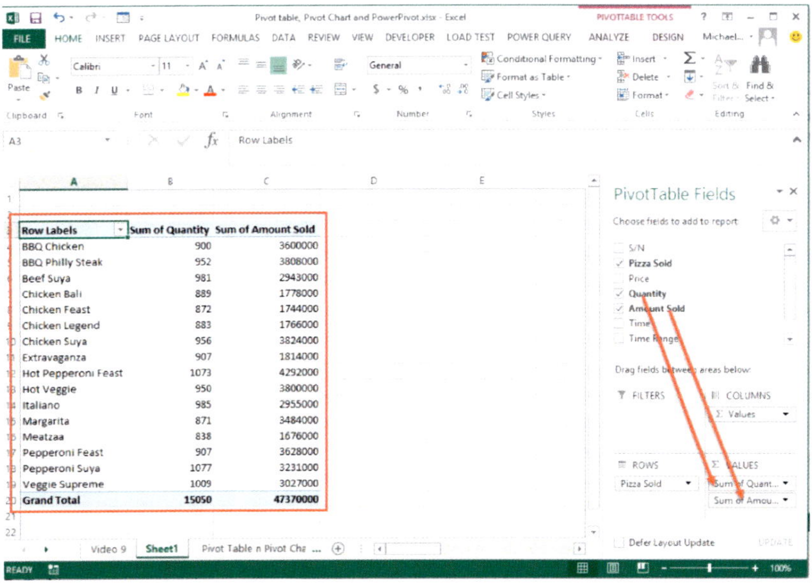

Can you see how quick this is? We have just analyzed a 5000 sales record table in seconds. Now we have a report that shows us how many of each Pizza type was sold and the total sales amount generated.

Those are the type of lightning fast analysis PivotTable allows you to do.

There is now one part we haven't touched: FILTERS. As the name suggests, it simply gives us the capability to filter our report. We will drag Time Range to FILTERS to see which sales occurred at the peak period (before 9:00am) and after the peak period.

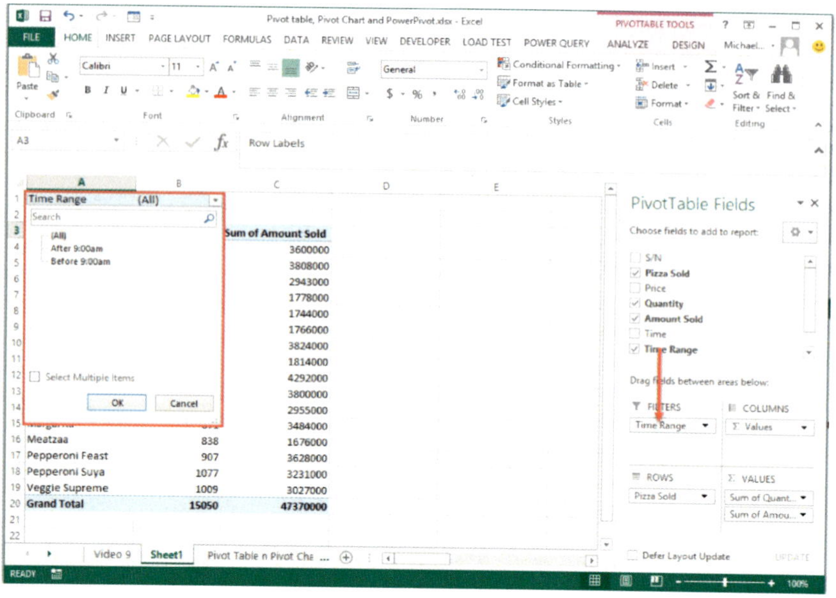

And that's how PivotTable works. Very easy to use and powerful.

PivotChart

Whenever you insert a chart using data generated via a PivotTable, that chart is a PivotChart. It has some extra functionalities it inherits from the PivotTable which makes it a little different from the regular charts we have already discussed.

Below is the PivotChart for the PivotTable we just created.

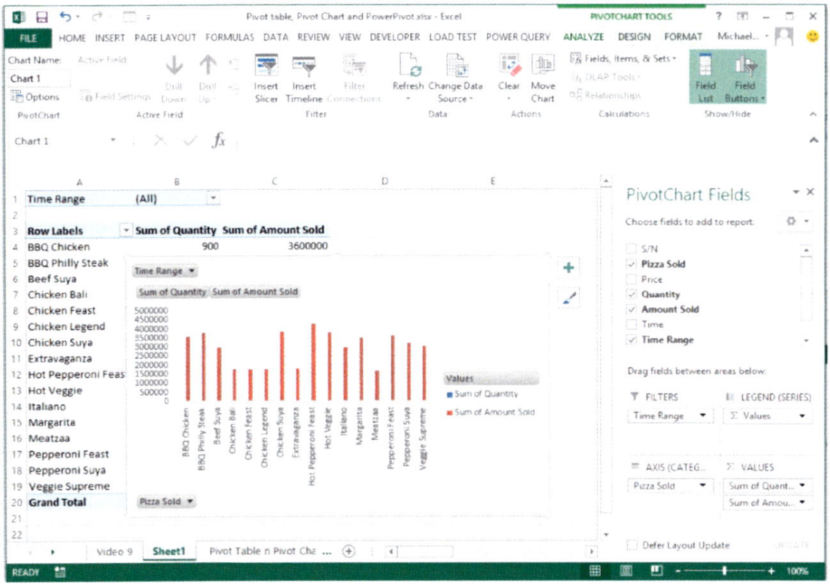

Notice the extra elements on it. Even the Time Range filter is showing on the chart. Besides those extra elements, a PivotChart is same as the regular charts and the same kind of formatting you can do on the regular charts work on PivotCharts.

Business Data Analysis

When using Excel to organize or analyze your business operations data, there are some tools you need to be aware of.

Linking Sheets

You often have to pull data into a report from another report or Excel file, the most effective way to do this is to link the sheets. You will be mirroring the value in the source sheet in your destination sheet.

An example is if there is a sheet that contains the internal revenue of all the states in Nigeria and you are doing a report on Kebbi state. You want to pull the values for Kebbi state from the sheet that has everything (source sheet), your best bet is to link the sheets. It is preferable to copying the values from the source sheet because if the source sheet is updated with new values your analysis sheet will not automatically update (will still be showing the now incorrect old values). So how do you link sheets?

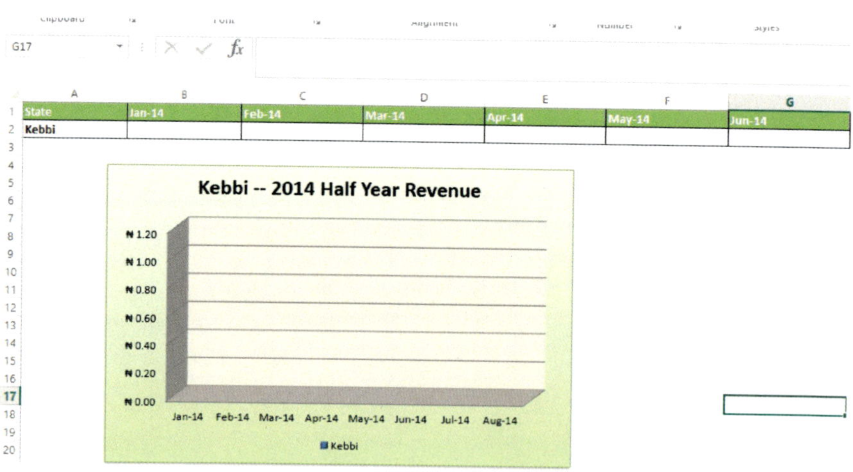

	A	B	C	D	E	F	G
1		Internally Generated Revenue of States in Nigeria					
2	State	Jan-14	Feb-14	Mar-14	Apr-14	May-14	Jun-14
3	Abia	₦ 1,297,498,300.00	₦ 821,123,500.00	₦ 1,175,454,800.00	₦ 967,327,400.00	₦ 2,265,644,000.00	₦ 4,544,916,100.00
4	Adamawa	₦ 4,022,792,500.00	₦ 4,317,641,300.00	₦ 1,627,470,600.00	₦ 1,023,694,700.00	₦ 3,493,691,500.00	₦ 1,973,059,900.00
23	Kano	₦ 2,981,980,300.00	₦ 2,021,735,600.00	₦ 3,016,518,600.00	₦ 4,411,651,000.00	₦ 2,387,291,000.00	₦ 530,613,400.00
24	Katsina	₦ 3,589,421,500.00	₦ 1,293,838,700.00	₦ 638,877,300.00	₦ 2,969,721,400.00	₦ 1,025,989,500.00	₦ 2,648,689,500.00
25	Kebbi	₦ 1,684,273,500.00	₦ 4,790,202,900.00	₦ 991,721,500.00	₦ 4,897,014,100.00	₦ 4,131,210,900.00	₦ 3,990,418,100.00
26	Kogi	₦ 2,812,863,300.00	₦ 2,734,189,600.00	₦ 2,306,601,300.00	₦ 867,264,000.00	₦ 2,104,687,400.00	₦ 2,825,512,800.00
27	Kwara	₦ 3,915,338,600.00	₦ 1,496,830,100.00	₦ 1,305,529,900.00	₦ 4,919,941,300.00	₦ 2,214,504,600.00	₦ 912,176,400.00
28	Lagos	₦ 6,239,473,500.00	₦ 7,319,183,000.00	₦ 6,211,689,500.00	₦ 3,351,178,500.00	₦ 11,610,307,000.00	₦ 22,681,984,500.00
29	Nasarawa	₦ 450,732,700.00	₦ 4,852,095,900.00	₦ 1,411,838,200.00	₦ 743,233,200.00	₦ 492,081,500.00	₦ 1,310,892,700.00
30	Niger	₦ 3,002,387,100.00	₦ 4,592,318,900.00	₦ 3,219,870,900.00	₦ 1,086,334,400.00	₦ 3,979,805,300.00	₦ 1,826,747,300.00
31	Ogun	₦ 3,434,714,900.00	₦ 2,586,000,100.00	₦ 3,907,557,600.00	₦ 1,642,410,200.00	₦ 2,265,022,600.00	₦ 3,200,451,900.00
32	Ondo	₦ 716,222,900.00	₦ 1,690,422,800.00	₦ 4,362,953,800.00	₦ 977,876,300.00	₦ 4,300,936,900.00	₦ 4,925,747,700.00
33	Plateau	₦ 4,527,323,100.00	₦ 2,371,220,000.00	₦ 4,471,653,300.00	₦ 932,778,800.00	₦ 3,593,441,000.00	₦ 4,894,816,200.00
34	Rivers	₦ 2,423,028,900.00	₦ 4,860,256,800.00	₦ 4,148,808,900.00	₦ 859,719,700.00	₦ 4,882,684,300.00	₦ 4,459,705,200.00
35	Taraba	₦ 531,248,900.00	₦ 785,603,400.00	₦ 2,475,480,400.00	₦ 878,820,400.00	₦ 1,389,495,200.00	₦ 3,244,525,900.00
36	Yobe	₦ 2,187,894,400.00	₦ 2,500,320,500.00	₦ 3,497,511,100.00	₦ 829,030,800.00	₦ 3,799,677,800.00	₦ 2,986,053,000.00
37	Zamfara	₦ 4,767,284,200.00	₦ 1,622,967,600.00	₦ 4,509,006,600.00	₦ 1,308,237,500.00	₦ 3,350,176,900.00	₦ 756,637,100.00

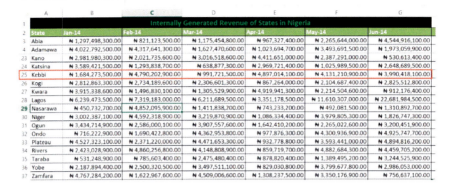

It's very easy. In the fields in the analysis sheet, for the different months values you will type = and select the cell with the actual figure in the source sheet.

In the end you will have the following or similar:

	A	B	C	D	E	F	G
1	State	Jan-14	Feb-14	Mar-14	Apr-14	May-14	Jun-14
2	Kebbi	=Datasheet!B25	=Datasheet!C25	=Datasheet!D25	=Datasheet!E25	=Datasheet!F25	=Datasheet!G25

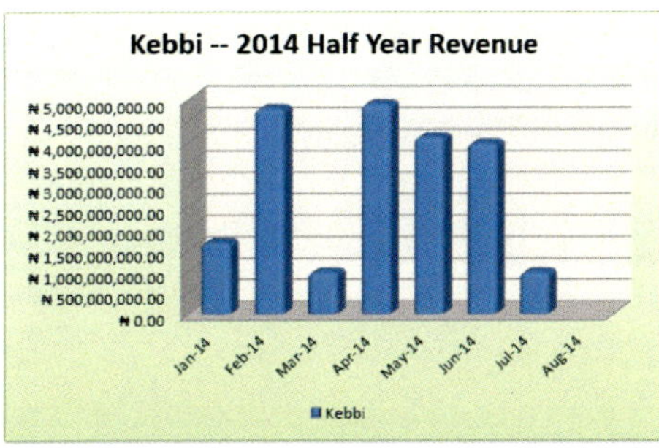

	A	B	C	D	E	F	G
1		Internally Generated Revenue of States in Nigeria					
2	State	Jan-14	Feb-14	Mar-14	Apr-14	May-14	Jun-14
3	Abia	₦ 1,297,498,300.00	₦ 821,123,500.00	₦ 1,175,454,800.00	₦ 967,327,400.00	₦ 2,265,644,000.00	₦ 4,544,916,100.00
4	Adamawa	₦ 4,022,792,500.00	₦ 4,317,641,300.00	₦ 1,627,470,600.00	₦ 1,023,694,700.00	₦ 3,493,691,500.00	₦ 1,973,059,900.00
23	Kano	₦ 2,981,980,300.00	₦ 2,021,735,600.00	₦ 3,016,518,600.00	₦ 4,411,651,000.00	₦ 2,387,291,000.00	₦ 530,613,400.00
24	Katsina	₦ 3,589,421,500.00	₦ 1,293,838,700.00	₦ 638,877,300.00	₦ 2,969,721,400.00	₦ 1,025,989,500.00	₦ 2,648,689,500.00
25	Kebbi	₦ 1,6 B25 ,500.00	₦ 4, C25 2,900.00	₦ 9 D25 ,500.00	₦ 4, E25 4,100.00	₦ 4,1 F25 0,900.00	₦ 3,9 G25 ,100.00
26	Kogi	₦ 2,812,863,300.00	₦ 2,734,189,600.00	₦ 2,306,601,300.00	₦ 867,264,000.00	₦ 2,104,687,400.00	₦ 2,825,512,800.00
27	Kwara	₦ 3,915,338,600.00	₦ 1,496,830,100.00	₦ 1,305,529,900.00	₦ 4,919,941,300.00	₦ 2,214,504,600.00	₦ 912,176,400.00
28	Lagos	₦ 6,239,473,500.00	₦ 7,319,183,000.00	₦ 6,211,689,500.00	₦ 3,351,178,500.00	₦ 11,610,307,000.00	₦ 22,681,984,500.00
29	Nasarawa	₦ 450,732,700.00	₦ 4,852,095,900.00	₦ 1,411,838,200.00	₦ 743,233,200.00	₦ 492,081,500.00	₦ 1,310,892,700.00
30	Niger	₦ 3,002,387,100.00	₦ 4,592,318,900.00	₦ 3,219,870,900.00	₦ 1,086,334,400.00	₦ 3,979,805,300.00	₦ 1,826,747,300.00
31	Ogun	₦ 3,434,714,900.00	₦ 2,586,000,100.00	₦ 3,907,557,600.00	₦ 1,642,410,200.00	₦ 2,265,022,600.00	₦ 3,200,451,900.00
32	Ondo	₦ 716,222,900.00	₦ 1,690,422,800.00	₦ 4,362,953,800.00	₦ 977,876,300.00	₦ 4,300,936,900.00	₦ 4,925,747,700.00
33	Plateau	₦ 4,527,323,100.00	₦ 2,371,220,000.00	₦ 4,471,653,300.00	₦ 932,778,800.00	₦ 3,593,441,000.00	₦ 4,894,816,200.00
34	Rivers	₦ 2,423,028,900.00	₦ 4,860,256,800.00	₦ 4,148,808,900.00	₦ 859,719,700.00	₦ 4,882,684,300.00	₦ 4,459,705,200.00
35	Taraba	₦ 531,248,900.00	₦ 785,603,400.00	₦ 2,475,480,400.00	₦ 878,820,400.00	₦ 1,389,495,200.00	₦ 3,244,525,900.00
36	Yobe	₦ 2,187,894,400.00	₦ 2,500,320,500.00	₦ 3,497,511,100.00	₦ 829,030,800.00	₦ 3,799,677,800.00	₦ 2,986,053,000.00
37	Zamfara	₦ 4,767,284,200.00	₦ 1,622,967,600.00	₦ 4,509,006,600.00	₦ 1,308,237,500.00	₦ 3,350,176,900.00	₦ 756,637,100.00

The source sheet has the name Datasheet, hence the **=Datasheet!B25** in January value cell in the analysis sheet. You don't type anything beyond = into the values cells in the analysis sheet, once you select the right cell in the source sheet, Excel will write everything you see in the cell.

Duplicating Sheets

Sometimes you will want an exact copy of a sheet to work with or email to someone (especially if the Excel file contains other sheets you don't want the person to access). Excel has a nifty tool for duplicating sheets. And it's very easy to use.

Right click on the name of the sheet you want to duplicate. Click on **Move or Copy…**

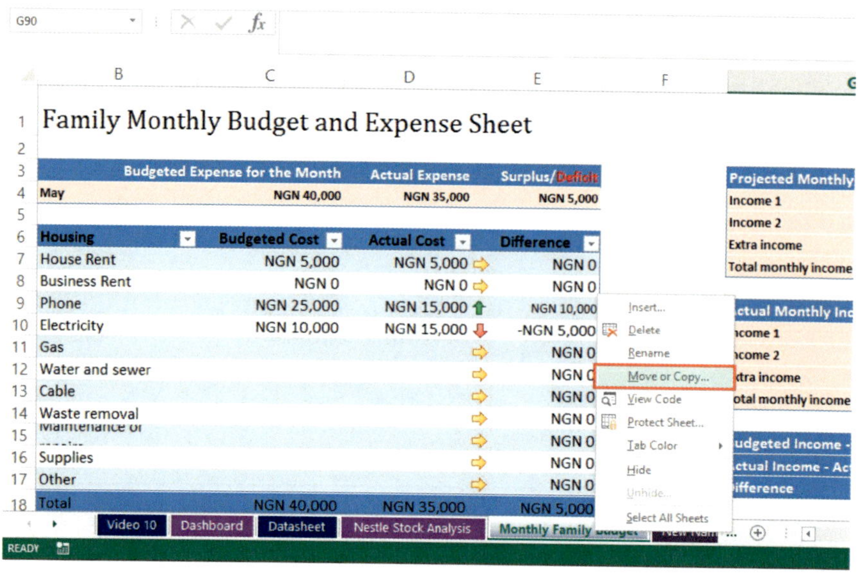

You'll see a dialog box. Select **new book** and tick **Create a Copy**.

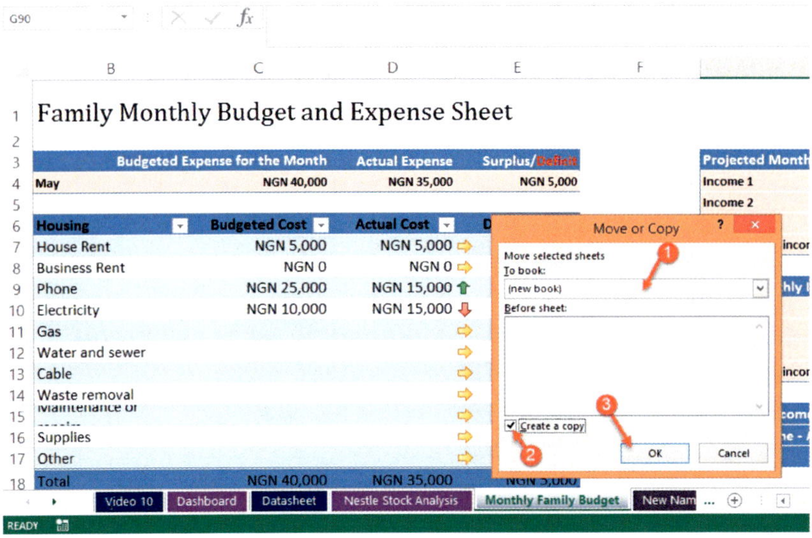

And the sheet will be duplicated in a new Excel file for you.

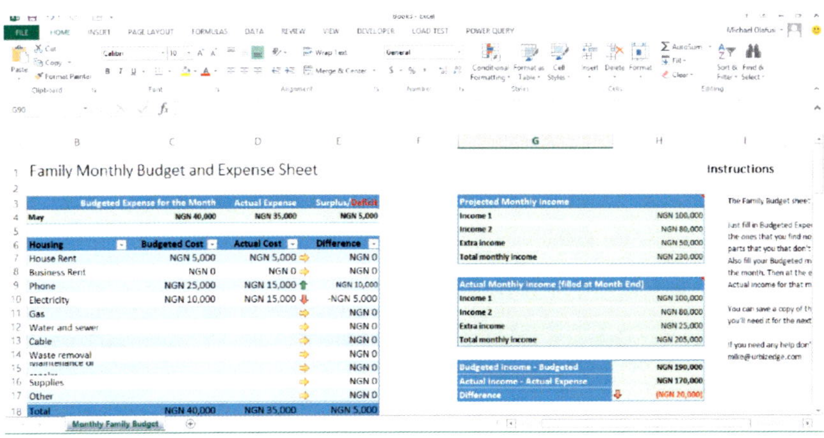

Inserting Sheets, Renaming Sheets and Changing Sheet Tab color

You can insert a new Sheet in an Excel file. Just click on the new sheet icon at the right of the last sheet tab in the file.

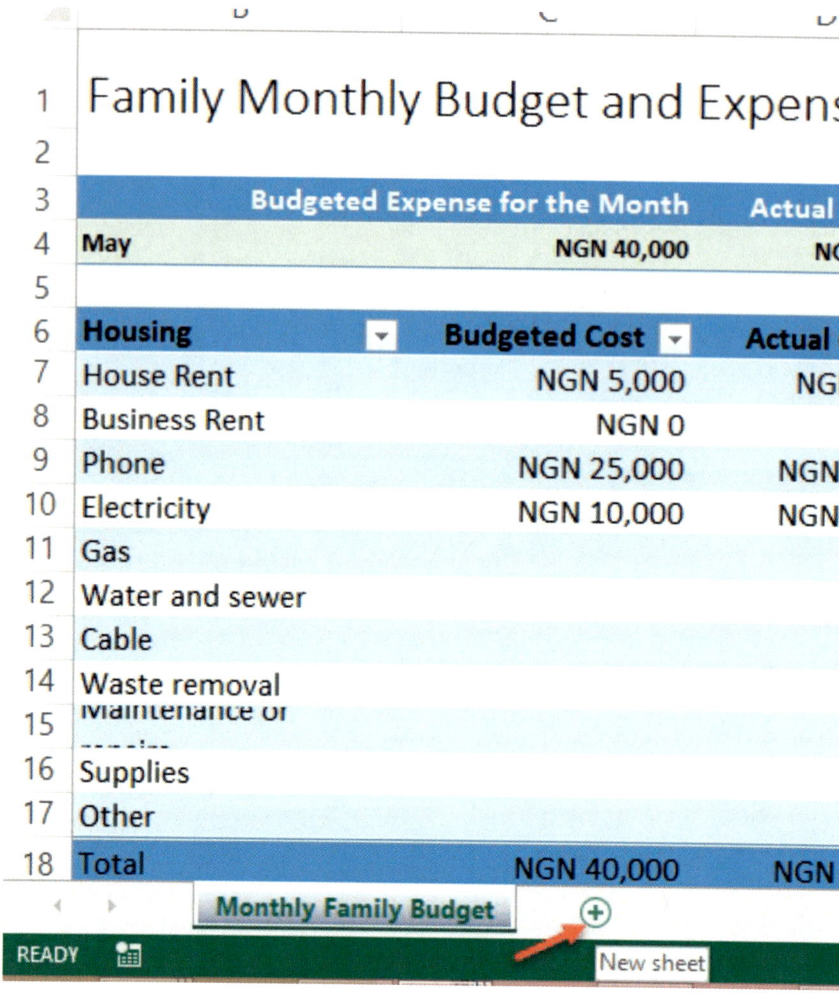

Family Monthly Budget and Expens
Budgeted Expense for the Month
Actual
May
NGN 40,000
Housing
Budgeted Cost
Actual
House Rent
NGN 5,000
Business Rent
NGN 0
Phone
NGN 25,000
Electricity
NGN 10,000
Gas
Water and sewer
Cable
Waste removal
Supplies
Other
Total
NGN 40,000
Monthly Family Budget
READY
New sheet

You can also rename the new Sheet to what you want. Just right click on the sheet tab and select Rename.

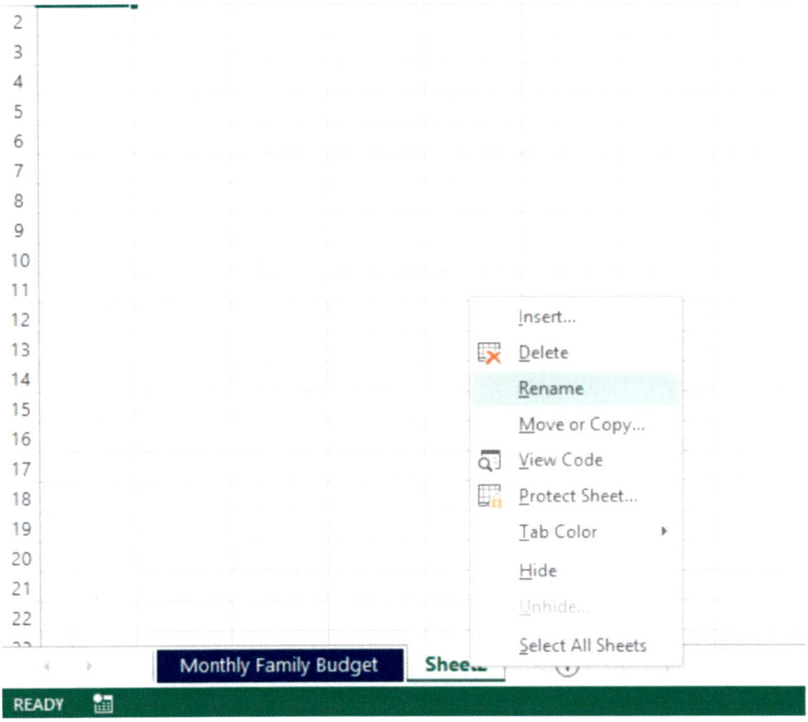

Finally, you can give it the color you want. Again, right click on the sheet name and click on Tab Color. Choose the color you want.

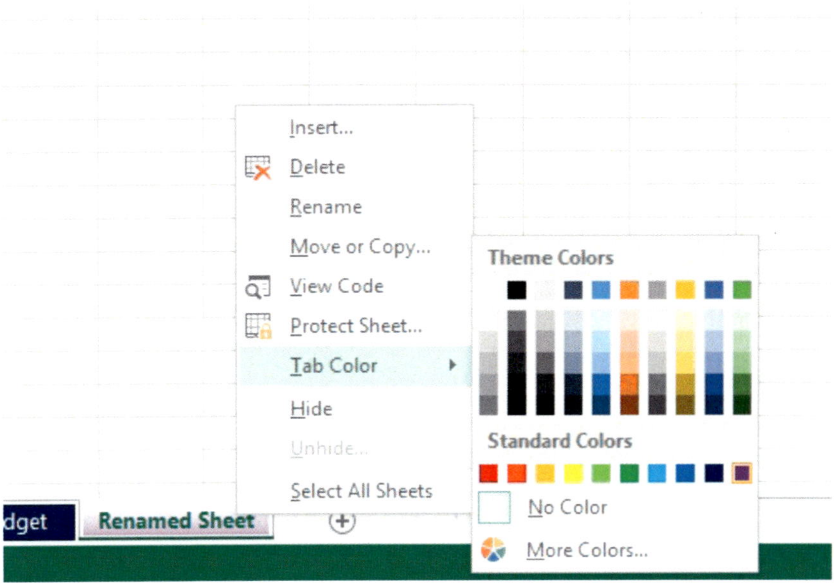

Freezing Panes

There will be times you have a table to with lots of entries and will require a lot scrolling up and down, and even left and right. Often you will want some part of the table to never scroll out of view. This is usually the headers. Achieving this requires enabling a tool called Freeze Panes.

It freezes the part of your report you don't want to scroll out of view. Below is an example. You access it from the View menu.

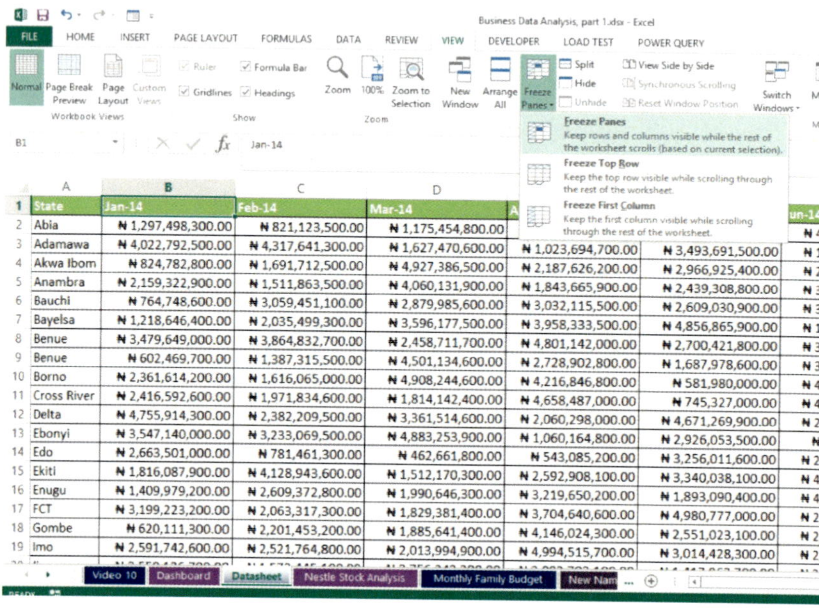

There are three options:

1. **Freeze Panes.** To use this option you have to select a cell in the table. This option will freeze all the rows above the cell you selected and all the columns to the left of the cell you selected. So you have to select just the right cell. If you want to freeze rows 1 and 2, then you will select cell A3.
2. **Freeze Top Row.** This freezes the top row in your Excel's current view.
3. **Freeze First Column.** This freezes the first column in your Excel's current view.

Below is the result of freezing row 1. It doesn't scroll out of view even when I scroll way down.

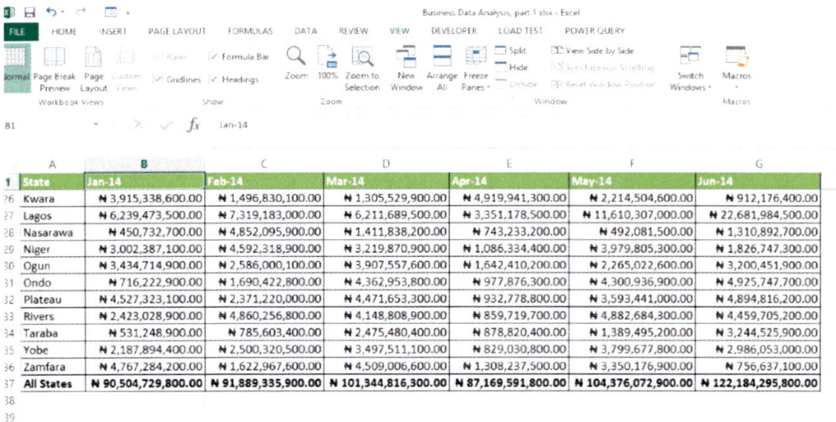

State	Jan-14	Feb-14	Mar-14	Apr-14	May-14	Jun-14
Kwara	₦ 3,915,338,600.00	₦ 1,496,830,100.00	₦ 1,305,529,900.00	₦ 4,919,941,300.00	₦ 2,214,504,600.00	₦ 912,176,400.00
Lagos	₦ 6,239,473,500.00	₦ 7,319,183,000.00	₦ 6,211,689,500.00	₦ 3,351,178,500.00	₦ 11,610,307,000.00	₦ 22,681,984,500.00
Nasarawa	₦ 450,732,700.00	₦ 4,852,095,900.00	₦ 1,411,838,200.00	₦ 743,233,200.00	₦ 492,081,500.00	₦ 1,310,892,700.00
Niger	₦ 3,002,387,100.00	₦ 4,592,318,900.00	₦ 3,219,870,900.00	₦ 1,086,334,400.00	₦ 3,979,805,300.00	₦ 1,826,747,300.00
Ogun	₦ 3,434,714,900.00	₦ 2,586,000,100.00	₦ 3,907,557,600.00	₦ 1,642,410,200.00	₦ 2,265,022,600.00	₦ 3,200,451,900.00
Ondo	₦ 716,222,900.00	₦ 1,690,422,800.00	₦ 4,362,953,800.00	₦ 977,876,300.00	₦ 4,300,936,900.00	₦ 4,925,747,700.00
Plateau	₦ 4,527,323,100.00	₦ 2,371,220,000.00	₦ 4,471,653,300.00	₦ 932,778,800.00	₦ 3,593,441,000.00	₦ 4,894,816,200.00
Rivers	₦ 2,423,028,900.00	₦ 4,860,256,800.00	₦ 4,148,808,900.00	₦ 859,719,700.00	₦ 4,882,684,300.00	₦ 4,459,705,200.00
Taraba	₦ 531,248,900.00	₦ 785,603,400.00	₦ 2,475,480,400.00	₦ 878,820,400.00	₦ 1,389,495,200.00	₦ 3,244,525,900.00
Yobe	₦ 2,187,894,400.00	₦ 2,500,320,500.00	₦ 3,497,511,100.00	₦ 829,030,800.00	₦ 3,799,677,800.00	₦ 2,986,053,000.00
Zamfara	₦ 4,767,284,200.00	₦ 1,622,967,600.00	₦ 4,509,006,600.00	₦ 1,308,237,500.00	₦ 3,350,176,900.00	₦ 756,637,100.00
All States	**₦ 90,504,729,800.00**	**₦ 91,889,335,900.00**	**₦ 101,344,816,300.00**	**₦ 87,169,591,800.00**	**₦ 104,376,072,900.00**	**₦ 122,184,295,800.00**

Splitting Windows

Excel lets you split your current Excel view into two independent windows that you can scroll separately. This is useful if you want to monitor changes in two different far away parts of your Excel file that are dependent.

An example is shown below. The Excel file is a stock analysis file and at the top far right are projected values based on assumptions made far down the Excel sheet. So in order to see instantaneously the effect of a change in an assumption on the projected values, splitting window was used.

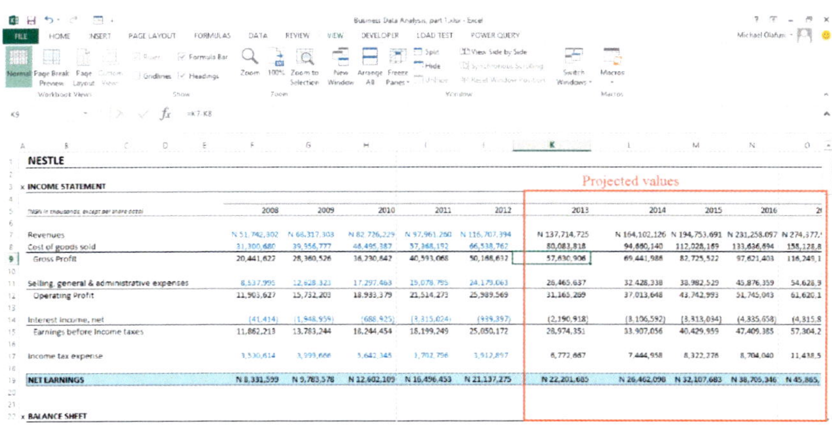

And the assumptions far down

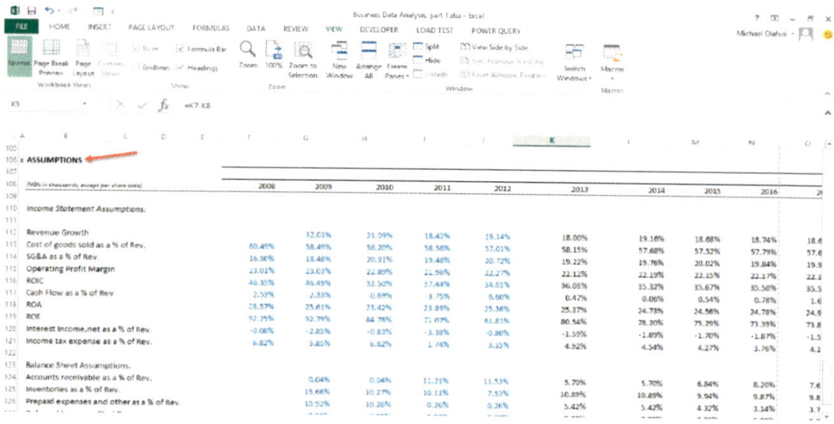

Splitting window allows us to view this two far away parts of the Excel sheet at once.

To do this, select the middle row in the Excel sheet and go to View menu and click on Split.

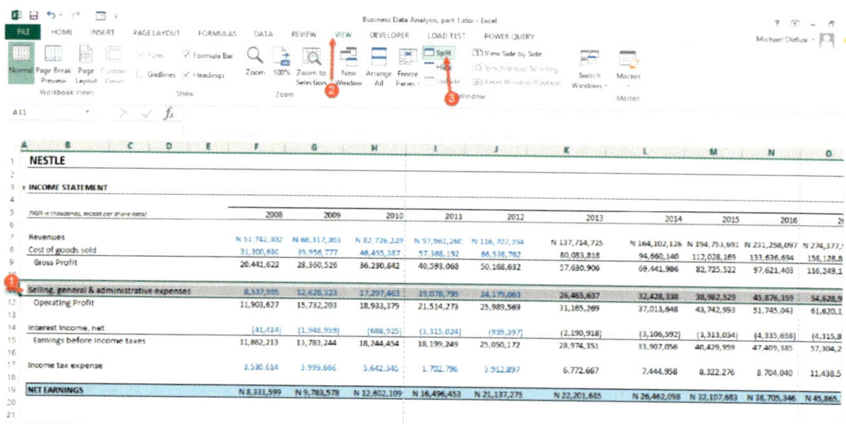

Then scroll the section below the splitting point down to the assumptions part. It will scroll independent of the part above the split line.

Notice the jump from row 10 to row 104.

Now whenever you alter the assumptions you won't have to scroll up to see the effect on the projected revenue and projected profit.

Conditional Formatting

Conditional formatting is another power tool in the power Excel user's toolbox. It allows you to indicate the relative performance of metrics (KPIs). Below is a simple example of its use.

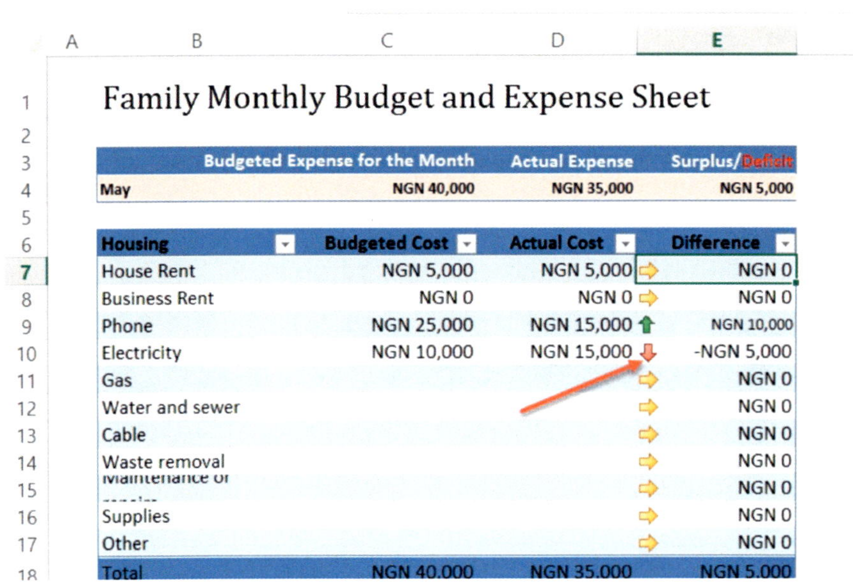

Notice the green, yellow and red arrows. They are conditional formats that let you visually see where you are spending below your budget, where you are spending exactly what you budgeted and where you are spending above your budget.

Those are type of practical visual analysis conditional formatting provides.

You can access it via the Home menu. And it has the following formatting groups.

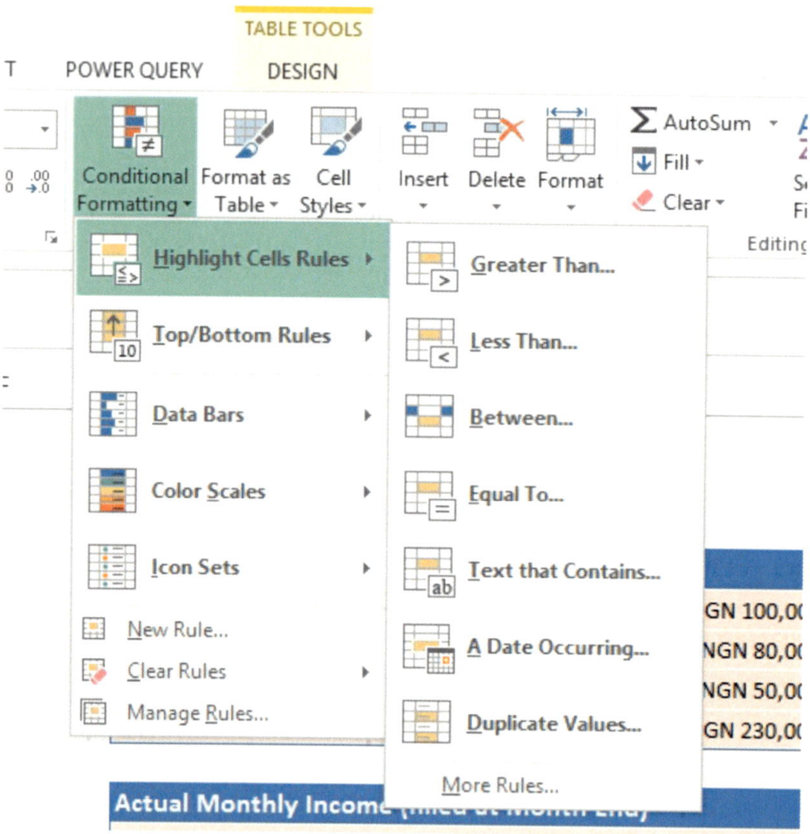

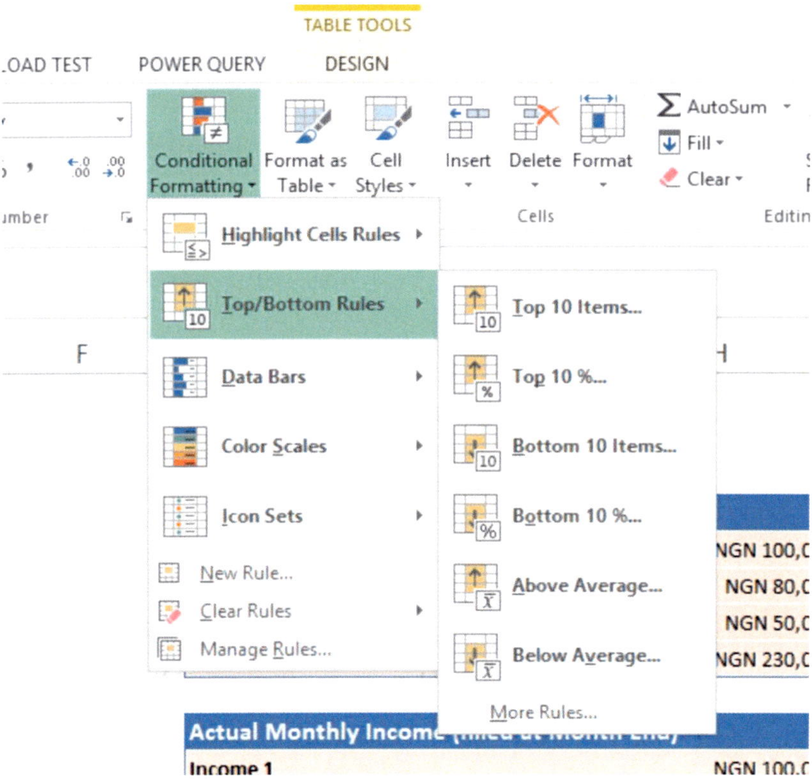
TABLE TOOLS
LOAD TEST
POWER QUERY
DESIGN
Conditional Formatting
Format as Table
Cell Styles
Insert
Delete
Format
AutoSum
Fill
Clear
Cells
Editin
Highlight Cells Rules
Top/Bottom Rules
Data Bars
Color Scales
Icon Sets
New Rule...
Clear Rules
Manage Rules...
Top 10 Items...
Top 10 %...
Bottom 10 Items...
Bottom 10 %...
Above Average...
Below Average...
More Rules...
NGN 100,0
NGN 80,0
NGN 50,0
NGN 230,0
Actual Monthly Income
Income 1

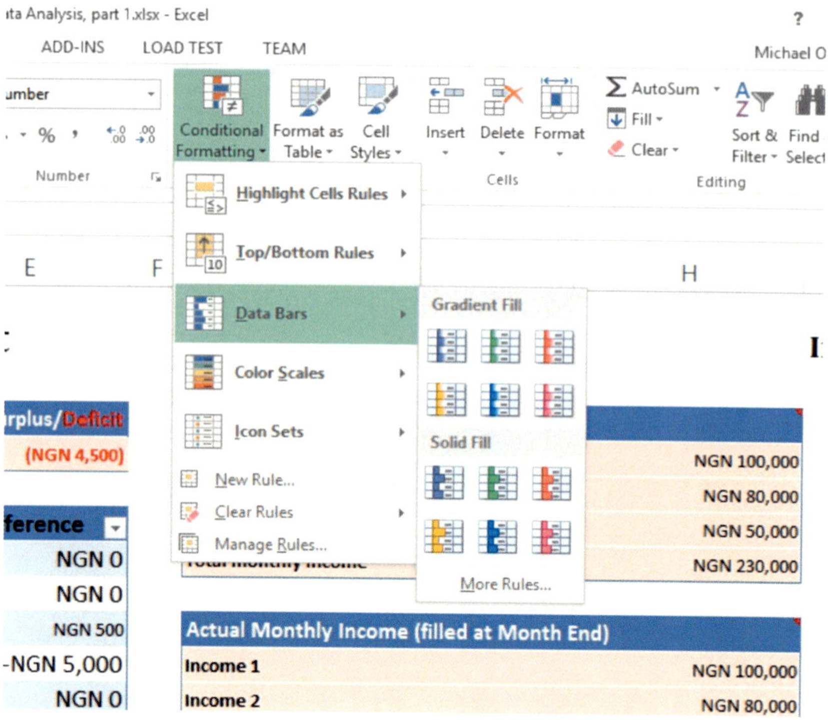
ata Analysis, part 1.xlsx - Excel
ADD-INS
LOAD TEST
TEAM
Michael O
Conditional Formatting
Format as Table
Cell Styles
Insert
Delete
Format
AutoSum
Fill
Clear
Sort & Filter
Find & Select
Number
Cells
Editing
Highlight Cells Rules
Top/Bottom Rules
Data Bars
Color Scales
Icon Sets
New Rule...
Clear Rules
Manage Rules...
Gradient Fill
Solid Fill
More Rules...
rplus/Deficit
(NGN 4,500)
ference
NGN 0
NGN 0
NGN 500
-NGN 5,000
NGN 0
NGN 100,000
NGN 80,000
NGN 50,000
NGN 230,000
Actual Monthly Income (filled at Month End)
Income 1
NGN 100,000
Income 2
NGN 80,000

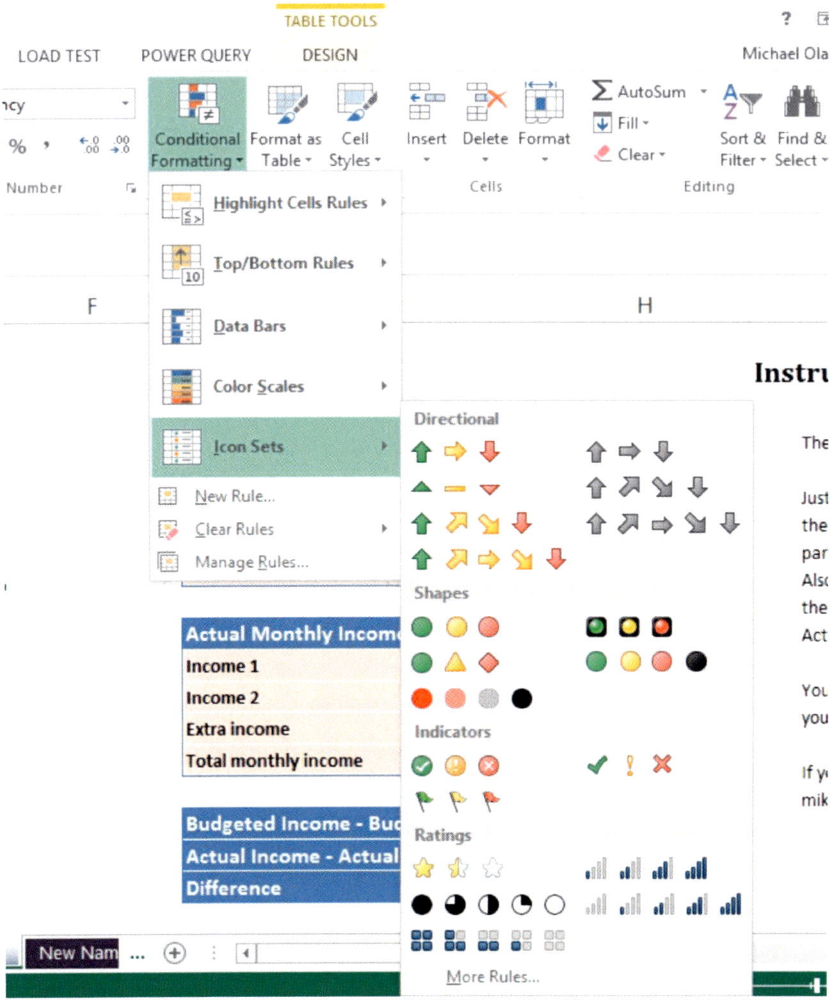

Excel 2016 Forecast Tool

There is a forecast tool in Excel 2016. It helps you make time series forecast.
To show you how it works, I have prepared a sample sales data.

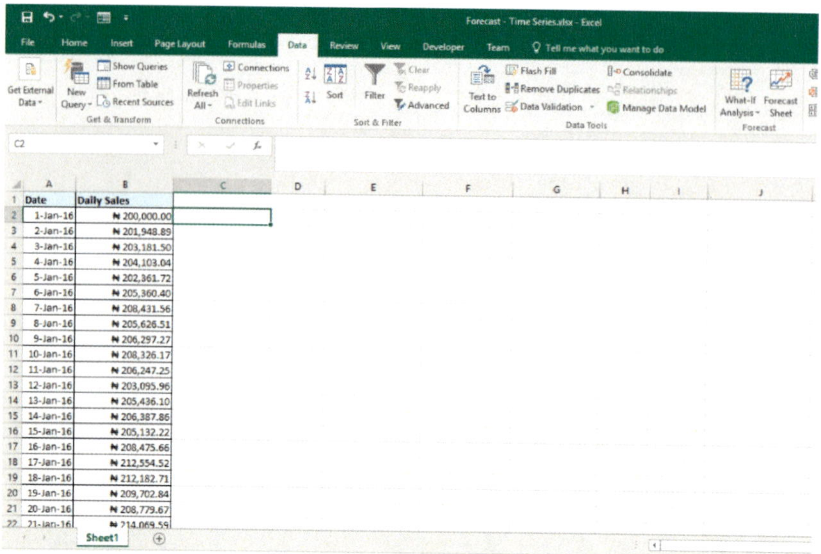

It is the daily sales record of a grocery store for this year. The store has been hit by the current economic downturn and sales are not as good as they used to be. The owner is very worried and wants to see what the future will be like if the trend continues.

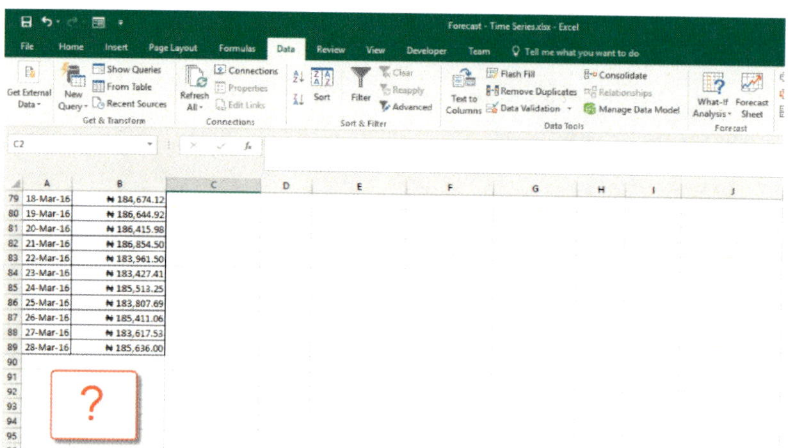

This is what the forecast tool in Excel 2016 is built for. And here's how to use it.

Select the historical data, go to Data menu and select "Forecast Sheet".

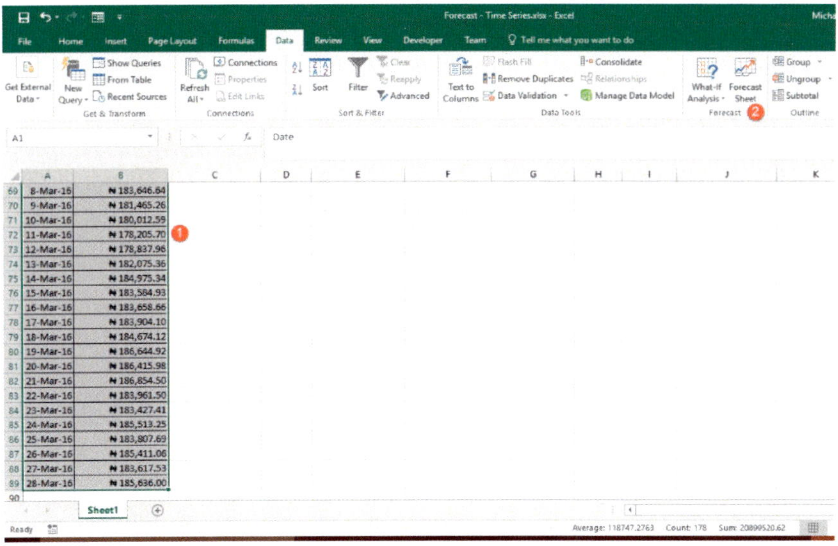

The forecast dialog box comes up. Set the date you want the forecast to end (Forecast End).

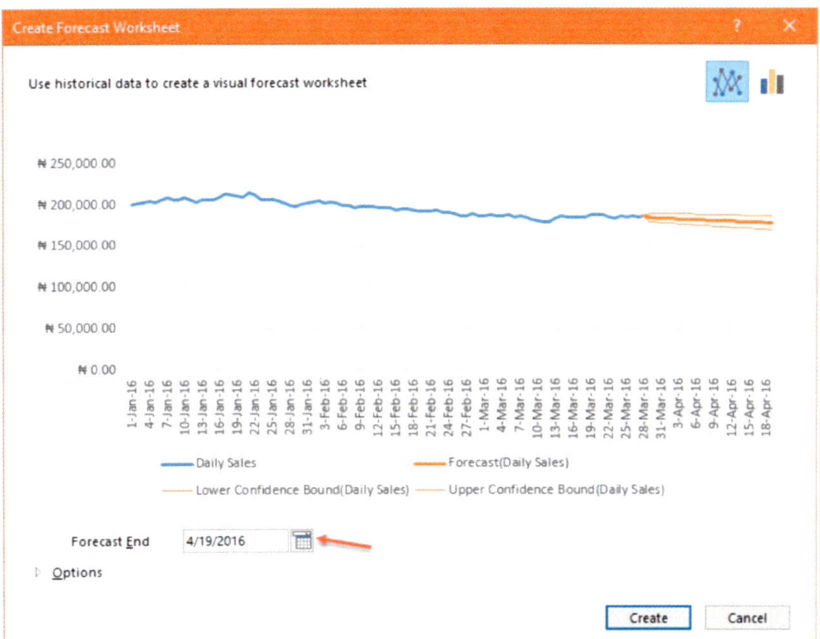

If you are familiar with time series, it is a triple exponential smoothing capable time series tool. You can expand the options and set things as you want.

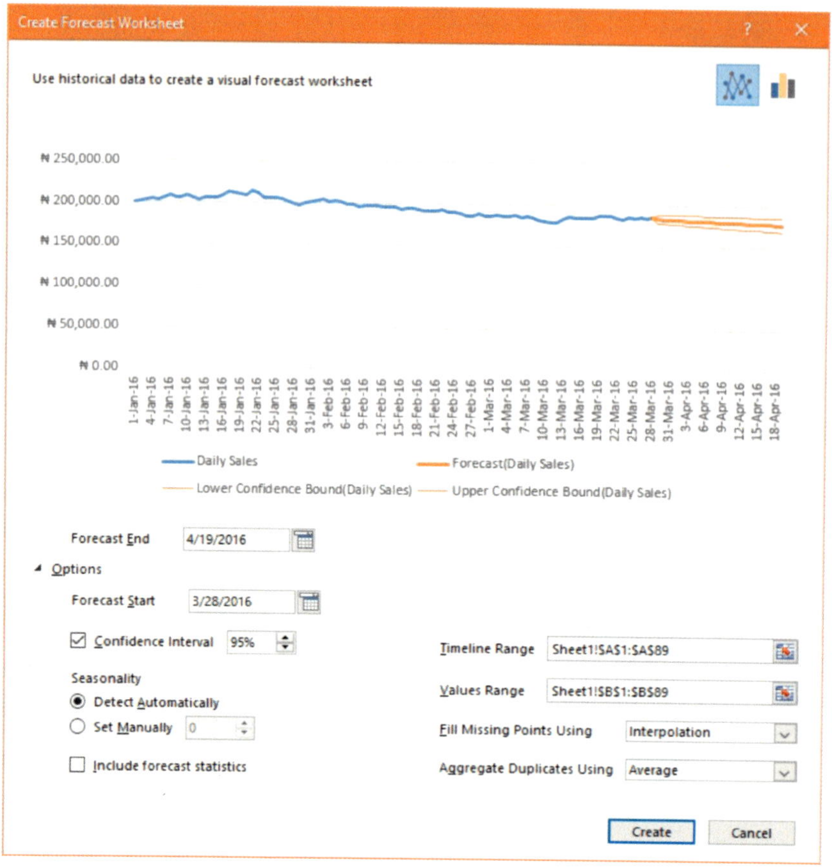

And for the setting above (default setting), here is the result.

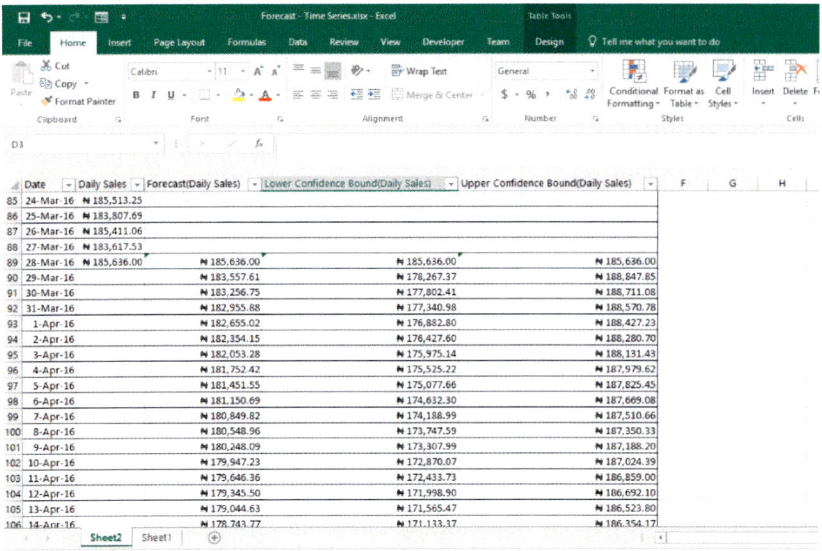

	Date	Daily Sales	Forecast(Daily Sales)	Lower Confidence Bound(Daily Sales)	Upper Confidence Bound(Daily Sales)
85	24-Mar-16	₦ 185,513.25			
86	25-Mar-16	₦ 183,807.69			
87	26-Mar-16	₦ 185,411.06			
88	27-Mar-16	₦ 183,617.53			
89	28-Mar-16	₦ 185,636.00	₦ 185,636.00	₦ 185,636.00	₦ 185,636.00
90	29-Mar-16		₦ 183,557.61	₦ 178,267.37	₦ 188,847.85
91	30-Mar-16		₦ 183,256.75	₦ 177,802.41	₦ 188,711.08
92	31-Mar-16		₦ 182,955.88	₦ 177,340.98	₦ 188,570.78
93	1-Apr-16		₦ 182,655.02	₦ 176,882.80	₦ 188,427.23
94	2-Apr-16		₦ 182,354.15	₦ 176,427.60	₦ 188,280.70
95	3-Apr-16		₦ 182,053.28	₦ 175,975.14	₦ 188,131.43
96	4-Apr-16		₦ 181,752.42	₦ 175,525.22	₦ 187,979.62
97	5-Apr-16		₦ 181,451.55	₦ 175,077.66	₦ 187,825.45
98	6-Apr-16		₦ 181,150.69	₦ 174,632.30	₦ 187,669.08
99	7-Apr-16		₦ 180,849.82	₦ 174,188.99	₦ 187,510.66
100	8-Apr-16		₦ 180,548.96	₦ 173,747.59	₦ 187,350.33
101	9-Apr-16		₦ 180,248.09	₦ 173,307.99	₦ 187,188.20
102	10-Apr-16		₦ 179,947.23	₦ 172,870.07	₦ 187,024.39
103	11-Apr-16		₦ 179,646.36	₦ 172,433.73	₦ 186,859.00
104	12-Apr-16		₦ 179,345.50	₦ 171,998.90	₦ 186,692.10
105	13-Apr-16		₦ 179,044.63	₦ 171,565.47	₦ 186,523.80
106	14-Apr-16		₦ 178,743.77	₦ 171,133.37	₦ 186,354.17

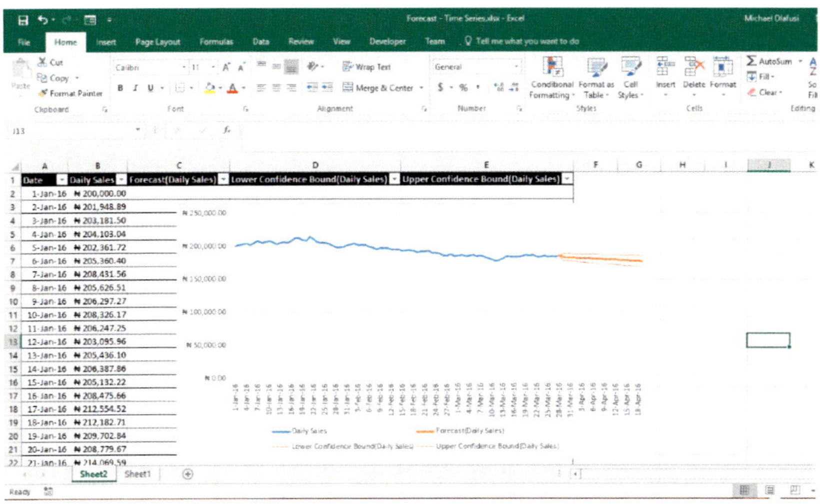

	Date	Daily Sales
2	1-Jan-16	₦ 200,000.00
3	2-Jan-16	₦ 201,948.89
4	3-Jan-16	₦ 203,181.50
5	4-Jan-16	₦ 204,103.04
6	5-Jan-16	₦ 202,361.72
7	6-Jan-16	₦ 205,360.40
8	7-Jan-16	₦ 208,431.56
9	8-Jan-16	₦ 205,626.51
10	9-Jan-16	₦ 206,297.27
11	10-Jan-16	₦ 208,326.17
12	11-Jan-16	₦ 206,247.25
13	12-Jan-16	₦ 203,095.96
14	13-Jan-16	₦ 205,436.10
15	14-Jan-16	₦ 206,387.86
16	15-Jan-16	₦ 205,132.22
17	16-Jan-16	₦ 208,475.66
18	17-Jan-16	₦ 212,554.52
19	18-Jan-16	₦ 212,182.71
20	19-Jan-16	₦ 209,702.84
21	20-Jan-16	₦ 208,779.67
22	21-Jan-16	₦ 214,069.59

Now the store owner can see that things will get worse if he doesn't do something to halt the downward sales trend. And that is how easy it is to run a time series forecast in Excel 2016. Unfortunately, it is not available in Excel 2013, Excel 2010, Excel 2007 and, obviously, older Excel versions.

Power Excel Formulas

Excel has thousands of formulas but a select few stand out as very versatile and useful for day to day business data analysis and reporting. We are going to focus on those formulas in this section.

VLOOKUP

This is perhaps Excel's most popular function. In interviews it is used to sieve the power Excel users from the occasional Excel user. Its popularity lies in its ease of use and capability to get you the data you need from another table if you provide it a clue.

Below is an example of its use.

PMT =VLOOKUP(A2,A5:G24,2,FALSE)

	A	B	C	D	E	F	G
1	Clients\Month	Jan-14	Feb-14	Mar-14	Apr-14	May-14	Jun-14
2	Dangote	=VLOOKUP(A2,A5:G24,2,FALSE)					
3		VLOOKUP(lookup_value, table_array, col_index_num, [range_lookup])					
4							
5	Monthly Revenue from Clients						
6	Clients	Jan-14	Feb-14	Mar-14	Apr-14	May-14	Jun-14
7	Mobil	₦ 4,129,000	₦ 3,695,000	₦ 2,770,000	₦ 4,520,000	₦ 2,223,000	₦ 3,929,000
8	Nestle	₦ 1,688,000	₦ 3,300,000	₦ 4,880,000	₦ 3,730,000	₦ 2,046,000	₦ 2,326,000
9	NBC	₦ 3,701,000	₦ 4,361,000	₦ 4,254,000	₦ 4,550,000	₦ 4,834,000	₦ 3,116,000
10	Exp Nigeria	₦ 2,587,000	₦ 4,198,000	₦ 2,146,000	₦ 1,062,000	₦ 2,341,000	₦ 4,713,000
11	Insight Nigeria	₦ 1,688,000	₦ 4,759,000	₦ 1,300,000	₦ 4,426,000	₦ 3,521,000	₦ 3,171,000
12	Radisson Blu	₦ 2,485,000	₦ 2,025,000	₦ 1,603,000	₦ 3,089,000	₦ 2,841,000	₦ 3,156,000
13	Guinness	₦ 2,703,000	₦ 1,888,000	₦ 1,360,000	₦ 1,664,000	₦ 1,097,000	₦ 4,920,000
14	Chevron	₦ 3,516,000	₦ 2,988,000	₦ 4,788,000	₦ 2,425,000	₦ 4,689,000	₦ 4,080,000
15	Etisalat	₦ 4,475,000	₦ 3,459,000	₦ 2,701,000	₦ 2,058,000	₦ 3,562,000	₦ 3,096,000
16	Dangote	₦ 1,457,000	₦ 3,241,000	₦ 4,441,000	₦ 1,544,000	₦ 3,749,000	₦ 3,544,000
17	Dana Group	₦ 2,984,000	₦ 1,882,000	₦ 2,898,000	₦ 4,618,000	₦ 2,372,000	₦ 3,723,000
18	LaFarge	₦ 2,111,000	₦ 3,293,000	₦ 1,427,000	₦ 3,953,000	₦ 1,616,000	₦ 2,885,000
19	NB	₦ 3,396,000	₦ 4,148,000	₦ 4,569,000	₦ 3,893,000	₦ 3,871,000	₦ 3,045,000
20	MTN	₦ 4,410,000	₦ 2,391,000	₦ 4,180,000	₦ 3,788,000	₦ 2,669,000	₦ 4,262,000
21	Monacom	₦ 4,190,000	₦ 2,228,000	₦ 4,615,000	₦ 2,756,000	₦ 3,123,000	₦ 1,464,000
22	ARM	₦ 4,536,000	₦ 1,412,000	₦ 4,313,000	₦ 1,130,000	₦ 3,700,000	₦ 3,196,000

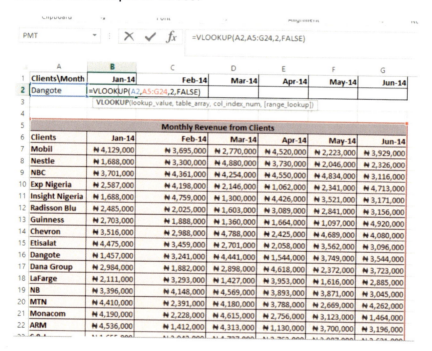

The formula breakdown is

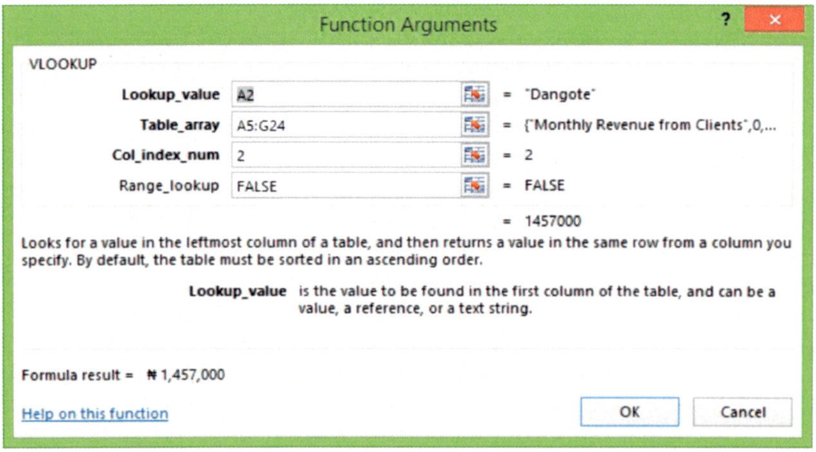

Lookup_value
=VLOOKUP(**A2**,A5:G24,2,FALSE)
Basically, it is asking you for the clue you have. What piece of information do you have that I should look for in the table that has everything.

Table_array
=VLOOKUP(A2,**A5:G24**,2,FALSE)
Where is the table that has everything? So here you are selecting the table that has everything.

Col_index_num
=VLOOKUP(A2,A5:G24,**2**,FALSE)
When I see the clue, what data should I bring back? That data is in what column counting from the leftmost column in the selected table.

Range_lookup
=VLOOKUP(A2,A5:G24,2,**FALSE**)
If I am unable to find the clue, should I take a guess? Usually, you wouldn't want Excel to take a guess, that could cause you trouble. So say no by typing FALSE.

And that is how VLOOKUP works. It will look through the first column in the table you selected for the clue that you provided and when it finds it, it will bring back the data you specified for it to get.

It makes a lot of reports easy to do and very helpful with making dashboards.

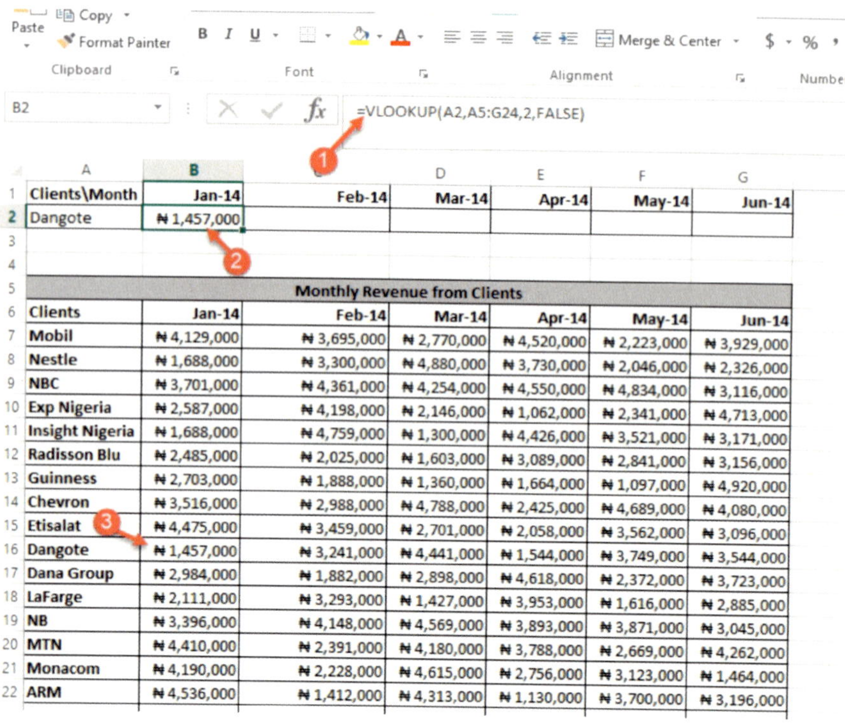

	A	B	C	D	E	F	G
1	Clients\Month	Jan-14	Feb-14	Mar-14	Apr-14	May-14	Jun-14
2	Dangote	₦ 1,457,000					
3							
4							
5	Monthly Revenue from Clients						
6	Clients	Jan-14	Feb-14	Mar-14	Apr-14	May-14	Jun-14
7	Mobil	₦ 4,129,000	₦ 3,695,000	₦ 2,770,000	₦ 4,520,000	₦ 2,223,000	₦ 3,929,000
8	Nestle	₦ 1,688,000	₦ 3,300,000	₦ 4,880,000	₦ 3,730,000	₦ 2,046,000	₦ 2,326,000
9	NBC	₦ 3,701,000	₦ 4,361,000	₦ 4,254,000	₦ 4,550,000	₦ 4,834,000	₦ 3,116,000
10	Exp Nigeria	₦ 2,587,000	₦ 4,198,000	₦ 2,146,000	₦ 1,062,000	₦ 2,341,000	₦ 4,713,000
11	Insight Nigeria	₦ 1,688,000	₦ 4,759,000	₦ 1,300,000	₦ 4,426,000	₦ 3,521,000	₦ 3,171,000
12	Radisson Blu	₦ 2,485,000	₦ 2,025,000	₦ 1,603,000	₦ 3,089,000	₦ 2,841,000	₦ 3,156,000
13	Guinness	₦ 2,703,000	₦ 1,888,000	₦ 1,360,000	₦ 1,664,000	₦ 1,097,000	₦ 4,920,000
14	Chevron	₦ 3,516,000	₦ 2,988,000	₦ 4,788,000	₦ 2,425,000	₦ 4,689,000	₦ 4,080,000
15	Etisalat	₦ 4,475,000	₦ 3,459,000	₦ 2,701,000	₦ 2,058,000	₦ 3,562,000	₦ 3,096,000
16	Dangote	₦ 1,457,000	₦ 3,241,000	₦ 4,441,000	₦ 1,544,000	₦ 3,749,000	₦ 3,544,000
17	Dana Group	₦ 2,984,000	₦ 1,882,000	₦ 2,898,000	₦ 4,618,000	₦ 2,372,000	₦ 3,723,000
18	LaFarge	₦ 2,111,000	₦ 3,293,000	₦ 1,427,000	₦ 3,953,000	₦ 1,616,000	₦ 2,885,000
19	NB	₦ 3,396,000	₦ 4,148,000	₦ 4,569,000	₦ 3,893,000	₦ 3,871,000	₦ 3,045,000
20	MTN	₦ 4,410,000	₦ 2,391,000	₦ 4,180,000	₦ 3,788,000	₦ 2,669,000	₦ 4,262,000
21	Monacom	₦ 4,190,000	₦ 2,228,000	₦ 4,615,000	₦ 2,756,000	₦ 3,123,000	₦ 1,464,000
22	ARM	₦ 4,536,000	₦ 1,412,000	₦ 4,313,000	₦ 1,130,000	₦ 3,700,000	₦ 3,196,000

IF

IF is arguably the most powerful function in Excel. It can do almost the impossible. And it's only limited by the creativity of the user. It allows you to check for a condition and specify what should be done when the condition is met and also what should be done when it is not met.

Here is the structure.

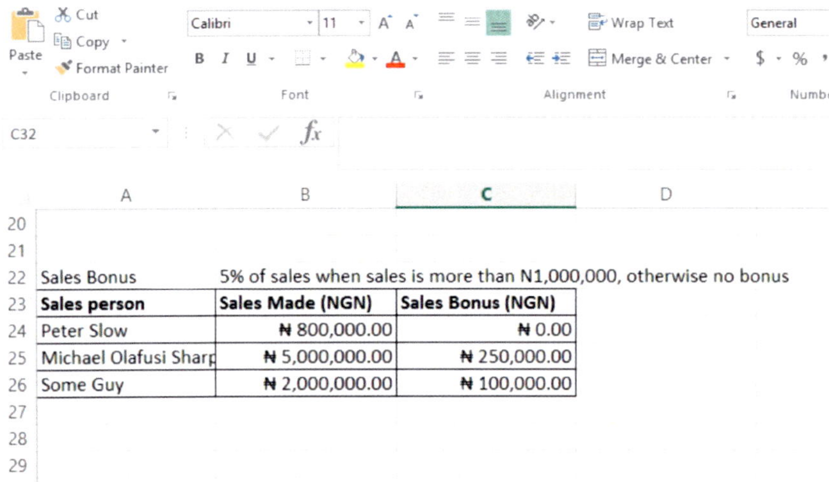

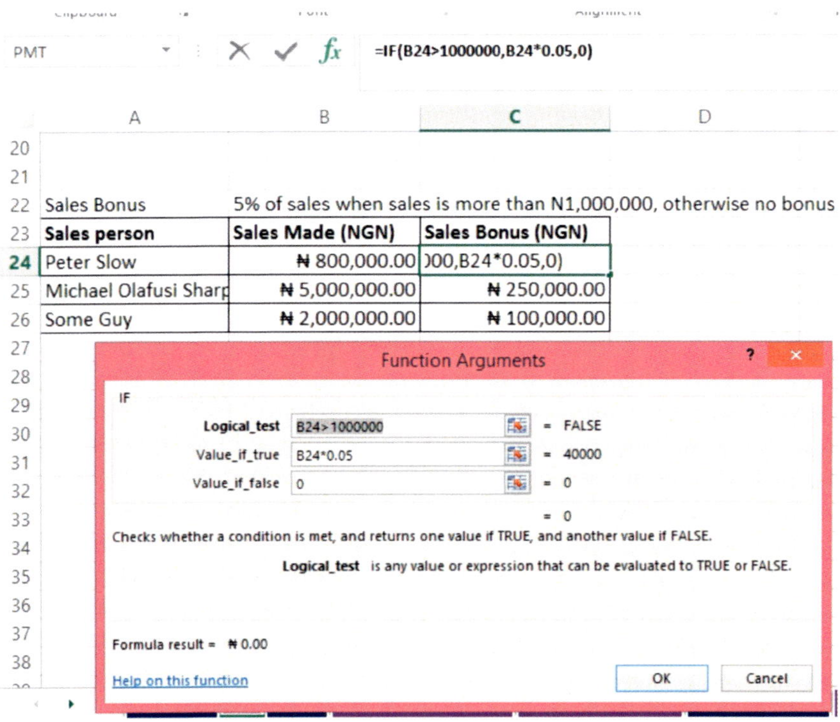

In the example above, we have specified a condition that only when the salesman makes more than 1 million naira worth of sales should he get the sales bonus of 5%. If he fails to meet that condition he is not entitled to any sales bonus.

COUNTIFS and SUMIFS

These combine an inbuilt if function with simple functions like count and sum.

A relevant example is the Pizza Sales record we used for PivotTable. We could have generated the same analysis without PivotTable by using the COUNTIFS and SUMIFS functions.

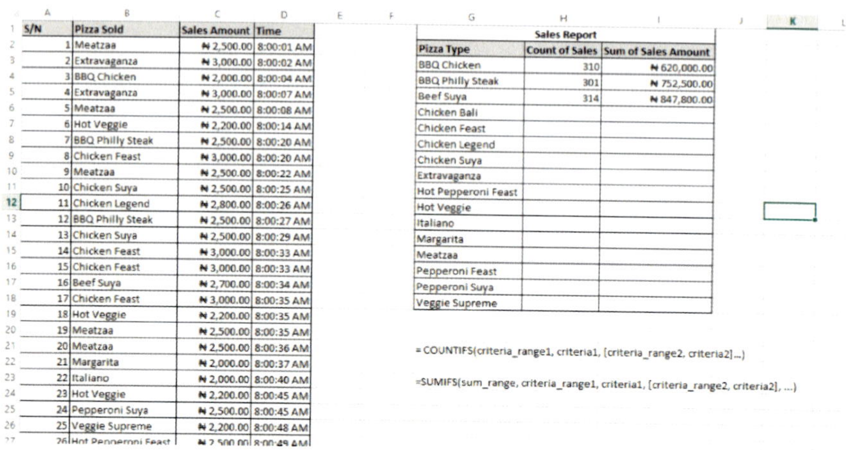

For the Count of Sales, the COUNTIFS structure is

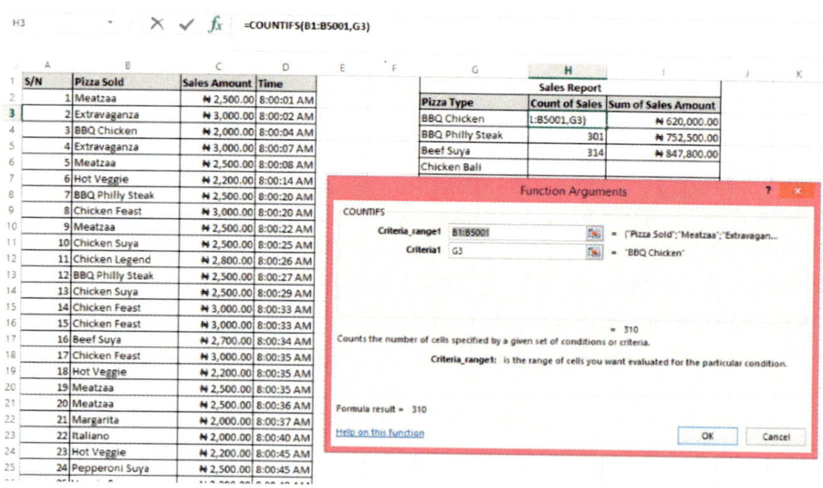

This will count cells between range B1 and B5001 where the cell entry is equal to the G3 value (BBQ Chicken). And it was replicated for the other pizza types.

For the Sum Of Sales Amount, the SUMIFS structure is

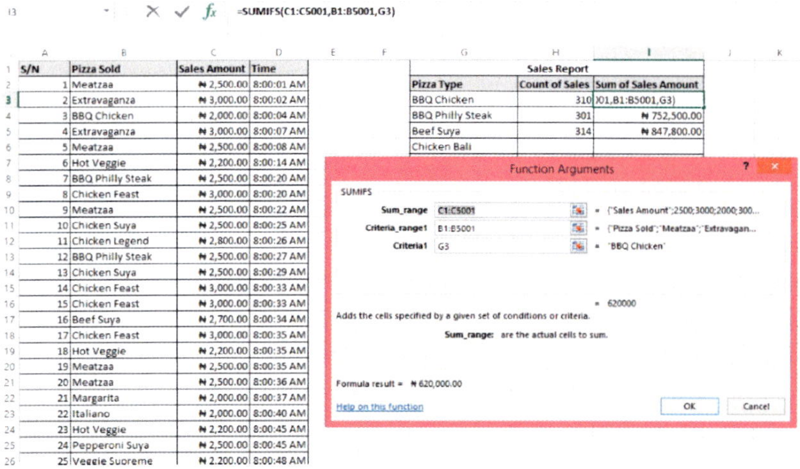

It will sum values in cells C1 to C5001 where the cells in B1 to B5001 has cell entry equal to G3 (BBQ Chicken).

AVERAGEIFS

AVERAGEIFS is similar to SUMIFS. Generally, I think it is much less used than SUMIFS. In my several consulting jobs for clients I have used more of COUNTIFS and SUMIFS than AVERAGEIFS. It is particularly useful in performance analysis. An example is if you are a stock analyst and you want to find the profit margin for a particular industry. You will need to use AVERAGEIFS to specify which companies to include in the computation of the profit margin, and statistically, you can’t count or sum the individual profit margins, you have to average them.

Below is an example we’ll use for illustration.

Company	Industry	Profit Margin
Mobil	Oil & Gas	23%
Dangote Cement	Manufacturing	15%
Access Bank	Finance	10%
Julius Berger	Construction	15%
Oando	Oil & Gas	23%
Arik Air	Airline	12%
NBC	Food & Beverage	7%
Nigerian Breweries	Food & Beverage	10%
La Casera	Food & Beverage	21%
Lafarge	Manufacturing	12%
GTBank	Finance	23%
Aero Contractors	Airline	6%
Aiico Insurance	Finance	17%
Berger Paints	Manufacturing	25%
Cadbury	Food & Beverage	13%
Nestle	Food & Beverage	23%
PZ	Manufacturing	21%
Unilever	Manufacturing	24%
Total	Oil & Gas	22%
First Bank	Finance	14%
Dana Air	Airline	11%

So how do we find the profit margin performance for the Airline Industry? We have to use AVERAGEIFS.

Here is how it works: =AVERAGEIFS(average_range, criteria_range, criteria)

The average range in our case is the Profit Margin field. That is where the profit margin values we want to average are.

The criteria range is the Industry field. It is where we will identify the companies that fall under the airline industry.

The criterion we are looking for is Airline. But remember to put it in double quotes. All texts in a formula must be in double quotes.

The resulting formula will be: =AVERAGEIFS(C1:C22,B1:B22,"Airline")

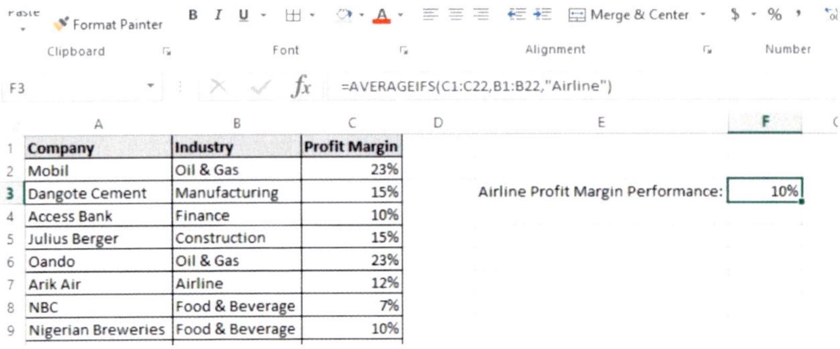

Company	Industry	Profit Margin
Mobil	Oil & Gas	23%
Dangote Cement	Manufacturing	15%
Access Bank	Finance	10%
Julius Berger	Construction	15%
Oando	Oil & Gas	23%
Arik Air	Airline	12%
NBC	Food & Beverage	7%
Nigerian Breweries	Food & Beverage	10%

IFERROR

A lot of times your formulas in Excel will generate an error. It could be for reasons beyond your control: a missing record, wrong value type or a problematic entry. IFERROR lets you trap errors and display something more meaningful or less annoying than the cryptic error entry Excel gives you.

Its syntax is: =IFERROR(value, value_if_error)

An example to illustrate its use is given below.

	A	B	C	D
1	**State**	**Population**	**%age Value**	
2	Lagos	16,768,590	26%	
3	Kano	13,001,029	20%	
4	Kaduna	12,912,425	20%	
5	Enugu	NA	#VALUE!	
6	Ogun	9,096,178	14%	
7	Rivers	6,507,834	10%	
8	Niger	6,193,390	10%	
9	**Total**	**64,479,446**	**100%**	
10				
11				

Notice that we have no value for Enugu state and it is generating an error in the %age value field. It would be nicer to have left a blank space or a hyphen instead of an error code in the Enugu row.

IFERROR can help us with that. And here is how we would do it.

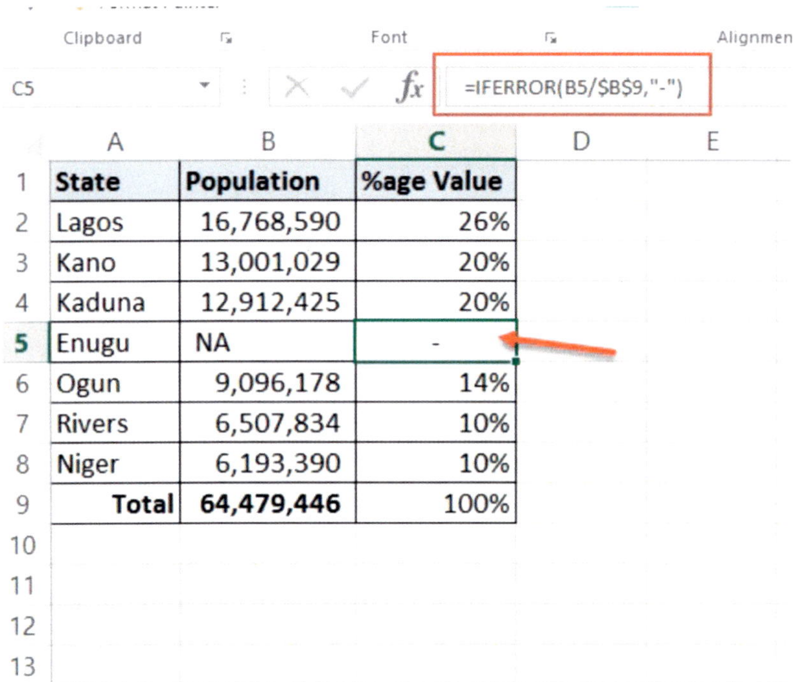

	A	B	C
1	**State**	**Population**	**%age Value**
2	Lagos	16,768,590	26%
3	Kano	13,001,029	20%
4	Kaduna	12,912,425	20%
5	Enugu	NA	-
6	Ogun	9,096,178	14%
7	Rivers	6,507,834	10%
8	Niger	6,193,390	10%
9	**Total**	**64,479,446**	100%

=IFERROR(B5/$B$9,"-") which is simply telling Excel to calculate B5/$B$9 and if the result is an error it should put a hyphen in the cell instead of an error code.

CONCATENATE

Concatenate lets you join entries in different cells.

The syntax is =CONCATENATE(text1, text2, ...)

A clear example is what we have below.

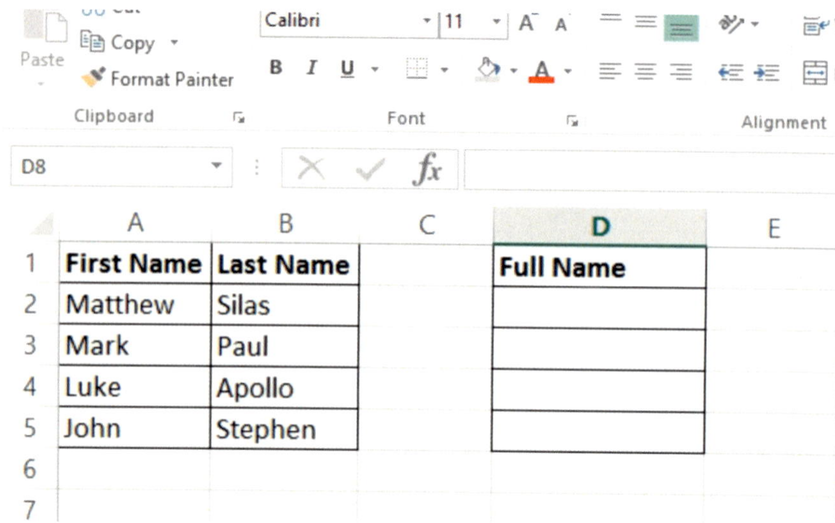

How do we join the First Name and Last Name to get the Full Name? This is what CONCATENATE does for us.

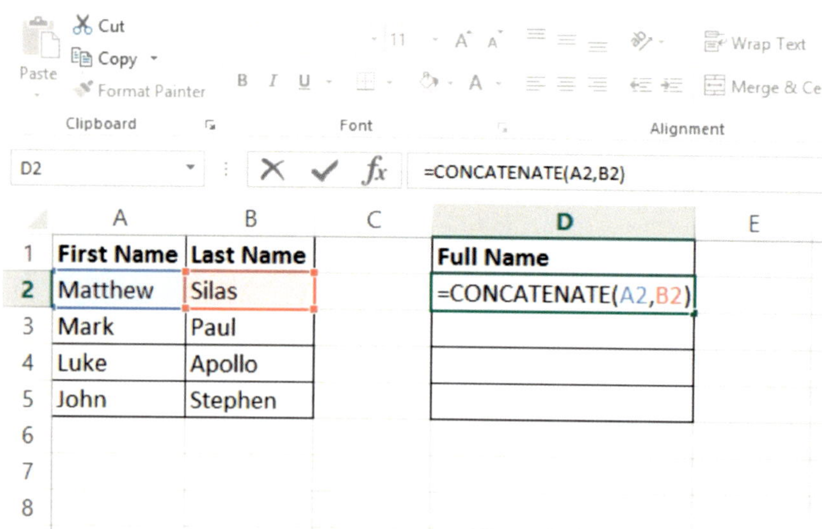

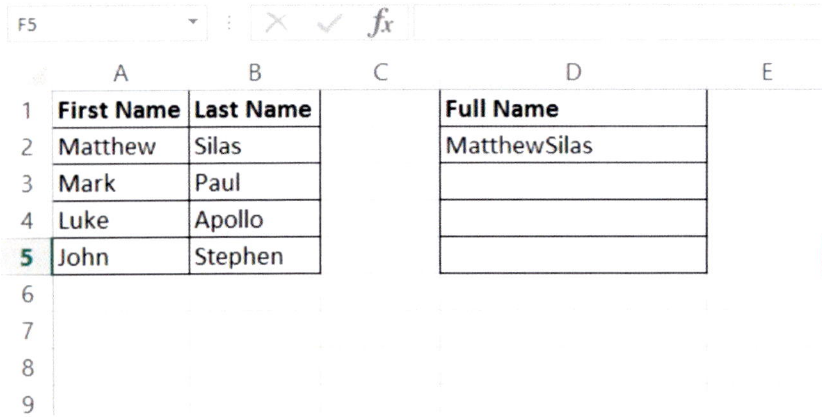

But there is a small problem: no space between the first name and the last name. How do we fix this?

CONCATENATE can handle that. You are not restricted to joining cell entries. You can put in your own text and that's what we will do to fix the problem we have.

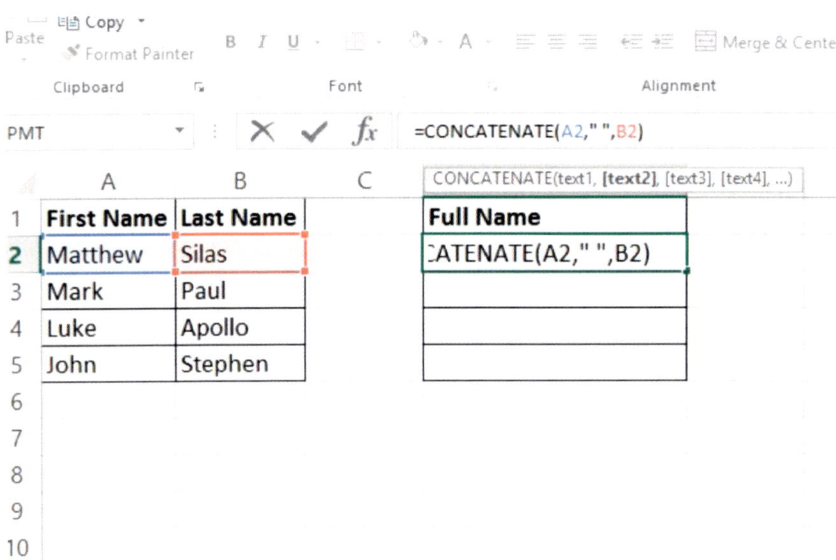

We have added a space between the first name and the last name. We added it as a text entry, hence the double quotes encapsulating it.

=CONCATENATE(A2," ",B2)

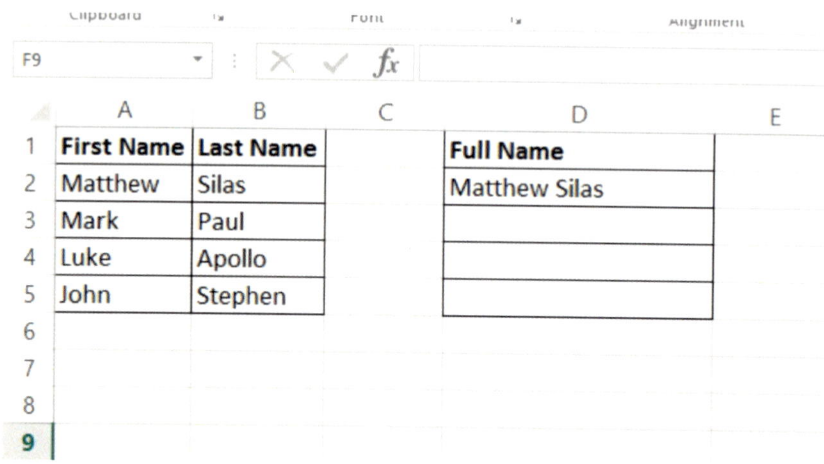

	A	B	C	D	E
1	**First Name**	**Last Name**		**Full Name**	
2	Matthew	Silas		Matthew Silas	
3	Mark	Paul			
4	Luke	Apollo			
5	John	Stephen			
6					
7					
8					
9					

And that's how you can join different cell entries using CONCATENATE.

I'm sure you are wondering why the formula had to be a long name one. Well, there is a very short alternative operator: &.

We can simply join the different cell entries by putting an ampersand (&) between the entries. So replacing our long formula, we will have: =A3&" "&B3

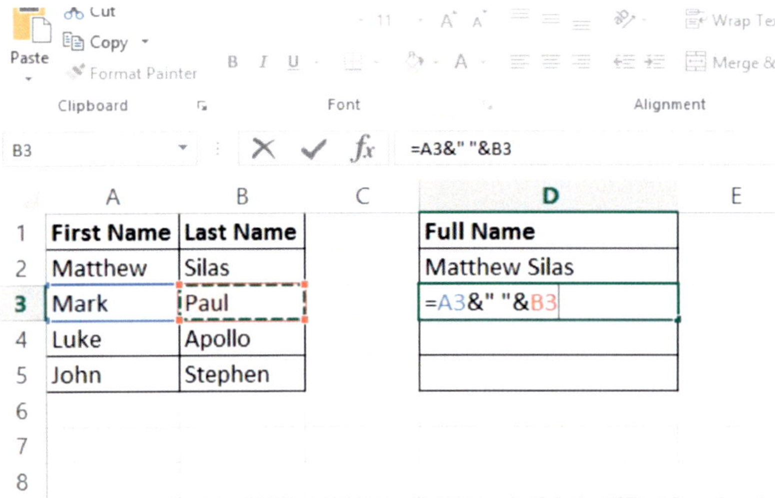

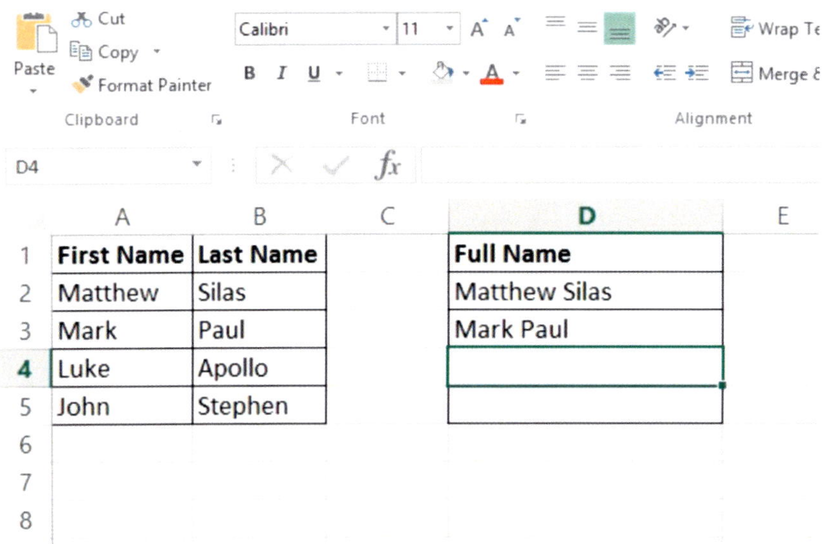

Great, right?

All that is left is to drag the formula down for the other entries.

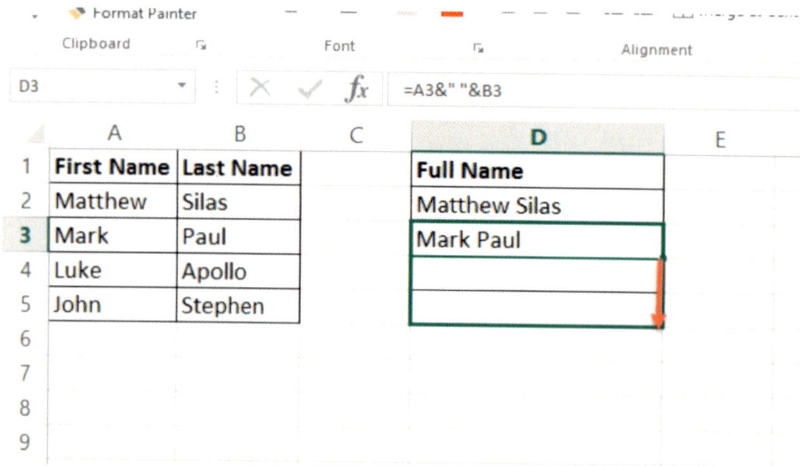

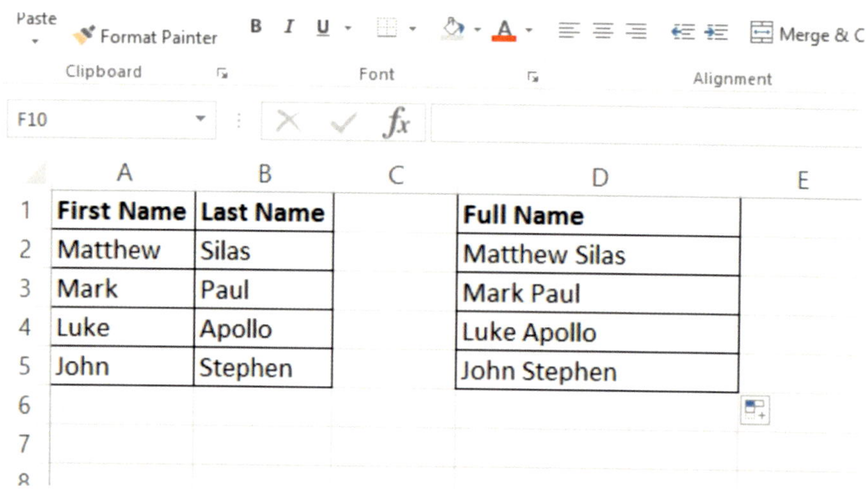

LEFT, RIGHT and MID

There will be times you need to extract a portion of a cell's entry. A practical case was a template I built for a telecoms company to determine the least cost partner to use for each international call destination. So I had to use a formula to pick out the country codes and check which provider is the cheapest to use to that destination.

I have prepared a sample data for a simple illustration. It is the matriculation number of the university I attended. It is a clever combination of department name, year of admission and candidate number.

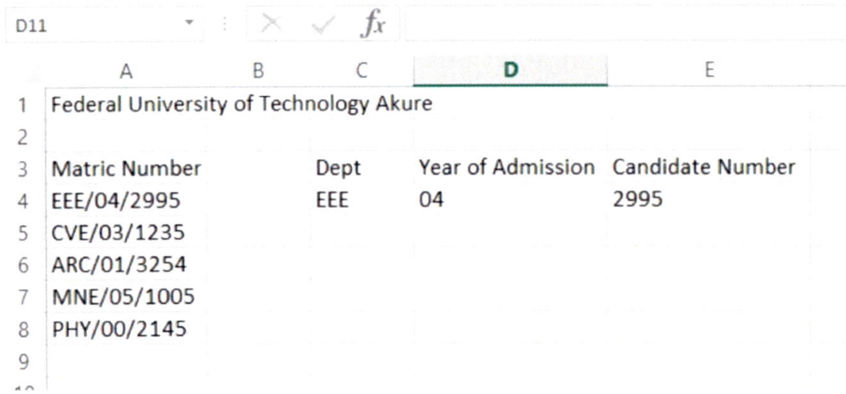

D11

	A	B	C	D	E
1	Federal University of Technology Akure				
2					
3	Matric Number		Dept	Year of Admission	Candidate Number
4	EEE/04/2995		EEE	04	2995
5	CVE/03/1235				
6	ARC/01/3254				
7	MNE/05/1005				
8	PHY/00/2145				
9					

The first three characters are the department acronym. The two digits sandwiched between two forward slashes are the year of admission and the last four characters are the candidate number.

We are going to use LEFT to extract the department name, RIGHT to extract the candidate number and MID to extract the admission year.

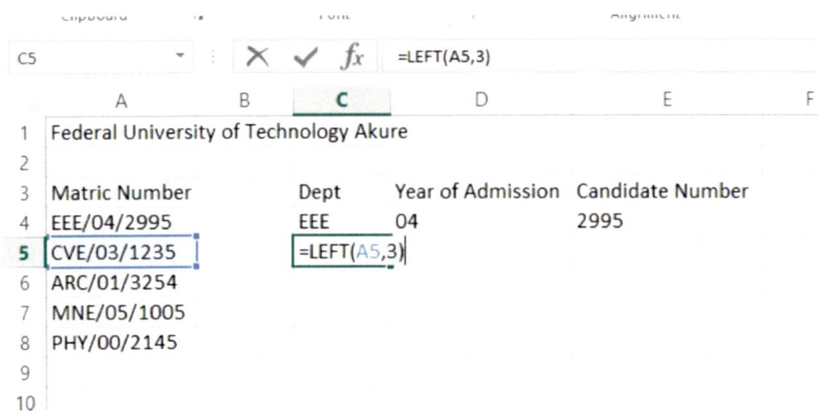

C5 =LEFT(A5,3)

	A	B	C	D	E	F
1	Federal University of Technology Akure					
2						
3	Matric Number		Dept	Year of Admission	Candidate Number	
4	EEE/04/2995		EEE	04	2995	
5	CVE/03/1235		=LEFT(A5,3)			
6	ARC/01/3254					
7	MNE/05/1005					
8	PHY/00/2145					
9						
10						

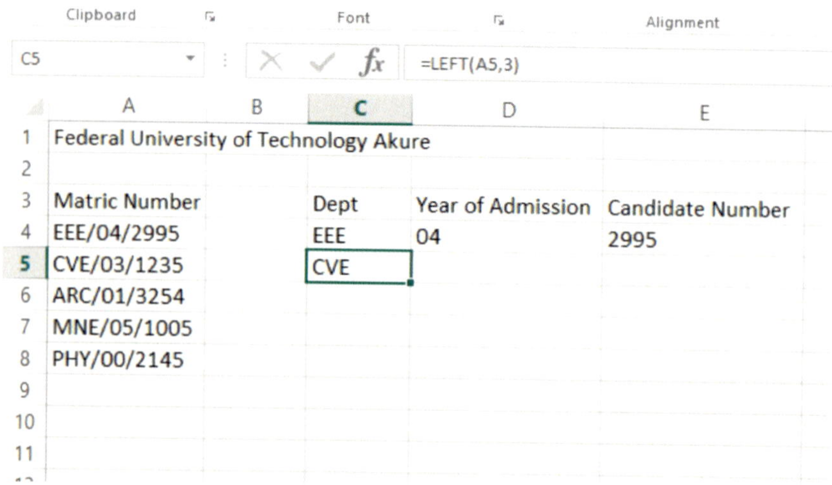

It is a very easy to understand formula: =LEFT(A5,3). You simply specify the cell you want to extract from and specify the number of characters you want to extract starting from the leftmost character.

In this example, it's three characters we want to extract starting from the left (beginning of the cell entry).

Now let's proceed to extracting the candidate number. This time we want to extract starting from the right, four characters. So we will use RIGHT.

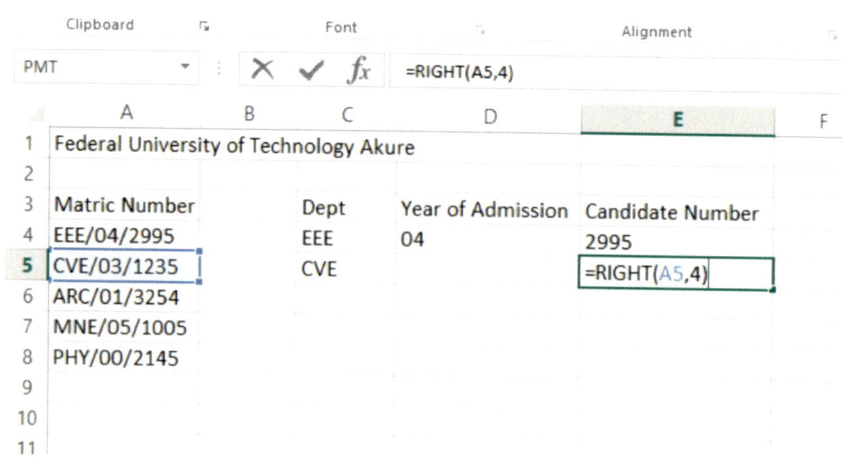

G7 fx

	A	B	C	D	E	F
1	Federal University of Technology Akure					
2						
3	Matric Number		Dept	Year of Admission	Candidate Number	
4	EEE/04/2995		EEE	04	2995	
5	CVE/03/1235		CVE		1235	
6	ARC/01/3254					
7	MNE/05/1005					
8	PHY/00/2145					
9						
10						
11						

=RIGHT(A5,4)

Also very easy to understand.

Finally, let's extract the admission year. It requires the MID formula. It's a little not easy to grasp like the LEFT and RIGHT. It requires that you specify the starting point for the extraction. The concept is very easy to understand, the part that trips a lot of people up is how the starting point is determined. You have to count from the first character (from the left) to the first character you want to extract.

In this example, we will count till the first character of the year. It is the character number 5. Then you'll proceed to specify the number of characters you want to extract (2 in our case).

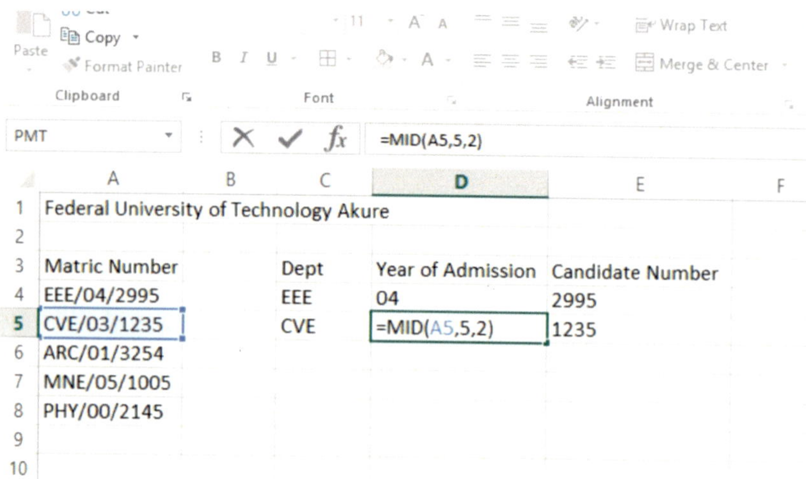

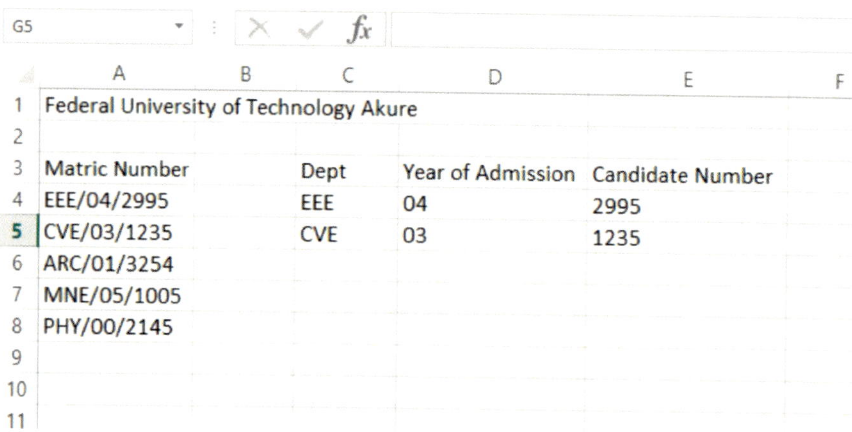

=MID(A5,5,2)

A5 is the cell we are extracting from.

5 is the starting point.

2 is the number of characters we want to extract.

TODAY, DAY, MONTH and YEAR

Excel allows you to do a lot on dates. There is even a formula to call up today's date; it is aptly named TODAY(). You have to enter the brackets.

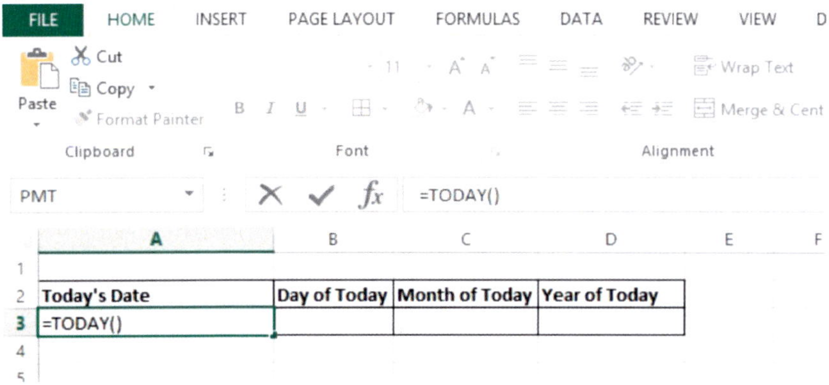

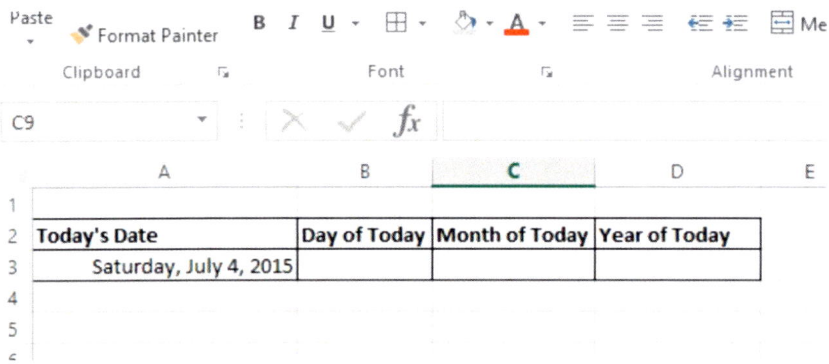

Then you can extract the day of the date, the month of the date and the year of the date very easily.

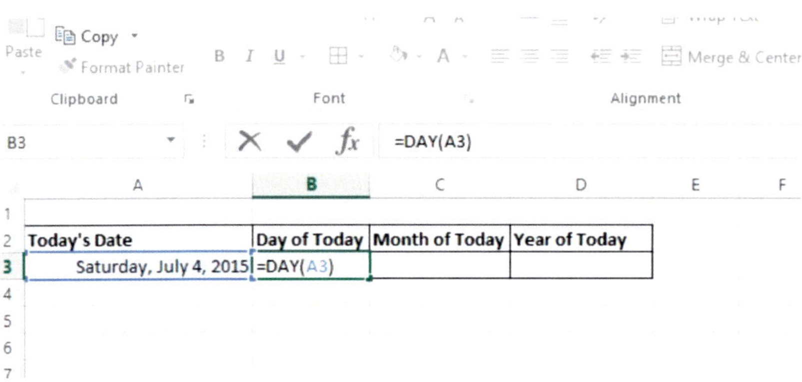

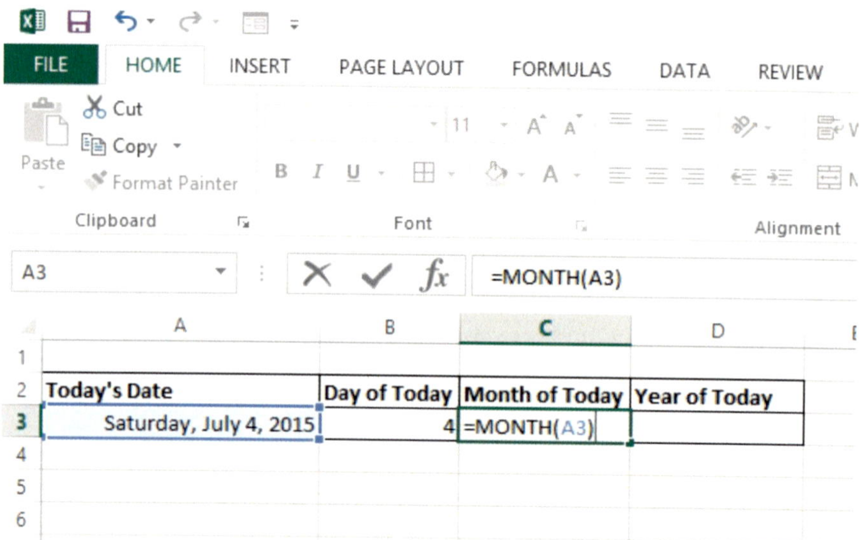
FILE
HOME
INSERT
PAGE LAYOUT
FORMULAS
DATA
REVIEW
Cut
Copy
Paste
Format Painter
Clipboard
Font
Alignment
A3
=MONTH(A3)
Today's Date
Day of Today
Month of Today
Year of Today
Saturday, July 4, 2015
4
=MONTH(A3)

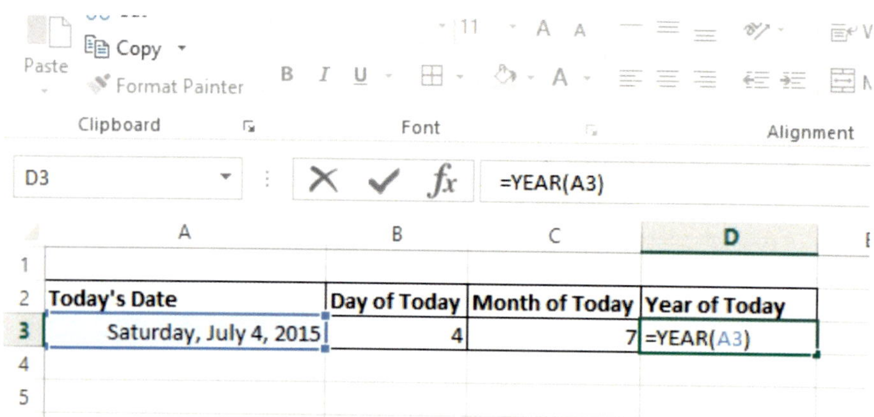
Copy
Paste
Format Painter
Clipboard
Font
Alignment
D3
=YEAR(A3)
Today's Date
Day of Today
Month of Today
Year of Today
Saturday, July 4, 2015
4
7
=YEAR(A3)

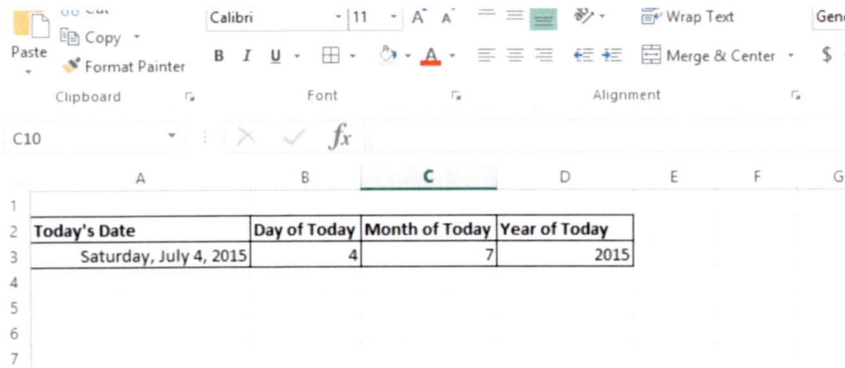

=DAY(A3)

=MONTH(A3)

=YEAR(A3)

A3 is the cell that has the date. And it works on dates you manually type or copy into Excel and not just the ones we use a formula like TODAY() to generate.

Finally, Excel lets you choose how a date should be displayed. Right click on the cell housing the date and click on Format Cells.

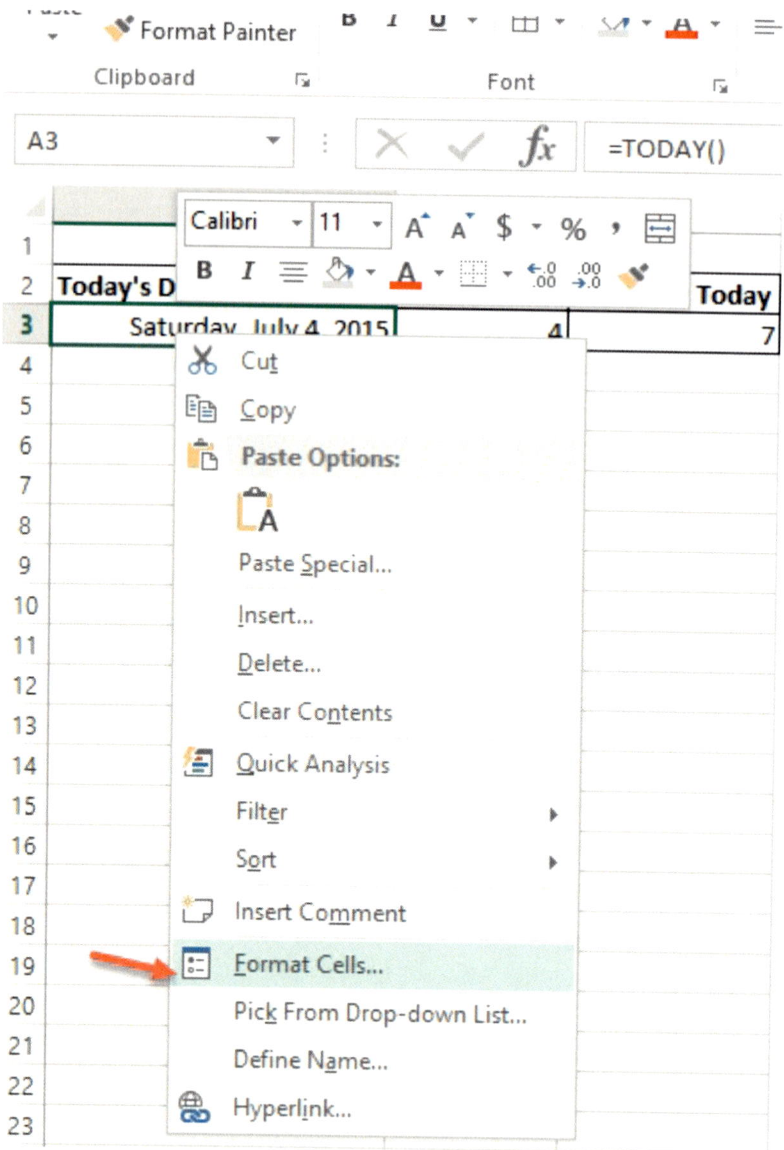
Format Painter
Clipboard
Font
A3
=TODAY()
Calibri
11
Today's D
Today
Saturday, July 4, 2015
4
7
Cut
Copy
Paste Options:
Paste Special...
Insert...
Delete...
Clear Contents
Quick Analysis
Filter
Sort
Insert Comment
Format Cells...
Pick From Drop-down List...
Define Name...
Hyperlink...

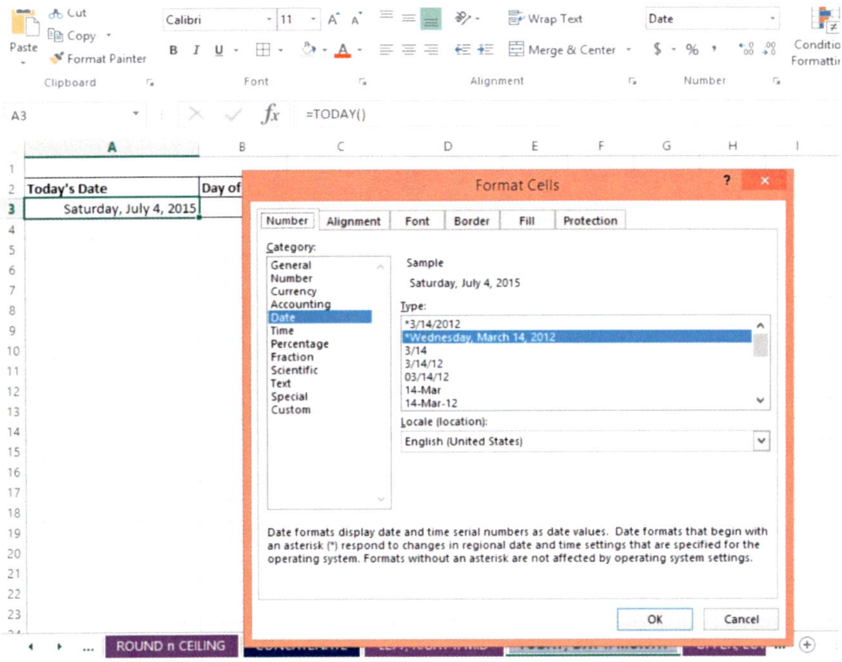

You can specify how it should be displayed.

UPPER, LOWER and PROPER

Ever tried changing a text from upper case to lower case in Excel? Too quickly people give up and conclude that it's not possible in Excel. Well, Excel has that functionality but as a formula.

UPPER converts a cell entry to all upper case.

LOWER converts a cell entry to all lower case.

Proper capitalizes the first letter of each word in the cell.

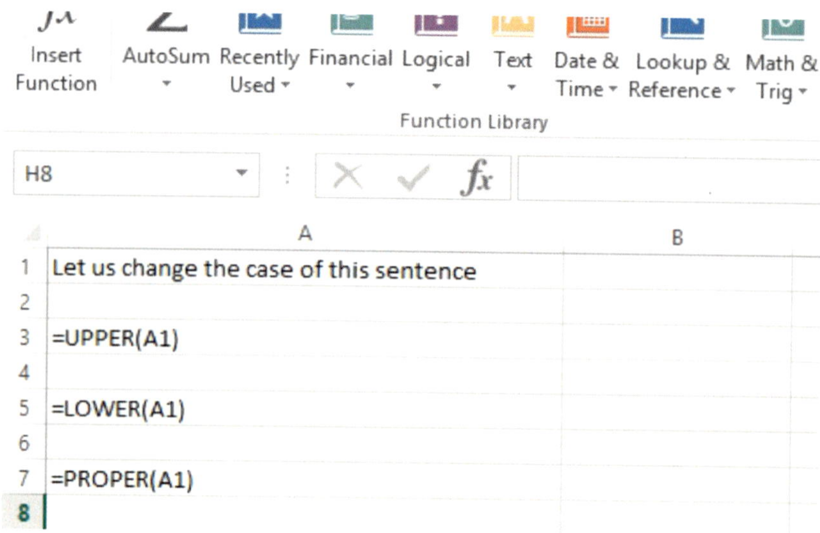

A1 is the cell entry we want to change the caps of.

See the results of the UPPER, LOWER and PROPER formulas below.

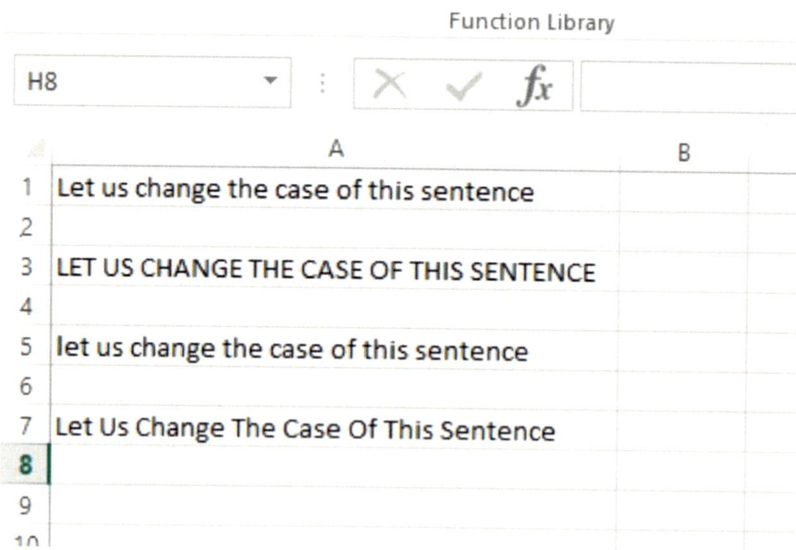

RAND and RANDBETWEEN

Wondered how I generated all the data I have been using for illustrations? Well, I used RAND and RANDBETWEEN for most of the numbers and even some of the texts (in conjunction with a magic formula called INDIRECT).

RAND() generates random decimal numbers that are greater than 0 but less than 1. Essentially, decimal numbers between 0 and 1 (0 and 1 non-included).

RANDBETWEEN(bottom_number, top_number) generates numbers between the bounds you specified as bottom and top.

Below is a relevant example. I have used the formulas to generate sales number and profit margin.

2			
3	**Sales Man**	**Sales Made**	**Profit Margin**
4	Mark David	=RANDBETWEEN(400000,800000)	=RAND()
5	Tunde Seun	=RANDBETWEEN(400000,800000)	=RAND()
6	Akeem Saliu	=RANDBETWEEN(400000,800000)	=RAND()
7	Ahmed Tafa	=RANDBETWEEN(400000,800000)	=RAND()
8	Obi Okonkwo	=RANDBETWEEN(400000,800000)	=RAND()
9	Uche Mba	=RANDBETWEEN(400000,800000)	=RAND()
10	Inam Effiong	=RANDBETWEEN(400000,800000)	=RAND()
11	Segun Azeez	=RANDBETWEEN(400000,800000)	=RAND()
12	Kola Adesida	=RANDBETWEEN(400000,800000)	=RAND()
13	Mark Femi	=RANDBETWEEN(400000,800000)	=RAND()
14	Seun Akinde	=RANDBETWEEN(400000,800000)	=RAND()
15	Lola Adigun	=RANDBETWEEN(400000,800000)	=RAND()
16	Nana Lolu	=RANDBETWEEN(400000,800000)	=RAND()

2			
3	**Sales Man**	**Sales Made**	**Profit Margin**
4	Mark David	₦ 401,083	73%
5	Tunde Seun	₦ 720,482	8%
6	Akeem Saliu	₦ 456,036	91%
7	Ahmed Tafa	₦ 716,166	76%
8	Obi Okonkwo	₦ 739,312	74%
9	Uche Mba	₦ 564,919	13%
10	Inam Effiong	₦ 544,028	94%
11	Segun Azeez	₦ 702,257	20%
12	Kola Adesida	₦ 799,302	1%
13	Mark Femi	₦ 693,876	59%
14	Seun Akinde	₦ 657,925	52%
15	Lola Adigun	₦ 487,943	99%
16	Nana Lolu	₦ 682,111	84%

CHOOSE

CHOOSE is one of the formulas dedicated to making your analysis life easier. You can easily do dynamic reports just by using CHOOSE.

I have an illustration we can all easily understand. It is Sam's todo list for the day. A list of 10 tasks he has arranged in the order he intends to carry them out today.

Task No	Description	Remark

Task No	Description	Remark
1	Call Customer XYZ	Done
2	Mail CEO about the deal requirements	Done
3	Call John's school principal	
4	Read a chapter in my MBA course material	
5	Finish the Strategy PPT Slides	
6	Send reminder about the 3:00pm meeting	
7	Send reminder about the 3:00pm meeting	
8	Skype call Ashish about the web app	
9	Call Wifey about the Mechanic's visit	
10	Do a 10mins brisk walk	

In reality, you would want to use CHOOSE for something more complex. But the concept is the same and once you grasp how to use it here, you can use it anywhere -- even for a list of 100,000 entries in a different Excel file.

Back to our illustration. Sam wants a simple way to see the progress he is making. He wants to type in a task number and see what it is about and if he has done it. And this where CHOOSE comes in very handy.

The way CHOOSE works is you specify the position of an item you want to pick and then the list of all the items. See below how Sam has used it to solve is problem.

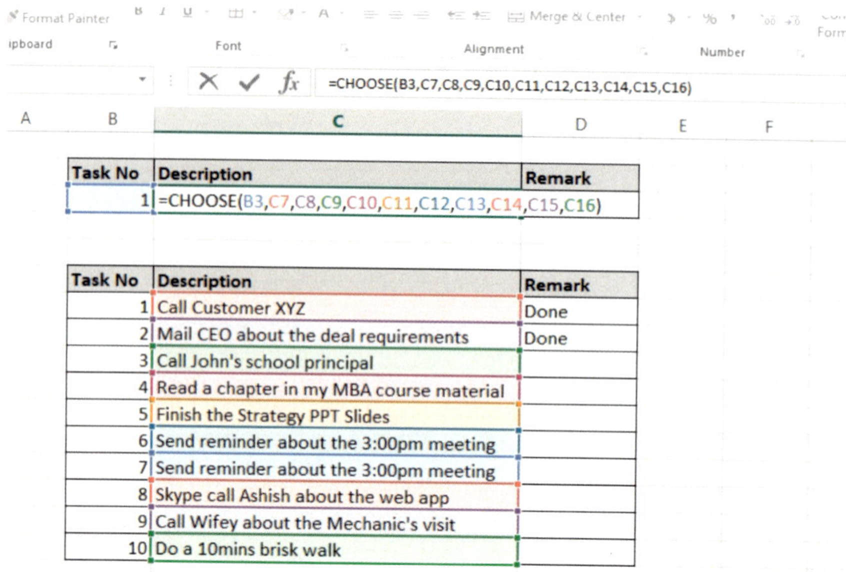

=CHOOSE(B3,C7,C8,C9,C10,C11,C12,C13,C14,C15,C16)

Task No	Description	Remark
1	=CHOOSE(B3,C7,C8,C9,C10,C11,C12,C13,C14,C15,C16)	

Task No	Description	Remark
1	Call Customer XYZ	Done
2	Mail CEO about the deal requirements	Done
3	Call John's school principal	
4	Read a chapter in my MBA course material	
5	Finish the Strategy PPT Slides	
6	Send reminder about the 3:00pm meeting	
7	Send reminder about the 3:00pm meeting	
8	Skype call Ashish about the web app	
9	Call Wifey about the Mechanic's visit	
10	Do a 10mins brisk walk	

CHOOSE checks for what number is in cell B3 and looks through the orderly list of Description field items, then returns the one that is in the position specified in cell B3. The one above should return "Call Customer XYZ" as that is what is in the position 1 in the Description field items.

And below is a similar formula for the Remark.

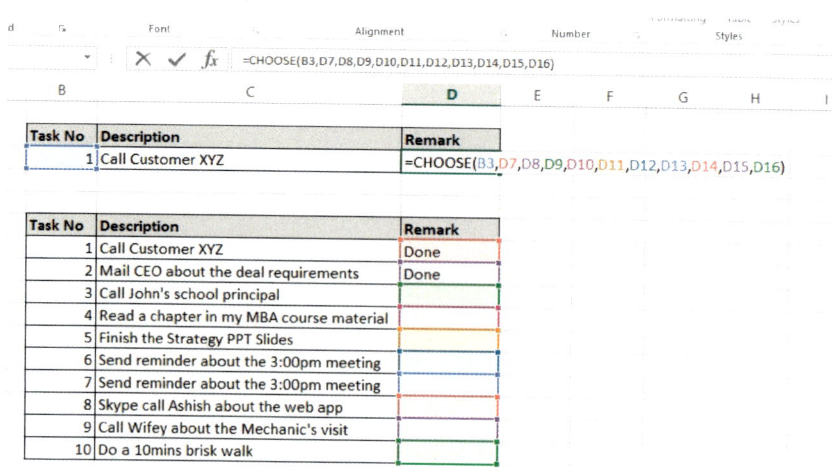

=CHOOSE(B3,D7,D8,D9,D10,D11,D12,D13,D14,D15,D16)

Task No	Description	Remark
1	Call Customer XYZ	=CHOOSE(B3,D7,D8,D9,D10,D11,D12,D13,D14,D15,D16)

Task No	Description	Remark
1	Call Customer XYZ	Done
2	Mail CEO about the deal requirements	Done
3	Call John's school principal	
4	Read a chapter in my MBA course material	
5	Finish the Strategy PPT Slides	
6	Send reminder about the 3:00pm meeting	
7	Send reminder about the 3:00pm meeting	
8	Skype call Ashish about the web app	
9	Call Wifey about the Mechanic's visit	
10	Do a 10mins brisk walk	

Let's specify Task number 4.

Task No	Description	Remark
4	Read a chapter in my MBA course material	-

Task No	Description	Remark
1	Call Customer XYZ	Done
2	Mail CEO about the deal requirements	Done
3	Call John's school principal	
4	Read a chapter in my MBA course material	
5	Finish the Strategy PPT Slides	
6	Send reminder about the 3:00pm meeting	
7	Send reminder about the 3:00pm meeting	
8	Skype call Ashish about the web app	
9	Call Wifey about the Mechanic's visit	
10	Do a 10mins brisk walk	

Let's specify Task number 8.

Task No	Description	Remark
8	Skype call Ashish about the web app	-

Task No	Description	Remark
1	Call Customer XYZ	Done
2	Mail CEO about the deal requirements	Done
3	Call John's school principal	
4	Read a chapter in my MBA course material	
5	Finish the Strategy PPT Slides	
6	Send reminder about the 3:00pm meeting	
7	Send reminder about the 3:00pm meeting	
8	Skype call Ashish about the web app	
9	Call Wifey about the Mechanic's visit	
10	Do a 10mins brisk walk	

Another interesting use of CHOOSE is in a Financial Model to select different projections scenarios. And that's it for choose.

SUMPRODUCT

SUMPRODUCT is one of Microsoft Excel's magic tool. It is just as powerful as the user's creativity (like the IF formula). I will start with a simple example to help you grasp how it works.

Let's say you own a grocery store and sell five product types. Every day you fill an Excel report template that already has the product names and prices. All you have to do is fill in the respective quantities bought and have the total sales for that day automatically computed for you.

N	O	P
Grocery Store A		
Product	Price	Quantity Sold
Product A	100	143
Product B	50	73
Product C	200	65
Product D	250	133
Total Sales:		

Ordinarily, you will have to compute the sales for each product by multiplying the price by quantity, and then sum them up to get the total sales.

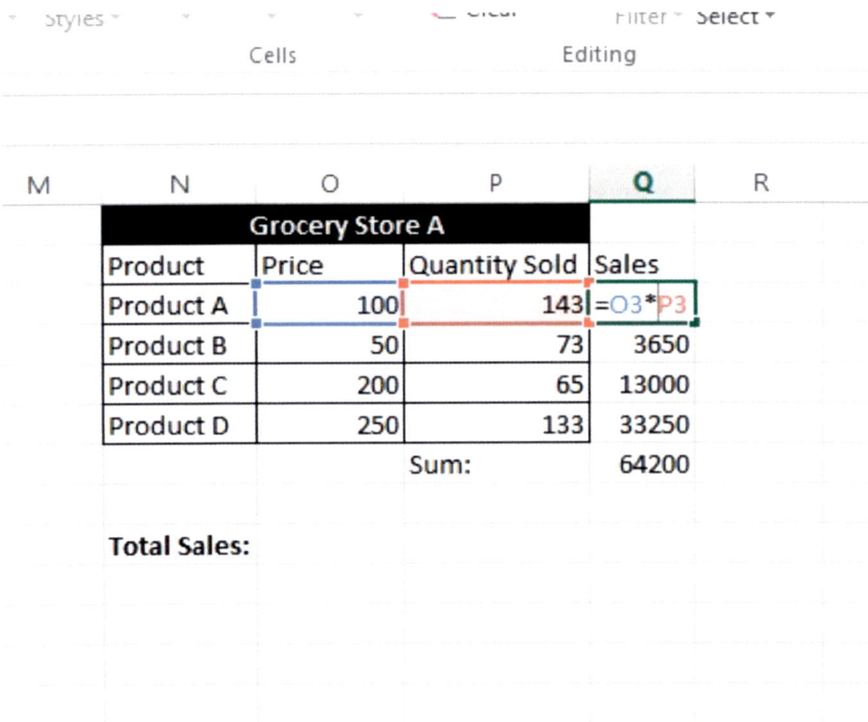

Grocery Store A			
Product	Price	Quantity Sold	Sales
Product A	100	143	=O3*P3
Product B	50	73	3650
Product C	200	65	13000
Product D	250	133	33250
		Sum:	64200

Total Sales:

However, with SUMPRODUCT you can get it done in one step without having to compute the sales of each product individually.

You simply tell Excel to sum the products of Price and Quantity: SUMPRODUCT

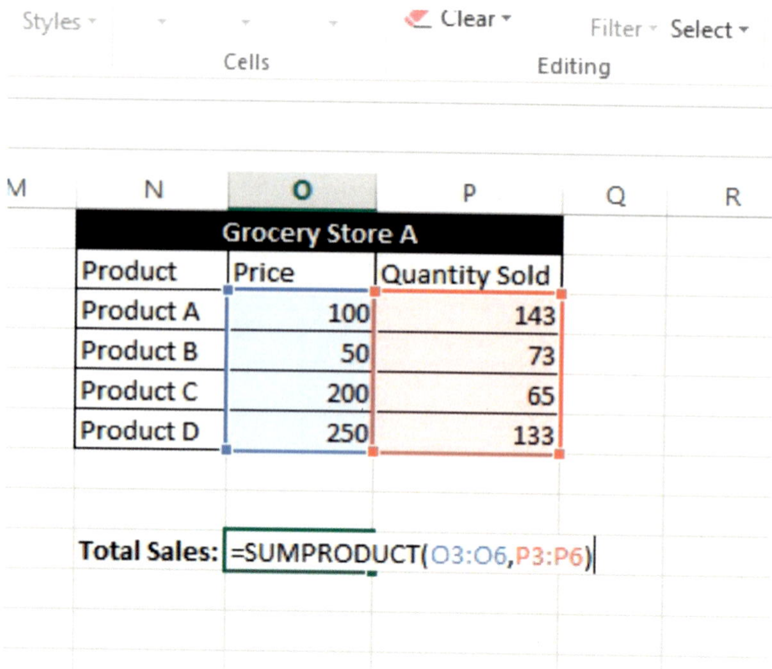

Grocery Store A		
Product	Price	Quantity Sold
Product A	100	143
Product B	50	73
Product C	200	65
Product D	250	133

Total Sales: =SUMPRODUCT(O3:O6,P3:P6)

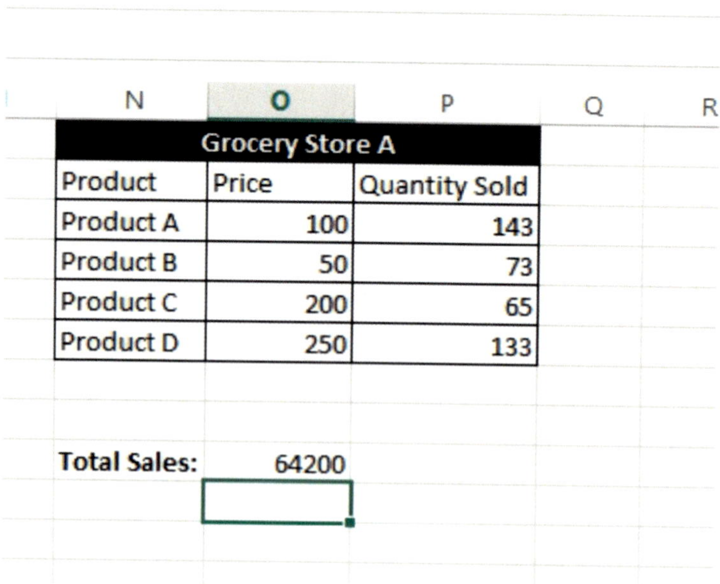

Grocery Store A		
Product	Price	Quantity Sold
Product A	100	143
Product B	50	73
Product C	200	65
Product D	250	133

Total Sales: 64200

Now you get how SUMPRODUCT works. Next, I will show you the more magical use of SUMPRODUCT

So let's say you manage a sales team and they sell two products. Every month, you get the report of the sales from each person which you combine to have a consolidated sales report.

Sales Person	Product	January	February	March	May	June	July
John	Detol	208	182	107	253	134	259
Mark	Close Up	109	246	381	280	250	143
Kenny	Detol	253	311	336	209	134	177
Taiwo	Close Up	353	356	348	301	305	211
Toyin	Detol	85	134	270	209	183	247
Felix	Close Up	145	375	336	194	113	254
John	Detol	206	260	244	109	320	344
Mark	Close Up	125	341	80	264	146	248
Kenny	Detol	247	155	376	208	210	89
Kenny	Close Up	111	271	322	106	244	111
Taiwo	Detol	193	357	164	278	255	180
Toyin	Close Up	337	249	110	120	178	222

As part of your team building strategy and sales improving tactic, you do an in-depth monthly performance report of each sales person per product with recommendations of what they could have done better. And to make this report, you constantly find yourself picking the sales for a month for a product by each salesperson. Like a probe into each person's sales figures. So what if you want something that will help you automate part of that probing by showing you total sales by a particular sales person per specified product and specified month.

N9

	A	B	C	D	E	F	G	H	I	J	K
1	Sales Person	Product	January	February	March	May	June	July			
2	John	Detol	208	182	107	253	134	259		Probe Panel	
3	Mark	Close Up	109	246	381	280	250	143		Sales Person	John
4	Kenny	Detol	253	311	336	209	134	177		Product	Detol
5	Taiwo	Close Up	353	356	348	301	305	211		Month	March
6	Toyin	Detol	85	134	270	209	183	247		Sales Quantity	
7	Felix	Close Up	145	375	336	194	113	254			
8	John	Detol	206	260	244	109	320	344			
9	Mark	Close Up	125	341	80	264	146	248			
10	Kenny	Detol	247	155	376	208	210	89			
11	Kenny	Close Up	111	271	322	106	244	111			
12	Taiwo	Detol	193	357	164	278	255	180			
13	Toyin	Close Up	337	249	110	120	178	222			

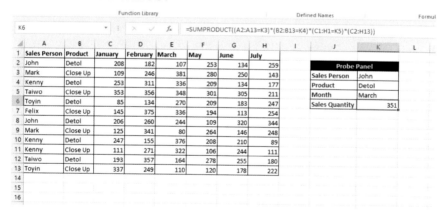

A formula that you can supply the person, the product and the month, and it will pick for you the total sales figure. Something like VLOOKUP except that VLOOKUP doesn't accept multiple lookup criteria and do a sum. So what formula would you use?

The answer: SUMPRODUCT

Function Library   Defined Names   Formul

K6   =SUMPRODUCT((A2:A13=K3)*(B2:B13=K4)*(C1:H1=K5)*(C2:H13))

	A	B	C	D	E	F	G	H	I	J	K
1	Sales Person	Product	January	February	March	May	June	July			
2	John	Detol	208	182	107	253	134	259		Probe Panel	
3	Mark	Close Up	109	246	381	280	250	143		Sales Person	John
4	Kenny	Detol	253	311	336	209	134	177		Product	Detol
5	Taiwo	Close Up	353	356	348	301	305	211		Month	March
6	Toyin	Detol	85	134	270	209	183	247		Sales Quantity	351
7	Felix	Close Up	145	375	336	194	113	254			
8	John	Detol	206	260	244	109	320	344			
9	Mark	Close Up	125	341	80	264	146	248			
10	Kenny	Detol	247	155	376	208	210	89			
11	Kenny	Close Up	111	271	322	106	244	111			
12	Taiwo	Detol	193	357	164	278	255	180			
13	Toyin	Close Up	337	249	110	120	178	222			

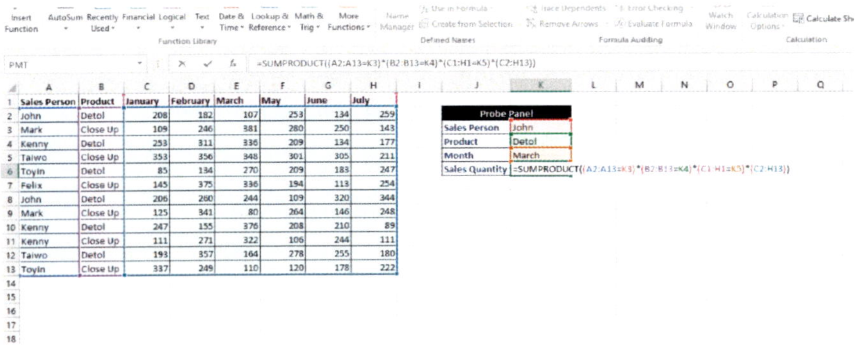

Sales Person	Product	January	February	March	May	June	July
John	Detol	208	182	107	253	134	259
Mark	Close Up	109	246	381	280	250	143
Kenny	Detol	253	311	336	209	134	177
Taiwo	Close Up	353	356	348	301	305	211
Toyin	Detol	85	134	270	209	183	247
Felix	Close Up	145	375	336	194	113	254
John	Detol	206	260	244	109	320	344
Mark	Close Up	125	341	80	264	146	248
Kenny	Detol	247	155	376	208	210	89
Kenny	Close Up	111	271	322	106	244	111
Taiwo	Detol	193	357	164	278	255	180
Toyin	Close Up	337	249	110	120	178	222

Probe Panel	
Sales Person	John
Product	Detol
Month	March
Sales Quantity	=SUMPRODUCT((A2:A13=K3)*(B2:B13=K4)*(C1:H1=K5)*(C2:H13))

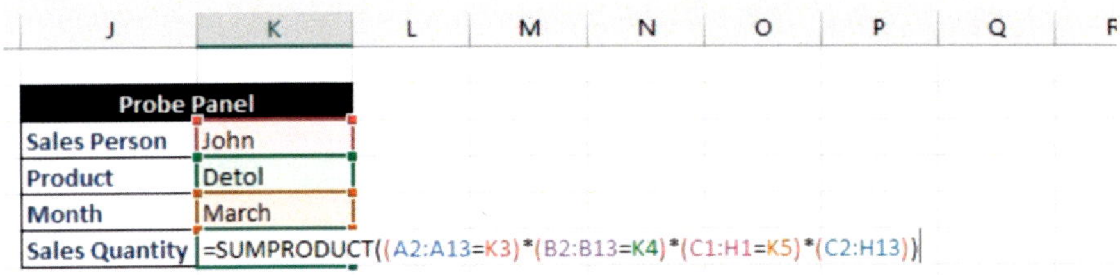

Probe Panel	
Sales Person	John
Product	Detol
Month	March
Sales Quantity	=SUMPRODUCT((A2:A13=K3)*(B2:B13=K4)*(C1:H1=K5)*(C2:H13))

Don't be put off by the length or complexity of the formula. It is easy to grasp. What I more importantly want you to pay attention to is that whenever you have a table and want to pick a value (numeric value and involving a summation) based on multiple criteria that VLOOKUP can't handle, then turn to SUMPRODUCT.

And here is how the formula works:
=SUMPRODUCT((A2:A13=K3)*(B2:B13=K4)*(C1:H1=K5)*(C2:H13))

(A2:A13=K3) checks for where the Sales Person field matches the name you provided in cell K3. Likewise, (B2:B13=K4) checks for where the Product field matches the product name provided in cell K4. And (C1:H1=K5) checks for where the month field has the month provided in cell K5. Finally, by multiplying them together and with the sales value range, (C2:H13), Excel will only pick values that match the criteria we have set-up and sum them up.

To make it clearer, here is the screenshot of what Evaluate Formula shows towards the last calculation step. Notice that only places that don't match our conditions have zeros.

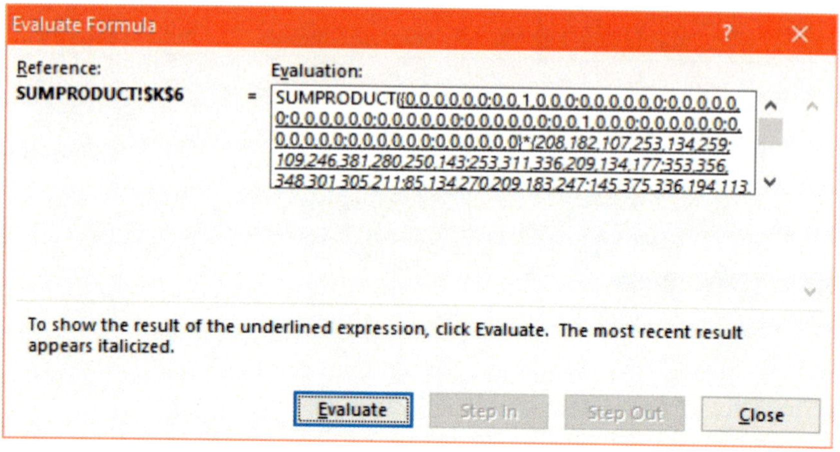

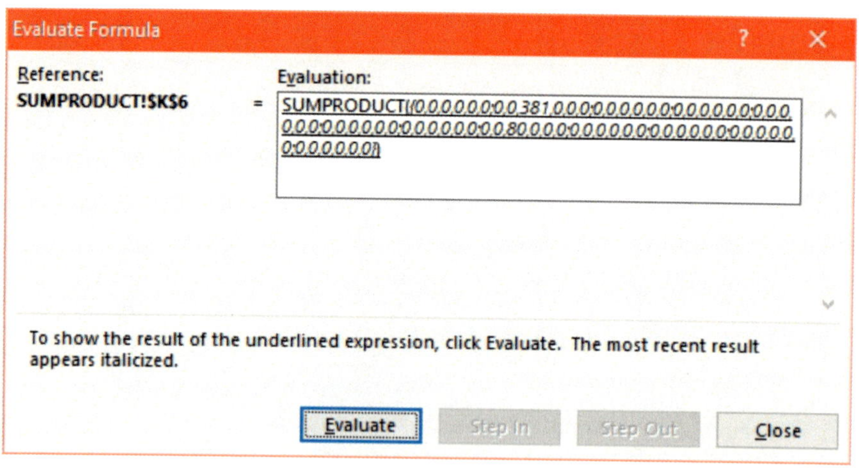

And that's the beauty of SUMPRODUCT. I find myself using it a lot for creating dashboards/templates where I am summing values that meet many conditions across rows and columns (like we have for product name across rows and month across columns) which SUMIFS cannot do (SUMMIFS can only work across rows or columns but not both at once).

SIX NEW USEFUL FORMULAS IN EXCEL 2016

Microsoft added 6 new very useful functions to Microsoft Excel 2016. They are mainly based on Microsoft Excel user community requests. You too can request for any new function or tool in Excel via https://excel.uservoice.com/

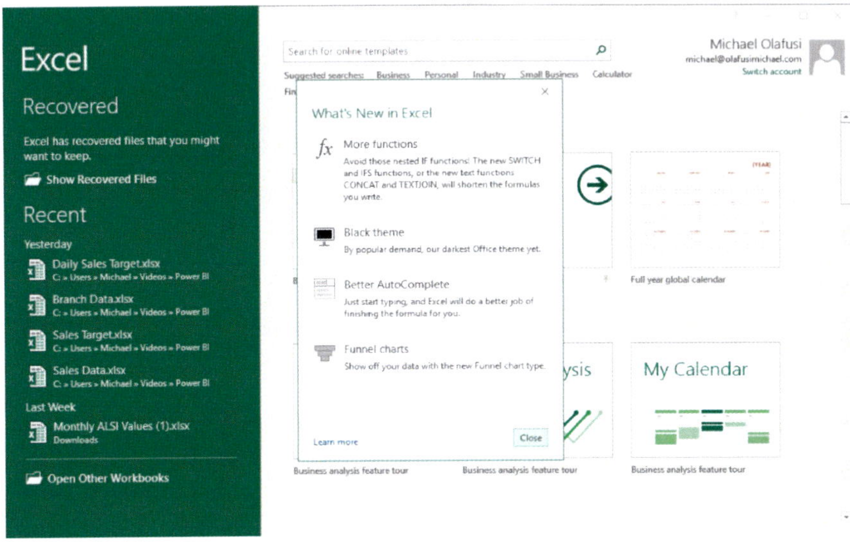

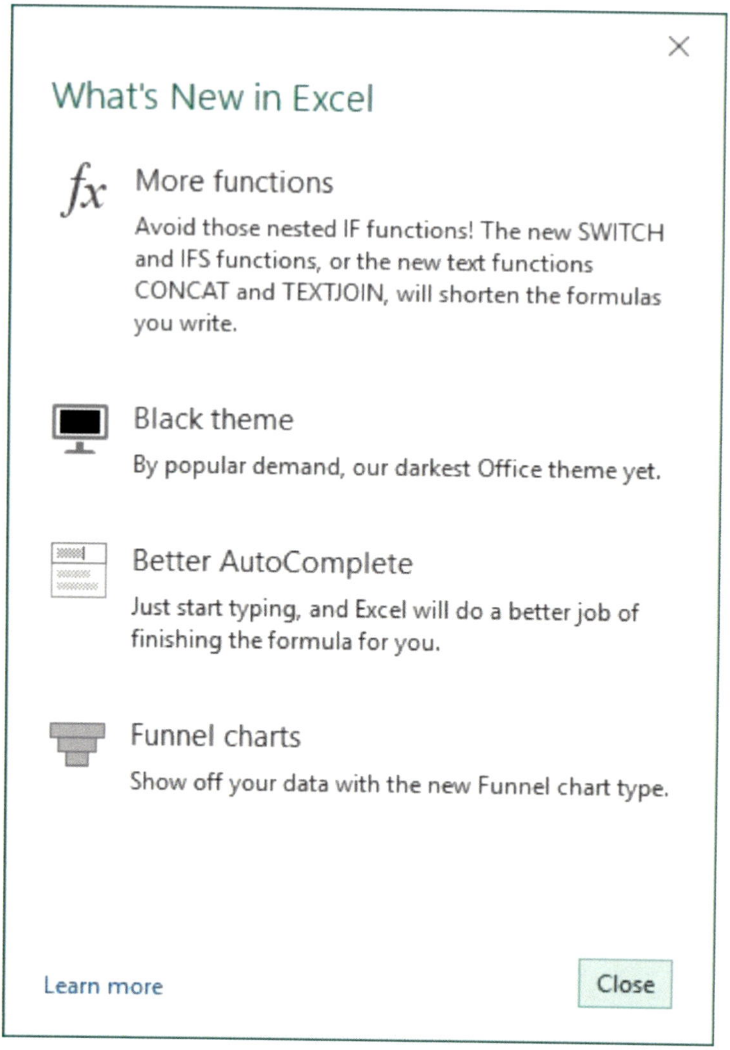

CONCAT

Two complaints I hear people make a lot about CONCATENATE (the Excel function that lets you join the values/texts in different cells) are that why is the name that long? and can't we select a range?

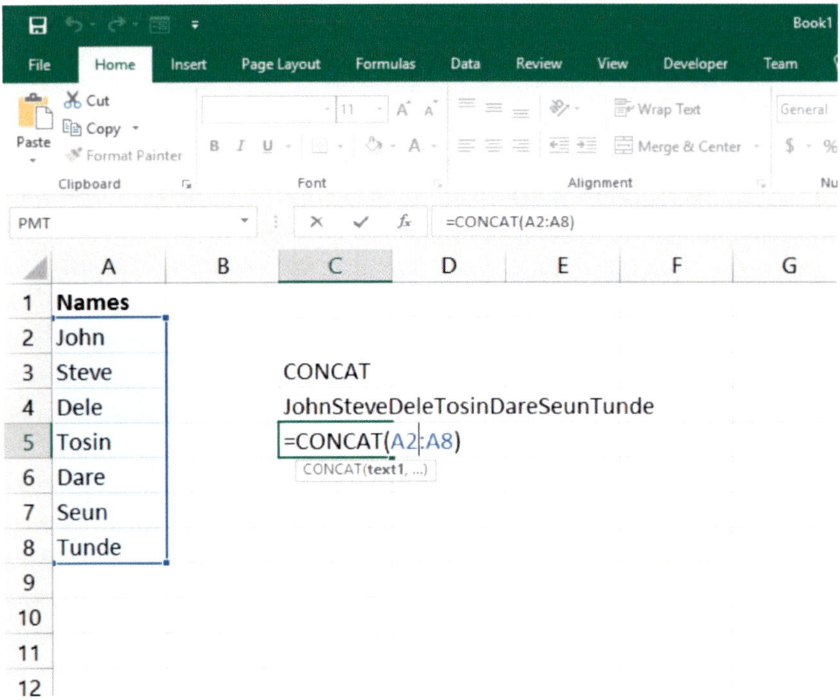

Now Microsoft has nifty fixed those two issues in one cool function: CONCAT

CONCAT is short to write and allows you join entries selected as a range.

TEXTJOIN

This takes CONCAT to a new level. So what if you want to put a comma and a space between the names as you are joining them? That is what TEXTJOIN enables you to do.

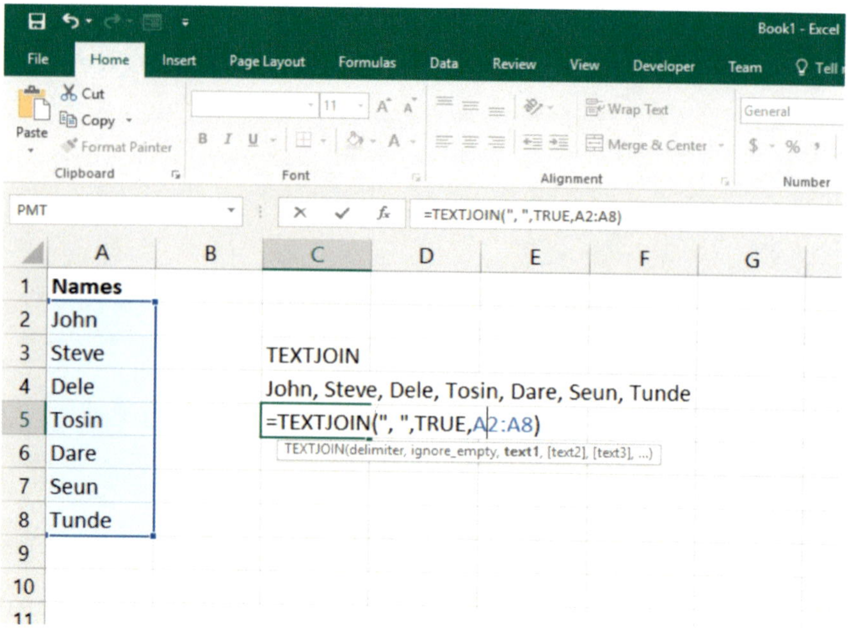

IFS

The formula that gets most people confused the most in Excel is nested IF. People find it hard to process the numerous brackets and IF statements that characterize a nested IF function. Now there's some relief. Excel has introduced IFS to help combat the strain of untangling brackets.

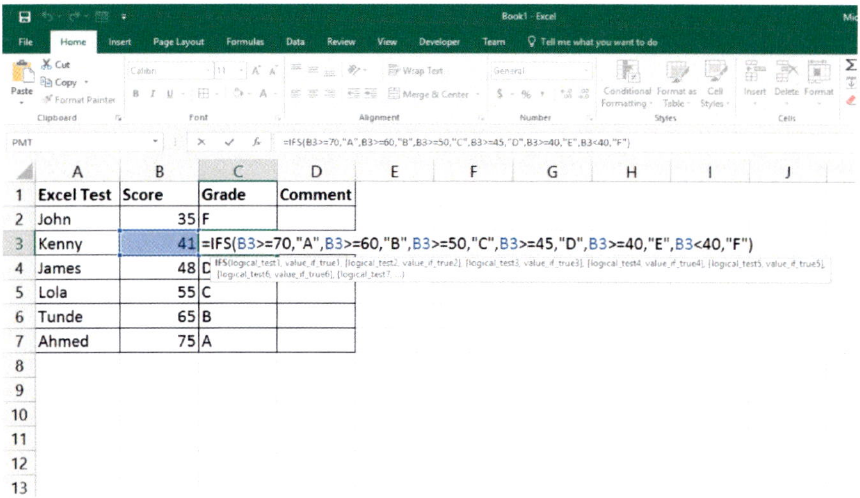

If you have a report and need to grade the performance with some conditions like we do for school marks to grades, then IFS is your new friend.

SWITCH

So what if you want to pass a comment on the grade performance? You want to say grade A means Excellent, grade B means Very Good, and so on. Well, that is what SWITCH allows you to do. It was borrowed from the programming community.

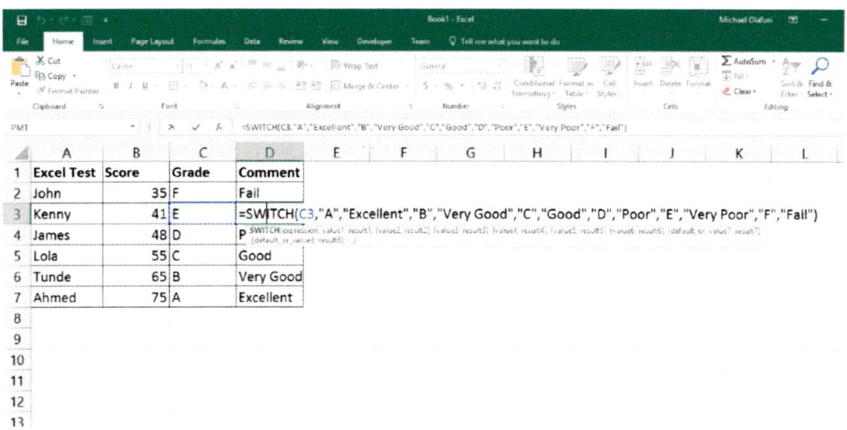

MAXIFS

And there is also MAXIFS to let you do want you've been doing with SUMIFS and COUNTIFS, just this time you are picking the highest value that meets your criteria.

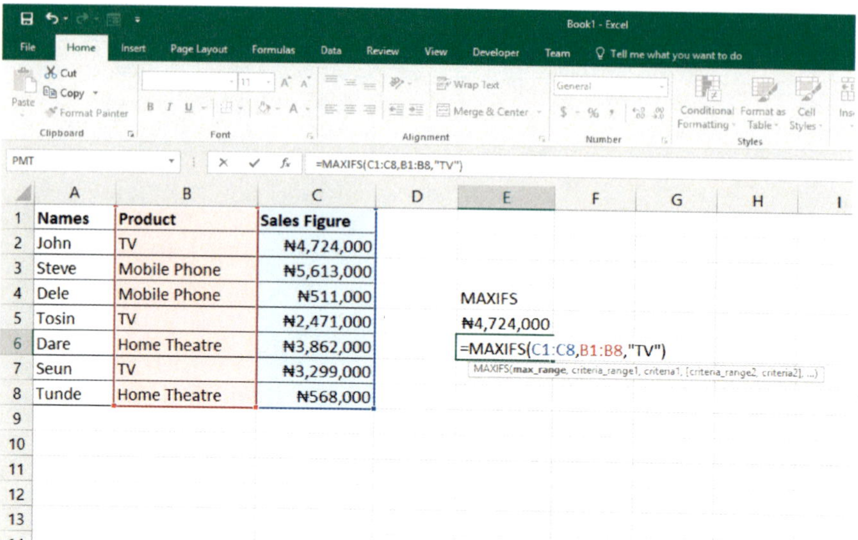

MINIFS

And this is the sixth and last: MINIFS. You've guessed right! It does similar stuff as MAXIFS but returns the minimum value that meets your criteria.

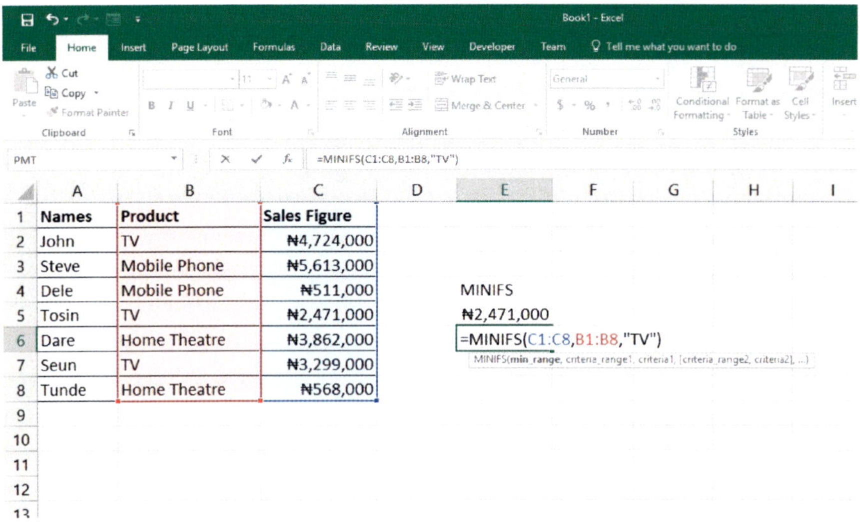

	A	B	C
1	**Names**	**Product**	**Sales Figure**
2	John	TV	₦4,724,000
3	Steve	Mobile Phone	₦5,613,000
4	Dele	Mobile Phone	₦511,000
5	Tosin	TV	₦2,471,000
6	Dare	Home Theatre	₦3,862,000
7	Seun	TV	₦3,299,000
8	Tunde	Home Theatre	₦568,000

Named Range, Goal Seek, Data Table and Scenario Manager

Excel has some what-if-analysis tools that greatly help with business decision analysis. You can easily simulate effect of changes in circumstances on your business projections and create compelling business case analysis.

Named Range

Excel lets you name a cell or a selection of cells. It's very useful when you are building models in Excel as it makes the model formulas easy to write and troubleshoot.

They are two ways to create a named range and I will start with the very quick and easy way.

Just select the cell or group of cells you want to name. Go to the name box and type in the name, replacing the cell address in the name box.

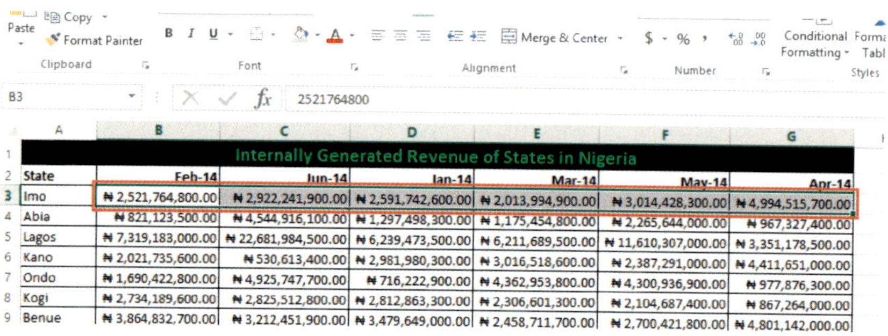

State	Feb-14	Jun-14	Jan-14	Mar-14	May-14	Apr-14
Imo	₦ 2,521,764,800.00	₦ 2,922,241,900.00	₦ 2,591,742,600.00	₦ 2,013,994,900.00	₦ 3,014,428,300.00	₦ 4,994,515,700.00
Abia	₦ 821,123,500.00	₦ 4,544,916,100.00	₦ 1,297,498,300.00	₦ 1,175,454,800.00	₦ 2,265,644,000.00	₦ 967,327,400.00
Lagos	₦ 7,319,183,000.00	₦ 22,681,984,500.00	₦ 6,239,473,500.00	₦ 6,211,689,500.00	₦ 11,610,307,000.00	₦ 3,351,178,500.00
Kano	₦ 2,021,735,600.00	₦ 530,613,400.00	₦ 2,981,980,300.00	₦ 3,016,518,600.00	₦ 2,387,291,000.00	₦ 4,411,651,000.00
Ondo	₦ 1,690,422,800.00	₦ 4,925,747,700.00	₦ 716,222,900.00	₦ 4,362,953,800.00	₦ 4,300,936,900.00	₦ 977,876,300.00
Kogi	₦ 2,734,189,600.00	₦ 2,825,512,800.00	₦ 2,812,863,300.00	₦ 2,306,601,300.00	₦ 2,104,687,400.00	₦ 867,264,000.00
Benue	₦ 3,864,832,700.00	₦ 3,212,451,900.00	₦ 3,479,649,000.00	₦ 2,458,711,700.00	₦ 2,700,421,800.00	₦ 4,801,142,000.00

Internally Generated Revenue of States in Nigeria

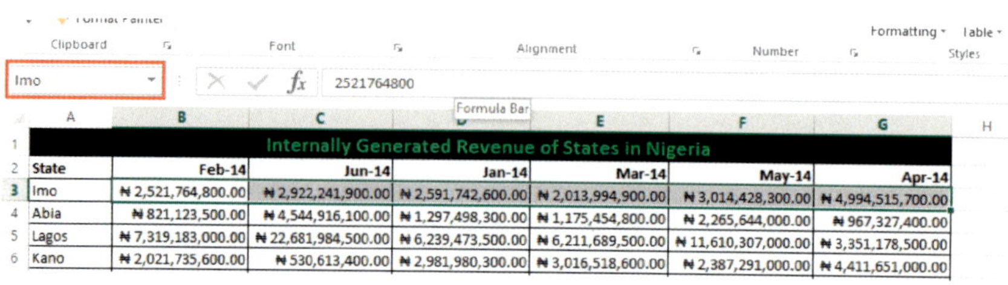

State	Feb-14	Jun-14	Jan-14	Mar-14	May-14	Apr-14
Imo	₦ 2,521,764,800.00	₦ 2,922,241,900.00	₦ 2,591,742,600.00	₦ 2,013,994,900.00	₦ 3,014,428,300.00	₦ 4,994,515,700.00
Abia	₦ 821,123,500.00	₦ 4,544,916,100.00	₦ 1,297,498,300.00	₦ 1,175,454,800.00	₦ 2,265,644,000.00	₦ 967,327,400.00
Lagos	₦ 7,319,183,000.00	₦ 22,681,984,500.00	₦ 6,239,473,500.00	₦ 6,211,689,500.00	₦ 11,610,307,000.00	₦ 3,351,178,500.00
Kano	₦ 2,021,735,600.00	₦ 530,613,400.00	₦ 2,981,980,300.00	₦ 3,016,518,600.00	₦ 2,387,291,000.00	₦ 4,411,651,000.00

Internally Generated Revenue of States in Nigeria

We've successfully named all the Imo state revenue values as Imo. As benefit number 1, we can use it in a SUM formula instead of highlighting the entire range.

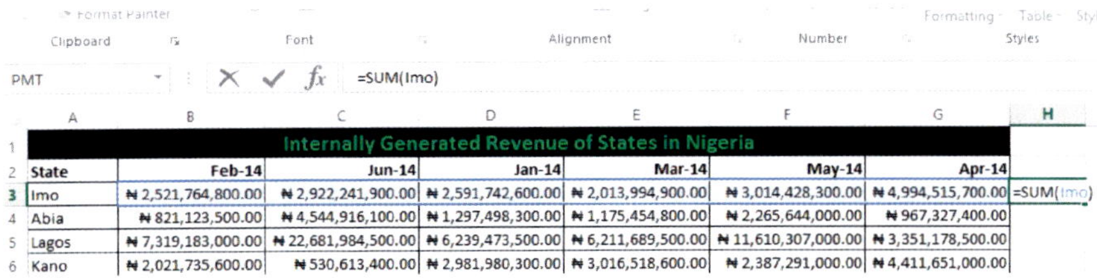

Another advantage will become obvious later when we do Scenario Manager.

So what is the second way of creating a named range?

It is, in fact, the standard way. It's also the only way that allows you to edit an already created named range.

Go to Formulas menu and click on the Name Manager.

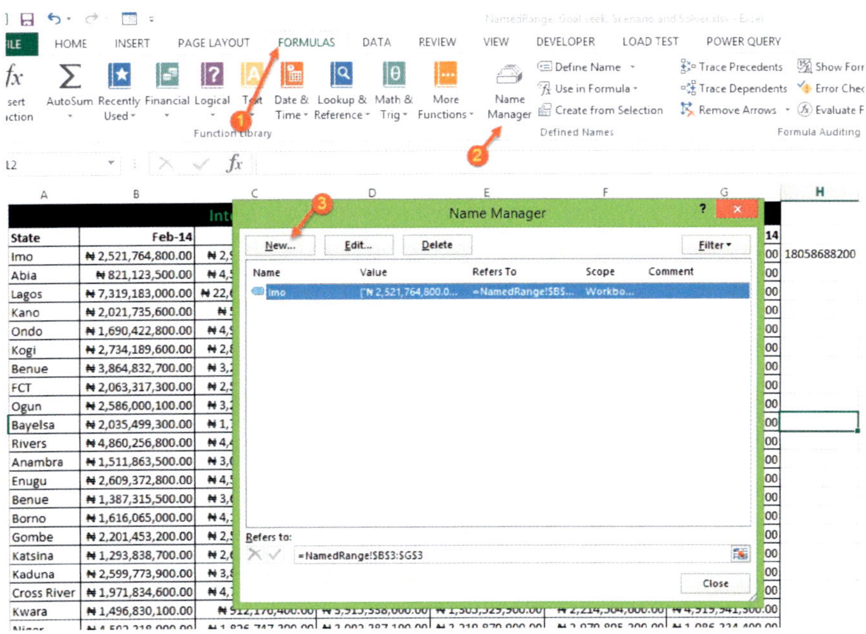

You can create new named range, edit already created ones and delete a named range.

GOAL SEEK

Goal seek is one of those powerful but seldom used tools in Excel.

It allows you to set-up a small model and tell Excel to optimize it for you based on one variable input and one set output. It's the perfect introduction to a model and linear programming in Excel.

Let's a simple and common use case. Below is a loan calculation table. Let's say I have found a huge business opportunity in large scale cocoa farming and I want to borrow N100 million from the bank. And the table below is the conditions the bank gave me: a payment period of 10 years and annual interest rate of 24%.

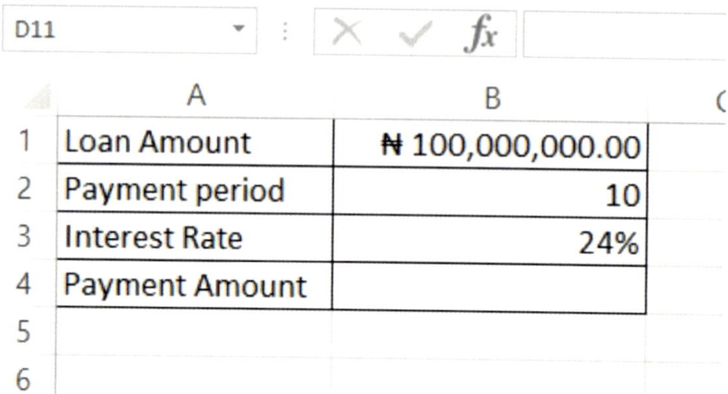

D11
A
B
Loan Amount
₦ 100,000,000.00
Payment period
10
Interest Rate
24%
Payment Amount

Excel has a formula for calculating the annual payment amount.

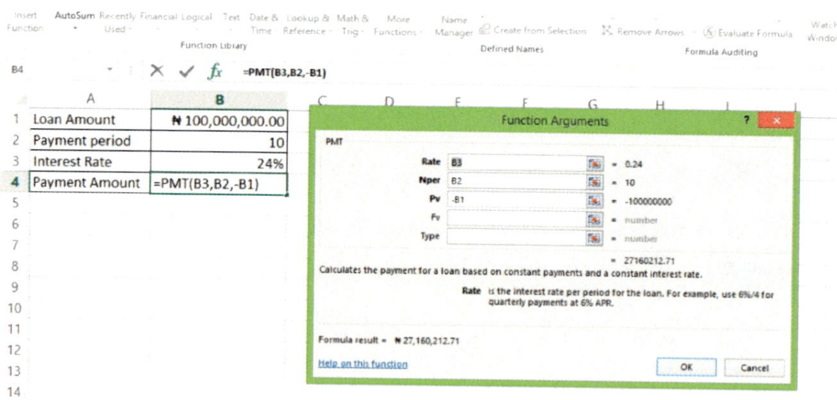

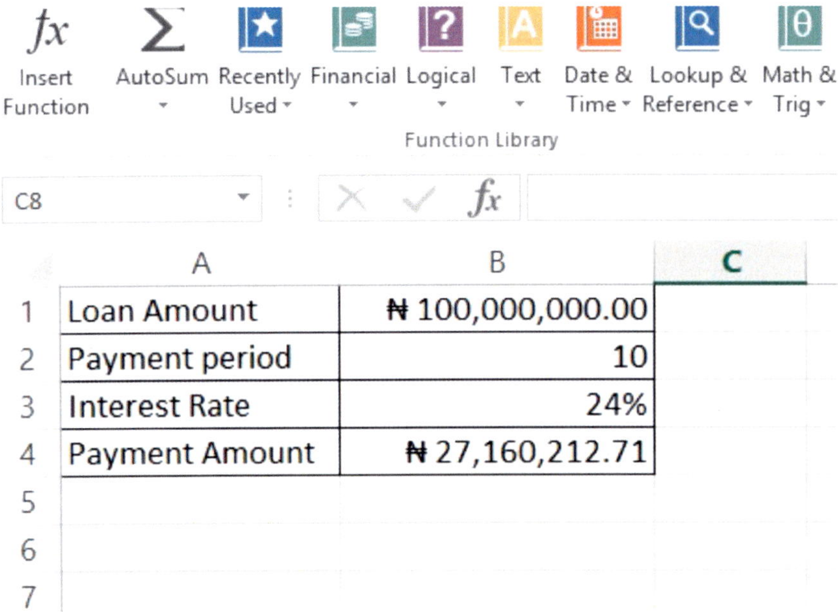

So I go and check my business financial projection, and find out that I can only afford to make N20 million annual payment. What rate will I negotiate with the bank?

This is where Goal Seek comes in. We simply tell it to find out what interest rate will evaluate to N20 million annual payment.

To access Goal Seek, go to Data menu and What-If-Analysis.

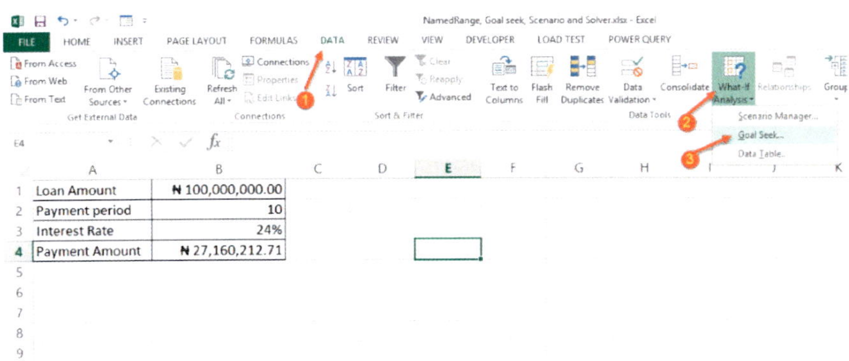

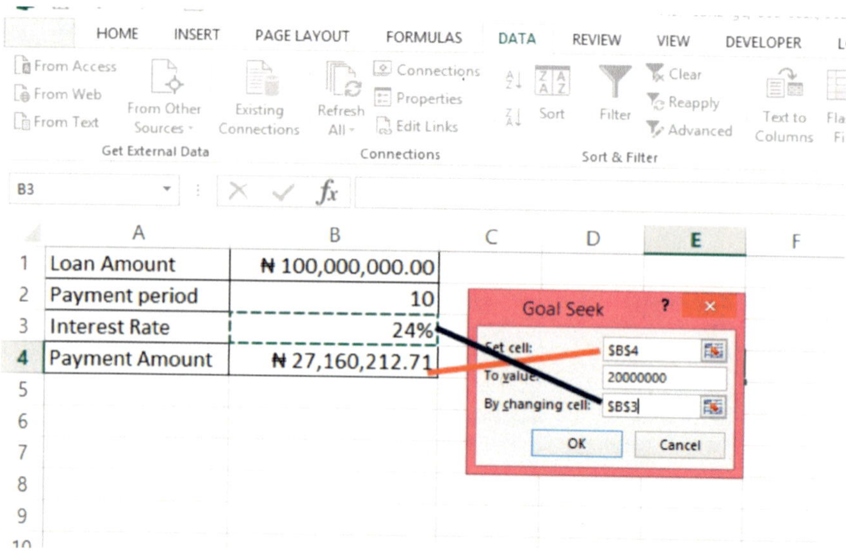

I set payment amount cell to N20 million and tell Goal Seek to vary the interest rate.

Once I click on OK, it does a series of iteration and gives me the result.

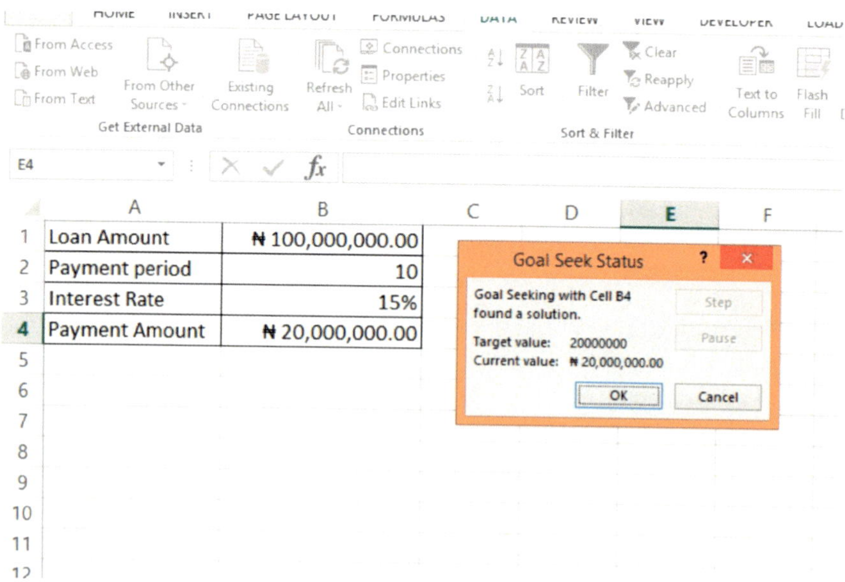

I should ask for 15% annual interest rate.

Data Table

Excel has an amazing tool called Data Table. It lets you sort of simulate a lot of predefined conditions.

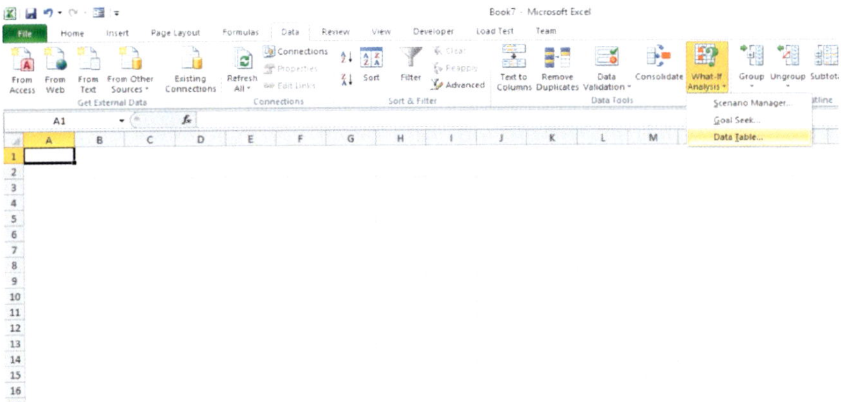

For illustration, I'll create an example we can all relate with. It's the revenue projections of a small vibrant company.

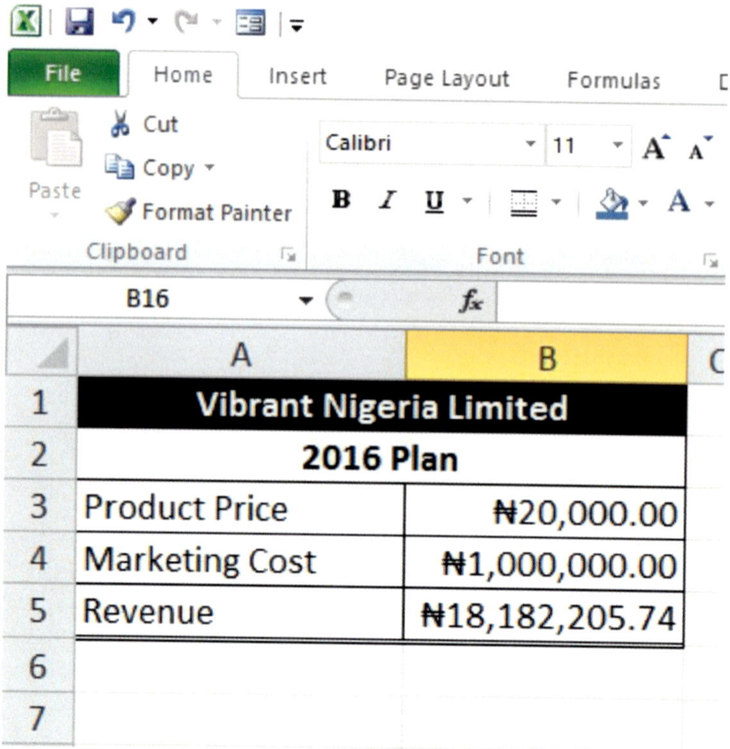

There is a formula in the Revenue field that depends on the Product Price and Marketing Cost.

The next thing, we will do is help the management simulate what the Revenue will be for different combinations of Product Price and Marketing Cost.

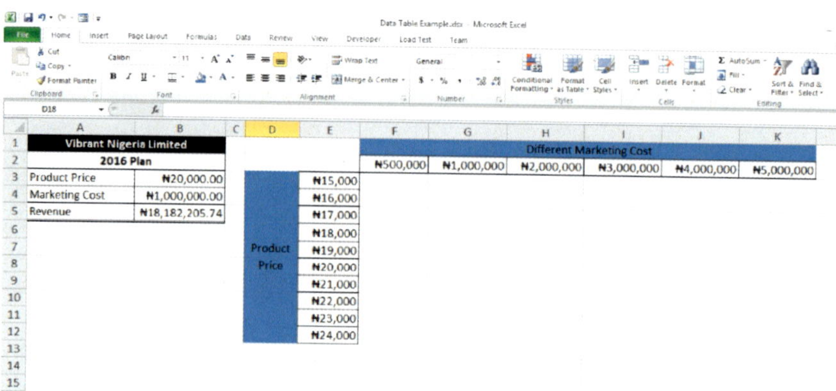

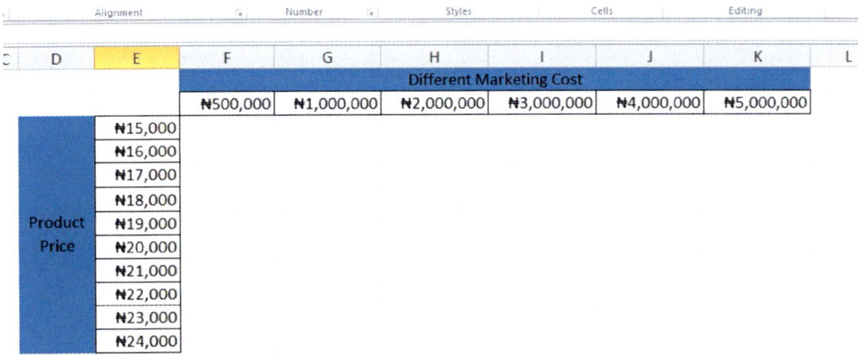

This is the sort of task Data Table is great at.

All we have to do is link the cell at the junction of the simulated Product Price and simulated Marketing Cost to the calculated Revenue cell. See the screenshot below for what I mean.

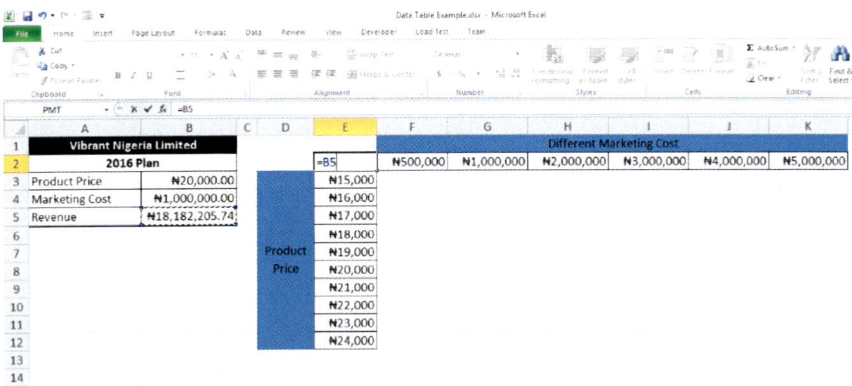

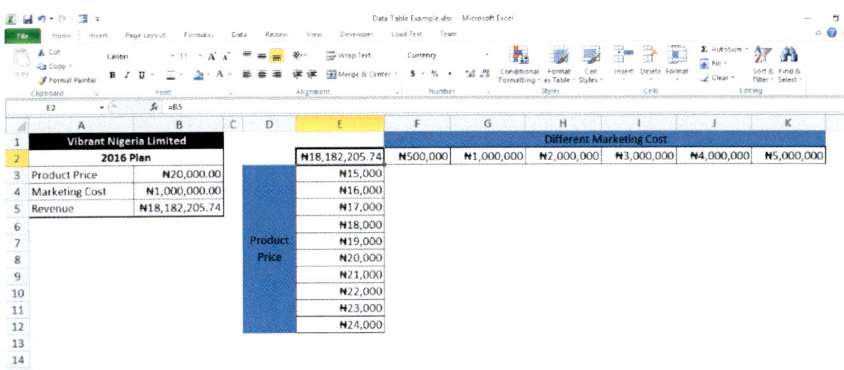

Now we are ready to use Data Table.

Select the entire simulation table.

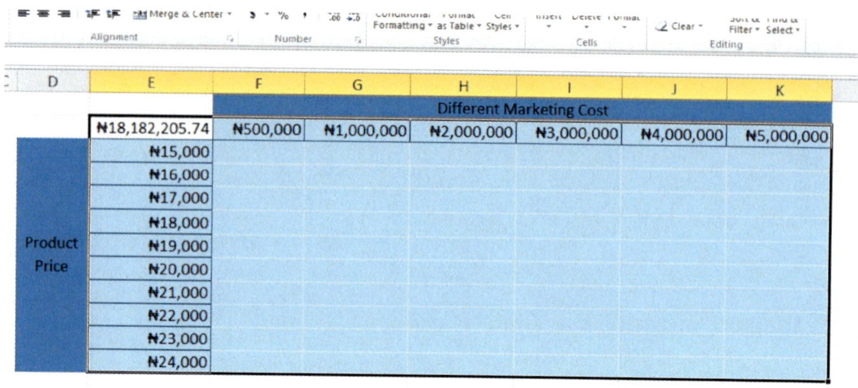

Then go to Data menu, What-If Analysis and Data Table.

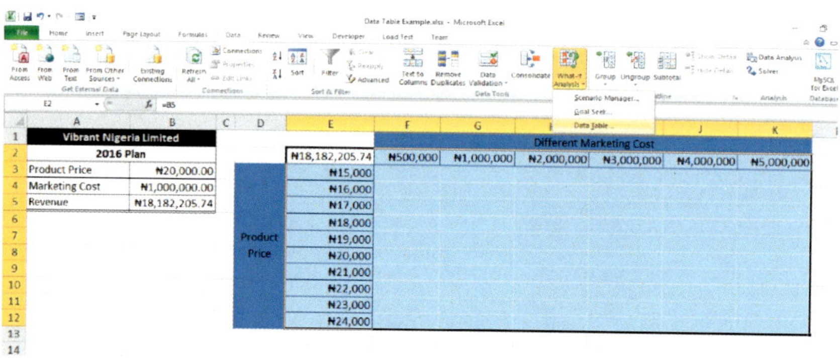

In the small dialog box that comes up, set the Row Input Cell to the Marketing Cost value in the analysis table. And set the Column Input Cell to the Product Price in the analysis table.

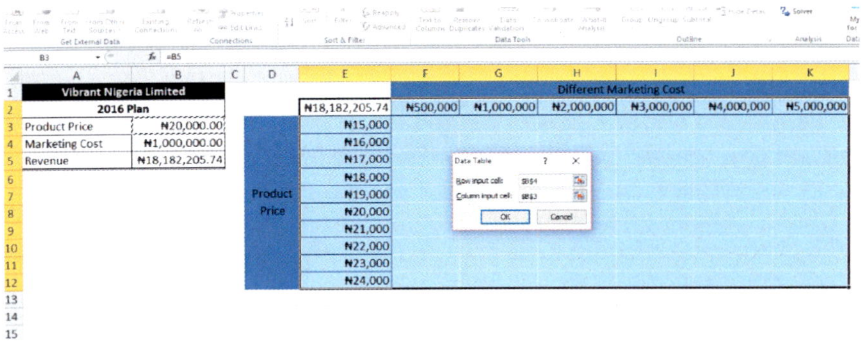

And you get what the Revenue will be for the different combinations of Product Price and Marketing Cost.

		Different Marketing Cost					
	₦18,182,205.74	₦500,000	₦1,000,000	₦2,000,000	₦3,000,000	₦4,000,000	₦5,000,000
Product Price	₦15,000	₦7,381,956	₦21,386,047	₦65,413,425	₦127,665,286	₦206,040,721	₦299,210,891
	₦16,000	₦7,160,504	₦20,603,282	₦62,780,343	₦122,363,596	₦197,350,527	₦286,473,414
	₦17,000	₦6,963,871	₦19,902,898	₦60,417,960	₦117,603,309	₦189,544,968	₦275,030,199
	₦18,000	₦6,788,247	₦19,272,333	₦58,285,152	₦113,302,283	₦182,489,915	₦264,685,089
	₦19,000	₦6,630,577	₦18,701,502	₦56,348,885	₦109,394,526	₦176,077,604	₦255,280,475
	₦20,000	₦6,488,378	₦18,182,206	₦54,582,296	₦105,826,366	₦170,220,381	₦246,688,158
	₦21,000	₦6,359,612	₦17,707,709	₦52,963,303	₦102,553,673	₦164,846,173	₦238,802,716
	₦22,000	₦6,242,590	₦17,272,420	₦51,473,571	₦99,539,805	₦159,895,124	₦231,536,601
	₦23,000	₦6,135,899	₦16,871,659	₦50,097,741	₦96,754,061	₦155,317,089	₦224,816,457
	₦24,000	₦6,038,346	₦16,501,475	₦48,822,846	₦94,170,514	₦151,069,711	₦218,580,324

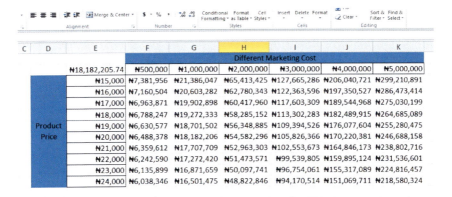

It's now left for the management of Vibrant Nigeria Limited to choose which combination of Product Price and Marketing Cost will get them the best Profit after factoring the Cost of Sales.

And now you understand how Data Table works in Excel and when you might want to use it.

Scenario Manager

Scenario Manager is one of Excel's decision analysis tool. It allows you compare outcome for different business scenarios.

Below is a practical business use case of the scenario manager. It is taken from our business circumstance and you'll find it very interesting.

We run a Microsoft Excel and Business Data Analysis business. Our major income streams are consulting for big multinational firms on data analysis and business process automations, and Microsoft Excel training. So let's say we decide to run a special one day Microsoft Excel training. It was specifically my idea. I had stumbled on a training advert on Punch newspaper. A one day training at VCP Hotel and costing N80,000. So I felt we should try it too. But I needed to build a convincing business case for the idea. And in doing this I used scenario manager.

I called up the hotel to get the details of the cost of hosting a full day training in their conference hall. I then went to work on the other costs that would be incurred in putting together the training. And below is the sheet of the cost details.

	A	B	C	D	E
1	High Quality Full Day Excel Training				
2					
3	**Cost Item**	**Amount**			
4	Hotel Conference Room	₦ 600,000.00			
5	Feeding per participant	₦ 12,500.00			
6	Training Material	₦ 3,000.00			
7	Certificate	₦ 2,000.00			
8	Prize for best participant	₦ 100,000.00			
9					
10	**Analysis based on estimates**	**Figure**			
11	Number of participants	40			
12	Course Fee	₦ 100,000.00			
13	Total Feeding cost	₦ 500,000.00			
14	Conference Room cost	₦ 600,000.00			
15	Training Materials cost	₦ 120,000.00			
16	Certificate Costs	₦ 80,000.00			
17	Prize Award cost	₦ 100,000.00			
18					
19	Total Revenue	₦ 4,000,000.00			
20	Total Cost	₦ 1,400,000.00			
21	VAT Fee (5%)	₦ 200,000.00			
22	Contigencies (7%)	₦ 280,000.00			
23	**Gross Profit**	**₦ 2,120,000.00**			
24					

And the underlying formulas are:

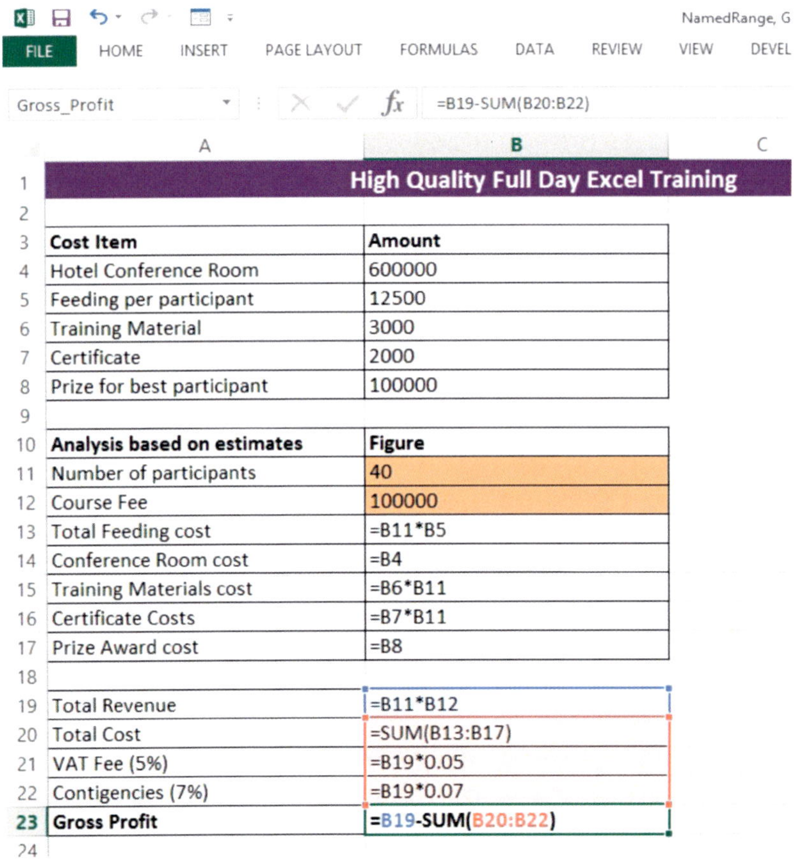

	A	B
1	High Quality Full Day Excel Training	
2		
3	**Cost Item**	**Amount**
4	Hotel Conference Room	600000
5	Feeding per participant	12500
6	Training Material	3000
7	Certificate	2000
8	Prize for best participant	100000
9		
10	**Analysis based on estimates**	**Figure**
11	Number of participants	40
12	Course Fee	100000
13	Total Feeding cost	=B11*B5
14	Conference Room cost	=B4
15	Training Materials cost	=B6*B11
16	Certificate Costs	=B7*B11
17	Prize Award cost	=B8
18		
19	Total Revenue	=B11*B12
20	Total Cost	=SUM(B13:B17)
21	VAT Fee (5%)	=B19*0.05
22	Contigencies (7%)	=B19*0.07
23	**Gross Profit**	**=B19-SUM(B20:B22)**
24		

As you can see, I have gotten every cost item listed; the estimated number of participants and the course fee too. But to build a convincing business case I need to create different scenarios. Maybe three scenarios.

- Scenario 1: The worst that could happen if we don't market the training well and put the course fee enticingly low.
- Scenario 2: The most likely thing to happen if we do our regular marketing and put up a fair course fee.
- Scenario 3: What would happen if everything goes extremely well. Which will be our marketing aim.

So how do you set up this scenarios in Excel? You use Scenario Manager.

But first we need to use Named Range for the most important cells in our scenario. They are the Gross Profit cell, the Number of Participants cell and the Course Fee cell. In our scenarios we want to monitor what the Gross Profit will be for different combinations of Number of Participants and Course Fee.

I hope you remember how to do Named Range. You simply select the cell or range, go to the name box and type in the name you want to name the selection as.

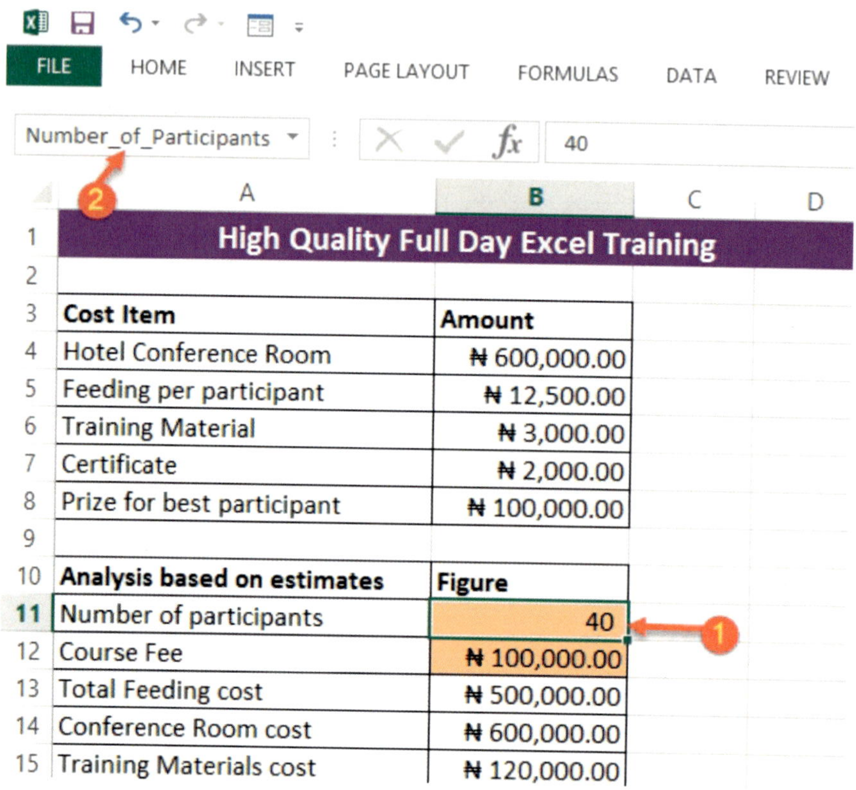

We do same for Course Fee.

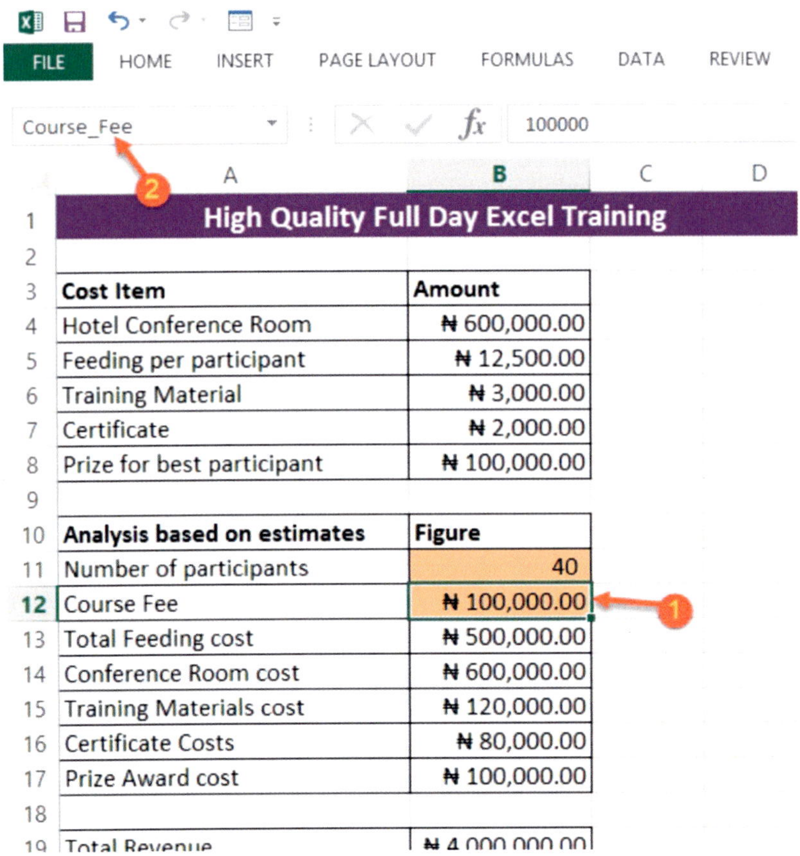

And for Gross Profit.

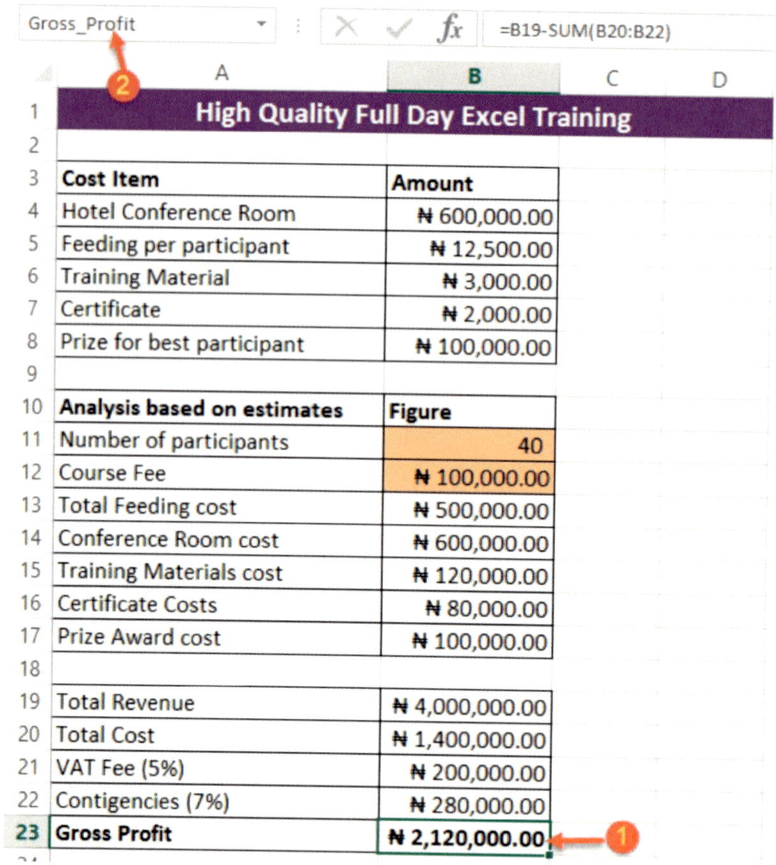

Now, we launch the Scenario Manager.

It is under Data Menu, What-If-Analysis.

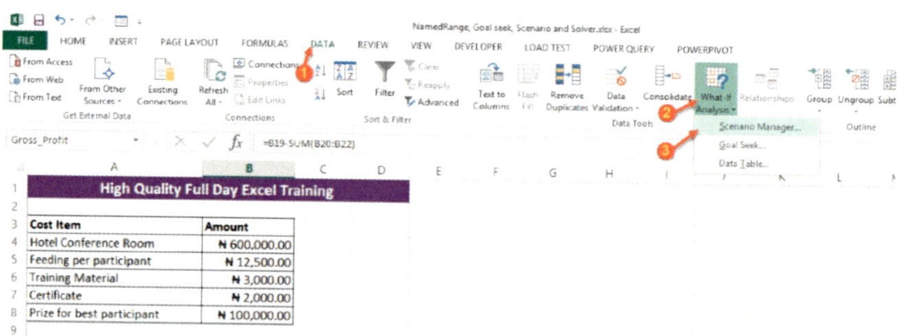

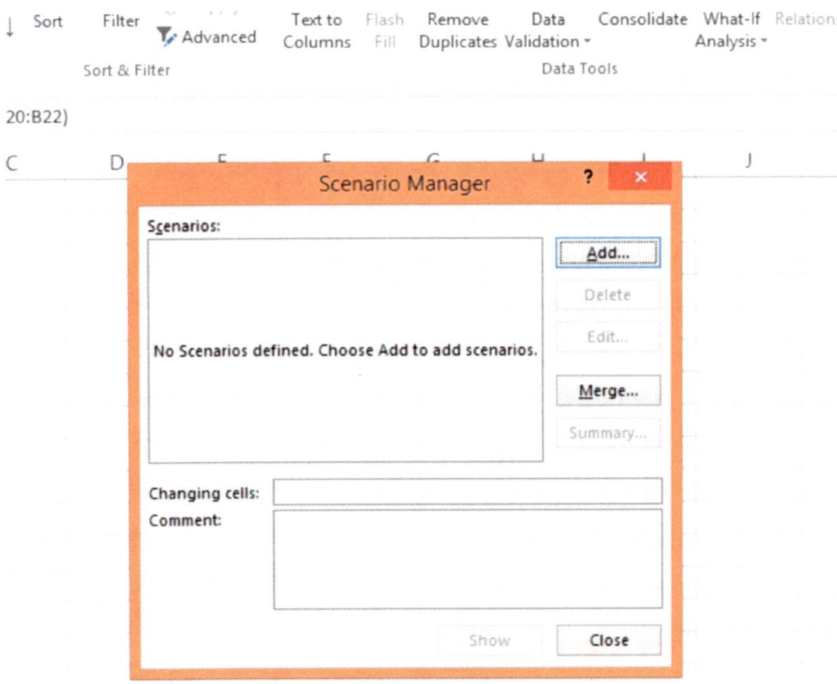

So let's add the three different scenarios.

I'll start with the worst. Click on Add and give the Scenario name as Worst. The cells we will vary are the Number of Participants and Course Fee cells.

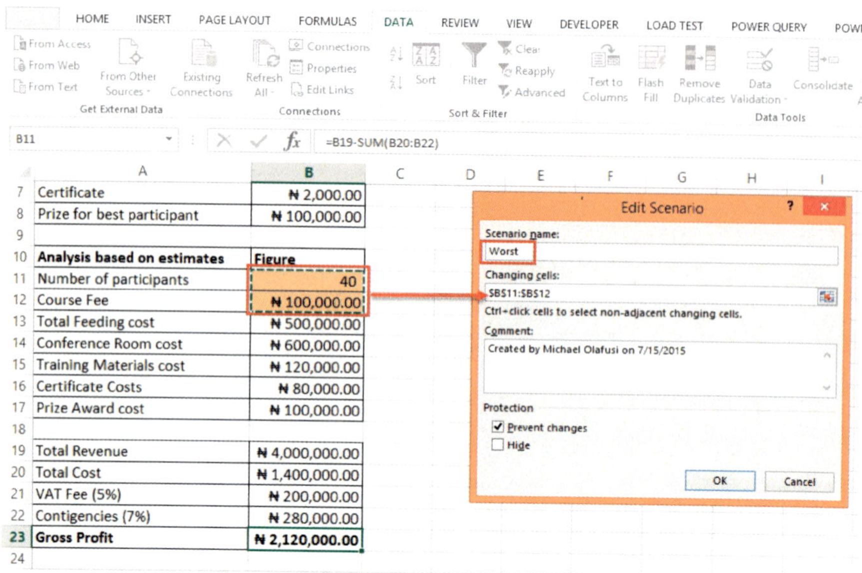

Click on OK.

It will ask you to set the number of participants and course fee. So based on experience, I know that if we do no serious marketing and set the price to N45,000 we can get 20 people. And that is the worst that can happen.

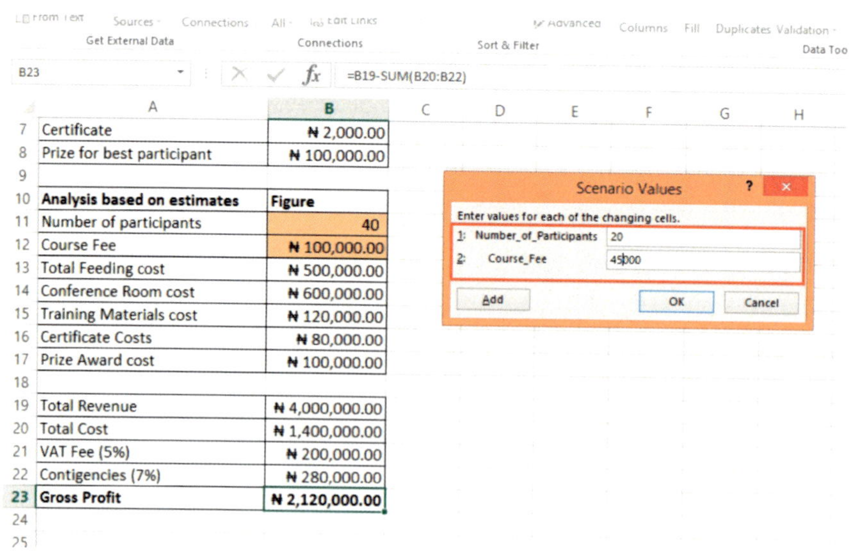

Click on OK.

Create a second scenario. Name it "Probable". It will be what we will most likely achieve. Give the number of participants as 30 and the cost as N70,000.

Finally, do the last scenario. Name it "Ideal". It will be our marketing aim if we decide to go ahead with the training idea. Give the number of participants as 40 and the cost as N100,000

Once you are done, the Scenario Manager dialog box would look like the one below.

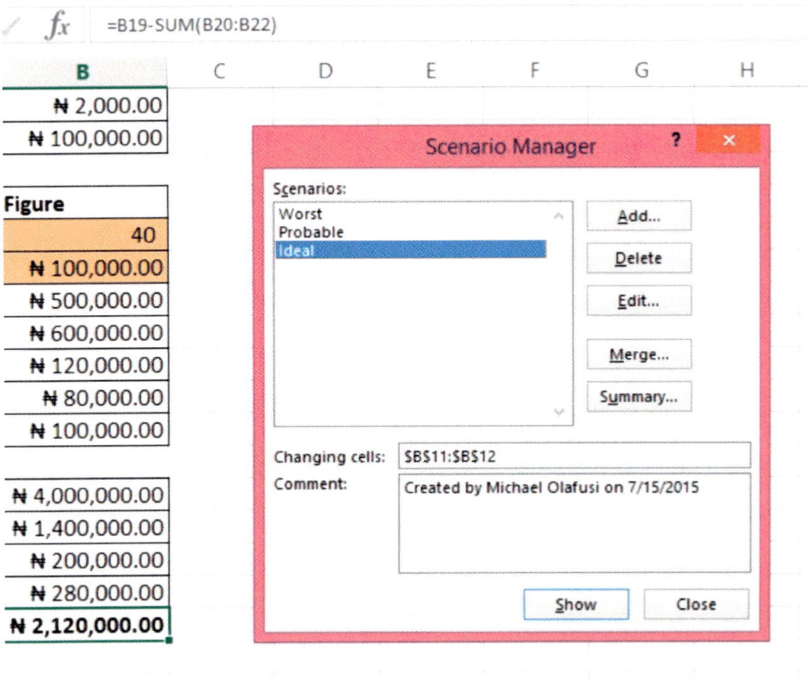

Click on Summary. It will ask you for the Result cell to monitor. That is the Gross Profit cell.

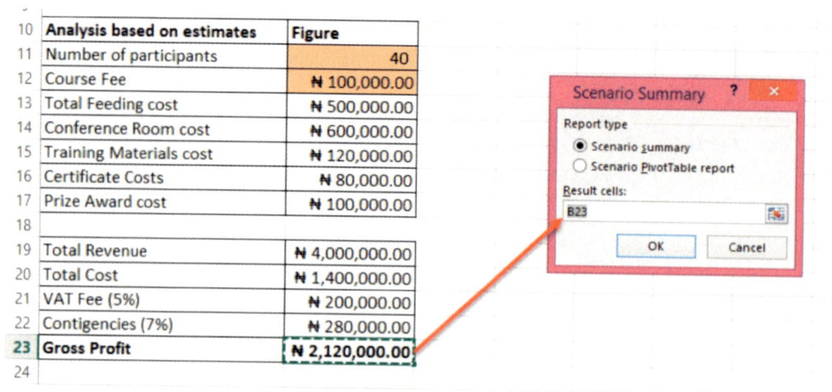

Click on OK.

You will be taken to a new sheet showing the comparison of the different scenarios.

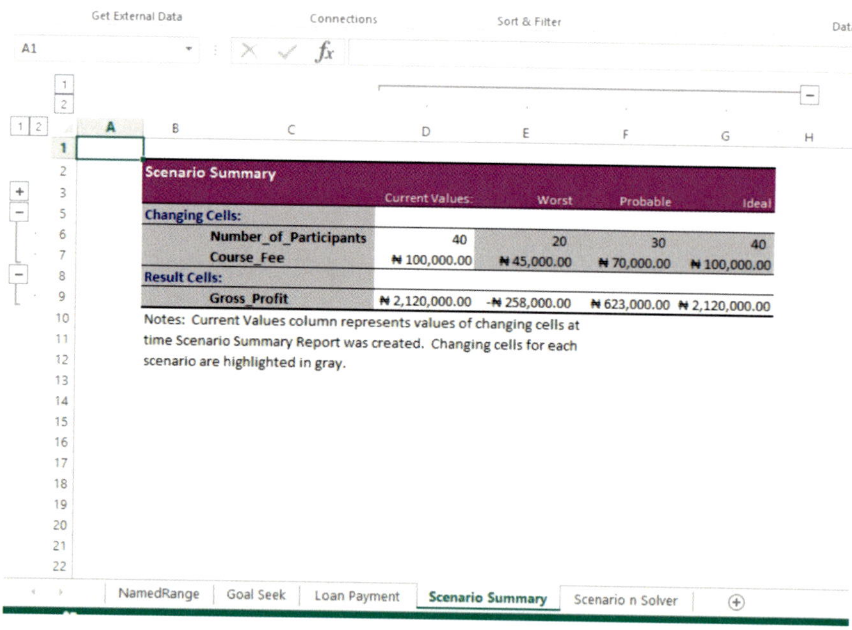

And as you can see, I now have a convincing case to show my partners and make them agree to organizing the one day training.

That’s how easy and powerful the Scenario Manager is.

Introduction To Excel VBA (macros)

A lot of people feel making macros in Excel is extremely hard and should be left only people who make a living from doing it full-time. If you are one of such people, I have a pleasant surprise for you. Macros in Excel are very easy and in the next five minutes I will guide you into making one.

So just before we start, let me do a brief explanation of what a macro is, why you might need to make one and the benefits of being able to make one.

Macros are simply a means of automating tasks in Excel. It's no more than that. You might need to do it when you have a daily or weekly report you make that is of an unvarying standard format, input and output-wise. Having a macro can cut your analysis time from hours to 15 seconds. It's like magic and everyone in your office will see you as a special being.

To be able to make macros, you need to make a small settings change in your Microsoft Excel.

Go to Files, Options and Customize Ribbon. Check the box beside Developer.

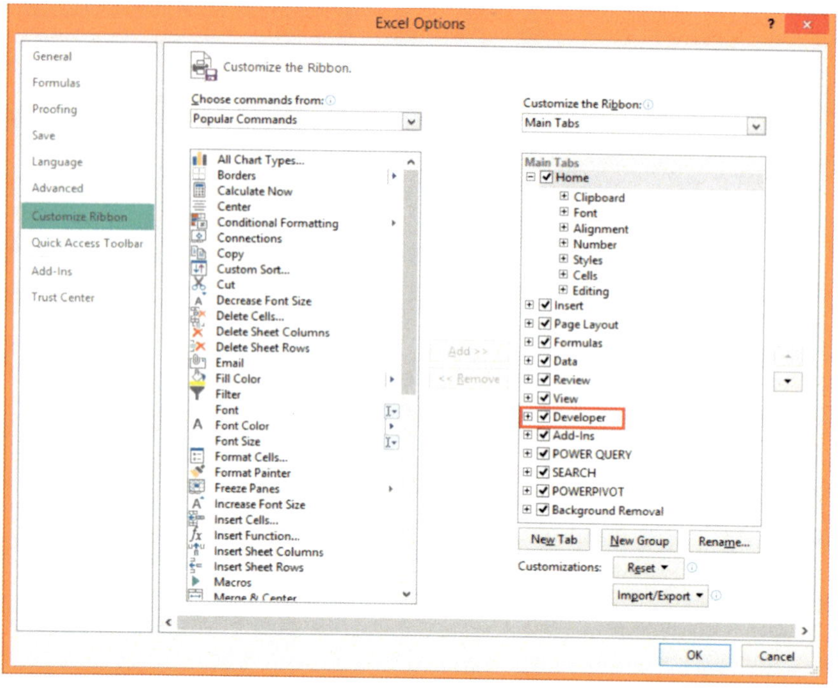

Now you will be able to access the Developer menu.

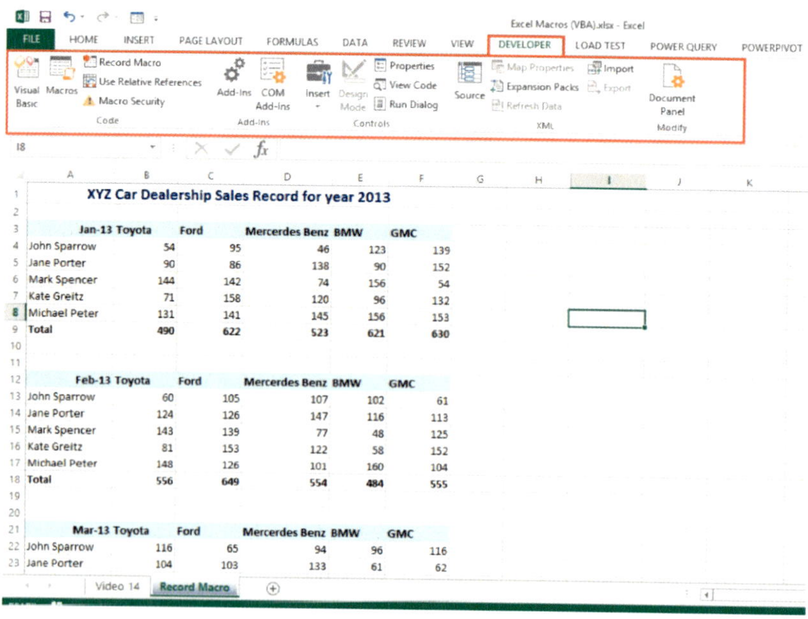

Jan-13	Toyota	Ford	Mercerdes Benz	BMW	GMC
John Sparrow	54	95	46	123	139
Jane Porter	90	86	138	90	152
Mark Spencer	144	142	74	156	54
Kate Greitz	71	158	120	96	132
Michael Peter	131	141	145	156	153
Total	490	622	523	621	630

Feb-13	Toyota	Ford	Mercerdes Benz	BMW	GMC
John Sparrow	60	105	107	102	61
Jane Porter	124	126	147	116	113
Mark Spencer	143	139	77	48	125
Kate Greitz	81	153	122	58	152
Michael Peter	148	126	101	160	104
Total	556	649	554	484	555

Mar-13	Toyota	Ford	Mercerdes Benz	BMW	GMC
John Sparrow	116	65	94	96	116
Jane Porter	104	103	133	61	62

Also enabling the Macro record button which we will use in this introduction to Excel VBA.

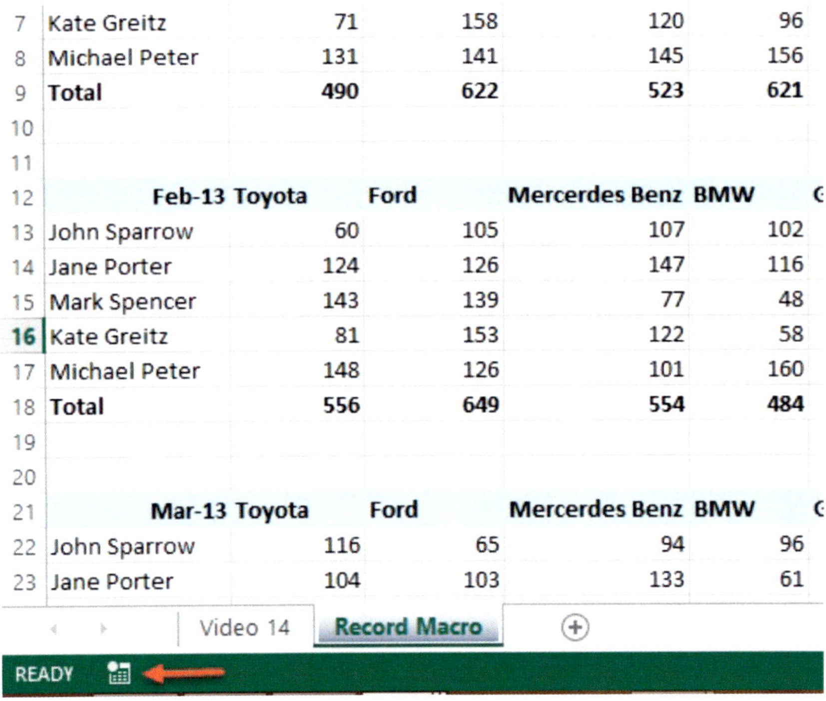

7	Kate Greitz	71	158	120	96	
8	Michael Peter	131	141	145	156	
9	**Total**	**490**	**622**	**523**	**621**	
10						
11						
12	**Feb-13**	**Toyota**	**Ford**	**Mercerdes Benz**	**BMW**	**G**
13	John Sparrow	60	105	107	102	
14	Jane Porter	124	126	147	116	
15	Mark Spencer	143	139	77	48	
16	Kate Greitz	81	153	122	58	
17	Michael Peter	148	126	101	160	
18	**Total**	**556**	**649**	**554**	**484**	
19						
20						
21	**Mar-13**	**Toyota**	**Ford**	**Mercerdes Benz**	**BMW**	**G**
22	John Sparrow	116	65	94	96	
23	Jane Porter	104	103	133	61	

Next, I will show you how to create a macro by clicking the right button twice – the macro record button.

I have prepared a sample illustration data.

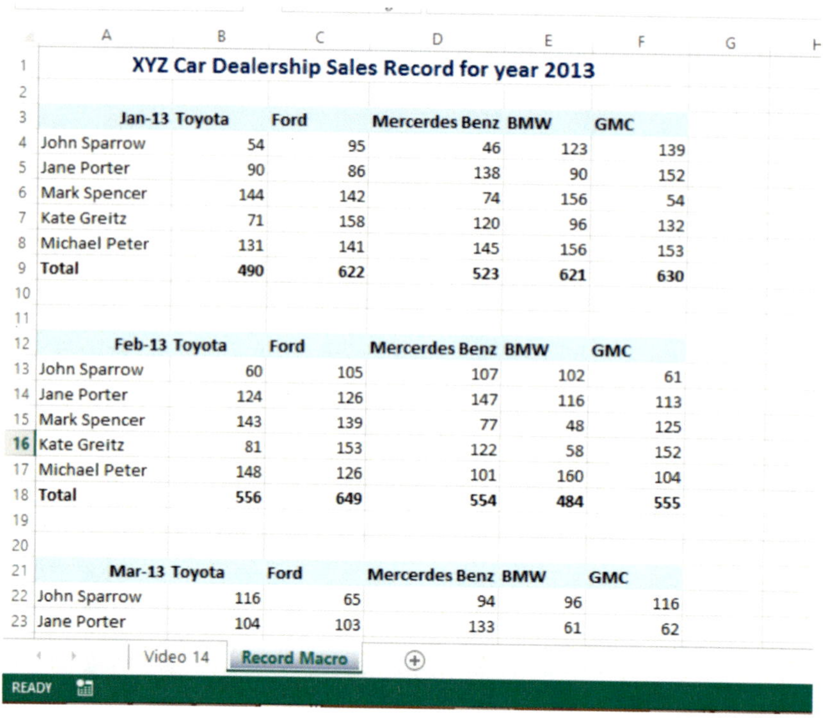

	A	B	C	D	E	F
1	XYZ Car Dealership Sales Record for year 2013					
2						
3	Jan-13	Toyota	Ford	Mercerdes Benz	BMW	GMC
4	John Sparrow	54	95	46	123	139
5	Jane Porter	90	86	138	90	152
6	Mark Spencer	144	142	74	156	54
7	Kate Greitz	71	158	120	96	132
8	Michael Peter	131	141	145	156	153
9	**Total**	**490**	**622**	**523**	**621**	**630**
10						
11						
12	Feb-13	Toyota	Ford	Mercerdes Benz	BMW	GMC
13	John Sparrow	60	105	107	102	61
14	Jane Porter	124	126	147	116	113
15	Mark Spencer	143	139	77	48	125
16	Kate Greitz	81	153	122	58	152
17	Michael Peter	148	126	101	160	104
18	**Total**	**556**	**649**	**554**	**484**	**555**
19						
20						
21	Mar-13	Toyota	Ford	Mercerdes Benz	BMW	GMC
22	John Sparrow	116	65	94	96	116
23	Jane Porter	104	103	133	61	62

It is fictitious table of Sales at an Autodealership by the different salesmen and the car make.

So the task I will use a macro to automate is a series of formatting steps.

Note: For the gurus, it would be obvious that copy pasting format would have done the same thing our macro will do. Yes. But we have to do the illustration with something not too complex to confuse anyone. The good thing is that you will learn all the steps required to make any complex recorded macro you desire.

So here are the easy steps to creating a macro.

First, I select the month I want to manually do the formatting for and have the macro recorder save my steps.

	A	B	C	D	E	F
1	XYZ Car Dealership Sales Record for year 2013					
2						
3	**Jan-13**	**Toyota**	**Ford**	**Mercerdes Benz**	**BMW**	**GMC**
4	John Sparrow	54	95	46	123	139
5	Jane Porter	90	86	138	90	152
6	Mark Spencer	144	142	74	156	54
7	Kate Greitz	71	158	120	96	132
8	Michael Peter	131	141	145	156	153
9	**Total**	**490**	**622**	**523**	**621**	**630**
10						
11						
12	**Feb-13**	**Toyota**	**Ford**	**Mercerdes Benz**	**BMW**	**GMC**
13	John Sparrow	60	105	107	102	61
14	Jane Porter	124	126	147	116	113
15	Mark Spencer	143	139	77	48	125
16	Kate Greitz	81	153	122	58	152
17	Michael Peter	148	126	101	160	104
18	**Total**	**556**	**649**	**554**	**484**	**555**
19						
20						
21	**Mar-13**	**Toyota**	**Ford**	**Mercerdes Benz**	**BMW**	**GMC**
22	John Sparrow	116	65	94	96	116
23	Jane Porter	104	103	133	61	62

Video 14 | **Record Macro**

Click on the macro record button.

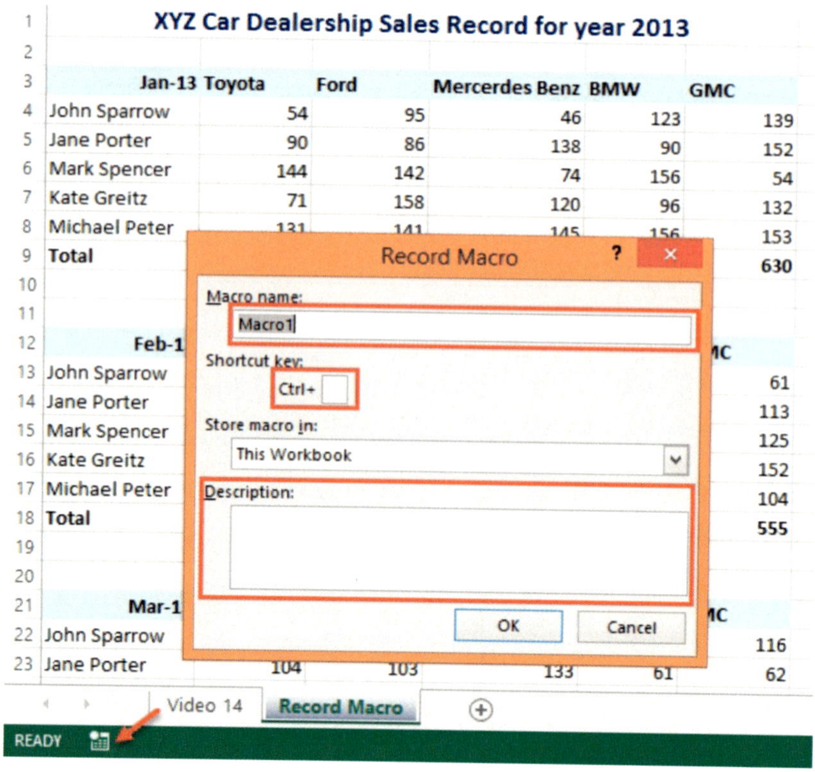

Give the macro a name, a keyboard shortcut and a description.

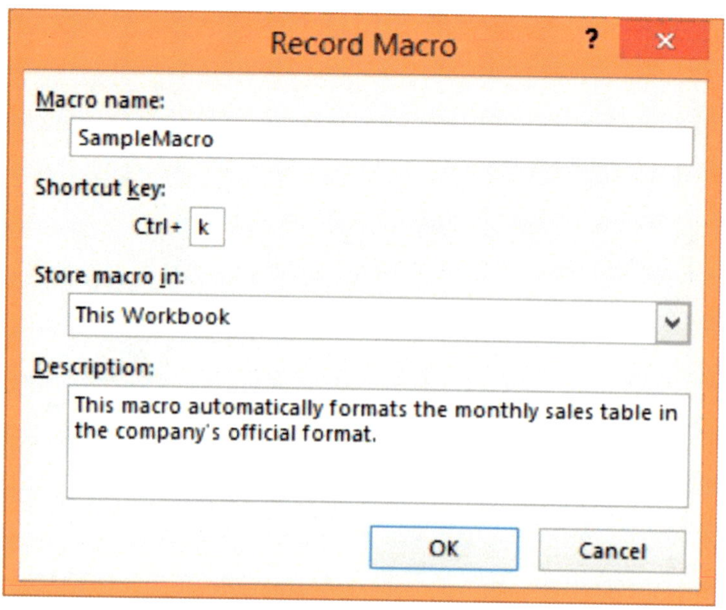

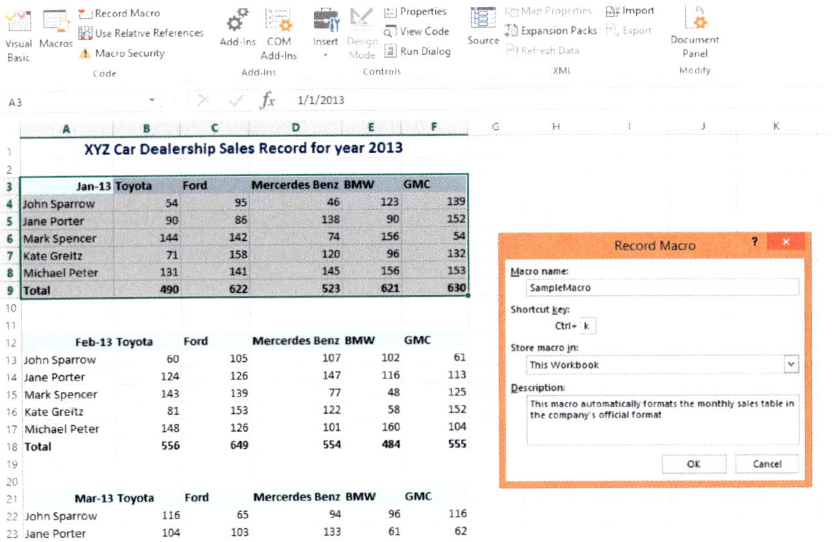

Click on OK.

Then begin doing the formatting steps. I change the font type, font color and add border, making it have our corporate color feel. Once I am done, I click on the stop recording button.

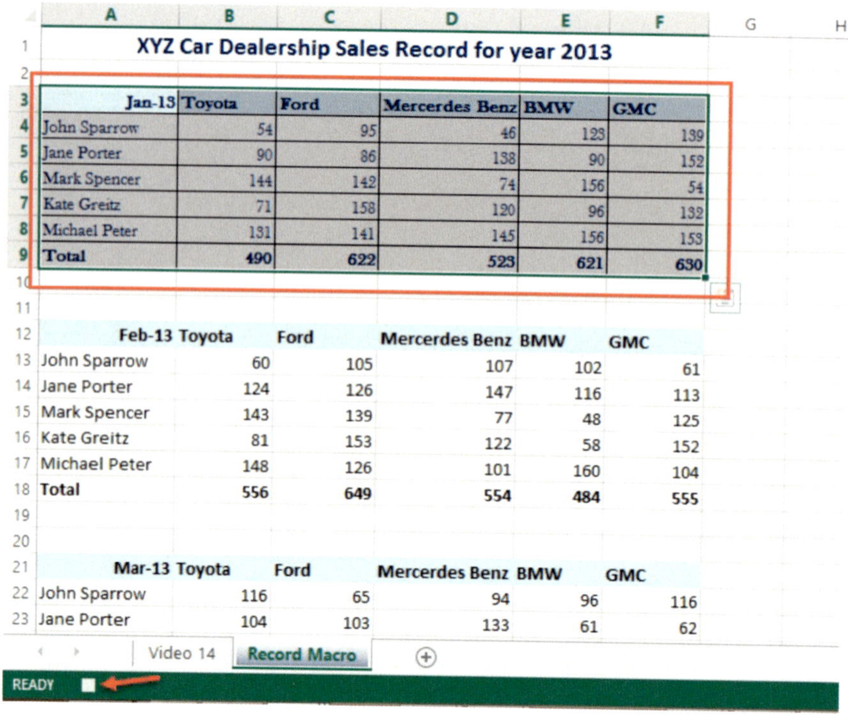

	A	B	C	D	E	F
1	XYZ Car Dealership Sales Record for year 2013					
2						
3	Jan-13	Toyota	Ford	Mercerdes Benz	BMW	GMC
4	John Sparrow	54	95	46	123	139
5	Jane Porter	90	86	138	90	152
6	Mark Spencer	144	142	74	156	54
7	Kate Greitz	71	158	120	96	132
8	Michael Peter	131	141	145	156	153
9	Total	490	622	523	621	630
10						
11						
12	Feb-13	Toyota	Ford	Mercerdes Benz	BMW	GMC
13	John Sparrow	60	105	107	102	61
14	Jane Porter	124	126	147	116	113
15	Mark Spencer	143	139	77	48	125
16	Kate Greitz	81	153	122	58	152
17	Michael Peter	148	126	101	160	104
18	Total	556	649	554	484	555
19						
20						
21	Mar-13	Toyota	Ford	Mercerdes Benz	BMW	GMC
22	John Sparrow	116	65	94	96	116
23	Jane Porter	104	103	133	61	62

And that's all. We have created a macro. Next is to try it out and see it work.

Select another month's record and press CTRL + k (the keyboard shortcut we used for the macro).

	A	B	C	D	E	F	G
1	XYZ Car Dealership Sales Record for year 2013						
2							
3	**Jan-13**	**Toyota**	**Ford**	**Mercerdes Benz**	**BMW**	**GMC**	
4	John Sparrow	54	95	46	123	139	
5	Jane Porter	90	86	138	90	152	
6	Mark Spencer	144	142	74	156	54	
7	Kate Greitz	71	158	120	96	132	
8	Michael Peter	131	141	145	156	153	
9	**Total**	**490**	**622**	**523**	**621**	**630**	
10							
11							
12	**Feb-13**	**Toyota**	**Ford**	**Mercerdes Benz**	**BMW**	**GMC**	
13	John Sparrow	60	105	107	102	61	
14	Jane Porter	124	126	147	116	113	
15	Mark Spencer	143	139	77	48	125	
16	Kate Greitz	81	153	122	58	152	
17	Michael Peter	148	126	101	160	104	
18	**Total**	**556**	**649**	**554**	**484**	**555**	
19							
20							
21	**Mar-13**	**Toyota**	**Ford**	**Mercerdes Benz**	**BMW**	**GMC**	
22	John Sparrow	116	65	94	96	116	
23	Jane Porter	104	103	133	61	62	

Video 14 | **Record Macro** | (+)

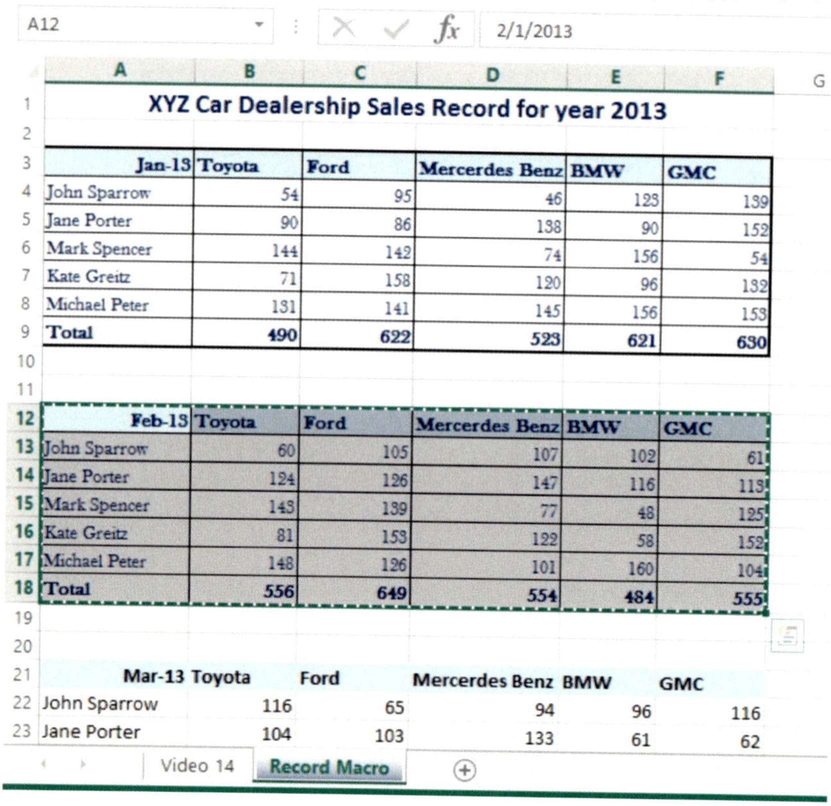

Voila! It works!

So let's insert a macro button. A button you will click to run the macro. I am sure you've seen one before. They are super easy to create.

Go to the Developer menu, Insert and select Button under Form Controls.

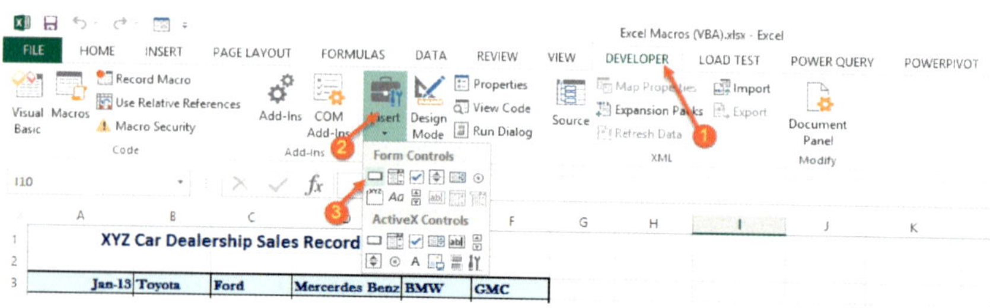

Draw a rectangular button where you want the macro button to be. Immediately, Excel will ask you to select the macro to link it to. Select the macro we just created.

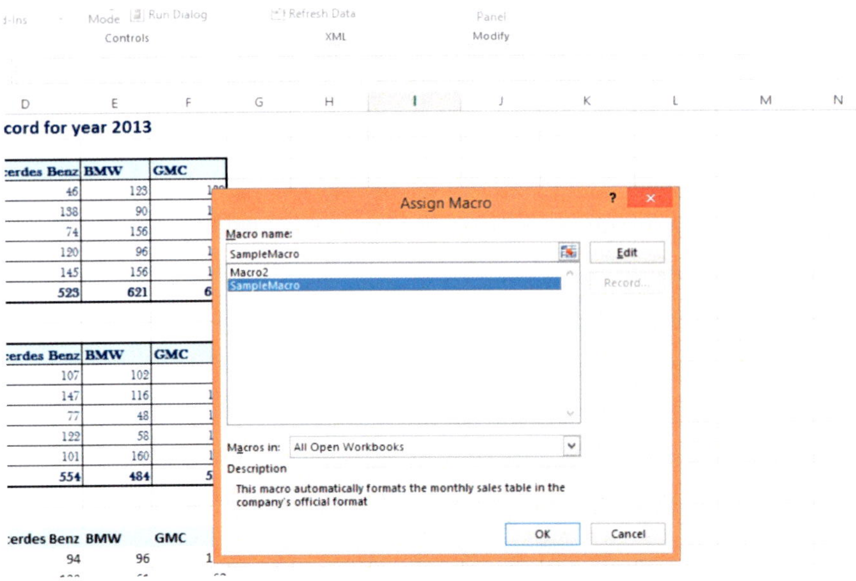

Click on OK.

Then edit the name of the rectangular button.

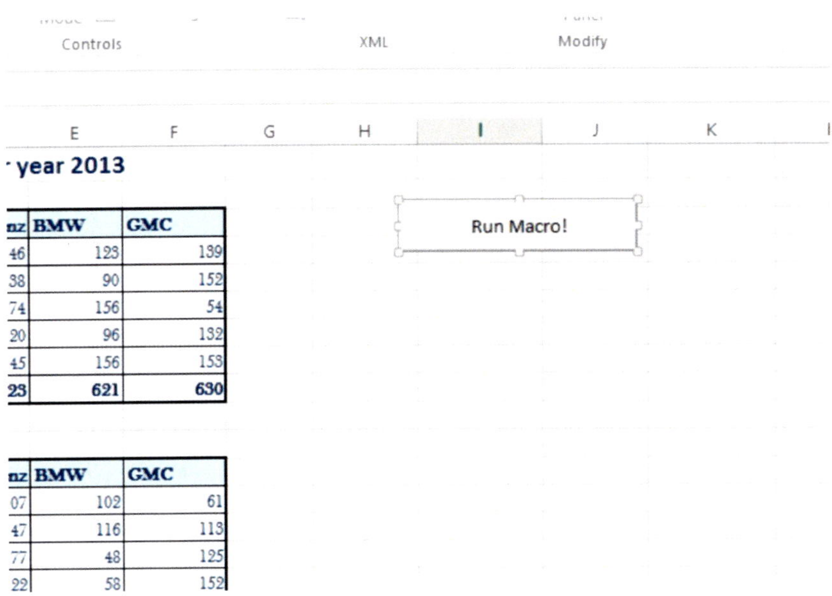

And that's it! You've created a macro button.

Now select another month's data and click on the macro button to see it work the magic we configured it for.

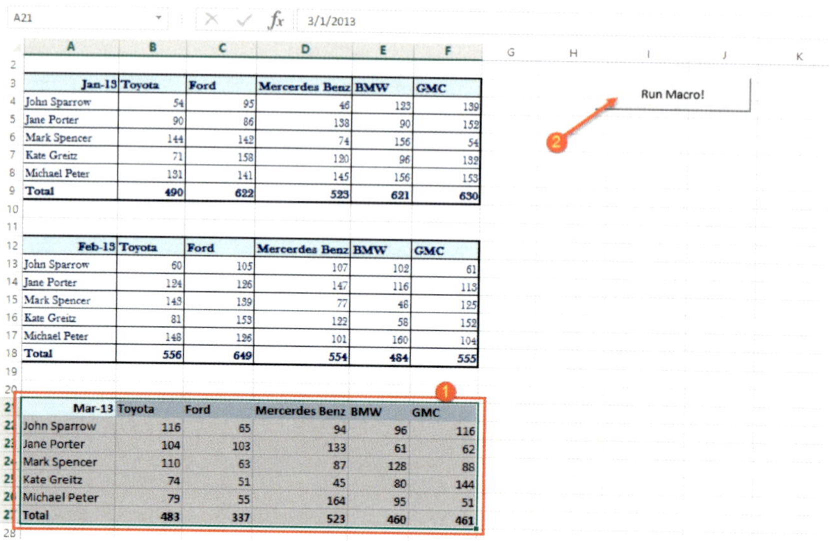

Jan-13	Toyota	Ford	Mercerdes Benz	BMW	GMC
John Sparrow	54	95	46	123	139
Jane Porter	90	86	138	90	152
Mark Spencer	144	142	74	156	54
Kate Greitz	71	158	120	96	132
Michael Peter	131	141	145	156	153
Total	**490**	**622**	**523**	**621**	**630**

Feb-13	Toyota	Ford	Mercerdes Benz	BMW	GMC
John Sparrow	60	105	107	102	61
Jane Porter	124	126	147	116	113
Mark Spencer	143	139	77	46	125
Kate Greitz	81	153	122	58	152
Michael Peter	148	126	101	160	104
Total	**556**	**649**	**554**	**484**	**555**

Mar-13	Toyota	Ford	Mercerdes Benz	BMW	GMC
John Sparrow	116	65	94	96	116
Jane Porter	104	103	133	61	62
Mark Spencer	110	63	87	128	88
Kate Greitz	74	51	45	80	144
Michael Peter	79	55	164	95	51
Total	483	337	523	460	461

See the result!

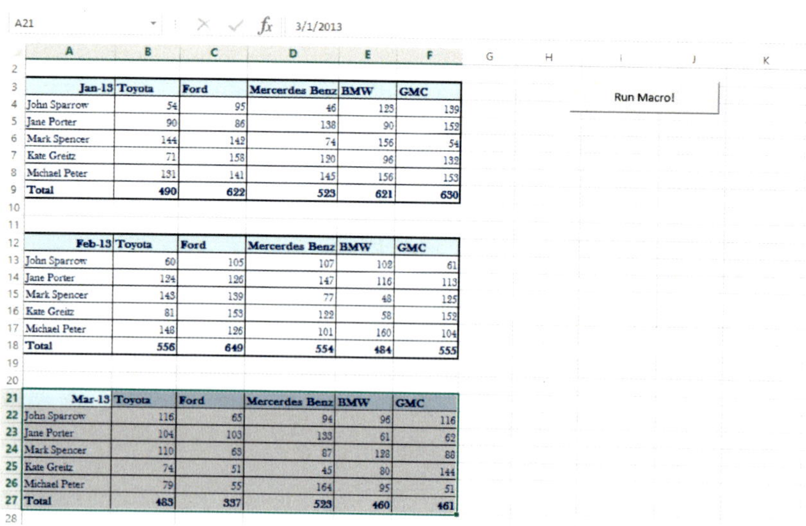

Jan-13	Toyota	Ford	Mercerdes Benz	BMW	GMC
John Sparrow	54	95	46	123	139
Jane Porter	90	86	138	90	152
Mark Spencer	144	142	74	156	54
Kate Greitz	71	158	120	96	132
Michael Peter	131	141	145	156	153
Total	**490**	**622**	**523**	**621**	**630**

Feb-13	Toyota	Ford	Mercerdes Benz	BMW	GMC
John Sparrow	60	105	107	102	61
Jane Porter	124	126	147	116	113
Mark Spencer	143	139	77	46	125
Kate Greitz	81	153	122	58	152
Michael Peter	148	126	101	160	104
Total	**556**	**649**	**554**	**484**	**555**

Mar-13	Toyota	Ford	Mercerdes Benz	BMW	GMC
John Sparrow	116	65	94	96	116
Jane Porter	104	103	133	61	62
Mark Spencer	110	63	87	128	88
Kate Greitz	74	51	45	80	144
Michael Peter	79	55	164	95	51
Total	**483**	**337**	**523**	**460**	**461**

Amazing, isn't it?

I hope you are now convinced that creating a macro in Excel is very easy.

It's now time for you to think up other creative ways to use a recorded macro.

Bonne chance!

Engage Us Today

Register for Training
We have the only Microsoft Excel MVP in Africa (as at 2015) and have held training for people from Vodacom, Airtel, IBM, SABMiller, Nestle & Lafarge.

Custom Programs
We can build you programs to fix your unique business and data analysis issues.

Outsource Your Data Analysis
Don't have the internal resources or want an expert to show the insights in your business data. We are who you need.

UrBizEdge

UrBizEdge Limited,
20, Kofoworola street, Off Lagoon Hospital,
Obafemi Awolowo road, Ikeja,
Lagos. Nigeria

+234-808-938-2423; +1-941-312-2094

info@urbizedge.com

www.urbizedge.com

Made in the USA
Middletown, DE
21 May 2023

31067155R10128